Enterprise IoT

Enterprise IoT will be the dominant theme for industrial companies in the coming decade. This book provides actionable guidelines for business and IT executives to master the challenges and reap the rewards of this transformation.

—*Anand Mahindra,*
Chairman and Managing Director of Mahindra Group

The *Enterprise IoT* project looks set to become the primary source for answers to the big IoT questions that are challenging enterprises right now: where to start? What do you do first? What steps are necessary not only from a technical perspective, but from a product and workforce perspective? The collaborative and open approach is a perfect match for the open nature of the IoT.

—*Dr. Richard Soley,*
Executive Director of the Industrial Internet Consortium (IIC)

The industrial internet of things is a union of two domains, each with its own distinct history and culture. Manufacturing tends to focus on quality and long product lifespans. The software world tends to focus on speed and agility. This book reveals the benefits and potential risks of combining the two cultures on a truly global scale. Based on best practices culled from real-world case studies, the Ignite Methodology offers a blueprint for transitioning into the IoT economy.

—*William Ruh,*
Vice President of GE Software

Enterprise IoT

Dirk Slama, Frank Puhlmann,
Jim Morrish, and Rishi M. Bhatnagar

Beijing · Boston · Farnham · Sebastopol · Tokyo   O'REILLY®

Enterprise IoT

by Dirk Slama, Frank Puhlmann, Jim Morrish, and Rishi M. Bhatnagar

Printed in the United States of America.

Published by O'Reilly Media, Inc., 1005 Gravenstein Highway North, Sebastopol, CA 95472.

O'Reilly books may be purchased for educational, business, or sales promotional use. Online editions are also available for most titles (*http://safaribooksonline.com*). For more information, contact our corporate/institutional sales department: 800-998-9938 or *corporate@oreilly.com*.

Acquisitions Editor: Jon Bruner	**Indexer:** Ellen Troutman Zaig
Editor: Dawn Schanafelt	**Interior Designer:** David Futato
Production Editor: Matthew Hacker	**Cover Designer:** Edie Freedman
Copyeditor: Jasmine Kwityn	**Illustrator:** Rebecca Demarest
Proofreader: Sonia Saruba	

November 2015:   First Edition

Revision History for the First Edition

2015-10-28:   First Release

See *http://oreilly.com/catalog/errata.csp?isbn=9781491924839* for release details.

978-1-4919-2483-9

[LSI]

Table of Contents

Part I. IoT Application Domains and Case Studies

Part II. Ignite | IoT Methodology

Foreword

Dear Reader,

After 25 years of socioeconomic transformation driven by the Internet, we are now looking at the next wave of disruptive changes. The Internet of Things (IoT) is transforming the way we interact with physical products. Constant connectivity will enable new products and services that we have not even thought of today.

True to our own strategic imperative "Invented for Life," many IoT use cases have the potential to significantly improve quality of life in our society. Connected health devices can help to improve medical care. Urban eBike sharing services help reduce pollution and are fun to use! eCall Services reduce the time it takes to direct emergency services to the site of a car accident. Our Digital Horizon technology meshes traditional map data with additional data like traffic signs and road conditions to enable driving with foresight. Autonomous driving and its many precursors will change how we look at transportation. Smart Cities, Smart Buildings, and Smart Homes will improve people's quality of life and save energy.

For many companies, the IoT will accelerate the shift towards integrated product and service offerings. Connected Asset Lifecycle Management and digital services will become an integral part of this development. However, we have to be aware that in this context two very different worlds are meeting. On the one hand, we have the manufacturing and engineering companies that have traditionally been driven by very high quality standards and long-term product thinking, often resulting in long product development cycles and a general risk adversity. On the other hand, we have the Internet companies that often focus on point solutions ("minimum viable product"), work in a "perpetual beta" mode, and generally seem prepared to take bigger risks.

Successful IoT businesses on the enterprise level will require a little bit of both. In particular, we need to combine the service-thinking of the Internet world with the device-centric, quality-focused thinking of the manufacturing world.

This approach will have to encompass both the technical as well as the organizational level. If we want to move from the more obvious, Remote Condition Monitoring-like services towards new, disruptive, data-driven business models in the IoT, we need to ask ourselves:

- Which new services could make use of existing products and product data? How can the optimal interaction between new products and services be ensured? How does this affect my product design?

- What impact does the new value proposition have on my marketing and sales organization? How can the data from connected products be used for better market segmentation, product tailoring, and cross-selling?

- How can I adapt my after-sales processes to leverage the newly won customer usage data?

- How can my service organization best leverage product data to help customers improve Operational Equipment Efficiency?

- How can we as a company define efficient policies and governance mechanisms to ensure that customer data is used responsibly and in accordance with the customer's wishes?

On the technological side, for example, we have to understand:

- If my hardware development cycles are five times as long as my software rollout cycles, how can I decouple hardware and software on the asset more efficiently?

- How can I manage these different lifecycles on a global scale?

- What infrastructure is required to manage software on remote assets?

These are only some of the pressing questions that we need to address if we want to be successful in the Internet of Things. In my opinion, *Enterprise IoT* has taken a very good first step towards the development of a methodology that helps to identify the most critical issues, and to create answers by collecting best practices from experts and early adaptors in the IoT. The Ignite | IoT methodology is a very valuable tool for IoT product managers, IoT project managers, and IoT solution architects. Open sourcing Ignite | IoT and allowing for crowd-sourced input perfectly fits the open philosophy of the IoT. This approach will help to ensure that Ignite | IoT becomes a tried and tested delivery methodology for the Internet of Things.

With best regards,

Dr. Volkmar Denner

Chairman, Board of Management of Robert Bosch GmbH

Preface

We live in fast-moving times, so not everybody will read this book from cover to cover. To help you to better navigate this book, we have provided a visual overview of the book's structure (see "Structure of This Book" on page xiii), along with some advice on where different types of readers should focus. Think of it as the program you might get at the opera.

Just as the overture warms up the crowd, Chapter 1 provides some background, introduces the main characters, and asks a number of questions that we hope to answer as we progress. By the way, spectators are allowed to talk during an overture (but not during a prelude, or so we are told), so comments in the online edition are very welcome.

Like in any good opera, there are numerous characters, each linked by complex relationships. Chapter 2 provides definitions of the main elements of IoT and introduces different IoT scenarios to explain the relationships between the different elements.

Structure of This Book

This section provides an overview of the three main parts of this book:

Part I: IoT Application Domains and Case Studies
   The first part of the book introduces some important IoT application domains and case studies. The focus here is on the enterprise side of the IoT, with applications such as automotive and transportation, manufacturing and supply chain, energy, and other industrial uses (hence the name "Enterprise IoT"). This is followed by a set of associated case studies. Our analysis of these case studies provides the basis for our Ignite | IoT Methodology, which we introduce in Part II.

Part II: Ignite | IoT Methodology
   The second part of the book outlines the Ignite | IoT Methodology. This methodology is based on the best practices and lessons learned from the case studies in Part I. Ignite | IoT looks at the enterprise level as well as the product and project levels. The general aim

is to provide IoT practitioners with actionable guidelines on how best to implement an IoT strategy and related projects.

Part III: Detailed Case Study

The final part of the book presents a detailed case study of a project that was implemented using the Ignite | IoT Methodology. Most of the case studies in Part I were analyzed retrospectively, as our methodology was not available when these projects were first started. The case study in Part III was implemented using Ignite | IoT Methodology right from the outset.

Figure P-1 provides a visual overview of the book.

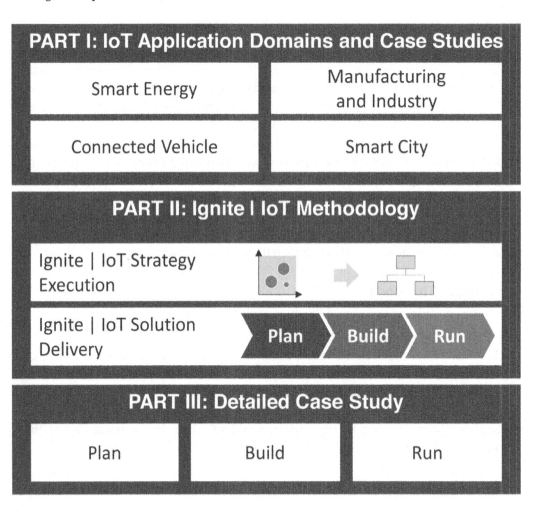

FIGURE P-1. Structure of this book

How to Use This Book

Depending on your specific background and interests, we recommend that you use this book as follows:

IoT strategist

IoT strategists will most likely be interested in Part I and the first element of the Ignite | IoT Methodology (IoT Strategy Execution).

IoT project and product managers

IoT project managers and product managers will also like Part I, and will find a lot of value in the Ignite | IoT Solution Delivery section in particular.

IoT solution architects

IoT solution architects can browse through Parts I and II, but might want to start by looking at Part III in more detail, as this is a hands-on example of the Ignite | IoT Methodology in use.

We will begin by introducing some key Enterprise IoT concepts before moving on to Part I. We hope you enjoy this book, and we look forward to receiving your feedback.

Safari® Books Online

 *Safari Books Online* is an on-demand digital library that delivers expert content in both book and video form from the world's leading authors in technology and business.

Technology professionals, software developers, web designers, and business and creative professionals use Safari Books Online as their primary resource for research, problem solving, learning, and certification training.

Safari Books Online offers a range of plans and pricing for enterprise, government, education, and individuals.

Members have access to thousands of books, training videos, and prepublication manuscripts in one fully searchable database from publishers like O'Reilly Media, Prentice Hall Professional, Addison-Wesley Professional, Microsoft Press, Sams, Que, Peachpit Press, Focal Press, Cisco Press, John Wiley & Sons, Syngress, Morgan Kaufmann, IBM Redbooks, Packt, Adobe Press, FT Press, Apress, Manning, New Riders, McGraw-Hill, Jones & Bartlett, Course Technology, and hundreds more. For more information about Safari Books Online, please visit us online.

How to Contact Us

Please address comments and questions concerning this book to the publisher:

O'Reilly Media, Inc.
1005 Gravenstein Highway North
Sebastopol, CA 95472
800-998-9938 (in the United States or Canada)
707-829-0515 (international or local)
707-829-0104 (fax)

We have a web page for this book, where we list errata, examples, and any additional information. You can access this page at *http://bit.ly/enterprise_iot*.

To comment or ask technical questions about this book, send email to *bookquestions@oreilly.com*.

For more information about our books, courses, conferences, and news, see our website at *http://www.oreilly.com*.

Find us on Facebook: *http://facebook.com/oreilly*

Follow us on Twitter: *http://twitter.com/oreillymedia*

Watch us on YouTube: *http://www.youtube.com/oreillymedia*

Acknowledgments

First of all, we would like to thank our executive sponsors, Dr. Volkmar Denner (Chairman, Bosch Group) and Mr. Anand Mahindra (Chairman, Mahindra Group), as well as Dr. Rainer Kallenbach (CEO, Bosch Software Innovations) and CP Gurnani (CEO, Tech Mahindra).

Many thanks also to our Keynote Contributors, including Peter Coffee (Salesforce.com), Wim Elfrink (Cisco), Jim Heppelmann (PTC), Mike Olson (Cloudera), and Alex Sinclair (GSMA).

A big "thank you" goes to all of the Enterprise IoT community members who are listed at the end of the book—it has been fun working with you, and we really appreciate the long days and nights and the challenging discussions! Special thanks is due to Thomas Stoffel from Siemens for kicking things off.

We spent a lot of time talking with technology and industry experts. Your input was invaluable! Many thanks to Alexander Grohmann (Kärcher), Allen Prohithis (Wot.io), Andre Nitzschmann (Fraunhofer IIS), Andres Rosello (PTC), Arthur Viegers (MongoDB), Berhard Schäfer (m3), Bernard Duprieu (Airbus), Bernard Kryszak, Bernd Gruber (indoo.rs), Bill Ruh (GE), Brian Hayes (Salesforce.com), Brian Philippi (NI), Brian Westcott (Purfresh), Christian Czauderna (Currenta), Christoph Schillo (Peiker), Christopher Dziekan (Pentaho), Elgar Fleisch (HSG), Enrique Gutierrez (Peiker), Felix Worthmann (IoT Lab @ HSG), Heiner Lasi (Steinbeis University), Ian Skerrett (Eclipse Foundation), James Dixon (Pentaho), James Smith (NI), Jason Garbis (RSA), Joe Drumgoole (MongoDB), Joe Salvo (GE), Kai Millarg

(Intellion), Laurenz Kirchner (mmi), Marc Jones (Aeris), Marc Sauter (Vodafone), Markus Weinberger (IoT Lab @ HSG), Michael Ganser (Cisco), Michael Lee (IIC), Micheal Jungmann (WJW), Mike Prince (Vodafone), Mitko Vasilev (Cisco), Nico Neufeld (CERN), Nigel Chadwick (Stream Technologies), Peter Fürst (five i), Rainer Eschrich (Oracle), Richard Soley (IIC), Rick Bullotta (PTC), Robin Smith (Oracle), Robin Smith (Oracle), Roman Wambacher (WJW), Sean O'Sullivan (LocalSocial), Sebastien Boria (Airbus), Stefanie Fischer (SmartFactoryKL), Stella Löffler (mmi), Stephan Otto (Fraunhofer IIS), Stephen Blackburn (Aeris), Sverre Jarp (CERN), Ted Willke (Intel), Torsten Winterberg (Opitz), and Volker Scholz (mmi).

From Machina Research, we would like to thank Jeremy Green and Emil Berthelsen.

From Tech Mahindra, we would like to thank Asit Goel, Devashish Bhatt, and Narayanan Ramanathan.

From Bosch Software Innovations, we would like to thank Daniela Hartmann-Ege, Didier Manning, Michael Schlauch, Stefanie Lipps, Steffen Schmickler, and Tom Srocke.

From the rest of the Bosch Group, we would like to thank Julian Bartholomeyczik (Bosch Connected Devices and Solutions), Martin Dölfs (Bosch Rexroth), Olaf Klemd (Bosch), Peter Busch (Bosch), Silke Vogel (Bosch), Stefan Schuster (Bosch Connected Devices and Solutions), Sven Kappel (Bosch), Tapio Torikka (Bosch Rexroth), Thomas Wollinger (ESCRYPT), Thorsten Müller (Bosch Connected Devices and Solutions), and Tim Kornherr (Bosch ST).

For review and production support, we would like to extend our thanks to Sinéad Healy and Anne Molloy from Nova Language Solutions, Ruth Townsend, and especially Christiane Prager, without whom we would have had no chance of surviving this project.

And, finally, we would like to thank our friends and family for their support and patience.

Dirk Slama
Frank Puhlmann
Jim Morrish
Rishi Bhatnagar

CHAPTER 1

Overture

Mission: 50 Billion Connected Devices by 2020

If you did a Google search for "IoT" in 2012, the top results would have included "Illuminates of Thanateros" and "International Oceanic Travel Organization." A search for "Internet of Things" would have produced a results page with a list of academic papers at the top, but with no advertisements—a strong indicator that in 2012, few people spent marketing dollars on the IoT.

Two years on, and this had changed dramatically. In 2014, the IoT was one of the most hyped buzzwords in the IT industry. IT analysts everywhere tried to outdo each other's growth projections for 2020, from Cisco's 50 billion connected devices to Gartner's economic value add of 1.9 trillion dollars (Figure 1-1).

Until we have reached this point in the future, no one can tell just how realistic these predictions are. However, the excitement generated around these growth numbers is significant, not least because it highlights a general industry trend while also creating a self-fulfilling prophecy of sorts.

We saw something similar happening with the auctioning of new mobile spectrum in the early 2000s. Literally billions were invested in the mobile Internet. And although it took longer than expected (remember the WAP protocol?), the mobile Internet eventually took off with the launch of Apple's iPhone, and has since exceeded market expectations.

Some Big Numbers:

Some Small Numbers:

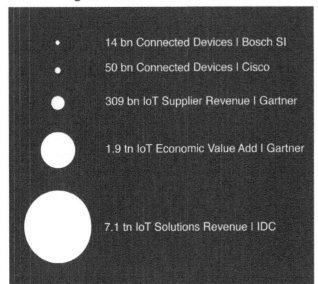

- 14 bn Connected Devices | Bosch SI
- 50 bn Connected Devices | Cisco
- 309 bn IoT Supplier Revenue | Gartner
- 1.9 tn IoT Economic Value Add | Gartner
- 7.1 tn IoT Solutions Revenue | IDC

Data from http://postscapes.com/internet-of-things-market-size

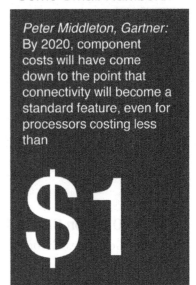

Peter Middleton, Gartner:
By 2020, component costs will have come down to the point that connectivity will become a standard feature, even for processors costing less than

$1

FIGURE 1-1. IoT predictions

Meanwhile, Google—another major player in the mobile Internet sphere—has bet heavily on the IoT with its acquisition of Nest and Nest's subsequent acquisition of DropCam. In addition, 2014 also saw many large IT vendors pushing themselves into pole position in the race for IoT supremacy, such as PTC with its acquisitions of ThingWorx and Axeda. On the industry side of things, many central European manufacturers and engineering companies rallied around the Industry 4.0 initiative, which promotes the use of IoT concepts in manufacturing. GE heavily promoted the Industrial Internet and spearheaded the establishment of the Industrial Internet Consortium. Many industrial companies began implementing IoT strategies and launching IoT pilot programs. And slowly the first real results emerged. Some were telematics or machine-to-machine (M2M) solutions dressed up as IoT solutions, while others were true IoT solutions according to our definition, which we will provide in Chapter 2.

Thus, at the time of writing, it seems that the final verdict on the significance of the IoT is still out. However, it looks as though industry is determined to seize the opportunities promised by the IoT. The authors of this book believe that the IoT (or whatever it will be called 5–10 years from now) will become as fundamental as the Internet itself. It took the Internet about 25 years to become as ubiquitous as television and the telephone system, and to transform a large number of industries. The situation in 2014 is reminiscent of the climate in the early 1990s, when we had our first exposure to Mosaic, and later Netscape, and the promises they stood for. Just think what a long way we have come since then, and where we stand with the IoT at the present time.

Customer Perspective: Value-Added Services

From the customer's point of view, the main benefit offered by the IoT will be new services enabled by connected products and (potentially) backend services based on Big Data. Figure 1-2 provides an overview. Within different ecosystems (we call them Subnets of Things, or SoTs), assets (or devices that are part of an asset) are connected to a cloud or enterprise backend. New services are emerging with software running both on the asset and in the backend. For example, the Connected Horizon [BoschCH14] is a technology that has been developed by Bosch. It provides a backend that combines traditional map data with additional data such as traffic signs and road conditions, and then uses this data in the car to provide the driver and the vehicle's various control devices with important advance information that enables safer driving. This is a good example of an SoT that already integrates a multitude of devices and external data sources.

Integration between different SoTs can occur at multiple levels. Assets can communicate with each other directly (e.g., in Car2Car, Car2X, etc.), or alternatively, integration can take place in the backend (e.g., Cloud2Cloud, Cloud2Enterprise, etc.)

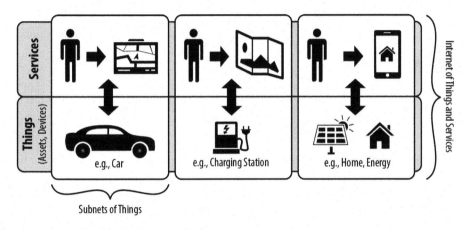

FIGURE 1-2. Internet of Things and Services (IoTS)

For the end user, the advantages are value-added services based on connected assets and devices. Big Data can provide contextual information, as seen in the Connected Horizon example. Furthermore, Big Data analytics can be used to initiate additional customer services, such as recommendations based on customer profile and current location. There is no shortage of ideas for new business models based on these new technological capabilities.

Manufacturer Perspective: Connected Asset Lifecycle Management

From the manufacturer's point of view, the potential impact of the IoT is equally as vast. Most manufacturers today hear very little about their products once they leave the factory. In fact, this was traditionally seen as the best possible outcome, the most likely alternative being a costly product recall.

The ability to connect (almost) any kind of product to the IoT has the potential to fundamentally transform the value chain of product manufacturers. The traditionally disconnected asset lifecycle will become a fully connected asset lifecycle (Figure 1-3).

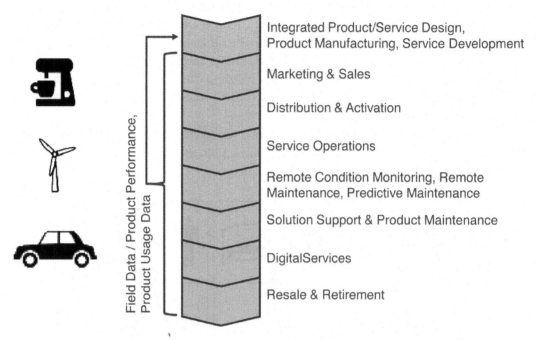

FIGURE 1-3. Connected asset lifecycle management

As we will discuss throughout this book, the capabilities provided by the IoT require a new appraisal of product design. How can new products leverage these new capabilities? How can value-added IoT services be created based on existing physical products? How can data received from connected products be used to optimize product design? How can we reconcile the different development times typically found in the worlds of physical products and software services? How can we align diverging development models (e.g., a Waterfall model for physical products and an Agile model for software services)?

New real-time and long-term analytics of usage data from connected products on the demands and behavior of product users will also have a dramatic impact on sales and marketing, as it provides new insights into usage patterns and value creation. Moreover, the IoT also has the potential to fundamentally change business models and value propositions, by moving from an asset-centric transactional sales model to a relationship-oriented service model, for example. In turn, this will require new organizational capabilities in sales and marketing.

Connected products also call for specialized processes for product or service activation, including the enablement of basic communication features (e.g., the activation of embedded SIM cards) as well as user account setup and management, and so on.

Following product activation, new remote-monitoring capabilities can be leveraged both by the service and the sales organizations. Particularly for industrial products, the use of remote condition monitoring in order to provide customers with advance warnings about potential problems, thus increasing Overall Equipment Efficiency (OEE), can be an important value add. Internally, product/service processes can be optimized by leveraging the same data. Analysis of product usage patterns could potentially help sales teams identify cross- and up-selling opportunities.

More than anything else, the combination of physical products and digital services has the potential to generate significant revenue after the sale of the initial product or service. Consider, for example, a service that allows customers to upgrade the engine performance of their cars for a weekend trip by temporarily reconfiguring the engine software.

Finally, connected products also make it easier to get involved in product resale and retirement activities, which is important from the point of view of customer retention.

Servitization: The Next Logical Step?

Taking things one step further, many people in the IoT community see servitization as the next logical progression in the evolution of the IoT. The concept of servitization has been around since the late 1980s [Van88], but is currently experiencing a boost thanks to new capabilities such as connected asset lifecycle management.

The basic idea of servitization is that manufacturers move from a model based on selling assets toward a model in which they offer a service that utilizes those assets. For example, Hilti offers a service that guarantees customers access to required power-tool capabilities for as long as they are needed, wherever they are needed. The monthly fee—which includes costs for tool provisioning, service, and repairs—makes financial planning much easier for customers. Similarly, Rolls-Royce, GE, and Pratt & Whitney offer aircraft engines as a service (for a fixed rate per flying hour). One immediate benefit of such models for customers is that instead of earning money for each repair, suppliers are now highly incentivized to reduce the need for repairs, because they have to carry the costs themselves. And fewer repairs means greater uptime for customers. In addition, customers can focus on their core competencies, such as running an airline. Finally, a recent study shows that servitization customers are reducing costs by up to 25%–30% [Aston14].

From a supplier perspective, servitization also has many benefits:

- Value-added services can generate additional revenue
- Continuous, service-based revenue streams allow for more predictable financial planning
- A recent study [Aston14] shows that servitization promises sustained annual business growth of 5%–10%
- Highly differentiated services increase competitiveness

However, servitization does not come for free. Many manufacturers are focusing on product features and capabilities instead of taking a customer perspective focused on outcomes (Figure 1-4).

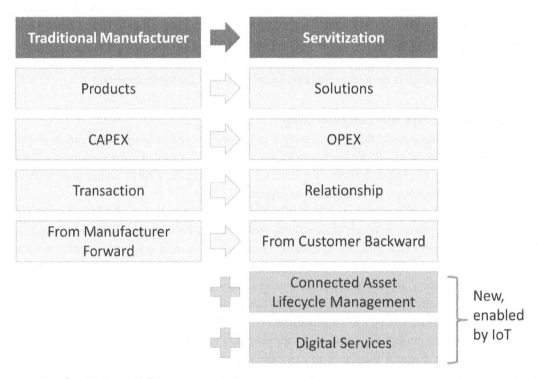

FIGURE 1-4. Servitization and IoT

Instead of focusing on products, the focal point of servitization must be solutions. Instead of emphasizing output, suppliers need to take a customer perspective and think about results. Single sales transactions are converted into long-standing customer relationships. All this requires numerous changes—from strategy and business models to technologies and organizational setup.

As already mentioned, servitization is not a new development, and has been successfully deployed outside of the IoT. However, the IoT is now adding interesting capabilities that could help make servitization more efficient, or even pave the way for servitization models that were previously unfeasible:

- The previously discussed concept of connected asset lifecycle management provides new insights into product usage, which can be leveraged to make servitization much more efficient for the supplier—for instance, by using remote condition monitoring instead of costly onsite equipment checks.

- New IoT-based digital services could create completely new service models, in which a predictive maintenance solution can be used to sell improved service-level agreements (SLAs) with greater guaranteed uptime, for example.

Prerequisite: Operator Approach

All of the approaches just discussed—from connected asset lifecycle management to servitization—have a common prerequisite: manufacturers must adopt an operator approach in order to implement them successfully. This is something that should not be underestimated, because it requires a completely different infrastructure, organizational setup, and set of processes from those found in a traditional manufacturing business. Operating an IoT-based service is not just a technical challenge; operational considerations can go far beyond the operation of an IT service infrastructure.

For example, the eCall service discussed later not only requires the operation of an IT infrastructure that can accept and process incoming distress signals from vehicles on the road; it also requires a physical business operation, mainly in the form of a call center that can receive incoming distress calls from drivers and ensure that these calls are answered in the right language, among other considerations.

Another example is provided by the real-time car-sharing services that we will discuss later. These services need an efficient fleet management process and service structure, which a manufacturer may not be able to establish and operate alone. For instance, it is no coincidence that BMW set up a joint venture with car rental company Sixt to operate the DriveNow service. It is clear that BMW is relying on Sixt's experience in operating a very large fleet of rental cars and car rental stations and in managing customer relationships.

Another interesting industry with a wealth of operator experience that may be hugely relevant to the IoT is the telecommunications industry. Few other sectors have as much experience in running an organization and infrastructure that supports millions of distributed, intelligent, connected devices with advanced backend services. Moreover, this industry has a great deal of experience in managing firmware and application updates for remote devices such as smartphones.

For companies striving to conquer the IoT, it will be vital to learn from these kinds of examples in their transition toward becoming service operators.

Impact: Disruption Versus Evolution

We believe that the IoT has the potential to disrupt many industries in the future, just as the Internet did over the last few decades. Take as an example real-time car-sharing services. A number of companies (e.g., DriveNow, Car2Go, and ZipCar) are now offering customers real-time car-sharing services. Instead of owning a car, customers can simply locate and reserve the nearest available car using an app on their smartphone, open the car with a chip card, use a specialized onboard unit in the car to manage the rental process, and simply lock and leave the car once they have reached their destination. Currently, these services are mainly limited to urban areas. However, with many young urban consumers no longer viewing a car as the ultimate status symbol, these kinds of services are becoming increasingly popular and have the potential to transform the entire automotive industry over the coming decades.

Another potential disruptive aspect of the IoT concerns data-driven business models in formerly asset-centric business areas. Google's Nest giving away thermostats for free, and then earning money by means of houseowners' behavior profiles, would be one example. Another scenario goes back to the example of car sharing. Imagine your service provider offering you 50% off the cost of a ride if you agree to listen to targeted advertisements while you drive. Combining your customer profile data with location-based information could be very attractive for local businesses eager to target you with special offers. In fact, this could even develop to the point where your local mall offers to sponsor your ride entirely, provided you use the car to drive to that specific mall. If we then add autonomous driving to the mix, the automotive industry will be changed beyond recognition, as it will truly have transformed into a transportation business.

There are many other examples of potentially disruptive business models driven by the IoT, from smart grids to smart homes and smart cities. However, a number of obstacles will also need to be overcome, including regulatory requirements (e.g., a lack of regulation permitting autonomous driving), an absence of standards to allow interoperability, and the complexity of some of the technologies required for some IoT applications.

Finally, not all use cases supported by the IoT are necessarily disruptive. Many companies today are looking at more evolutionary use cases—including remote condition monitoring (RCM), remote maintenance, and predictive maintenance—as well as highly specialized service add-ons for existing assets, such as the eCall Service, which notifies emergency services in the event of a car accident.

The important and potentially huge impact that these more evolutionary IoT-based servitization use cases will have on existing organizational structures should not be underestimated. Transforming a large service and support organization to make efficient use of remote services such as remote condition monitoring and remote maintenance will unquestionably require significant organizational change, and it may well take a number of years before the positive effects of these new capabilities are fully leveraged.

Clash of Two Worlds: Machine Camp Versus Internet Camp

As exciting as the opportunities presented by these "connected products with services" are, we need to bear in mind that they will require two fundamentally different worlds to work together: the physical world and the service world. And this is not as easy as it sounds.

The physical world has traditionally been dominated by what we will refer to (for simplicity's sake) as the "machine camp": manufacturers, engineering companies, and so on (Figure 1-5). On the other hand, we have the "Internet camp": companies that have, over the last 25 years, rapidly transformed several industries with their Internet-based service offerings.

"Machine Camp"	"Internet Camp"
▪ "Brown field" ▪ Strong company heritage, risk aversion ▪ Corporate career is the norm ▪ Domains: Physics, engineering ▪ "Think big" ▪ Waterfall approach ▪ Standards like DIN/ISO ▪ Long QA & release cycles ("defect free") ▪ Long lead times	▪ "Green field" ▪ High-risk, VC-driven culture ▪ Entrepreneurial management and employees ▪ Domains: IT, services ▪ Focus on point solutions/MVP ▪ Agile approach ▪ Open source ▪ Perpetual beta ("Fast patches")

FIGURE 1-5. "Machine camp" versus "Internet camp"

Most people in the machine camp work for companies that have a long heritage, some with roots in the early Industrial Revolution. To achieve such long-term success, careful risk management and long-term strategic thinking is paramount. Those in the Internet camp, on the other hand, usually start on a green-field site without the restrictions of existing product lines that must be maintained, or corporate governance rules that must be followed, and often with extremely big risks. The venture capital (VC) funds often backing these companies actually demand such high-risk/high-growth strategies. The VC business model is typically based on the assumption that only a small number of investments will succeed, but those that do will pay such a high dividend that it is acceptable to write off other failed investments (an approach described as "fail fast, fail often, fail cheap").

This also has a strong impact on corporate culture in these different environments. In the machine camp environment, a corporate career is the norm. Many managers will move between vastly different domains and roles over the lifetime of their career. This can lead to situations in which a longer learning curve is required in a new job. Members of the Internet camp are often more focused on subject matter, and tend to follow their passion rather than a long-term career development plan. This can be advantageous, in that they will push a project they strongly believe in much harder. On the other hand, many entrepreneurs generally tend to stay with a company during a specific phase only, often the early-growth phase.

Many of those in the machine camp have a background in physics or engineering, while the domain of the Internet camp is often IT and services—two key perspectives that need to be combined in the IoT world. Because of their background, people in the machine camp tend to think big in terms of complexity of solutions and global rollout (e.g., for cars, aircraft, or steel mills). The Internet camp usually also thinks big in terms of global rollout, but often starts with very focused point solutions (e.g., Skype, WhatsApp, Doodle, etc.) that evolve over time into more complex platforms (e.g., Amazon, eBay, or Salesforce.com). The concept of the minimum viable product (MVP) has become a common strategy for many startups, promoting an iterative process of idea generation, prototyping, field trial, data collection, analysis, and learning.

Another key difference that must be bridged in the IoT is the general approach to running projects. Many in the machine camp still run projects using a Waterfall model, while most in the Internet camp have by now adopted An agile approach. For many Internet companies, following a perpetual beta approach is the norm ("fast patches"). Large Internet portals commonly roll out multiple updates per day, often running test versions for smaller user groups in parallel. Those in the machine camp come from a world where a single failure can have potentially deadly consequences (e.g., malfunctioning car brakes) or, at the very least, result in costly and image-damaging product recalls. Naturally, therefore, lengthy QA and release cycles are the norm in this environment, the aim being "zero defects."

This is perhaps one of the biggest challenges for the IoT. However, it is clearly influenced not only by cultural differences, but also by technological restrictions. For decades, the machine camp had to deal with environments in which it was nearly impossible—or was otherwise cost prohibitive—to modify a product after it had been deployed in the field. With the ever-increasing digitization of products in the IoT, this is now changing. For example, it is now possible to remotely update the embedded software that controls a car engine. Of course, we are not suggesting that the perpetual beta approach should be applied to car engine control software. However, it is clear that there are many benefits to this new flexibility—for instance, the ability to simply roll out two million patches over a global, wireless network instead of having to recall two million products. Yet in order to take advantage of the new opportunities offered by digitized physical products, manufacturers will have to transform themselves into operators that are capable of managing these processes in a secure and highly reliable way. Incidentally, a lot can be learned from the telecommunications companies and smartphones platform operators here, as they are currently the only ones who understand how to operate networks comprising millions of intelligent, physical products and how to deal with issues such as software updates on this scale.

The pressure is on for many of those in the machine camp in this area. Customers do not understand why they can update their smartphone apps at the tap of a finger or purchase a new generation of powerful smartphone every year, but are stuck with their cars' onboard systems for years on end without the option to update hardware or software, or at least not easily. Nobody wants to spend an afternoon at the auto repair shop installing the new telematics unit required for a new, usage-based insurance (UBI) policy. Customers want the same experience they receive from their smartphones: "Do you want to allow the ACME Insurance app to access your driving behavior? Click 'yes' and save $100 a year on your car insurance."

Of course, the differences between the machine camp and the Internet camp are not just cultural or technological in nature. Another important area relates to standards and regulatory requirements. Those in the machine camp are accustomed to living in a world dominated by DIN, ISO, and the like. Whereas those in the Internet camp often take the liberty of ignoring these restrictions, especially in early development phases. Take, for example, the development of a truck fleet management solution with an integrated telematics unit. Regulations in different countries require the communication modules to use different frequencies. A startup might simply ignore this requirement and take the risk of rolling out a solution based on a single frequency in different countries, which may mean capturing markets faster, but at a higher risk. A large company simply cannot afford to take such a risk, and will attempt to build a multifrequency solution from the beginning. This means the solution will be much more complex to start with, and will probably be rolled out later and possibly at a higher cost. Managing such situations while also balancing cost efficiency and compliance is a key challenge for large companies, particularly in the context of the IoT.

Every company will need to find its own way of dealing with this "clash of two worlds." Some may try to build bridges and new capabilities internally; some may seek out partners; while others may decide to go down the acquisitions route. There are many different examples in practice, from Google's acquisition of Nest, to BMW's joint venture with Sixt for the new DriveNow car-sharing service.

Difficulty of Finding the Right Service

As we can see, bringing together the worlds of the machine and the Internet in the context of a single solution is challenging at the very least. Furthermore, in our experience, it is quite common for the development of an IoT solution to have one of the two perspectives as its starting point—i.e., either the Internet camp moves toward the physical world, or the machine camp moves toward the service world (Figure 1-6). Over the past few decades, the machine camp has transitioned from "things" to "intelligent things" by adding local intelligence using electronics. Now many are adding connectivity, and moving toward what we call "intelligent things with Internet services." The Internet camp, on the other hand, started off with Internet services, and is now moving toward "Internet services with (potentially intelligent) things." This means that we are essentially looking at two different versions of the same IoTS formula: one has a "thing" at its root, the other a service.

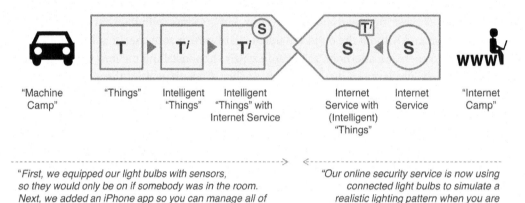

| "Machine Camp" | "Things" | Intelligent "Things" | Intelligent "Things" with Internet Service | Internet Service with (Intelligent) "Things" | Internet Service | "Internet Camp" |

"First, we equipped our light bulbs with sensors, so they would only be on if somebody was in the room. Next, we added an iPhone app so you can manage all of the electric lights in your home."

"Our online security service is now using connected light bulbs to simulate a realistic lighting pattern when you are away from home at night."

FIGURE 1-6. IoTS formula

Let's discuss the implications using a theoretical (and again exaggerated) example (inspired by [HSG14]): remote-controlled lightbulbs. In general, lightbulbs are a domain that has been dominated by the machine camp for the best part of a century, with high production volumes and usually low margins. Roughly 20 years ago, an interesting innovation took place whereby manufacturers added intelligence to lightbulbs by using motion detectors to switch on lights whenever movement was detected. And now we have the connected lightbulb, enabled by the IoT. So the question is: what happens if you ask people who have spent the last 20 years as a product manager for lightbulbs, focusing on improving things like energy consumption and product durability, to design a service that utilizes the new connectivity features? Our bet is that their immediate reflex would be to design a service that allows you to manage all of the lightbulbs in your home using your smartphone.

And what about the Internet camp? We expect that initially, they would not be interested, because remote management for lightbulbs is not the focus of their attention. But then one person in the Internet camp, who provides an Internet-based security service for homeowners, may pause and reconsider. What if you recorded the homeowners' light usage patterns and then played them back while they're on vacation? That way, the remote-controlled lightbulbs could be used to improve the security service by simulating the lighting pattern that would occur if the owners were at home.

Let's compare the two approaches. For the lightbulb manufacturer, adding the remote management service seems to make sense. The only question is this: will they be able to sell this service as a value add, and thus generate extra revenue? Or will customers simply assume this to be a standard feature of next-generation lightbulbs? Now take the security service that utilizes lightbulbs to provide an additional feature for a highly differentiated product. In this case, it seems more likely that the service owner will be able to charge extra for this feature, due to its innovative nature and the different context in which it is sold. However, they have no control over the technology used, and may run the risk of annoying their customers if the mechanism does not function properly—for example, if the lights stay on for the entire duration of the vacation, running up a big electricity bill. In summary, this means that we have two versions of our simplified IoTS formula for success:

- Intelligent Thing(s) with Service: $T^i + S$
- Service with Intelligent Thing(s): $S + T^i$

This example may not be perfect, but it helps to highlight some of the key points about the differences in thinking with regard to IoT business models. Many believe that truly transformative, IoT-enabled business models will require more out-of-the-box thinking in respect of new services, as our example demonstrates.

As outlined earlier, there are many other differences in the typical behavior of engineering-based companies versus Internet-based companies. Engineering companies would be well advised to adapt certain elements of the startup world, such as service thinking and a bit more of a "fail early, fail often" philosophy. Internet companies, on the other hand, will not succeed in the IoT unless they learn from engineering companies about how to ensure high product quality standards and integration with the lifecycles of nondigital products.

Foundation: Digitization of the Physical World

The foundation for the new business models enabled by the IoT is the digitization of the physical world. Billions of sensors that generate massive amounts of information, cost-effectively managed by utilizing state-of-the-art, scale-out, Big-Data architectures, provide the basis for new Internet-based services. Cost efficiency is probably the key word here; from telematics to M2M, connecting sensors and other components with backend databases is not a new phenomenon. However, as outlined earlier, previous solutions were costly and limited in both scope and functionality. Advances in technology such as processors for mobile devices, (almost) ubiquitous wireless communication infrastructures, scale-out cloud data management, and the emergence of IoT application platforms now seem likely to bring down the cost of creating a real-time digital image of the physical world to a level that will allow the emergence of several new data-driven business models. Of course, there won't be just one digital model of the entire physical world—we expect many different digital models to emerge, motivated by different use cases, company boundaries, partner ecosystems, and other parameters. We also expect these different digital models to develop along the lines of the Subnets of Things, which we described earlier. Using mashup technologies, different isolated digital models can be integrated to form more complex models that also help advance the transition from Subnets of Things to the IoT. These real-time digital models of the real world, enabled by sensors and Big Data, will provide the foundation for numerous different use cases, many of which are not even known yet.

Critical: Security and Data Privacy

The excitement surrounding digital models of the physical world, including the collection of new customer usage data and product data, also creates concerns for many users—and rightly so. Security is one such concern. Not only do we need to ensure that all of this "big" data in the backend is managed in a secure fashion; in a distributed environment such as the IoT, we need to secure the connections between the different participants, as well as the hardware and software running on the assets. Stuxnet [ST1] and the hacking of the Tesla Model S electric car [TH1] by Chinese students in 2014 illustrate just how important this issue will become. Imagine a hostage situation where criminals hacked into a pacemaker, or seized control of an aircraft in flight...

The other side of the equation is less concerned with external intruders and hackers, and more focused on the corporate policies and governance processes regulating the newly obtained customer and product data. One aspect here is compliance with regulatory and legal requirements in different countries. Another aspect is transparency and respect for customer rights and preferences. Many users rely on social networking services such as Facebook and LinkedIn to use their social media data to generate relevant updates and recommendations. However, these same users are frequently frustrated by the complex and ever-changing data usage policies enforced by such companies.

Given the nature of the data that could potentially be acquired by IoT solutions—not just social data submitted more or less voluntarily, but data captured by possibly hidden sensors and vital systems—it will be absolutely essential for the IoT industry to efficiently handle security and data privacy. Otherwise, there is a huge risk that customers will not accept these new IoT solutions, out of fear of an Orwellian dystopia.

Timing: Why Now?

Finally, many people ask: Why now? We have been waiting for hockey-stick growth curves in the M2M market for nearly a decade; why is the IoT taking off now? The answer to this question has partly to do with momentum, partly with business models, and partly with technology. In 2014, we could see that the IoT had gathered a momentum not shared by M2M. Business magazines like *Forbes* and *Der Spiegel* dedicated lengthy articles to the topic, creating a high level of visibility. Many large businesses have now instructed their strategy departments to devise IoT-based business models—even if we are still in the learning phase in this respect. Initial business successes can be seen, with examples such as ZipCar, DriveNow, and Car2Go. Most large IT players now offer dedicated IoT implementation services, IoT middleware, or IoT hardware (or a combination of all three). Finally, a combination of different technologies seems to have reached a point where managing the complexity of IoT solutions has now become more feasible and cost efficient:

Moore's law
Ever-increasing hardware performance enables new levels of abstraction in the embedded space, which provides the basis for semantically rich embedded applications and the decoupling of on-asset hardware and software lifecycles. The app revolution for smartphones will soon be replicated in the embedded space.

Wireless technology
From ZigBee to Bluetooth LE, and from LTE/4G to specialized low-power, wide-area (LPWA) IoT communication networks—the foundation for "always-on" assets and devices is either already available or in the process of being put in place.

Metcalfe's law
Information and its value grow exponentially as the number of nodes connected to the IoT increases. With more and more remote assets being connected, it looks like we are reaching a tipping point.

Battery technology
Ever-improving battery quality enables new business models, from electric vehicles to battery-powered beacons.

Sensor technology
Ever-smaller and more energy-efficient sensors integrated into multiaxis sensors and sensor clusters, an increasing number of which are preinstalled in devices and assets.

Big Data
Technology that is able to ingest, process, and analyze the massive amounts of sensor-generated data at affordable cost.

The cloud
The scalable, global platform that delivers data-centric services to enable new IoT business models.

While nobody knows for sure exactly how many billions of devices will be connected by 2020, it looks as though the technical foundation for this growth is maturing rapidly, inspiring new business models, and making this an extremely exciting space to work in.

Keynote Contribution: IoT and Smart, Connected Products

To conclude our Overture, we have included an interview with James (Jim) Heppelmann. He is the president and chief executive officer (CEO) of PTC and is responsible for driving PTC's global business strategy and operations. Previous to his appointment as CEO, Mr. Heppelmann served as PTC's president and chief operating officer, responsible for managing the operating business units of the company, including R&D, marketing, sales, services, and maintenance. He also serves on PTC's Board of Directors.

Mr. Heppelmann has worked in the information technology industry since 1985 and has extensive experience developing and deploying large-scale product development systems within the manufacturing marketplace. Prior to joining PTC, Mr. Heppelmann was cofounder and chief technical officer of Windchill Technology, a Minnesota-based company acquired by PTC in 1998.

Mr. Heppelmann travels extensively to customer sites around the globe and speaks regularly at product development and manufacturing industry forums on topics such as the IoT, PLM, and gaining competitive advantage through product development process improvement. He has also been published and quoted in numerous business and trade media, including *Harvard Business Review*, *The Wall Street Journal*, and *Bloomberg Television*.

Dirk Slama: PTC has long been known as a leader in computer-aided design (CAD) and product lifestyle management (PLM). However, most recently you seem to focus a lot on IoT. Your acquisition of ThingWorx and Axeda alone must have cost you nearly a quarter of a billion dollars.

Jim Heppelmann: We see IoT as a disruptive force that will transform existing industries, especially in our core markets like manufacturing and engineering. PTC responded earlier to the growth of software-intensive products and service-oriented business models with hundreds of millions of dollars of investments in those key areas over the last 10 years. Adding connectivity to the product and service lifecycle solutions we already provide enables our customer to close the loop and transform the way they create, operate, and service their products. These investments will enable us to provide the best possible support for our customers in this critical transformation process, and certainly charts a course for PTC that is quite different from other CAD and PLM providers.

Dirk Slama: We have seen many M2M applications in the last couple of years that were focused on retrofitting remote condition monitoring (RCM)–like applications onto existing assets. Your vision for IoT-enabled products seems to go much further.

Jim Heppelmann: Such retrofitting approaches are important and will continue to play an important role for many established long-lived assets and products; however, we also see a new breed of products emerging that have been specifically designed to leverage the IoT. For these products, connectivity is not an optional add-on; rather, it is designed into the product. Many of the core features of these new products will rely on this built-in connectivity. Physical products and related cloud services are forming new ecosystems, like Apple devices and iTunes cloud services. We call this new breed of products "smart, connected products."

Dirk Slama: So I assume that we need to rethink PLM for these smart, connected products?

Jim Heppelmann: Yes. Traditional PLM tools, in truth, really focus on the early stages of the product's lifecycle—product design and development. We need to look at the entire product and service lifecycle, including product design, manufacturing, sales/marketing, customer operations, and after-sales services.

Dirk Slama: Let's start with product design. What are the key issues here?

Jim Heppelmann: On the functional level, the product designers need to take a holistic systems engineering approach to design across the hardware and software layers of the physical product, and across the physical product and the related cloud services. Which new services can be enabled, and from where should they be enabled? And which existing functions can be optimized by leveraging connectivity—for example, by replacing clumsy onboard displays and buttons with a web interface that allows the operator or manufacturer to monitor, control, or configure the product from a new user interface, such as a smartphone? While enabling new capabilities, this approach dramatically increases the complexity of design and requires new design principles.

For example, to design for customization or personalization, designers need to capture the opportunity of hardware standardization through software-based customization. More and more of the variability of products today comes from the software layer, which drives down costs and enables customization later in the process. There is also a virtuous cycle here as innovations in the software layer drive increased value in the hardware, but hardware and software development have fundamentally different "clock speeds." We might see 10 software releases in the time it takes to create one new version of the physical product on which the software runs.

This leads to another new design principle, designing for continuous upgrades and enhancements so that smart, connected products leverage connectivity for software upgrades throughout the life of the product. Design principles now need to anticipate opportunities to add or enhance product capabilities, and allow for these upgrades to occur remotely and in an efficient manner. Basically, the product becomes a platform on which increasing amounts of value can be delivered via software over time.

We also need to understand the new capabilities required in the development organization. Formerly siloed development teams need to interact much more closely, integrating the products' hardware, electronics, software, and connectivity components. Agile software development processes need to be established and coexist with the more traditional hardware development cycles. New processes need to be defined to close the loop with product design. Direct, continuous, and often real-time data about how the product is being used will give engineering rapid feedback on how well their design functioned in the real world rather than simply using scenario-based simulation and testing. Value can be created from this data by using it to understand how to improve designs so that enhanced second and third generations of products are brought to market more quickly.

Dirk Slama: This also requires a new approach to sales and marketing?

Jim Heppelmann: Smart, connected products create new opportunities and reasons to transform your value proposition and even address completely different markets and refined customer segments.

This requires a different marketing approach and potentially new skill sets, too. The whole relationship with the customer is changing because companies are now able to stay in touch with the product after the initial sale. The product, in a sense, becomes a sensor for the relationship with the customer. Companies can gain amazingly detailed insights into the customer relationship by collecting and analyzing product usage data to understand how the product is performing, how much is it being utilized, which features are being used, and which features are not. This allows companies to improve segmentation, deploy more granular and targeted pricing models, deliver new, value-added services, and anticipate the needs of their customers. Recurring revenue streams can be created by combining physical products with digital content and services, which requires companies to transform the processes and culture across their marketing and sales organizations, and potentially their business models, to capture more of the newly created value. The implications of shifting from a discrete product sale to streams of upgrades and services over the product's life are dramatic.

Dirk Slama: So "after sales" becomes "sales after the initial sale"?

Jim Heppelmann: Correct. Because products are now connected, we can stay in touch with the customer throughout the entire lifecycle of the product. This creates tremendous potential for cross-selling and up-selling. Take, for example, car engines. Instead of manufacturing multiple engines with different levels of horsepower, the horsepower rating on the same physical engine can be modified using software alone. By connecting this smart capability with a cloud service, a customer could upgrade his car for his weekend trip up the coastal highway; hence smart, connected products.

Dirk Slama: But traditional after sales services are still important?

Jim Heppelmann: Yes, of course. Product usage data can reveal current and potential future problems. Preventive and predictive maintenance are enabling product users and service organizations to prevent machine downtimes and improve overall equipment effectiveness (OEE).

For example, most service events today require multiple passes. The first pass enables a technician to identify the nature of the failure and what will be required to correct the problem; the second pass is to perform the actual repair. With smart, connected products, service technicians can obtain all "first pass" information remotely, and may even be able to perform the repair remotely if the failure can be remedied via software. The savings associated with reduced service calls can be substantial, and the product usage data can also be used to validate warranty claims and to identify warranty agreement violations, another huge expense for most product companies today. These approaches allow a manufacturer to transform its service business from reactive to proactive and create substantial gains in both service and operational efficiency.

However, this doesn't come for free, and also has the potential to disrupt the high revenue, high profit service businesses that many companies have in place today. Service organizations that connect product condition and operations data with existing service processes can transform those processes, and potentially enable new processes and services that take advantage of the insights that come from the smart, connected products. By monitoring a product's condition and proactively delivering service, sometimes via software, a company can improve the reliability and availability of the product. The potential benefits are significant, including reductions in field-service dispatch costs and capital costs for spare-part inventories. The threat of disruption comes if the benefit of the reduced need for spare parts and service visits accrues to the end customer, who then pays less for the cost of service. This reduced service demand may create a kind of "service paradox" for companies pursuing a smart, connected product strategy.

Dirk Slama: You recently coauthored the Harvard Business Review article "How Smart, Connected Products Are Transforming Competition" (*http://bit.ly/smart_products*) with Prof. Porter from Harvard Business School. In this article, you identified 10 strategic choices derived from the push toward smart, connected products.

Jim Heppelmann: The transformation ahead of many companies requires a clear definition of the goals and strategy in this area. A strategy requires trade-offs that create a unique competitive position, which has to be defined at the executive level and communicated to all relevant stakeholders. There is no right or wrong answer, only choices that must reinforce one another and define a coherent and distinctive overall strategic position for the company. Our framework of 10 strategic choices can help to define that company-specific strategy (Figure 1-7).

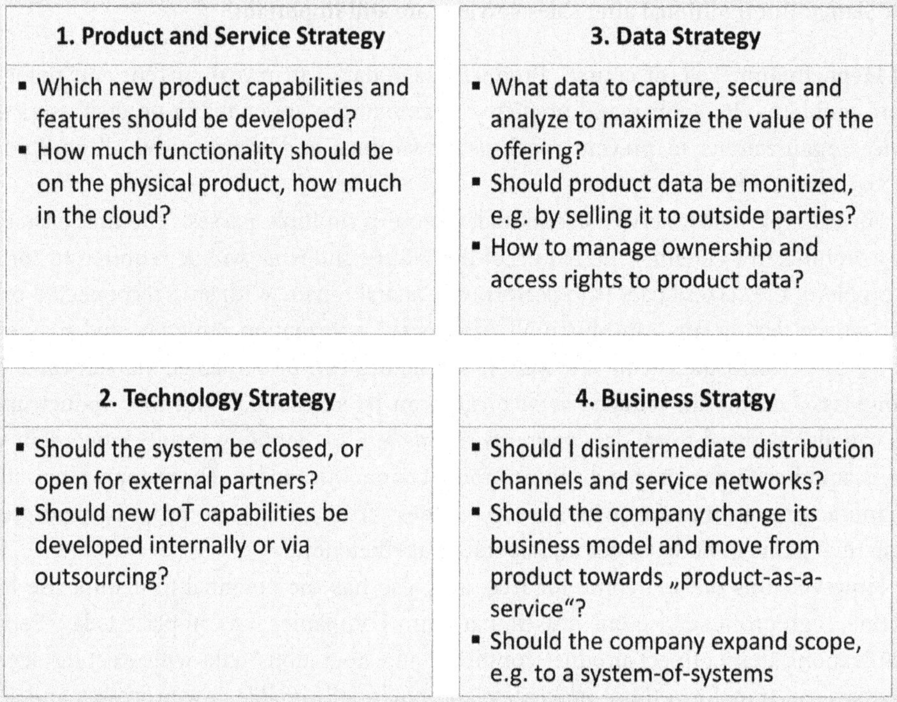

1. Product and Service Strategy	3. Data Strategy
• Which new product capabilities and features should be developed? • How much functionality should be on the physical product, how much in the cloud?	• What data to capture, secure and analyze to maximize the value of the offering? • Should product data be monitized, e.g. by selling it to outside parties? • How to manage ownership and access rights to product data?
2. Technology Strategy	4. Business Stratgy
• Should the system be closed, or open for external partners? • Should new IoT capabilities be developed internally or via outsourcing?	• Should I disintermediate distribution channels and service networks? • Should the company change its business model and move from product towards „product-as-a-service"? • Should the company expand scope, e.g. to a system-of-systems

FIGURE 1-7. 10 strategic choices for IoT, based on HBR article by Jim Heppelmann and Prof. Porter

The first set of questions is around the product and service strategy, starting with: Which capabilities should the company pursue? A smart, connected product drastically expands the number of potential product and service capabilities, but just because a company can offer many new capabilities doesn't ensure there is sufficient value for customers above the incurred costs to the company. Next is how to best deliver those new product and service capabilities by determining how much functionality should be embedded in the product versus the cloud. Factors like required response time, expected network availability, complexity of the user interface, and frequency of service events or product upgrades will impact those decisions. The next set of questions is around the technology infrastructure required to enable smart, connected products. Developing the technology stack for smart, connected products requires significant investment in specialized skills, technologies, and infrastructure that have not been typically present in manufacturing companies. Some of the early pioneers like General Electric and Bosch have invested heavily via a largely in-house route to capture first-mover advantages and retain greater control over features, functionality, and product data. However, just as Intel has specialized in microprocessors and Oracle in databases, new firms that specialize in components of the smart, connected products technology stack are already emerging, and some in-house efforts may overestimate the ability to stay ahead, turning an early lead into a long-term disadvantage. A related question is whether the system architecture should be open or closed, where key interfaces are proprietary and only chosen parties gain access. While this has clear benefits for the company to control and optimize the systems, over time we expect closed approaches to become more challenging as technology spreads, ecosystems develop, and customers resist limits on choice.

Dirk Slama: The increasing focus on product data also requires a strategic take?

Jim Heppelmann: Yes, we see data and the insights derived from analytics becoming the key differentiator in a smart, connected world. This is really key to capturing the full opportunity. There are three strategic choices specific to data, first of which is: What data do I need? Capturing and analyzing data is fundamental to value creation, but also imposes costs and risks. Variable product costs increase from additional sensors, carrier-based data transmission, and so on, and fixed costs from robust analytics capabilities and skills required to translate Big Data into insight. And almost any data collected brings with it the risk and burden of data stewardship to ensure that all the data is secure and protected over time.

This relates to the next data choice around how the company manages ownership and access rights to the data. Firms must determine their approach to data ownership, sharing, and transparency. For example, providing data access to upstream component suppliers may improve component quality and innovation but may lead to new competitive threats if the supplier develops value-added services for the end customer using the data. The services that GE Aviation provides directly to airlines based on data collected from the aircraft engine is a real-world example for Boeing and Airbus.

This brings us to the third data choice about monetizing the data. Companies may find that the data they capture is valuable to entities beyond their traditional customers, creating new services or even businesses. The challenge is in defining mechanisms that provide valuable data to third parties without alienating existing customers or increasing regulatory risks.

Dirk Slama: All of these choices seem to open up some corporate-level decisions around the company's business model and scope.

Jim Heppelmann: Yes, through the capabilities and data generated by smart, connected products, firms are now able to maintain direct and deep customer relationships through the products, which can reduce the need for distribution channel partners. Tesla Motors, for example, has disrupted the automotive industry by selling cars directly to consumers rather than through a dealer network. In an existing business, we would only caution not to underestimate the relationship that customers may have with existing channel and service partners.

Through those same capabilities, companies may be inclined to change their business model from product sales toward product-as-a-service. As customers pay for the performance of the product instead of the ownership of the asset, the value of the product improvements (like improving product quality or service efficiency) will be captured by the manufacturer.

Finally, as products continue to integrate in product systems and diverse networks, many companies will have to reexamine their core mission and determine what role they want to play in these larger systems; should they attempt to provide the platform and services for the entire system or play a supporting role in a broader industry landscape?

All difficult choices, but we believe that by providing the right strategic framework and ensuring the right environment for their execution, IoT and smart, connected products will be the foundation for the next era of IT-driven productivity growth for these companies and their customers.

CHAPTER 2

Enterprise IoT

THE TITLE OF THIS BOOK IS *Enterprise IoT* BECAUSE WE FOCUS ON A SPECIFIC SUBSET OF enterprise solutions within the larger realm of the Internet of Things. It is not our intention to invent yet another category, as there are already enough in this area—including Cisco's Internet of Everything, GE's Industrial Internet, and the German Industry 4.0 initiative. However, for a book such as this, we believe that it is helpful to have a clearly defined scope and give it an explicit name. In this section, we will explain the origins of Enterprise IoT and provide a definition.

From M2M Toward the IoT

The idea of connecting devices and applications is not new. Specialized telematics solutions have been around for a long time. Over the last decade, machine-to-machine (M2M) communication became widely established, a development driven by players such as telecommunications companies looking for new ways to leverage their existing mobile networks. So what is the difference between M2M and IoT? There is no black-and-white answer to this question, but Figure 2-1offers some general observations.

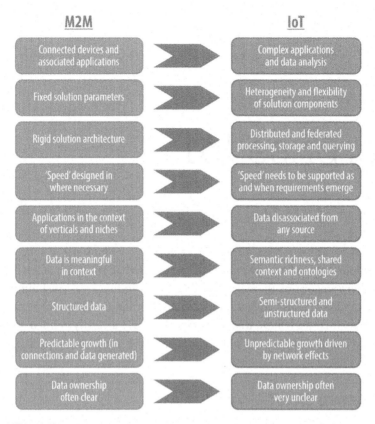

M2M

- Connected devices and associated applications
- Fixed solution parameters
- Rigid solution architecture
- 'Speed' designed in where necessary
- Applications in the context of verticals and niches
- Data is meaningful in context
- Structured data
- Predictable growth (in connections and data generated)
- Data ownership often clear

IoT

- Complex applications and data analysis
- Heterogeneity and flexibility of solution components
- Distributed and federated processing, storage and querying
- 'Speed' needs to be supported as and when requirements emerge
- Data disassociated from any source
- Semantic richness, shared context and ontologies
- Semi-structured and unstructured data
- Unpredictable growth driven by network effects
- Data ownership often very unclear

FIGURE 2-1. From M2M to IoT

The following excerpt from [MR13] summarizes what we feel to be the most important points:

Applications

M2M applications are about connecting devices and their associated applications—for instance, a smart meter and a smart metering application. IoT applications are potentially far more complex. They are characterized by complex event processing and data analysis and offer higher-level services.

Flexibility

While an M2M application is typically functionally specialized (dedicated) and quite inflexible, an IoT application needs to be more flexible in terms of its potential to evolve over time.

Architecture

Many M2M applications are deployed with a relatively rigid and unchanging solution architecture, while IoT applications are characterized by their need for distributed and federated processing, storage, and querying. In essence, when an M2M application is deployed, software engineers have a pretty good idea of what processing will need to take place over the entire lifetime of the solution. Conversely, because the range of IoT applications is ever-expanding and individual applications are often divorced from the underlying data feeds, different aspects of different IoT applications that may leverage the same data feeds might most efficiently be located in different places.

Speed

It is worth emphasizing the point about speed, by which we mean potentially minimizing transmission and processing delays to better support data analysis. "Speed" can be designed into an M2M solution as needed, and applications are capable of supporting the necessary "speed" requirements from Day 1. In an IoT environment, however, the need for speed in the delivery and processing of different data feeds may evolve and change over time.

Verticals

The discussion up to now highlights a related difference between M2M and IoT: M2M applications should be considered in the context of industry verticals and functional niches, whereas IoT applications have the potential to transcend these limitations to become cross-industry and cross-function applications.

Context

To support the flexibility of environment (discussed earlier in this list), it is necessary for IoT applications to be semantically rich and for associated contexts and ontologies to be clear. This is not the case for M2M applications, where data generated by an application only needs to be meaningful in the context of that specific application and within the boundaries of a known systems environment.

Structure

This leads to a wider point about the structure of data. In M2M, data is highly structured (and well documented). In an IoT environment, a developer may want to include CCTV feeds in an application, or crowdsourced information, or information derived from the Twittersphere. These information sources are at best semi-structured and at worst completely unstructured (depending to a great extent on the kind of information that the developer is trying to extract).

Growth

A related difference is the speed of growth that can be expected in M2M and IoT environments. In the case of an M2M application, growth is far more predictable. Typically, an M2M solution is designed for a specific market, or set of assets, and can be deployed in that addressable market in a relatively predictable way. Data generated by M2M solutions would typically grow linearly with device count. The growth in data volumes, transaction volumes, and applications in an IoT environment is driven by network effects between a diverse range of data sources. Accordingly, growth in the IoT space (on any measure) can be expected to be more exponential, rather than the more linear and predictable growth that characterizes the M2M space.

Data ownership

Lastly, it's worth touching on the topic of data ownership. While data ownership in the case of M2M connected solutions can often be unclear, the concept of data ownership in an IoT environment is far more complex. Fundamentally, in the case of M2M, the privacy of data can be considered within a known landscape of application, user, and regulatory requirements. In the case of IoT applications, however, data could potentially be used for contemporaneously unforeseen applications in unforeseen locations and for unforeseen beneficiaries. This is one of the major aspects of the IoT that large companies will have to deal with effectively if they do not want to lose their customers' trust.

Subnets of Things

Building on all of these points, [MR14] introduces the useful concept of Subnets of Things (SoTs) as a necessary step in the evolution from M2M to the IoT. M2M solutions can almost be regarded as Intranets of Things: closed environments with little connectivity outside of the device estate or solution in question. The natural next step for integrating these solutions into the "outside world" is to consider how these Intranets of Things could be integrated with what could be regarded as "adjacent" products, services, and, of course, (other) Intranets of Things (Figure 2-2).

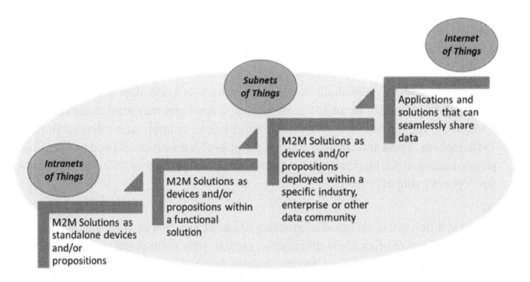

FIGURE 2-2. Subnets of Things

We believe that this stage of development will be driven by common ownership of data sources or common cause among data owners. An example might be a utility that builds connections between its smart metering solution and its field force solution. The utility can do this because it owns the smart meters, the field force capability, and the applications that support these capabilities, as well as the data that the applications generate. In short, the systems, the connected devices, and the IT environment within an enterprise can be regarded as a potential Subnet of Things.

The key point to consider in relation to these Subnets of Things is their unique ability to develop far more quickly than a full-scale Internet of Things. This is due both to the fact that stakeholders are more willing to share data and to the technical feasibility of sharing between applications.

A logical next step is to extend the concept to data communities, which we define as a community of devices, data sources, and data owners that could potentially give rise to a Subnet of Things. An example might be a group of intelligent building providers that come together to form a common platform.

It is clear that SoTs are a significant and critical step on the path to any future IoT. We believe it should be relatively easy to convince a defined group of people with similar motivations to standardize in order to create an SoT. However, it is likely to be far more difficult to take the next step to the IoT—that is, to convince all those in IT and related industries to standardize sufficiently to allow the emergence of a fully fledged IoT.

Focus of this Book

Simply put, Enterprise IoT focuses on the space that includes both advanced M2M solutions and Subnets of Things (with the exception of highly advanced SoTs). This is indicated in Figure 2-3.

Typically, an Enterprise IoT solution would focus on a single class of assets, but would often have multiple devices from different vendors deployed on this asset class. Enterprise IoT solutions will often have higher semantic richness than simple M2M solutions.

In this book, the scope of a typical Enterprise IoT solution is explicitly limited to a single enterprise that controls this solution, but that might collaborate with other partners for the backend in order to provide a complete solution. In this regard, Enterprise IoT is more limited than the full IoT vision, in which essentially every device can connect to any other device, either directly or through the cloud. This was a deliberate decision, as we feel that many enterprises will focus on these more tightly controlled, single-enterprise types of IoT solutions in the next couple of years.

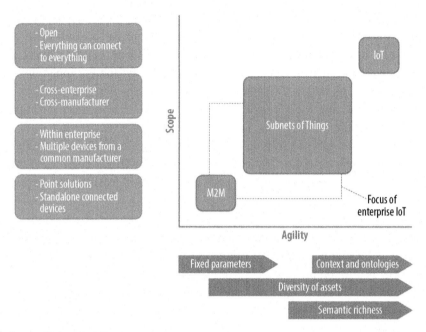

FIGURE 2-3. Focus of Enterprise IoT

DOMAIN FOCUS

Some people in the IoT community differentiate between the Industrial IoT (connected vehicles, machines, and other industrial equipment) and the Consumer IoT (smart wearables, connected dishwashers, etc.) [OR14]. However, it would be too simplistic to say that Enterprise IoT only focuses on the Industrial IoT. While it is true that most of the application domains and use cases in Part I of this book primarily deal with industrial examples, we believe that the key point of this book is its focus on solutions that are typically controlled by a single enterprise and that follow certain architectural patterns, which are described in more detail in Part II. Both of these criteria are fulfilled by numerous examples from the Consumer IoT as well. Take, for instance, the eCall service or the car-sharing facilities discussed in the previous section.

As you will see in Part I, our analysis to date has mainly focused on manufacturing and industry, connected vehicles, smart energy, and smart cities. The lessons learned from these domains provide the current basis for the Ignite | IoT Methodology. In the current edition of this book, at least, we didn't have time to include a case study on smart wearables. However, we would be curious to find out if this would be another suitable candidate for Enterprise IoT (possibly something we will explore in the next edition).

Definitions of Key Terms in IoT

In order to help make Enterprise IoT concepts more concrete, we have included a number of helpful definitions, which we will look at momentarily. Perhaps one of the most important decisions we made in devising our nomenclature was to drop the term "thing"—which sounds paradoxical, considering that the IoT is supposed to be all about connecting "things." However, in our experience, people in an enterprise rarely talk about "things." We have therefore opted for the terms "asset" and "device," as they are more commonly used.

Figure 2-4 provides an overview of the key elements of an Enterprise IoT solution scenario.

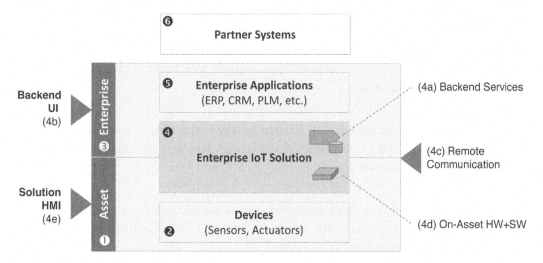

FIGURE 2-4. Enterprise IoT definitions

The elements in Figure 2-4 are defined as follows:

(1) Asset

In business terminology, we refer to numerous physical "things" as "assets" in order to emphasize their significance. An asset is a property or piece of equipment that is produced, operated, or managed in order to generate revenue or to help improve a company's operations; for example, vehicles, facilities, machines, or power tools. Assets are generally a key part of an enterprise's business model. Note that the asset itself is not generally considered to be part of the IoT solution (at least not in the Enterprise IoT context), whereas a device (described next) might well be part of the IoT solution.

(2) Device

Devices are another important type of "thing." Typically, devices are economically less significant and physically much finer grained than assets. Devices in the IoT mainly include sensors (for heat, temperature, pressure, flow, etc.) and actuators (such as electric motors or hydraulic components). In our Enterprise IoT scenarios, devices are typically deployed on the assets.

(3) Enterprise

"Enterprise" refers to the organizational scope of the entity that is operating the Enterprise IoT solution. In many cases, this is the same enterprise as the one operating the assets—for example, a fleet manager, a manufacturer, and so on. In some cases—like the eCall service—the enterprise operates the backend service only. Enterprises are increasingly adopting IoT solutions to support their core business processes as a means of establishing new business models and creating lasting relationships with their customers. An enterprise may use the IoT either to operate its own assets or to deliver a service for assets belonging to another organization.

(4) Enterprise IoT solution

An IT system that connects assets and their devices with backend application services. This includes the following:

(4a) Backend services

The backend services of an IoT solution usually enable remote monitoring and control of devices and assets, gather device-related data, and are integrated with other enterprise applications (5).

(4b) Backend UI

The backend services generally provide web or mobile interfaces to enable users to interact with the services—for example, a visual dashboard with an overview of the current operational status of all assets.

(4c) Remote communication

The communication mechanism between the asset and the backend service—for instance, via mobile network or satellite.

(4d) On-asset hardware + software (HW+SW)

The hardware and software components of the solution that are to be deployed on the asset. Often, the on-asset hardware is a form of gateway that enables local and remote communication, while the on-asset software acts as a local agent enabling local integration and remote messaging. For example, the gateway might use an industrial bus to integrate with local sensors, and a GSM module to communicate remotely with the backend. In many cases, the gateway/agent also performs translation and mapping services to create a bridge between the protocols used locally by the different devices and the formats supported by the backend system. Note that (4d) only refers to solution-specific HW+SW: many assets already have existing onboard HW+SW that enables local business logic but is not part of the solution.

(4e) Solution HMI

Some IoT solutions also include a solution-specific human–machine interface (HMI), such as the onboard display of a car-sharing service.

(5) Enterprise applications and (6) partner systems

Most IoT solutions have to integrate with a number of internal and external (i.e., partner) applications such as ERP, MES, PLM, CRM, legacy applications, and the like. In many cases, these applications also contain some data related to the assets. For example, an ERP system might contain vehicle configuration data, a CRM system will contain the vehicle owner's contact data, and the backend will contain data on the remote vehicle condition. Only by integrating all of these different data sources can a holistic view of the asset be obtained.

Figure 2-5 provides a concrete example of an Enterprise IoT solution. The solution is an eCall service that can detect and deal with emergency situations. The managed assets are cars. The enterprise is the eCall operator, in this case Bosch Security Technology. The solution contains an onboard telematics control unit (TCU), which has an integrated acceleration sensor. In addition, the TCU is integrated with the car's airbag via the controller area network (CAN) bus [CAN1]. Communication with the backend is based on GSM. The main backend service is the call center application. This application must integrate with the local telephony management solution, the vehicle database managed by the car manufacturer, and the public-safety answering point (PSAP), which is connected to the police station, fire department, or ambulance service closest to the scene of the accident.

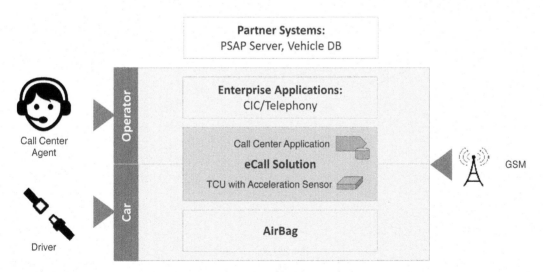

FIGURE 2-5. eCall example

We hope that these definitions and examples are helpful. They will be used throughout the book. In particular, you will see that they have been incorporated into one of our key architectural concepts, the Asset Integration Architecture (AIA). This concept is used to analyze most of the use cases and will be formally introduced in Part II (see "IoT Architecture Blueprints" on page 259).

IoT Application Domains and Case Studies

Part I of this book focuses on selected IoT application domains and provides detailed illustrative use cases for each one. It is virtually impossible to provide a complete and holistic overview of all possible applications for the IoT, because the IoT will affect nearly every aspect of our lives; application use cases are found within the areas of healthcare, smart homes, smart buildings, smart cities, energy, agriculture, transportation and connected vehicles, the military, logistics and supply chain, retail and wholesale, manufacturing, mining, and so on. The opportunities seem unlimited, and many application domains either overlap or have strong interdependencies. Machina Research's approach to mapping out the different applications and their overlaps on a high level is presented in Figure I-1. From a forecasting perspective, this already represents a detailed taxonomy of IoT use cases, and the underlying forecasts by Machina Research contain an even greater level of detail, spanning 223 different applications and market segments.

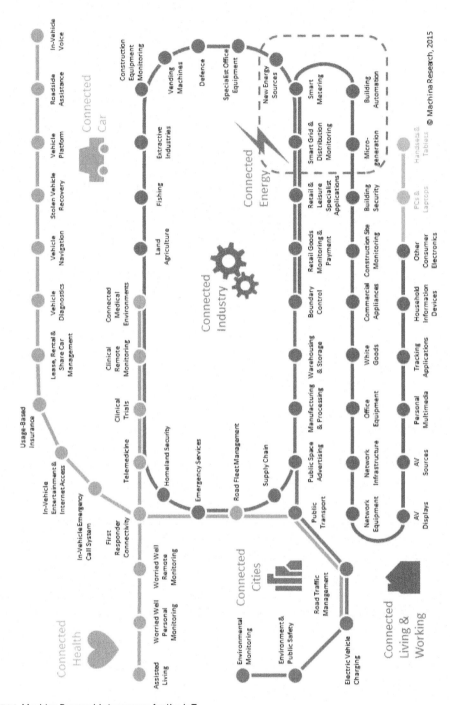

FIGURE I-1. Machina Research's taxonomy for the IoT

While this is an appropriate level of detail for forecasting our connected future world, the reality is likely to be far more fragmented. Even relatively standard and well-defined IoT applications can be implemented in radically different ways. Consider the example of smart electricity metering. This could be supported by cellular, power-line, radio mesh, or low-power, wide-area (LPWA) communications. Indeed, as we will see later, a single contract may include more than one of these technologies. But the fragmentation extends far beyond even this level, and includes treatment of the data provided by the smart meter (depending on whether readings are provided to a utility only, or to an in-home consumer device also), as well as the degree to which a smart meter can control in-home smart energy-consuming devices, and in what way. In some countries, the capability to support prepay options may be required, while in others, regulators are encouraging multiple utilities (electricity, gas, water, etc.) to "share" a single connection with the aim of increased efficiency. In some markets, integration with low-voltage generators (i.e., local or micro-generation) is a particular requirement. The list of technical and process-related factors by which two smart electricity metering solutions may differ is itself almost endless. And that's before we consider the list of commercial and contractual parameters that may differ between solutions, leading to differences in data sharing and management, support infrastructure, and even technical infrastructure, given the desire to optimize risks and returns.

The conclusion, however, is clear: while this taxonomy might be appropriate for forecasting IoT markets, the reality is that IoT project managers will be confronted with a great deal more complexity and fragmentation than this taxonomy even hints at.

The majority of this section of the book will focus on a detailed analysis of application domains and case studies. Before moving on to that discussion, however, it may be helpful to briefly discuss some of the forecast figures associated with our connected future. In terms of connected devices today, of course, PCs, tablets, and mobile handsets are by far the dominant category. These devices are almost ubiquitous in the developed world, and their adoption rates in the developing world are rising fast. As is often observed, the real growth in connected devices in the coming years will come from connecting "things," not people—hence the term "Internet of Things."

It is clear that some domains will give rise to a much greater number of connected devices than others. Fundamentally, this is a consequence of the size of addressable markets. In the case of connected consumer electronics, HVAC solutions, and building security, the number of connections can be analyzed at the level of individual households: a large number of households can be expected to have several of these connections. Figures for applications like connected vehicles and smart meters can also be estimated at 1–2 per adopting household. However, applications like connected ambulances will always be far fewer in number. That's not to say that there is no value in connecting ambulances—in fact, connecting an ambulance to a hospital so that patients' vital signs can be communicated is incredibly valuable—it's just that there will never be many connected ambulances, as the incidence rate of ambulances in developed economies seems to be roughly 1 per 10,000 population.

Another interesting observation is that particularly high-volume applications tend to be relatively homogeneous. Not only would a manufacturer of connected TVs expect to sell a large number of any one particular model, but one connected TV isn't really all that different from another. Conversely, low-volume industrial applications can be very diverse: there is a world of difference between a connected ambulance and a monitoring solution for ammonia (fertilizer) tanks for farms.

Figure I-2 highlights the forecast number of IoT device connections in certain key domains.

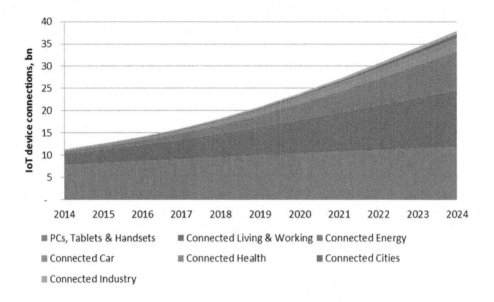

FIGURE I-2. IoT device connections

Instead of trying to cover all possible applications in all of these domains, we decided to delve a little deeper into a subset of them. Our selection was based on accessibility and the domain expertise of the authors, but also took into account growth projections and the perceived importance of particular applications in terms of their potential to define the pace of developments in the IoT space as a whole.

Naturally, these case studies represent different levels of maturity and innovation. Some are highly mature and widely deployed IoT solutions (especially those with their roots in M2M), while others are more innovative, less mature projects and pilots. For each case study, we tried to understand the problem domain, the specific problem, the way in which IoT (or sometimes M2M) helped to address the problem, and the lessons to be learned.

It was particularly important to us to collect the lessons learned and best practices drawn from these case studies in a structured way, because these form the basis for the Ignite | IoT Methodology presented in Part II. While working on the case studies and developing the methodology, we identified some useful tools for analyzing and designing IoT solutions. As you will see, we have tried to present as consistent a picture as possible by using the methodology tools from Part II to document the case studies in Part I. This represents a bit of a chicken-and-egg situation, as we will make use of certain tools in Part I before they are formally introduced in Part II. However, we believe that most examples are fairly self-explanatory, and help to make the case studies from all these different domains more accessible and easier for the reader to compare. If need be, you can always take a sneak peek at Part II—take a look at tools like the Asset Integration Architecture (AIA), for instance, which is introduced in "IoT Architecture Blueprints" on page 259.

The application domains we will focus on include:

- Smart energy, including generation, metering, and cross-energy management (CEM)
- Manufacturing and industry, including some unconventional case studies like the Large Hadron Collider at CERN
- The automotive sector (connected vehicles, in particular)
- Smart cities, including a detailed case study of the city of Monaco

CHAPTER 3

Smart Energy

THE FIRST POWER GRIDS EMERGED IN THE 1890S, DRIVEN BY PIONEERS SUCH AS THOMAS Edison and George Westinghouse and companies such as General Electric and Westinghouse Electric Corporation. These grids were highly centralized, isolated systems. Over the following decades, local grids became more and more interconnected. By the 1960s, electric grids had matured into highly interconnected systems. These grids were dominated by large power plants (usually based on fossil fuels such as coal, gas, and oil) that used high-capacity power lines to connect with the centers of electricity consumption, from which lower-capacity lines delivered electricity to the end users. Due to limitations in metering technologies, fixed tariffs were often used to bill end users.

From the very beginning, a key challenge faced by electric power grids involved dealing with varying energy demand. The main problems here related to very limited energy storage capacities and high costs for adding additional power-generation units on demand. Adding peak-time generators such as gas turbines with low startup times is a relatively costly solution, for example. Initial attempts were made to solve the problem on the demand side. For instance, dual tariffs were introduced to encourage customers to increase their usage of electric power at night, when demand is generally lower. Demand-aware devices (e.g., air conditioners, refrigerators, and heaters) were also introduced; these can sense the load in the grid using analog technologies, by monitoring changes in the power supply frequency, for example.

Nowadays, distribution networks accommodate an increasing share of (decentralized) generation, from sources such as small- and mid-sized wind power plants, combined heat and power plants, or solar power plants. This puts pressure on the power grids, making grid stability more difficult to maintain. Digitization is able to make the grid "smart" enough to deal with these new requirements. Figure 3-1 outlines the impact of digitization on the energy sector in more detail.

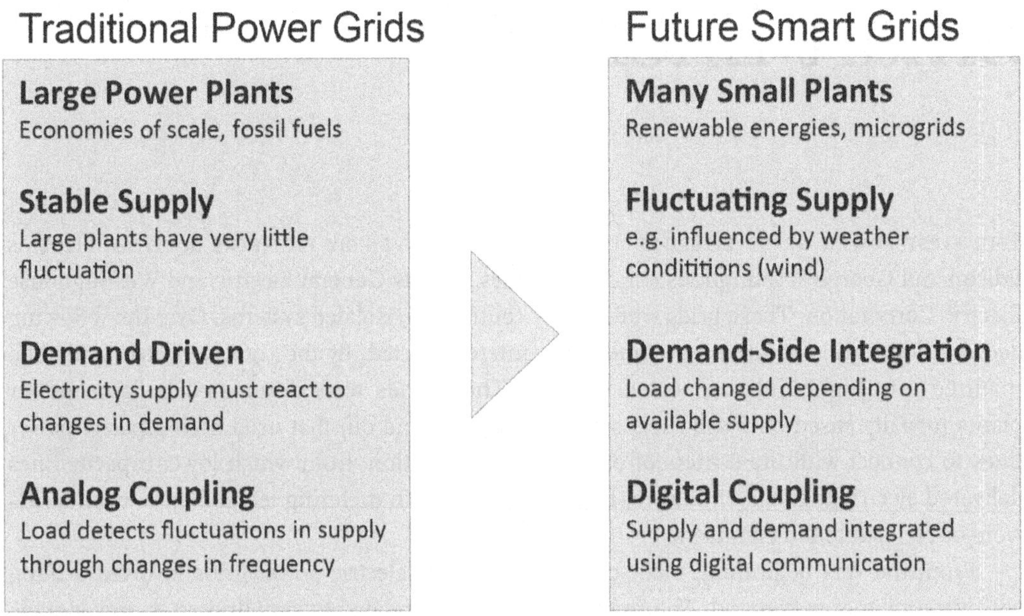

Traditional Power Grids

Large Power Plants
Economies of scale, fossil fuels

Stable Supply
Large plants have very little fluctuation

Demand Driven
Electricity supply must react to changes in demand

Analog Coupling
Load detects fluctuations in supply through changes in frequency

Future Smart Grids

Many Small Plants
Renewable energies, microgrids

Fluctuating Supply
e.g. influenced by weather condititions (wind)

Demand-Side Integration
Load changed depending on available supply

Digital Coupling
Supply and demand integrated using digital communication

FIGURE 3-1. Evolution of the electric power grid

Additionally, the last decade has seen a considerable increase in power trading both in national wholesale markets and across national borders, leading to new requirements for the transmission grid. The majority of consumers are connected to the distribution network, and metering services are used to record both consumption and feed-in.

Influence of Digitization

In recent years, the phenomenon of digitization has evolved into a genuine megatrend of cross-industry relevance. Although the energy industry initially lagged behind other industries, it is now rushing to catch up, with digital elements affecting more and more aspects of this market. The term "digitization" itself, however, is actually quite vague, so we need to define what we mean by it. Bernhard Schaefer, Senior Manager at m3 management consulting, defines digitization as:

> The comprehensive transformation of an energy company's products and services, its value chain (from generation to consumption), as well as its internal support functions (controlling, purchasing, HR, etc.) making use of new information and communication technologies and fulfilling related customer expectations.

The result is a "smart" utility, part of a "smart" energy world that will be embedded into the wider Internet of Things to an ever-greater extent.

A smart energy system will differ from the traditional system in many ways.

Data-led intelligence is entering more or less all steps of the energy value chain, with a pronounced focus on generation, distribution, metering, and consumption. This is illustrated in more detail in Figure 3-2, which maps IoT applications to the extended energy value chain. (Note that the value chain is different in some EU countries; for example, smart meters come under retail in the UK). In the following sections, we will examine each step in more detail.

Lessons Learned

Michael Schlauch from Bosch Software Innovations is the Bosch project manager supporting the Smart City Rheintal project. Here are his two key takeaways from the project:

> We still see major room for improvement in the forecasting process. That applies to the generation forecasts for the PV facilities as well as the consumption forecasts for consumers at home. Here, longer time frames are needed that go beyond the end of the project being funded. That's the only way to extrapolate practical and individualized consumption profiles for particular housing units, for example. Thanks to our collaboration with Vorarlberg University of Applied Sciences and specialized IT companies, we are well on our way to obtaining this type of forecast for a wide range of regional and structural parameters.

> Consumer devices such as washing machines are too small to make any reasonable headway with demand-side management. Devices integrated into the VPP have to be more flexible. This holds true for heat pumps as well as for electric boilers. And, of course, it's also helpful when we can bundle together facilities with widely varying degrees of flexibility.

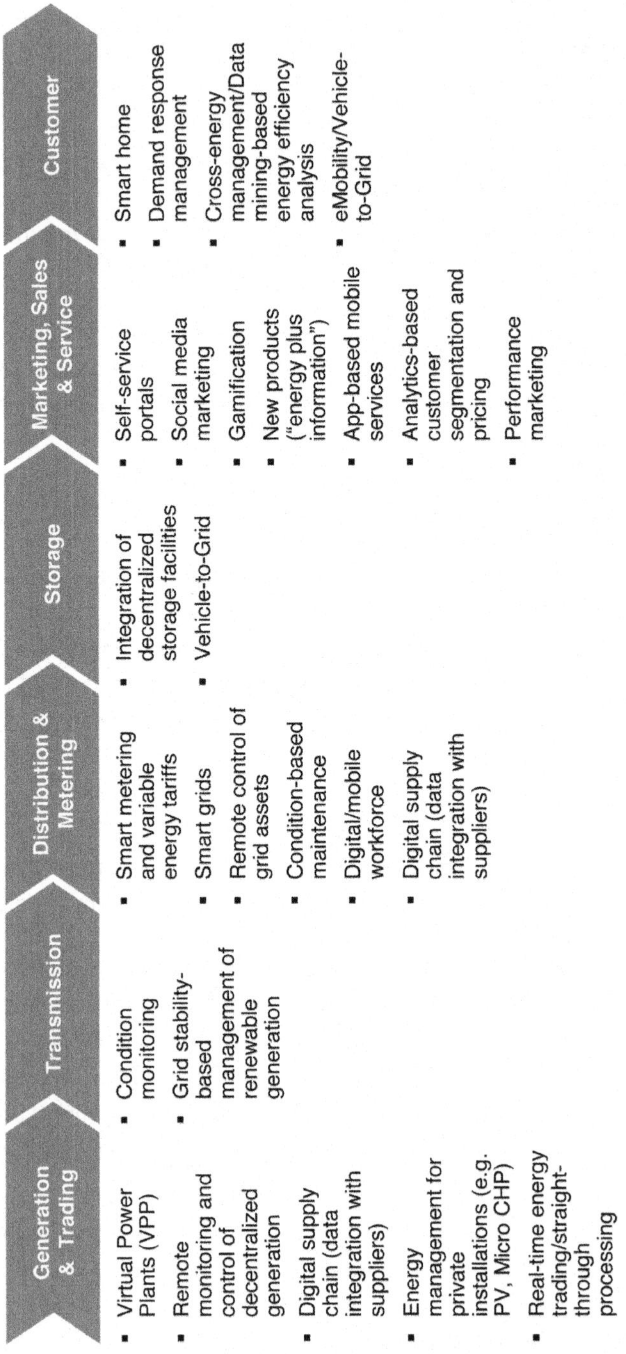

Generation & Trading
- Virtual Power Plants (VPP)
- Remote monitoring and control of decentralized generation
- Digital supply chain (data integration with suppliers)
- Energy management for private installations (e.g. PV, Micro CHP)
- Real-time energy trading/straight-through processing

Transmission
- Condition monitoring
- Grid stability-based management of renewable generation

Distribution & Metering
- Smart metering and variable energy tariffs
- Smart grids
- Remote control of grid assets
- Condition-based maintenance
- Digital/mobile workforce
- Digital supply chain (data integration with suppliers)

Storage
- Integration of decentralized storage facilities
- Vehicle-to-Grid

Marketing, Sales & Service
- Self-service portals
- Social media marketing
- Gamification
- New products ("energy plus information")
- App-based mobile services
- Analytics-based customer segmentation and pricing
- Performance marketing

Customer
- Smart home
- Demand response management
- Cross-energy management/Data mining-based energy efficiency analysis
- eMobility/Vehicle-to-Grid

FIGURE 3-2. Extended energy value chain and IoT use cases

Generation

Power generation is a field in which digitization can undoubtedly bring significant benefits. While in the past, the traditional electricity system was primarily fed by large, centralized power stations, today a huge and ever-increasing number of small, decentralized installations inject power into the grid. Most of these additional capacities are renewable generation sources like wind, solar, and biomass. However, production from wind and solar energy sources is highly volatile, and production forecasts—which rely on weather forecasts—are prone to inaccuracy. This presents a challenge for network operators, who must keep their networks stable and secure by ensuring, inter alia, a constant balance between power injection and power consumption. Energy expert Bernard Kryszak says:

> One option for meeting this challenge is to bundle a variety of small electricity generators into a coordinated "Virtual Power Plant" (VPP). Production of power by the VPP's individual entities (which may utilize solar, wind, biomass, small-scale water, or CHP energy sources) is centrally optimized using a single IP network to collect and analyze production data from the decentralized units, local weather forecasts, demand forecasts, and so on. This synergy-based approach makes it possible to minimize generation costs for required output. Furthermore, a VPP is able to provide a more stable overall power output in comparison to the individual sources, for example by ramping up biomass power at times when the sun is not shining and solar power cannot be generated. Particularly in markets with a high degree of volatile power generation, VPPs are economically attractive if the regulatory framework provides sufficient market signals to incentivize the provision of reserve capacity, which contributes to system stability.

Another field of application for a digital infrastructure concerns monitoring and diagnostics for remote generation assets. Imagine a large offshore wind farm far off the coast. Simple time-based maintenance would not be appropriate here, as the costs involved in traveling to this location are very high. Instead, operational data from sensors connected to components in each wind turbine (such as the blades, gear box, oil pumps, controls, motors, and generator parts) are continuously fed to a central control center. Here, the data is stored in a data historian in a structured way and made available for analysis. This makes it possible to monitor the condition of each part and tailor maintenance plans to address the turbines' actual condition.

In addition, digitization can make support processes for generation more effective and efficient. The concept of a "digital supply chain" describes close data integration with external suppliers. This helps to ensure that suppliers of essential spare parts, for example, can have access to transparent online information about a generator's additional supply requirements. As a result, spare parts are delivered subject to demand and warehouses are well stocked (with minimal excess), which leads to increased reliability for power plants.

Turning now to smart applications in the field of private power generation, we shift our focus to energy management solutions. These can be helpful for private energy "prosumers"—that is, private consumers who also produce energy by means of photovoltaics (PV) or micro CHP (combined heat and power). Imagine a household with a PV installation on the roof. With the help of weather forecasts, prosumers can forecast their installation's electricity output and—taking into account the variable power prices offered by their utility—optimize their consumption accordingly. This increases the share of self-consumed solar electricity while at the same time reducing usage of the external distribution network.

With fully integrated trading platforms and automated trading processes, energy trading is also becoming a lot smarter. Whereas market participants used to trade power on a day-ahead basis only, trading today can be conducted via system-to-system messaging without manual intervention. This enables real-time trading and short-term optimization, thus ensuring sufficient agility in the new volatile energy markets.

Transmission

Today, transmission system operators (TSOs) are faced with the mounting challenge of maintaining stable and secure grid operation despite the increasing pressure caused by the growing share of intermittent renewable energies. As grid stability is always paramount, TSOs are permitted to ensure load balancing (frequency and voltage) by obliging power producers to temporarily ramp up or down their generation assets, with the aim of achieving the necessary constant balance between production and consumption (the latter being more difficult to influence). In this context, generation assets that are directly connected to the TSO's transmission grid are directly and remotely controlled by the TSO's control center via dedicated data interfaces.

Distribution and Metering

Looking to the area of distribution and metering, we encounter what is probably the best-known element in the new intelligent energy landscape: the "smart meter." A smart meter is a metering device that is capable of recording power consumption at short intervals, such as every 15 minutes, and then transmitting this data to the supplying utility for monitoring and billing purposes. Smart meters also enable two-way communication between the utility and the metered electric load, allowing electrical appliances to be controlled so that their energy consumption is highest at times when energy prices are low due to high renewable energy production.

When smart meters and other sensors and actuators are installed at a large number of relevant load points and network assets (such as controllable transformer stations), with collected data being fed into a central distribution management system, this facilitates real-time analysis and control of the network. The resulting "smart grid" can be monitored in detail and controlled remotely by the network operator. Network operation can in fact be automated to a significant extent, which enables fast reactions to network events like local supply disruptions. As in the case of remote generation, this also greatly facilitates condition-based maintenance of grid assets based on real-time information about asset condition. Maintenance activities can be further optimized through predictive analytics—that is, the forecasting of asset condition based on historic data and learning analysis algorithms.

As Bernhard Schaefer, Senior Manager at m3 management consulting, points out:

> *There are a number of benefits associated with making a grid "smarter": electricity flows are optimized, system security is improved, network capacities are better utilized, and network assets are better protected from faults. Also, renewable energy sources are more easily integrated into the network. This reduces the amount of required investment in networks and cuts operating expenses for asset servicing, while at the same time minimizing network faults and—in the event of supply disruptions—allowing supply to be restored faster.*

Nevertheless, when viewed from the network operator's perspective, installing and operating smart metering devices is in many cases not cost effective in comparison to the use of conventional meters. Indeed, in Europe, only Sweden and Italy have undertaken a full rollout of smart meters. In other European countries, the installation of smart meters is still under debate and will generally need to be preceded by legislation and regulation. In the long term, however, the costs of communication and hardware should decrease significantly, which will improve the business case for smart meters.

Storage

Electricity storage is an option for accommodating excess energy produced by renewables at times of low demand. In addition to large, central storage installations like pumped-storage hydroelectricity, there is a lot of development activity around bringing small- and medium-scale storage to the market, with examples such as lithium-ion batteries or power-to-gas technology. One particularly interesting form of potential electricity storage is the "vehicle-to-grid" concept. With a growing fleet of plug-in electric vehicles, a digital infrastructure could be used to control the vehicles' battery charging process and release energy back into the grid for stability in the event of surplus energy or demand peaks.

Although most of these storage technologies have not (yet) become profitable in most market environments, it is evident that added benefit is to be derived from integrating distributed, small-scale storage devices into a smart grid. Dispatch is thus based on actual overall system needs and takes network and geographic constraints into account, in an effort to achieve overall economic optimization.

Marketing, Sales, and Service

Up to this point, we have addressed purely technical solutions. However, smart energy is not restricted to machine-to-machine (M2M) communication. The digital customer interface is another important element in the evolving smart energy world. First, *new* products can be designed by bundling energy and information services. Second, sales and/or margins associated with *existing* products and services can be improved through analytics-based optimization of customer segmentation and pricing, using the newly available data to better target customer needs. Third, after-sales support can be improved by leveraging customer insight obtained through an analysis of smart metering data, and also by introducing user-friendly mobile services and online self-service portals for billing, submitting meter readings, on-demand support, and energy efficiency initiatives. And finally, suppliers can expect to gain additional information about customer behavior and key marketing data, which can be provided to third parties for targeted sales and advertisements.

Customers

In terms of the end customer, at the end of the value chain, numerous initiatives center on reducing energy consumption through increased energy efficiency and reducing costs through intelligent load scheduling. This is typically done by means of flexible scheduling according to real-time market price changes. This goes so far as to offer customers financial incentives for increasing their electrical load during situations in which network stability is endangered due to excess power production.

Energy management solutions primarily apply to industrial and commercial customers, for whom energy bills (at least in Europe) represent a dominant part of most cost structures. Demand response management is used to monetize existing flexibilities in production processes—for instance, by reducing cooling and heating processes or other electrical loads during times when higher prices are charged. Internal synergies between different power plants and/or different energy forms are also exploited (e.g., power versus natural gas).

In the private sector, the issues of energy efficiency, personal comfort, personal health, and security are addressed by the "smart home" concept. In a smart home, integrated home-automation controls optimize the use of lighting, heating, electrical appliances like refrigerators and washing machines, as well as motorized blinds and security systems. Learning algorithms help to reduce energy consumption—for instance, by turning down the heating when the resident goes to work. Sensors can monitor movement and send alerts—for example, in a situation where an elderly person falls or doesn't move for an extended period of time. Smartphone apps allow users to monitor their home's security features remotely. Furthermore, e-mobility applications can be integrated into a smart home by incorporating charging and discharging processes into the overall home energy management concept.

When Is All This Going to Happen?

The adoption of smart electricity meters will be a key driver for the widespread adoption of smart home and other downstream devices. In several markets worldwide, this is subject to government intervention and regulatory decisions, while in other markets, network efficiency and "nontechnical losses" (i.e., theft) can be a significant factor influencing the adoption of smart electricity meters. The potential beneficial environmental impact of adopting smart electricity metering is a near-global driver.

The net result is that smart metering and smart grid management solutions will be among the first technologies to be adopted in the coming IoT era. A vast array of other solutions will subsequently gain traction as a result of the introduction of these technologies. One category of solutions will include applications and devices that are effectively part of the smart grid infrastructure and support low-voltage power generation, for instance. We will also see a range of devices that are part of the wider smart grid ecosystem, which will be used where there is potential to increase efficiency by modifying power consumption. This second category would include many smart home devices.

Figure 3-3 illustrates the total number of smart grid IoT connections represented by these two different categories of devices. It also illustrates the share of the total number of smart grid IoT connections that is contributed by smart grid infrastructure devices, and highlights the share of the total number of IoT devices that is in some way related to the emerging smart grid.

There are three clear messages to be drawn from these figures. First, the total number of devices included in the IoT smart grid can be expected to grow quickly, approaching a total of 12 billion in 2024 from a base of less than 1 billion today. Second, and perhaps unsurprisingly, devices related to the smart grid infrastructure will be adopted prior to devices that depend on smart grid functionality. Third, devices related to the smart grid will make up an increasing share of IoT-connected devices. These forecasts show that by 2024, more than 40% of all IoT device-cloud connections (excluding PCs, tablets, and handsets) are forecast to belong to the smart grid ecosystem, which places smart grid and VPP concepts firmly at the core of the IoT.

Conclusions

Most of the trends described in this chapter are still in the pilot or early commercialization phase. Yet energy expert Bernard Kryszak emphasizes:

> We are confident that a large number of use cases will turn out to be profitable. However, the success of many smart energy applications depends on both an integrated perspective in terms of the resulting benefits and a fair distribution of costs among those profiting from this smart technology—generators, network operators, sales entities, and customers. A common infrastructure is an important part of this integrated perspective.

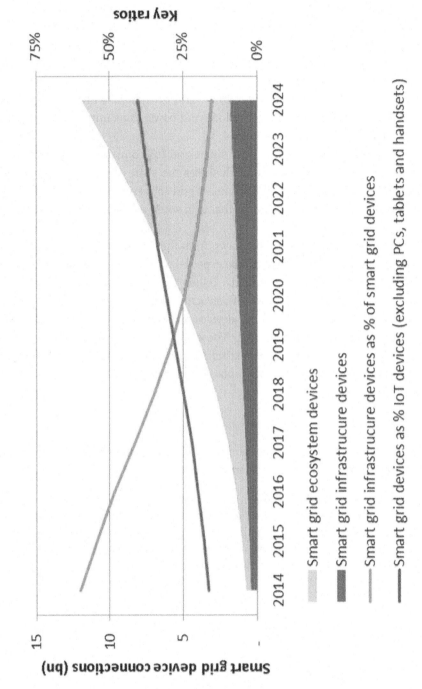

FIGURE 3-3. Smart grid IoT connections

Legend:
- Smart grid ecosystem devices
- Smart grid infrastrucure devices
- Smart grid infrastrucure devices as % of smart grid devices
- Smart grid devices as % IoT devices (excluding PCs, tablets and handsets)

Chart axes:
- Key ratios: 75%, 50%, 25%, 0%
- Smart grid device connections (bn): 15, 10, 5, -
- Years: 2014, 2015, 2016, 2017, 2018, 2019, 2020, 2021, 2022, 2023, 2024

Energy Case Studies

In the following sections, we will delve into some of these topics in more detail. To do so, we have collected a number of very interesting case studies on the use of IoT technologies in different segments of the smart energy value chain as discussed previously:

- Power generation
  - Smart monitoring and diagnostics systems at major power plants
- Metering
  - UK Smart Metering Implementation Programme (SMIP)
- Microgrids and virtual power plants
  - The Smart City Rheintal project
  - Smart energy in the chemical industry
- Cross-Energy management (CEM)
  - CEM in farms
  - CEM in steel production

Smart Monitoring and Diagnostics Systems at Major Power Plants

The electric power generation industry must use new technologies to shift how maintenance and diagnostic departments operate. More than 50% of the generation capacity within the United States is over 30 years old [NI1]. In many cases, these power plants depend on equipment that is operating close to the limits of its original, intended design lifetime (Figure 3-4). This increases the potential for equipment failure, which, depending on the type of equipment, can make the power being supplied more susceptible to outages and instabilities.

At one utility, a study claims that maintenance and diagnostic experts spend nearly 80% of their day traveling, sometimes across vast distances, to collect "health" information about equipment, and only 20% actually analyzing this data for potential failure points. This utility estimates nearly 60,000 operating points must be manually collected each month by personnel [NI2].

The aging infrastructure and inefficient use of experts' time, combined with the fact that the number of industry experts is dwindling due to an aging workforce, is quickly creating a critical resource bottleneck. This bottleneck may eventually cause more downtime on critical machines and lead to potential brownouts or blackouts across the grid.

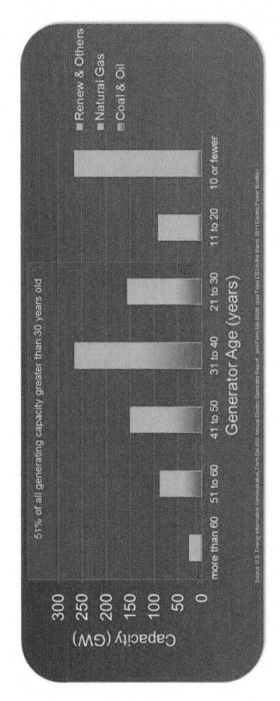

FIGURE 3-4. Capacity versus age of generation equipment [NI2]

Duke Energy, the Electric Power Research Institute (EPRI), NI, and a consortium of power generation producers are working on a solution to automate online equipment monitoring systems for decision support. The Smart Monitoring and Diagnostics Project (Smart M&D) [NI3] aims to continuously and remotely monitor plant equipment for changes in measured parameters, run prognostics and advanced pattern recognition routines, and enable more informed real-time decisions to optimize plant equipment and prevent failure (Figure 3-5).

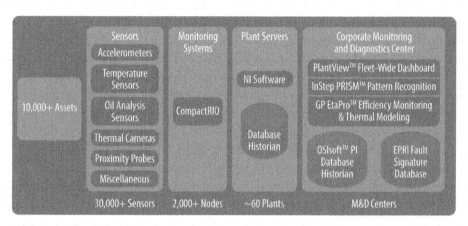

FIGURE 3-5. Smart generation architecture

Gathering analog sensory information, the core of this project, poses some unique challenges. For instance, vibration information is a good leading indicator of equipment breakdown. However, to collect vibration information, it may be necessary to capture anywhere from 10,000 to 100,000 samples per second for several seconds in order to obtain a good "measure" of the machine. Imagine, as the real-world scenario in Figure 3-5 highlights, if you had 30,000 vibration points each collecting five seconds' worth of data at 100,000 samples per second, every hour; that adds up to nearly 60 GB of data per hour! This collection of information, if not managed and architected properly, can quickly lead to a "Big Data" problem.

Another challenge is that analog sensory information on its own does not tell the operator whether a machine is "good" or "bad." Correlating multiple sensing types, processing data using mathematical algorithms, and using advanced pattern recognition techniques provide a true picture of the machine's health.

A core element of the Smart M&D Project is the CompactRIO platform from NI [NI4]. By connecting a field-programmable gate array (FPGA) and an onboard real-time processor to the sensor, raw analog waveforms can be reduced to conditions indicating the "health" of the system at the node itself.

FPGAs help analyze and process the high-speed sensory information in a very efficient, parallel manner for real-time decision making. Because the "smarts" in the system are close to the sensor and intelligent algorithms can be implemented directly on the CompactRIO system, data can immediately be reduced to known events. This prevents the data overload condition in which subject matter experts are stuck looking for problems that are difficult to locate.

The distributed, open, and reconfigurable nature of the system also plays an important part. Because the systems are distributed, a wide range of "health" information can be collected by similar systems (similar boiler feed pumps, fans, motors, and more) directly by the network of machines, and intelligence can immediately be applied to the data at the source. As the systems are analyzing data constantly, this means operator rounds can be greatly reduced while dramatically increasing the frequency of collection. Data no longer needs to be collected on a monthly, semiannual, or yearly basis—it can be collected several times *per day*. Issues can be discovered and tracked on a more frequent, consistent basis.

Further, advanced diagnostic and prognostic algorithms, such as those contained within the EPRI Asset Fault Signature Database and EPRI Remaining Useful Life Database, can be used to predict equipment failures before they occur. For example, the EPRI Asset Fault Signature Database characterizes equipment failure mechanisms by a collection of typical attributes or symptoms, such as temperatures, vibrations, lubrication analyses, and other diagnostic results. Using this type of real-time data generated by a Smart M&D system, comparisons can be made to diagnostic models contained in the EPRI Asset Fault Signature Database. When a set or subset of data coincides with the known attributes or symptoms of a known failure mechanism and/or location, these diagnostic tools can identify when a particular failure is impending (Figure 3-6).

Finally, the reconfigurable nature of CompactRIO means that as standards change, new algorithms are developed, or additional sensing technologies become prevalent, customers can update their intelligent nodes without having to physically go out into the plant to update them or having to reinvest new capital dollars in order to solve a new problem.

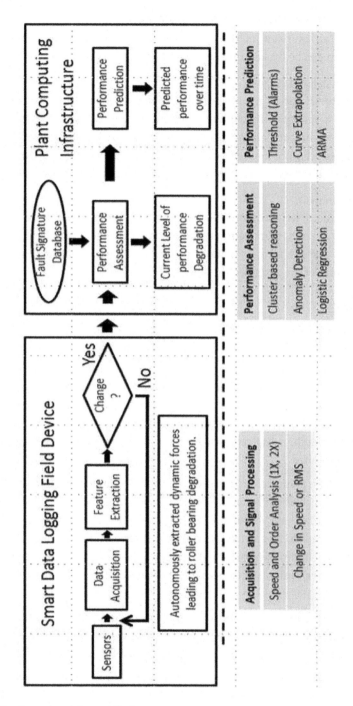

FIGURE 3-6. Smart logging and analytics architecture

ASSET INTEGRATION ARCHITECTURE OF SMART M&D

Figure 3-7 shows an overview of the Asset Integration Architecture for the Smart M&D Project. The system can be broken into two main components:

Data acquisitions systems (DAQs)

DAQs are a crucial part of the system and provide data from numerous different sensors hooked up to a variety of machinery components and types. The DAQs are distributed throughout a facility, region, or global geography. DAQ systems perform onboard processing and extraction of key sensory metrics for future trending, alarming, and analysis. They are intelligent devices that can perform in the absence of a network.

Sensor fusion and analysis

The piece of the system responsible for providing actionable data to system operators, subject matter experts, management, and others. Through a variety of open communication protocols and file formats, data from various sensors is fused together to provide a complete picture of the asset health.

LESSONS LEARNED

These points represent the key learnings from this project:

- The reconfigurable nature of the system provides interfaces so as new algorithms, industry protocols (61850, DNP3, etc.), and sensor types are created, the infrastructure does not need to change. Simply download new information to the embedded systems and begin collecting new fault signatures. The system can expand from the classical method of diagnosing machine faults with measurements such as temperature, vibration, pressure, and more, to incorporating advanced measurements like thermal imaging, ultrasonics, smell, and EMI interference.

- Providing an open platform encourages other system vendors to adopt the Smart M&D standard of connectivity. It is naïve to believe there will only be one type of acquisition system, backend database, enterprise analytic software, or more for a given facility. Therefore, a system needs to be created that can be inclusive of many systems. No longer is the data hidden away in proprietary formats; rather, it is open for users to run personalized algorithms, connect unique sensors in one package, and provide an ecosystem for expansion.

- The use of IoT technologies will provide an open, integrated, and flexible framework for service providers, suppliers, and users, thus increasing the operational efficiencies of plants, reducing downtime, and increasing the availability of energy on the grid.

- Currently, at Duke Energy, nearly 1,500 CompactRIO systems are deployed and managed by the Smart M&D architecture across 30 facilities.

We would like to thank Stuart Gillen and Jamie Smith from National Instruments for the contribution of this case study.

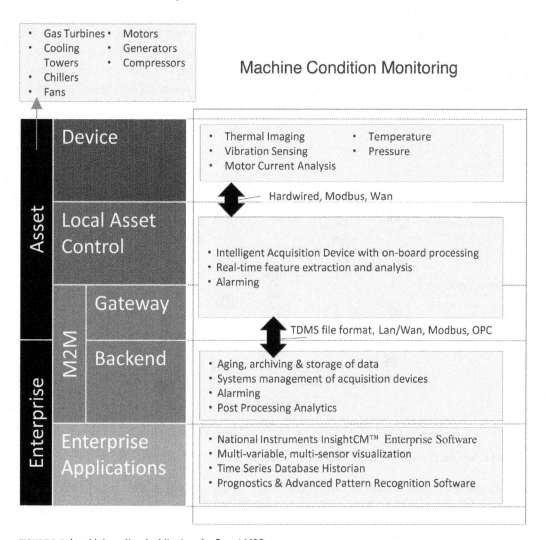

FIGURE 3-7. Asset Integration Architecture for Smart M&D

Microgrids and Virtual Power Plants

One of the key challenges for the future power grid will be coping with distributed energy resources (DERs) such as combined heat and power (CHP), photovoltaic systems, and wind turbines. In order to address this challenge, new concepts are currently being developed. However, the market is still in its early stages, and as yet there is no commonly accepted terminology. The terms *microgrid, virtual power plant (VPP), embedded generation,* and *smart distribution network* all describe similar concepts (Figure 3-8).

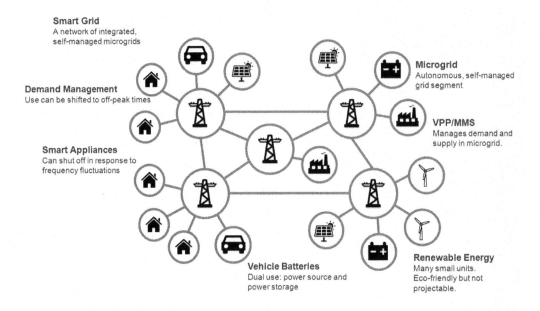

FIGURE 3-8. Overview of smart grids and microgrids

What these concepts have in common is that they all incorporate the idea of both energy resources and loads. Most VPP concepts also include the notion of load management, even though the term "power plant" generally refers to energy sources only. The U.S. Department of Energy Microgrid Exchange Group defines a microgrid [LBL1] as:

A group of interconnected loads and distributed energy resources within clearly defined electrical boundaries that acts as a single controllable entity with respect to the grid. A microgrid can connect and disconnect from the grid to enable it to operate in both grid-connected or island mode.

The Microgrids Group at Berkeley Lab describes three key features of a microgrid [LBL1]:

Designed around total system energy requirements
Microgrids optimize the overall energy system of the end user. For example, combined heat and power (CHP) systems can be used to limit heat waste by means of local thermal generation of electricity.

Provides a heterogeneous level of power quality and reliability (PQR) to end users
Microgrids provide high power quality to critical loads (such as lighting), while less critical loads (like refrigeration or ventilation) can receive lower PQR depending on availability. This is different from macrogrids, where consistent service quality is an important goal.

Presents itself to the macrogrid as a single controlled entity
A microgrid presents itself to the surrounding distribution grid as a single controlled system, acting as a "model citizen" that helps to reduce congestion, offset the need for new generation, supply local voltage support, and respond to rapid changes in load levels.

All of these features of a microgrid implicitly assume the existence of a local control function that is independent of the macrogrid. For lack of a widely established term (and in order to explicitly include the aspect of load management), we will use the term "virtual power plant/microgrid management system" (VPP/MMS) in the following paragraphs. This assumes that microgrids can be hierarchical and that a single VPP can manage multiple microgrids.

VPP/MMS: FUNCTIONAL OVERVIEW

The key functionalities of a virtual power plant/microgrid management system (VPP/MMS) include integration of different, heterogeneous energy sources and loads ("assets"), asset data management, energy management, and integration with external partners. Using our asset integration architecture (AIA) once again as a reference, Figure 3-9provides an overview of a typical VPP/MMS.

Integration with the different energy sources and loads ("assets," in the Ignite | IoT terminology) can either occur through the installation of a local gateway and/or agent directly on the asset, or—if the asset already provides remote integration capabilities— through a connector in the backend.

The VPP/MMS backend typically provides some kind of asset management functionality, which enables configuration and administration of the various integrated assets. Asset-related data, such as master data and asset history (including events, faults, and time series data), are managed centrally.

Building on this asset data, the VPP/MMS implements the logic required to manage the different assets and their energy supply and consumption levels. This includes modeling and forecasting, scheduling, and real-time optimization. As most microgrids will not be able to function completely autonomously, the VPP/MMS must also be integrated with external systems to receive information such as weather forecast data and market prices. In addition, the VPP/MMS will in many cases be integrated with external processes such as energy trading, billing, and other processes related to transmission system operators (DSOs) and distribution system operators (TSOs).

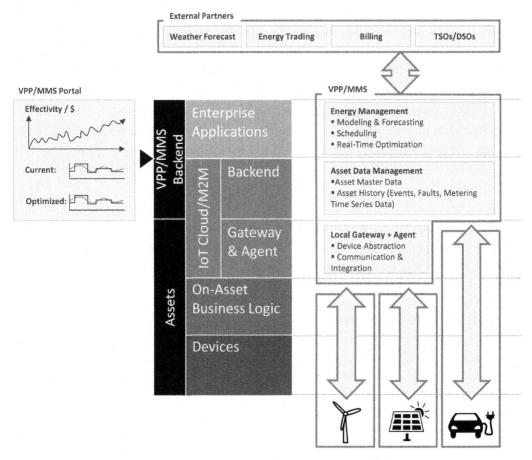

FIGURE 3-9. Overview of virtual power plant/microgrid management system (VPP/MMS)

CASE STUDY: SMART CITY RHEINTAL

The Vorarlberg Rhine Valley (*Rheintal*) is a densely populated metropolitan area in Austria, with a population of approximately 240,000. The Smart City Rheintal project was initiated by the federal state of Vorarlberg and the largest local utility, illwerke vkw. The goal is to leverage local renewable resources (such as hydropower) in order to make the region as energy-independent as possible by 2050 [SCR14].

One major subproject within this initiative is tasked with building a virtual power plant (VPP) to help balance out the different energy sources and loads involved. The current focus is more on functional integration rather than scalability. To date, the project has integrated the following components:

- Photovoltaic systems (PV)

- Consumer devices, including heat pumps and electric boilers equipped with storage units

- Electromobility infrastructure, including a charging infrastructure and electric vehicles from car-sharing companies

- Battery storage systems

Forecasting Photovoltaic Energy

The project is currently integrating PV facilities from one district into the VPP, with others soon to follow. Aggregated data is used to calculate day-ahead forecasts for PV power generation. The VPP monitors the facility's actual power output every 15 minutes. This is helpful for improving the accuracy of the forecasts. Figure 3-10 shows a comparison of the forecast and actual power output of a PV facility over a period of several days.

Consumer Devices: Load Management

The project has selected a number of flexible consumer devices that support active load management. These devices are less critical and support lower power quality and reliability. Moreover, they also support external control interfaces, which is a prerequisite for integrating them into an active load management scenario.

The basic idea is to use these more flexible consumer devices to take advantage of peak energy situations and then power down when supply is low. In order to support this, the VPP creates an operations schedule using the generation forecast series for the next 24 hours. The VPP coordinates technical integration, integration of external data (e.g., from the EXAA electricity exchange in Vienna), definition and implementation of threshold values, and prioritization of consumers.

Electromobility Infrastructure

For a smart grid, integration with the electromobility infrastructure is interesting for two different reasons:

Electric vehicles (EVs) as power consumers
  During the charging process, EVs act as power consumers (from the grid's perspective).

EVs as power storage units
  The batteries in EVs can also be used as power storage units, with the limitation that these units are only accessible as long as an EV is connected to a charging station.

The initial focus of the Smart City Rheintal project was to integrate EVs as power consumers. To support this, the project has integrated several charging stations operated by car-sharing providers into the VPP. In order to generate a viable charging schedule, the VPP must consider various inputs, including local power-generation forecasts, car reservation data, EV power requirements and state-of-charge (SOC) data, and the load profiles of the charging station.

Figure 3-11 provides an overview of the different elements of an EV infrastructure and how they integrate with one another in the context of a microgrid.

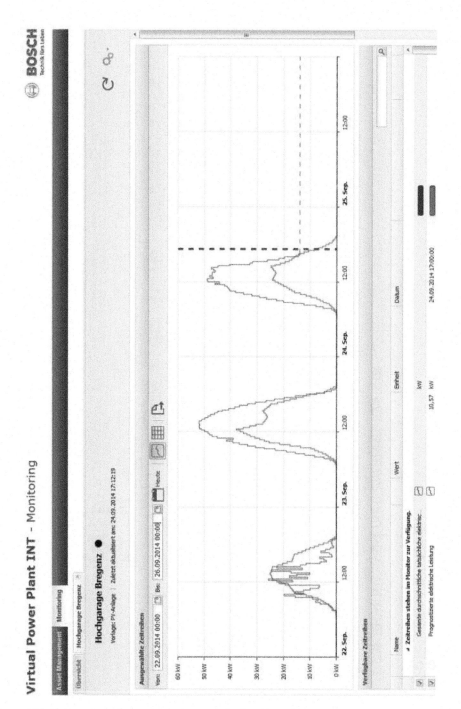

FIGURE 3-10. VPP dashboard: forecast versus actual energy

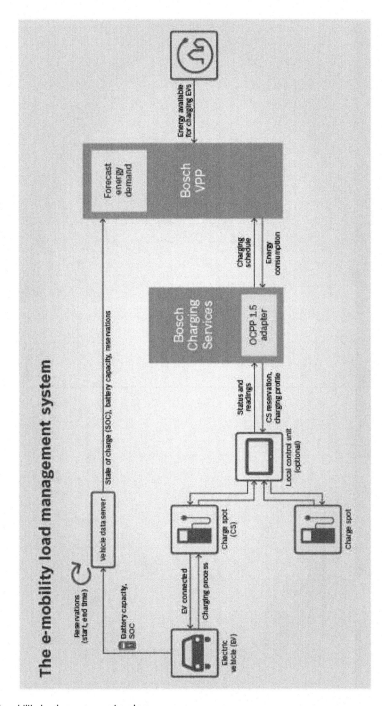

FIGURE 3-11. E-mobility load management system

Smart Energy in the Chemical Industry

The adoption of IoT-based solutions in industry is primarily motivated by commercial interests. The chemical industry is a perfect example of an industry that can benefit from the adoption of IoT-based solutions, as it combines a range of key characteristics that make adoption more attractive. These characteristics include the fact that chemical plants exist on a relatively small geographic scale, tend to consume significant quantities of power with a considerable degree of flexibility as to when power is used, and comprise multiple sophisticated and interlinked processes within a single site. Chemical parks increase the potential savings that can be achieved through IoT-based solutions by grouping multiple different chemical producers at a single site so that IoT solutions can be developed to encompass multiple participants. It should be no surprise that the chemical industry is already using IoT concepts in an advanced and effective way.

Currenta offers services for the chemical industry including utility supply, waste management, infrastructure, safety, security, analytics, and vocational training. Currenta is a joint venture between Bayer and Lanxess and operates CHEMPARK chemical park sites in Leverkusen, Dormagen, and Krefeld-Uerdingen, Germany. Its three sites account for around one-third of total chemical production in North Rhine-Westphalia. More than 70 companies specializing in production, research, and services help to create synergies at CHEMPARK sites. Currenta CHEMPARKs are thus ideal environments for the testing and implementation of smart energy applications, effectively creating a "smart CHEMPARK."

The following interview with Dr. Christian Czauderna, head of Business Management at Currenta, sheds some light on a fascinating industrial application of smart energy. The interview was conducted by Bernhard Schaefer, Senior Manager at m3 management consulting.

Bernhard Schaefer: Mr. Czauderna, what are the key aspects of the "smart CHEMPARK" concept? What targets is Currenta aiming to reach?

Christian Czauderna: Every chemical park is based on the principle of combining different parts of chemical value chains by grouping together and connecting plants that use each other's products. A *smart* chemical park provides additional features like the integration of new data sources and analysis algorithms to allow for a better understanding of the system and the potential for enhanced automation. Smartness for us means "using efficient structures in an efficient way"—for example, by optimizing energy use across different plants or even sites, taking into account external information like market prices. So why are we doing this? It's all about preserving our natural resources and at the same time improving the competitiveness of the German chemical industry by optimizing energy production and procurement costs.

Bernhard: In what respect is a smart chemical park different from a smart grid as we know it from pilot projects by public distribution network operators? Are there any specific challenges?

Christian: Indeed, an example of what sets us apart from a normal smart grid is the integration of different forms of energy into the overall optimization process. This includes not only electricity but also gas, steam, and raw materials that are used for production of chemicals. Another peculiarity is that our customers are all large companies with significant energy consumption and complex production processes. Many of these processes are characterized by flexibilities (i.e., the possibility to shift, postpone, or reduce energy consumption in accordance with external constraints). We also tend to see a high degree of automation in our customers' production facilities. Most assets, like reactors, pumps, and fans are already integrated into a local communication system—so the basic infrastructure for a smart chemical park is already available.

Bernhard: So is the planned "smartness" really a new and innovative development? Presumably, cost optimization in the interest of your customers is already an established practice for you?

Christian: This is absolutely correct. We have already reaped the low-hanging fruits by designing the CHEMPARK and its energy infrastructure efficiently. However, due to rising costs in the chemical industry and the current climate of the energy market, we need to do more. Smart technologies will help us to uncover remaining potential by better understanding interactions between energy production and consumption in the numerous facilities located here.

Bernhard: Could you give some specific examples of smart elements in your industrial park? How do you manage the smart integration of value chains?

Christian: Basically we are bundling our own generation flexibilities with those of our customers' energy consuming processes—and then we offer it on energy markets like the intra-day market or the electricity balancing market. One of our customers, for example, can provide a flexibility of ±10% of his energy consumption by shifting production between different production sites and through storage of the produced chemicals. This is more difficult than it sounds, as you need to adapt established production processes and install buffer capacities. Another example would be the installation of electrode boilers that create steam by heating water. A system of distributed boilers can be used to generate steam in times of low power prices and to back up the existing central steam generation. They can also help to contribute to negative power capacity on the balancing market (i.e., boiler operators are paid to consume electricity whenever there is surplus power on the grid, destabilizing supply and demand). We are also thinking about establishing a system of distributed high-temperature heat pumps to convert our clients' waste heat into useable steam that would feed into the steam network and be controlled by overall optimization in the network.

Bernhard: What competencies are needed to make this kind of project a success?

Christian: The chemical production processes involved are highly complex. To understand their inherent potential for energy savings and flexibilities, we need a thorough understanding of chemical process engineering. Also, we need to respect any operational limitations, keeping in mind that the primary purpose of our clients' facilities is to produce chemicals, not to offer power on energy markets. These analytical skills need to be complemented by IT and software skills for developing the algorithms we have to incorporate into our control systems. But, needless to say, we are not a software company, so for many applications we are partnering with external service providers. Another key skill is being able to assess the commercial viability of a new or innovative idea, based on a detailed understanding of external energy markets such as the markets for electricity balancing. Finally, we need good communication skills to help our customers understand the targets we are aiming for and the technical-commercial concepts we can implement.

Bernhard: What is the role of dedicated software solutions—for example, for modeling, simulation, and optimization of the energy infrastructure? Can you purchase such tools on the market?

Christian: To date, we have not found a commercial tool that would be able to support us sufficiently. As a result, we have to rely on heavily customized tools supplemented by in-house developments, which in fact limits our options. I imagine that dedicated tools could be developed jointly by chemical park operators; however, this is not yet a reality.

Bernhard: What is your approach to projects? Do you set up a single, all-encompassing project or rather a set of smaller projects? How do you integrate your customers into the project?

Christian: We rely on a number of solution-oriented pilot projects with significant customer integration. A key requirement is that we consider the solution to be suitable in terms of both time and profitability. Our customers are fully integrated into the pilot project as project partners. We are aiming at creating a high level of transparency for them, so that we can base the project on a joint understanding of the related challenges and benefits.

Bernhard: What have you accomplished to date? Are there any quick wins you have achieved?

Christian: First of all, we have significantly enhanced the flexibility of our power generation. We are now running our plants in a completely different way, no longer strictly coupling power and steam production in our cogeneration plants. We are also successfully offering the resulting flexibilities on the market for secondary and tertiary control power. Another successful innovation was the redesign of the production processes of one of our customers, which resulted in the creation of significant flexibilities in the region of 10 MW.

Bernhard: To conclude, what lessons have you learned? Do you foresee any major challenges in the near future?

Christian: A basic prerequisite is making the system you are looking at really transparent so that economic levers can be identified. Here we can make use of our proximity to our customers and our understanding of the processes we encounter in the CHEMPARK. However, the smartness we are aiming for is more than just technological; it entails a real change in habits—for example, running a power plant completely differently than you are used to. With a view to the future, a major challenge will be to scale up the solutions developed in pilots, creating more standardized products that are applicable to most of our customers. IT security is something we have to look at together with our customers, ensuring that production data is handled safely. Finally, it will be essential to implement robust technological solutions that do not have to be replaced every three years or so when new technologies or data protocols are introduced.

CHAPTER 4

Manufacturing and Industry

THE APPLICATION OF IoT CONCEPTS TO INDUSTRIAL ENVIRONMENTS HAS ATTRACTED A LOT OF interest. GE has coined the term "Industrial Internet," IBM is pushing the concept of "smart factories," German industry uses the term "Industry 4.0," while Airbus talks about the "factory of the future." Precise definitions are few and far between, and many of these concepts go beyond the notion of next-generation manufacturing to include logistics and supply chain management, mining and offshore drilling, and even smart grids and building automation.

In some cases, a worthwhile distinction is made between the Industrial IoT and the Consumer IoT. As we saw in Chapter 1, our definition of Enterprise IoT is less about specific application domains and more about openness and integration maturity. In this chapter, we will take a closer look at some of the more industrial applications of Enterprise IoT, starting with a discussion about how IoT will transform manufacturing from the perspective of both product engineering and production technology.

Integrated Production for Integrated Products

We believe that the IoT will have two main areas of impact on the current manufacturing landscape. The first concerns the organizational structure that is required to produce truly integrated IoT solutions. As discussed in Chapter 1, the IoT involves a clash between two worlds in which those in the machine camp and those in the Internet camp will be required to work together to create products that combine physical products with Internet-based application services. In an IoT world, many companies will discover that being just a manufacturing company or just an Internet company will no longer be sufficient; they will need to become both—or become subsumed in an ecosystem in which they play a smaller role.

For manufacturing companies, this means they will have to build up capabilities in IoT service development and operation; in other words, the achievement of "integrated production for integrated products" (Figure 4-1). Many of these companies will find this challenging, because it is not in their DNA. Nor is it just a question of developing additional IT skills (beyond the embedded skills most will likely already have); value propositions will have to evolve too, which will necessitate change in almost all parts of the organization, from engineering to sales right through to aftermarket services.

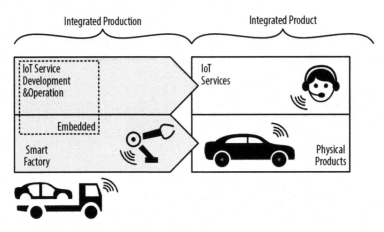

FIGURE 4-1. Integrated production of integrated products

The second area where the IoT will have a significant impact on manufacturers is of course in the area of manufacturing technologies. As promoted by initiatives such as the German government's Industry 4.0 strategy, connected manufacturing equipment, connected logistic chains, cyber–physical systems, and Big Data-based analytics of production processes will help improve the way the physical parts of a connected IoT solution are produced. In a sense, this second area of impact can benefit from the first; what might be considered an integrated product to one company (e.g., a machine component manufacturer) is an advanced production technology to another (e.g., a manufacturer using the connected machine component in their assembly lines).

Drawing on these two key assumptions, Figure 4-2 provides a detailed overview of the manufacturing value chain of tomorrow. Note, in particular, the integration of IoT service implementation with IoT service operation.

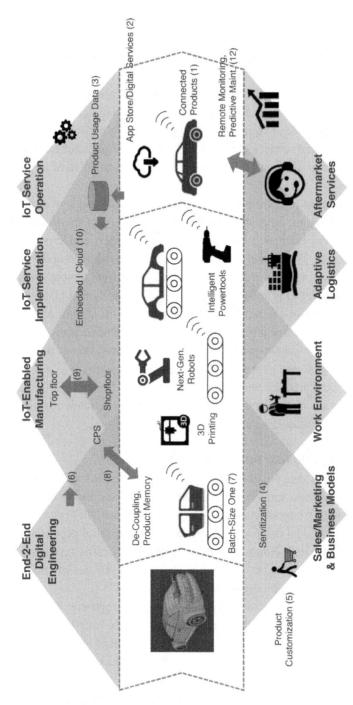

FIGURE 4-2. Factory of the future, Industry 4.0, and the IoT

Before we look at how new production technologies will help improve manufacturing processes in the future, we need to briefly recap on what we know about the products of tomorrow; because, ultimately, the nature of these new products will have an impact on all other processes, from design to manufacturing right through to aftermarket services.

As discussed in Chapter 1, the assumption is that the products of the future will be connected (1) and become part of what we call the Internet of Things. We are also assuming that products will have embedded computing capabilities, enabling local intelligence and digital services (2). These digital services can be applications or content. For example, a car app store might provide a new navigation application, and the application itself allow the purchase of additional maps.

The combination of physical product and connected backend service will have a sizeable impact on product design. First, it's possible that the design of the physical products themselves will change. For example, a product's embedded display and keys could be dropped in favor of a mobile app. This would constitute a significant redesign of the product's physical components. Second, products will be increasingly reliant on remote services, often in the cloud. Building these kinds of related IT services is not usually part of the traditional product engineering process. It will require someone to oversee the design of both elements—the physical product and its associated backend software services or platform— and ensure that everything results in a nicely integrated product offering. See also our discussion in "Clash of Two Worlds: Machine Camp Versus Internet Camp" on page 9.

Finally, connected products will provide a rich source of product usage data (3), which will serve as input for all other stages of the value chain, from sales, marketing, and product design through to manufacturing and after-sales services.

SALES/MARKETING AND NEW BUSINESS MODELS

New business models made possible by the emergence of the IoT will drive the future of product design. These business models will also have a significant impact on the sale and marketing of these products. As we discussed in Chapter 1, servitization (4) involves transforming a company's business model from one focused on selling physical products to one focused on services. For example, Rolls-Royce now earns roughly 50% of its revenue from services—by leasing jet engines to airlines on a "power-by-the-hour" basis, for example. This completely transforms the way in which products are sold and serviced.

However, it also means that sales teams will have to completely adjust their sales strategy. Incentive models based on upfront revenues will have to be revisited in favor of models that support recurring revenues, which allow for the stabilization of revenue forecasting.

Marketing teams will be able to leverage detailed product usage data (3) to drive marketing campaigns and define precise market segments. This direct link to the customer via the product can be of huge value for sales and marketing teams, making it easier for them to run targeted cross-selling and up-selling campaigns, for example.

Another key driver is product customization (5). More and more markets are demanding fully customized products. Ranging from custom-designed sneakers to cars built to customer specifications, this trend has two key implications. First, products are now being sold *before* they have been produced, and not the other way around. In Figure 4-2, we can see that sales comes *before* manufacturing, contrary to what we would normally expect. Second, this trend has a major impact on the manufacturing process itself; for example, "batch size 1" production is a basic requirement of custom manufacturing (7).

END-TO-END DIGITAL ENGINEERING

Digital engineering is a reality in most large manufacturing organizations today. These organizations have invested heavily in the integration of tool chains that support the entire product lifecycle. Computer-aided design (CAD) tools are used for product design and simulation, computer-aided production engineering (CAPE) tools support the design and simulation of manufacturing systems, while manufacturing execution systems (MES) tools help ensure the integration of product data right across the product lifecycle while also supporting resource scheduling, order execution and dispatch, material tracking, and production analysis.

3D models are also playing an increasingly important role that transcends the traditional domain of product design. Modern 3D PLM systems have integrated CAD design data with bill of material (BOM) data and other information to better support end-to-end digital engineering. The 3D model becomes the master model for all product-related data (6). 3D data also support the simulation of entire assembly lines, helping to optimize manufacturing efficiency and minimize the risk of costly changes after the assembly line has been set up.

One of the key benefits promised by the IoT is that it will help link the virtual world with the physical world. 3D models are a very important type of virtual model. The use of sensors, lasers, and localization technologies has enabled the creation of links between the virtual 3D world and the physical world. For example, Airbus uses 3D data to emit laser projections over aircraft bodies in order to guide assembly line workers [AB1]. Similarly, at the Hannover industrial trade fair in 2014, Siemens showcased a complete (physical) assembly line with an associated virtual model in their 3D factory simulation environment. Sensors on the moving parts of the assembly line send movement data back to the IT system, which then updates the position data in the 3D system in real time. As can be seen in Figure 4-3, the virtual 3D model is fully in synch with the actual production line.

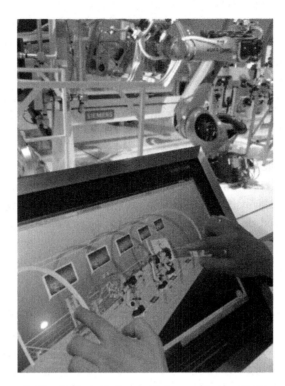

FIGURE 4-3. 3D simulation synchronized with physical assembly line, as showcased by Siemens at HMI 2014

Augmented reality is another interesting area in which we are seeing convergence between 3D models and the physical world, especially in the context of training and quality assurance. For example, Airbus's mixed reality application (MiRA) allows shopfloor workers to access a 3D model using a specialized device consisting of a tablet PC with integrated sensor pack. Leveraging location devices on the aircraft and on the tablet PC, MiRA can show a 3D model of the aircraft from the user`s perspective, "augmenting" it with additional, production-related data. Airbus's adoption of MiRA has allowed them to reduce the time needed to inspect the 60,000–80,000 brackets in their A380 fuselage from three weeks down to three days [AB1].

MANUFACTURING

We've already discussed the need to become increasingly flexible and capable of supporting highly customizable products. From a manufacturing point of view, this means that concepts like "batch size 1" (7) and "one-piece flow" are becoming even more important. One of the visions of Industry 4.0 is that it will enable the decoupling of production modules to support more flexible production. One potential way of achieving this is through the use of product memory. Products, semifinished products, and even component parts will be equipped with an RFID chip or similar piece of technology that performs a product memory function (8).

This product memory can be used to store product configuration data, work instructions, and work history. Instead of relying on a central MES system to manage all aspects of production, these intelligent products can tell the production modules themselves what needs to be done. This approach could be instrumental in paving the way for cyber–physical systems (CPS), another key element of the factory of the future. This is discussed in more detail in "Case Study: Smart Factory" on page 81.

Improved "top floor to shop floor" integration is another important benefit promised by Industry 4.0 (9). Concepts like manufacturing operations management (MOM) have emerged to help integrate and analyze data from different levels, including the machine, line, plant, and enterprise level. With IoT, additional data will be provided from the machine level directly.

The extent to which the IoT movement will deliver new technologies and standards in this area also makes for an interesting discussion. For example, one already widely established standard for integrating machine data is OPC/OPC-UA [OP1]. It remains to be seen whether OPC and similar standards will be simply relabeled as "IoT-compliant," or whether an entirely new set of standards will emerge.

Similarly, many machine component suppliers are already providing either standards-based interfaces (e.g., OPC) or proprietary interfaces (e.g., DB-based) for accessing machine data. Again, the question is whether it is necessary to invent new standards and protocols, or whether in this particular case it is more important to drive integration at a higher level, based on an enterprise application integration (EAI) or service-oriented architecture (SOA) approach, for example. One of the main issues here seems to be heterogeneity—the very issue that EAI and SOA were specifically developed to address.

Another interesting discussion relates to the integration that needs to take place one level down (i.e., at the bus level). For decades, industrial bus systems (EtherCAD, Modbus, Profibus, SERCOS, etc.) have been used for production automation, enabling communication with and control of industrial components, often via programmable logic controllers (PLCs). Most of these bus systems are highly proprietary, because they are required to support extremely demanding real-time requirements—which is difficult to achieve using the Internet Protocol (IP). This, again, poses a problem for the overall vision promised by the IoT—the IP-enabled integration of devices of all shapes and sizes. So it will be interesting to see if the efforts of the IEEE's Time-Sensitive Networking (TSN) task group [TS1]) succeed in establishing technologies for machine and robot control based on IP networking standards.

Other important examples of technologies that could become relevant for the factory of the future include:

3D printing

Especially in the area of prototyping and the production of nonstandard, low-volume parts, 3D printing is set to become very important in the not-so-distant future.

Next-generation robots

Robots are already being used in many high-volume production lines today. In terms of how they will evolve, one interesting area is the ability of robots to work in dynamic environments and ensure safe collaboration with humans.

Intelligent power tools

As we will see in more detail in Part III, power tools such as those used for drilling, tightening, and measuring are becoming increasingly intelligent and connected. The tracking and tracing of these tools is an important IoT use case.

High-precision indoor localization

The tracking and tracing of moving equipment and products in a factory environment will be primarily achieved through the use of high-precision indoor localization technology.

IOT SERVICE IMPLEMENTATION

The ability to combine manufacturing with IT service implementation is not yet widely established. Apple is still seen as a leader in the field, because of its ability to produce physical products (iPod, iPhone, etc.) that are tightly integrated with IT services (iTunes, iCloud, etc.). As we discussed in Chapter 1 in the introduction, many manufacturers today are still struggling to establish organizational structures where both capabilities are available and integrated to a sufficient degree. Regardless, the ability to combine physical product design and manufacturing with embedded, cloud/backend-based software service development is seen as a key capability of the IoT.

This integration must take place on both an organizational and technical level. The Ignite | IoT Methodology described in Part II specifically addresses this issue from an IT service implementation perspective.

IOT SERVICE OPERATIONS

The ability to make the transition from manufacturer to service operator is essential to the achievement of success in an IoT world. This applies not just to the technical operation of the service, but also to the operation of a business organization capable of supporting strong customer relationships. The DriveNow car-sharing service discussed in Chapter 1 is a good example of this. Formed as a result of a joint venture between BMW and Sixt, the service successfully combines BMW's car manufacturing expertise with Sixt's expertise in running a considerably more service-oriented car rental operation.

Another good example is the eCall service, an IoT service that requires a call center capable of manually processing incoming distress calls from vehicles and/or vehicle drivers. For more information, see Chapter 5.

Apart from the business operation itself, there is the question of operating the IT services associated with the IoT solution. Some of the capabilities required here include traditional IT operations capabilities, such as operating the call center application used in the eCall service described earlier. However, some of the capabilities required are also very IoT-specific. Managing remote connections to hundreds of thousands of assets and devices is challenging from an operational point of view, not least in terms of scalability and security.

Remote software distribution is another area worthy of discussion. It offers a huge opportunity for many manufacturers, but also requires the provision and operation of a suitable infrastructure. A good case in point is the recent recall of 1.9 million vehicles by a large OEM due to problems with the onboard software [TY1]. This OEM could have saved itself massive amounts of money if it had been able to distribute the required software update remotely. Smartphone platforms also provide a good insight into the challenges involved in running remote software updates on a very large scale. Although they are now much better at handling software updates than they were in the past, the situation is far from perfect and occasional problems still persist. In the case of in-car software, this would be unacceptable.

AFTERMARKET SERVICES

In an era of IoT-fueled "servitization" especially, aftermarket services are becoming increasingly important.

Remote condition monitoring (RCM) is one of a number of basic services that can have a fundamentally positive impact on customer service quality. The ability to access product status information in real time is invaluable for support services, not least because it makes for much more efficient root cause analysis and solution development. RCM is not new; it is most likely one of the most widely adopted M2M use cases. The challenge for many large manufacturers today is one of heterogeneity. A large manufacturer with thousands of product categories can easily have hundreds of different RCM solutions. The issue here is not so much the need for new and improved RCM for next-generation products, it's about the implementation of efficient IT management solutions that are capable of managing this heterogeneity. This could be achieved by automating virtualization and improving secure connection management, for example.

The next step in the evolution of RCM is predictive maintenance. The use of sensors for thermal imaging, vibration analysis, sonic and ultrasonic analysis, oil and liquid analysis, as well as emission analysis allows the detection of problems before they even occur. For buyers of industrial components, predictive maintenance has the potential to significantly improve operational equipment efficiency (OEE). For end-consumer products, predictive maintenance is a great way of improving customer service and ensuring extra sales or commission ("You should replace your brakes within the next 5,000 kilometers. We can recommend a service station on your way to work.").

In general, product usage data will really help with the identification of cross-selling and up-selling opportunities. When combined with the ability to sell additional digital services, the proposition becomes even more compelling. For example, the performance of many car engines today is controlled by software. We could have a scenario where a car manufacturer produces one version of an engine (the high-end version), and then uses configuration software to create a lower-performing version. The digital service in this case could be the option to temporarily upgrade engine performance for a weekend trip ("You have just programmed your navigation system for a drive to the country. Would you like to upgrade your engine performance for this trip?").

Naturally, this newly won customer intimacy will require solid security and reasonable data access policies in order to retain customer trust in the long term.

End-of-lifecycle data can be used for remanufacturing and recycling offers, or simply to make the customer an attractive product replacement proposals.

The boundary between IoT services and aftermarket services is not always clear. From our perspective, IoT services are part of the original value proposition. Take the eCall service, for example. In this case, the service is essentially the product that is being sold. Aftermarket services generally take the form of value-added services (which can also be IoT-based).

WORK ENVIRONMENT

Some people are concerned that these new manufacturing concepts will threaten the workplace of the future, bringing with them increased automation and the wider use of robots. While there is strong evidence that automation may actually reduce the amount of tedious and repetitive labor, there is also an argument that work will become more specialized and thus more interesting and varied. In particular, the flexibility inherent in the factory of the future will demand an approach that is more geared toward problem solving and self-organization. Robots that help with strenuous, manual labor are viewed by many as an improvement for the work environment. Airbus's wearable robotic devices or exoskeletons, which are intended to help with heavy loads and work in difficult spaces, provide a good case in point [AB1].

ADAPTIVE LOGISTICS AND VALUE-ADDED NETWORKS

Finally, one key element synonymous with the Industrial Internet and advanced Industry 4.0 concerns adaptive logistics and value-added networks. The idea here is that traditional supply chains will evolve into value networks. For example, these networks will need to have structures that are capable of adapting rapidly in order to address batch-of-one requests between different customers and suppliers.

The ability of the IoT to monitor containers, trucks, trains, and other elements of modern transportation systems in real time will also help optimize logistics processes. Improved integration at the business process level will also help make logistics systems more adaptive.

Other Industrial Applications

Of course, the Industrial IoT presents many opportunities beyond those related purely to manufacturing. Some of the opportunities covered in this book include:

Mobile equipment tracking
> The tracking of industrial equipment and containers was one of the first application areas of telematics and M2M, and will evolve and contribute to value-added IoT solutions. The Intellion, Kärcher, and PurFresh case studies at the end of this chapter provide some great examples of this.

Nuclear physics research
> As we will see in the CERN case study, one of the areas in which sensor technologies are most widely used is in nuclear physics research, where they are deployed to reconstruct digital images of nuclear collisions.

Energy
> Because it is such a large application domain for IoT, we have dedicated an entire chapter to energy (see Chapter 3).

And of course there are many other potential applications of the Industrial IoT, from cross-energy management (see Chapter 3) to mining right through to offshore drilling.

Industry Initiatives

Given the momentum of the Industrial IoT and its related concepts, it is no surprise that the raft of industry initiatives in this area has become a little confusing. Some examples of these initiatives include the Smart Manufacturing Leadership Coalition (SMLC), the Open Connect Consortium (OIC), the European Research Cluster on the Internet of Things (IERC), the M2M Alliance, and the IEEE Industrial Working Group, to name just a few. In this section, we will focus on two initiatives that are gathering strong momentum: Industry 4.0 and the Industrial Internet Consortium.

INDUSTRY 4.0

Industry 4.0 began as a special interest group supported by German industry heavyweights and machine manufacturers. Its goal was to promote the vision of a fourth industrial revolution, driven by the digitization of manufacturing. Today, the initiative is mostly led by the Industry 4.0 Platform, a dedicated grouping comprising industry members such as ABB, Bosch, FESTO, Infineon, PHOENIX CONTACT, Siemens, ThyssenKrupp, TRUMPF, Volkswagen, and WITTENSTEIN; as well as IT and telecoms companies such as Deutsche Telekom, HP, IBM Germany, and SAP. Government agencies and industry associations have also lent their support. The main focus of Industry 4.0 is on smart factories and related areas such as supply chains and value networks, as opposed to wider Industrial IoT use cases such as smart energy, smart building, and more. The initial report that defined the Industry 4.0

vision [141] defined use cases such as resilient factory, predictive maintenance, connected production, adaptive logistics, and others.

The following interview provides some background on the adoption of Industry 4.0 at Bosch, a large, multinational manufacturing company. Olaf Klemd is Vice President of Connected Industry at Bosch, where he is responsible for coordinating all Industry 4.0 initiatives across the different business units within Bosch.

Dirk Slama: Industry 4.0, Industrial Internet, Internet of Things—are these all referring to the same thing?

Olaf Klemd: The Internet of Things and Services (IoTS) is a global megatrend. Whether it's cars, household appliances, or medical devices, more and more devices are becoming connected via the Internet. Of course, this trend will also affect the way we produce things in the future. Industry 4.0 marks a shift away from serial production in favor of the manufacture of small lots and individualized products. Machines and automation modules will need to be closely interconnected, both with each other and with the required IT systems. It involves linking physical components with associated virtual data in a way that will change the underlying value chain—from product design and engineering, to manufacturing and logistics, right through to product recycling. It will also change traditional value chains, transforming them into comprehensive value networks in the industry of the future.

Dirk Slama: What is Bosch's main focus of activity in this area?

Olaf Klemd: Bosch has adopted a dual strategy based on two main pillars. First, Bosch is a leading provider of connected products and services to our customers around the globe. Second, Bosch is a leading plant operator with more than 220 factories worldwide, all of which stand to benefit significantly from these trends.

In terms of connected products and services, we leverage Bosch's vast and well-established product portfolio. We have developed new connected solutions in many Bosch divisions, covering a wide range of applications.

For example, our Drive and Control Technology Division already offers the decentralized, intelligent components required to meet the needs of the future. This is a result of the technological evolution that has been taking place in recent decades. Not without its challenges, the team faced one major obstacle: automation systems and IT systems use completely different programming languages, which makes the exchange of information difficult. They responded to this challenge by developing what we call Open Core Engineering (OCE). This innovative solution is a game changer for the industry, because for the first time it offers a universal translator that allows the exchange of information

---

between IT and machine controls. Machine manufacturers and end users now have the freedom to seamlessly integrate and adapt machines to specific Industry 4.0 solutions by themselves.

Our Packaging Technology (PT) division provides another good example. Its ATMO team has launched the Autonomous Production Assistant. Providing new collaboration opportunities for human/machine interaction in the area of robotics, the Autonomous Production Assistant reduces the overhead for traditional safety mechanisms and dramatically increases flexibility. Another good example is the virtual power plant, developed by our own Bosch Software Innovations division.

As the first to deploy these solutions, Bosch is using its first-mover advantage to build up unique expertise in Industry 4.0 on two fronts. As a leading plant operator, we are actively improving our competitiveness, and by giving open feedback internally, we are improving our products and solutions before they hit the market.

We have identified supply chain management as a critical element of the process. One Industry 4.0 approach is to virtualize the supply chain by using RFID technologies. This not only enables us to make material and product flows more transparent, it's also an important prerequisite for reducing inventory and ensuring just-in-time delivery. Pilot projects have shown that the use of RFID technologies has helped us to reduce inventory by up to 30%. In 2014, our internal Kanban processes benefited from the integration of data from more than 20 million RFID-driven transactions.

Dirk Slama: What are the key technical drivers of Industry 4.0?

Olaf Klemd: There are many: Big Data, IoT middleware, the increasing trend to use more embedded, integrated systems that allow for the creation of decentralized solutions. However, one very important driver is the proliferation of sensors in the industrial environment. Sensors allow us to capture product, machine, and environment behavior. This data can then be analyzed and correlations derived to help optimize products and processes. Sensors are a key enabler of cyber–physical systems because they help translate physical events into cyber data.

Dirk Slama: So in terms of timeline, where does this all fit in?

Olaf Klemd: Industry 4.0 is the next logical step in the evolution of automation. We started some years back with connected manufacturing, so it is still an ongoing process really. The German government's Industry 4.0 initiative was helpful in focusing our efforts, encouraging us to set up more than 50 initial pilot projects in 2013. At the time, it was very much a bottom-up effort. Today, we take a more holistic approach to ensuring that these trends are leveraged across our entire internal value chain and international production network.

Dirk Slama: What does this mean for people working in Bosch factories?

Olaf Klemd: Our main goals include the creation of sustainable workplaces and a good work environment. From the company's viewpoint, sustainable workplaces depend on product innovation and process efficiency. From the viewpoint of workers, the continuous development of new skills through the use of new technologies is also important. Ultimately, Industry 4.0 is more than just a tool for improving efficiency—it is an important driver for improving the work environment in general. For example, new human–machine interfaces represent a significant improvement for the work environment. The reduction of heavy, monotonous labor is a good example of how physical work can be supported effectively. In terms of collaborative work, the availability of more reliable, real-time data is generally welcomed as it helps people to make better decisions and be more successful in their work. In keeping with our own strategic imperative, "Invented for Life," we believe that Industry 4.0 will provide significant contributions in this area.

INDUSTRIAL INTERNET CONSORTIUM

Another noteworthy organization promoting the adoption of Industrial Internet–related topics is the Industrial Internet Consortium. GE, which coined the term "Industrial Internet," initiated the creation of the Industrial Internet Consortium in 2014, with AT&T, Cisco, Intel, and IBM joining as founding members. While initially driven by US-headquartered companies, the Industrial Internet Consortium takes a global take on the Industrial Internet, with more than 100 new members from many different countries joining the Industrial Internet Consortium in its first year.

The Industrial Internet Consortium takes a relatively broad perspective on the Industrial Internet: in addition to manufacturing, the Industrial Internet Consortium also looks at energy, healthcare, public sector, and transportation. The Industrial Internet Consortium sees itself more as an incubator for innovation. Its Working Groups address the architecture and security requirements for the Industrial Internet, but the Industrial Internet Consortium itself is not a standardization body.

An important tool to drive the adoption of new technologies and business models in the Industrial Internet is the so-called testbed. A testbed is a member-sponsored innovation project that supports the general goals and vision of the Industrial Internet Consortium and is compliant to the Industrial Internet Consortium reference architecture. An example for an Industrial Internet Consortium testbed is the Track & Trace Solution, which is described in detail in Part III of the book. This Industrial Internet Consortium testbed is utilizing the Ignite | IoT methodology for solution delivery.

Case Studies: Overview

The remainder of this chapter provides a number of case studies to illustrate some of the different facets of the Industrial IoT. We are always on the lookout for additional case studies, so if you feel you have something to offer in this space, contact us via our website:

SmartFactoryKL
This case study is an industrial-grade research project that showcases key elements of the smart factory, including decoupling of production modules and product memory.

Tracking of mobile equipment
This subject includes two case studies:

Intelligent lot handling
This case study describes the use of high-precision indoor localization technology to optimize wafer production.

Cleaning equipment
This case study looks at fleet management for mobile cleaning equipment and an innovative management dashboard.

Cool chain management
This case study goes beyond traditional container tracking and looks at actively managing the environment inside the container.

Nuclear particle physics
This case study looks at one of the largest pieces of industrial machinery built by mankind and its extremely advanced use of sensors.

Part III of this book provides a further Industrial IoT case study on the Trace & Trace solution for handheld power tools.

Case Study: Smart Factory

The increasing flexibility of production processes, associated customization requirements, and the push for "batch size 1" production are key drivers of the concepts of the smart factory and Industry 4.0. A leading research organization in this space is SmartFactoryKL, a special interest group specialized in the practical validation of theoretical manufacturing concepts. In collaboration with industry partners, SmartFactoryKL develops and tests industrial systems in realistic industrial production environments. This case study relates to the Industry 4.0 demonstration system that was showcased at the Hannover Messe industrial technology fair in 2014 [DF1].

The Industry 4.0 demonstration platform is a production line that allows the automatic assembly of customized business card holders from various components, the engraving of business names via laser, and the automatic completion of basic test functions. Bosch Rexroth and Harting modules are used for assembly, a Festo module is used for the engraving, and a

PhoenixContact module is used for laser writing. Quality assurance is provided by a module developed by Lapp Kabel. MiniTec has provided a manual workstation with integrated augmented-reality guidance features. Figure 4-4 shows the assembly line, as demonstrated in Hannover in 2014.

FIGURE 4-4. Industry 4.0 assembly line (Source: SmartFactoryKL)

What makes the assembly line so special is that it can be reassembled dynamically thanks to its modular structure. As demonstrated in Hannover, the sequence of the production modules can be changed in a matter of minutes. All production modules are fully autonomous; there is no central MES or other production control system involved. This is achieved using digital product memory, which stores product configurations as well as the corresponding work instructions and work history.

The Festo module is responsible for starting the production process. This is where the base casing of the business card holder is unloaded and customer-specific data is engraved onto an RFID tag, which is then attached to the base plate. The module then engraves the base of the holder itself as per customer specifications. Next, the Rexroth module mounts the clip to the base casing of the business card holder. Depending on the customer's specifications, the Harting module then places either a blue or black cover onto the base plate and force fits the two components together. The PhoenixContact module then takes over, using a laser system to add an individual QR code and lettering to the product.

The last module in the assembly line is the LappKabel module, which performs a quality check and releases the final product. Other partners such as Cisco, Hirschmann, ProAlpha, and Siemens have also contributed their expertise to the project. This has allowed the integration of different IT systems and the creation of a backbone structure to feed the individual modules of the assembly line. The key elements of the assembly line are shown in Figure 4-5.

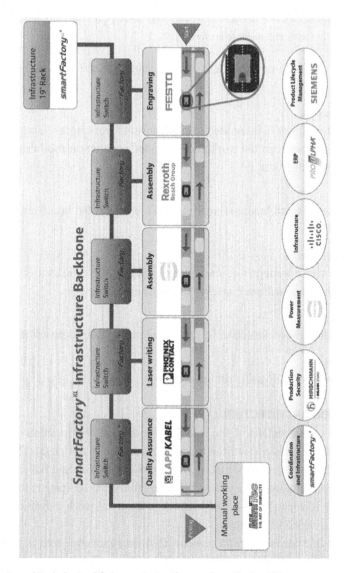

FIGURE 4-5. Architecture of the Industry 4.0 demonstrator (Source: SmartFactoryKL)

A key objective of the Industry 4.0 demonstration platform was to show how standardized production modules can be easily integrated and exchanged. Project initiator and chairman of the SmartFactoryKL board, Prof. Dr. Dr. h.c. Detlef Zühlke explains:

To ensure the modularity of production systems, the mechanical, electrical, and communication interfaces need to follow standards. Useful standards can only emerge on the basis of actual requirements and experience. This means that standards have to develop simultaneously with the adoption of Industry 4.0. Already there are a number of standards available at different levels, and we should use these standards. We do not need to start from scratch. It's only at higher interoperability levels that a lot more work still needs to be done.

For the Industry 4.0 demonstration platform, standardization was achieved at a number of levels:

Digital product memory
Digital product memory is integrated into the various workpieces using RFID technology. Data is exchanged between the workpieces and the production modules based on a standardized cross-manufacturer.

Vertical integration
Production modules and business applications are integrated based on the OPC UA standard.

Transportation of workpieces
An innovative sluice system was devised to facilitate the interconnection of production modules and the standardized conveyor belts within them.

Assembly line topology
Automatic neighborhood detection for independent topology derivation.

Production modules
All modules support EUR-pallet dimensions.

ASSET INTEGRATION ARCHITECTURE

Figure 4-6 provides more details of the solution's individual components. Each product has an RFID tag that can be read and written to and from a remote device (a). The tag stores product configuration data and the work history. Each production module has an integrated RFID unit that accesses this data from the product in order to read work instructions and create new entries in the work history (b). The ERP system creates the work definition for the product using the Festo module's RFID unit.

The use of product memory and a standardized data exchange format to control the production process across multiple production modules is very interesting, because it simplifies integration. Instead of having to integrate all modules into one complex central system, the interfaces are loosely coupled and relatively simple. The product controls its own flow and the work that has to be done in this flow. Especially in cases where products are worked on in multiple organizations, this has the potential to greatly simplify integration and provide for much greater flexibility.

The modules in the demonstration platform have different architectures. Some follow a more traditional approach; for example, module A has a PLC for controlling the pick-and-place units, and uses an OPC UA server to provide access to the business logic in the backend.

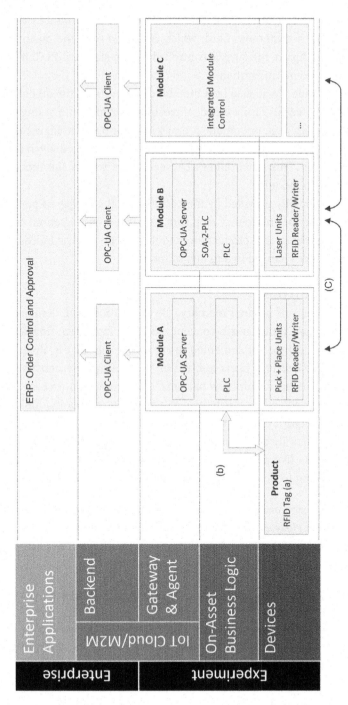

FIGURE 4-6. AIA for SmartFactoryKL demonstrator

Module B reads the customer name and address from the product's RFID tag and then uses this data to create a customer vCard, which is lasered onto the business card holder in the form of a QR code. Again, the laser is controlled from a standard PLC. It is also planned to use SOA-2-PLC for backend integration.

In the future, Module C will also be a little bit different from the other modules in that it will use a small but powerful Linux-based microcontroller to create a single, integrated network of actuators/sensors (e.g., pneumatic press) with their own intelligence.

The physical coupling of the modules is based on a standardized hatch through which the products are moved (c). This hatch allows conveyor belts within the modules to move the product from module to module.

The central functionality provided by the backbone is the supply of power, pressured air, industrial Ethernet, and an emergency stop function. There is no central SCADA or similar system involved. This means that production modules can be used as individual plug-and-play units, and their sequence changed in a matter of minutes.

CONCLUSIONS AND OUTLOOK

Thanks to the integration of product memory, the SmartFactoryKL demonstration platform has shown that important Industry 4.0 concepts such as single-item flow and loose coupling of production modules can be implemented using technology that is already available today. The SmartFactoryKL consortium plans to build on the concepts demonstrated in the system, and to add additional modules from new partners. The production process used for the demonstration will be extended and its capabilities enhanced on an ongoing basis. The first update is set to be unveiled at Hannover in April 2015.

The industry partners involved in the project are keen to transfer these concepts from a research environment to live production environments. However, this is unlikely to happen any time soon. According to Prof. Zühlke, there is more work to be done:

> In some areas, like in semiconductor production, we have made considerable advances in establishing module standards. However, I think it will be at least another three years before we start seeing initial implementations of the Smart Factory in a live production environment. In terms of full implementation, I think we are talking 10 years or even more.

However, Prof. Zühlke is keen to stress that companies should not miss the boat:

> Some companies are already under pressure to keep up with ongoing developments. Industry 4.0 is not just a minor trend; these concepts and technologies represent a fundamental paradigm shift that will completely transform the manufacturing landscape as we know it today.

Case Study: Intelligent Lot Tracking

Modern semiconductor chip factories are among the most advanced production facilities in existence today. The cost of building a next-generation chip factory can easily exceed $1 billion. 24/7 production involving hundreds of employees in large clean-room facilities yields billions of chips per year. The semiconductor production process is extremely complex. Typically, multiple circuits are grouped on a single wafer, which undergoes complex chemical processes in a clean-room environment to build up the circuits in layers. Several wafers are then placed in a wafer carrier for processing. These wafer carriers hold the wafers between the processing stages. Advanced wafer carriers such as a state-of-the-art FOUP (Front Opening Unified Pod) can be used to automatically unload the wafers in the next production bay and reload them again after processing. Up to 500 production steps per wafer may be required, using hundreds of different machines. Some of the larger semiconductor factories have full-scale material handling systems that automatically move wafer carriers between production bays. In many factories which require more flexibility and support for a broad product mix, wafer carriers still need to be transported between production bays manually.

Figure 4-7 shows an example of an FOUP wafer carrier (sometimes called a "lot box") and its path through a factory, also known as a "wafer fab."

In wafer factories that don't have an automated material handling system, the production process is generally managed on the basis of dispatch lists. The dispatch list defines the order in which the production lots have to be processed. One of the main problems here relates to the localization of individual wafer carriers, as many factories use thousands of these carriers. Manual processing is costly and prone to error.

This is where intelligent lot-handling solutions come in. These use indoor localization technology to automatically track the position of each wafer carrier in a production facility. Positioning data is managed in a central database, which is closely integrated with the manufacturing execution system (MES).

Signaling devices, such as LEDs or markers (which change colors from black to yellow), indicate whether a wafer carrier is currently scheduled for further processing. A display panel on the wafer carrier shows additional processing information, such as the lot number, next production operation, or next destination of a lot box. However, implementing this kind of solution presents multiple challenges, as we will soon see.

FIGURE 4-7. Logistical challenge: path of a lot box through a fab (Source: Infineon Technologies AG)

A good example of an intelligent lot-tracking solution is LotTrack, developed by Swiss company Intellion, which we will examine in more detail in this case study. LotTrack is a system designed to improve the overall workflow in manually operated wafer fabs. It consists of three key components:

DisTag

A smart device placed on each wafer carrier, which enables wafer carriers to be located within the factory to an accuracy of approximately 0.5 meters. The DisTag also has a control panel for local interaction with the factory operators. Signaling devices like an LED and a marker provide priority and search functions. Battery lifetime is approximately two years.

Antenna lines

The modular antenna line contains all the hardware modules required for indoor localization, assistance, and load port compliance. It is usually mounted to the ceiling of the clean room along the factory's interbay and intrabay.

Control suite

The backend software is the link between shop-floor activities and the MES. It provides a dashboard for visualizing all transport and storage activities.

Customers like Infineon, STMicroelectronics, and OSRAM use the LotTrack solution to reduce cycle times and work-in-progress (WIP), increase operator efficiency, digitize and automate paper-based administration processes, and enable automatic authentication of production lots at the equipment.

TECHNICAL ARCHITECTURE

The Infineon plant in Villach, Austria, is the headquarters of Infineon's Automotive and Industrial Business Group, which mainly develops integrated circuits (ICs) for use in cars, such as engine control ICs. Flexibility is important for this factory, which produces approximately 800 different products with a total volume of 10 billion chips per year [LT1]. Because of the high number of different products and associated production process variations, the factory uses a manual transportation process for wafer carriers. Over 1,000 wafer carriers have to be managed simultaneously. In storage areas, over 16 wafer carriers can be stored per square meter. The clean room contains numerous elements that can cause electromagnetic reflection, such as the walls, production equipment, and storage racks.

These factors all make this kind of factory a highly challenging environment for a tracking solution. In particular, finding a technical solution for indoor localization that combines an acceptable cost factor with sufficiently high resolution is still a challenge (see section on indoor localization systems in "Wireless Indoor Localization" on page 395). To address this problem, the LotTrack solution uses active and passive radio-frequency identification (RFID) in combination with ultrasound technology (Figure 4-8). The antennas on the ceiling contain ultrasound emitters that periodically send out a ping signal. These ping signals are received by the DisTags on the wafer carriers. The DisTags compute the outward travel time of the ultrasound waves and temporarily store the results locally, together with the signal strengths. Using RFID communication, the ping signal analysis data is communicated back to the RFID receivers in the antenna lines. From here, this data is sent back to the central server. In the backend, a complex algorithm derives the real-time position information from the UHF (Ultra-High Frequency) pings sent from the antennas to the DisTags [LT1].

The system in place at Infineon Austria now processes three billion UHF pings per day! From this, around 270 million positions are calculated, to an accuracy of approximately 30 centimeters. About 500,000 position updates are communicated to the client systems each day. The system operates in near real time, with the result that position changes by wafer carriers are recognized by the backend system within 30 seconds [LT1].

CONCLUSIONS AND OUTLOOK

These are the key lessons learned from Intellion:

- Wafer factories with a diverse product portfolio are particularly in need of solutions that are more flexible than fully automated conveyor belts. Intelligent lot handling can provide the required flexibility if delivered as a modular system.

- These types of environments have very strict requirements. Ensuring 100% availability calls for significant investment and a sound infrastructure design.

- High precision for indoor localization depends on a combination of technologies (in this case, ultrasound and RFID). This is especially feasible in wafer fabs due to fab setup (i.e., long floors with straight branches between them).

- The need for maximum efficiency in system management should not be underestimated.

- Customers require long-term support, which means that the solution design and roadmap must be capable of dealing with multiple system versions in the field. The challenge facing product management teams is to efficiently manage advances in new technology and product versions. Downward compatibility becomes a major concern.

We would like to thank Kai Millarg, Managing Partner at Intellion, for his support in writing this case study.

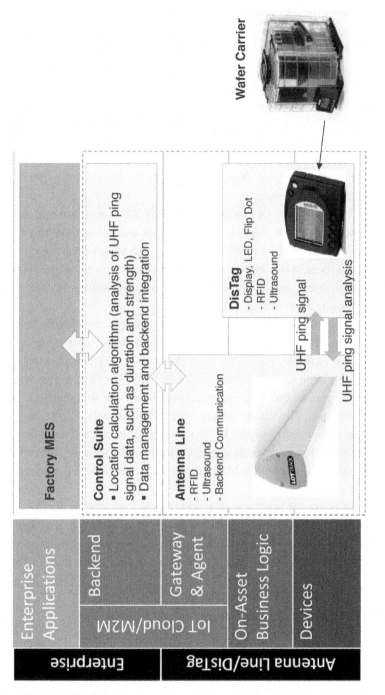

FIGURE 4-8. AIA for intelligent lot tracking

Case Study: Cleaning Service Industry and Technology

The global cleaning service industry is a huge and growing market. According to Frost and Sullivan, revenues in North America alone will reach USD 14 billion in 2015 [FS09]. The cleaning service industry is highly competitive. A small number of multinational companies account for a large share of the market, complemented by small—not only specialized—operators. Demand is mainly driven by building service contractors, commercial offices, hospitals, hotels, and industrial facilities. Among all facility maintenance services, janitorial services are the most commonly outsourced services. Main competitive factors include cost savings, strong customer relationships, geographic reach, service quality, experience, and reputation. In order to meet customers' cost expectations, large cleaning service providers constantly push for technological innovations.

This demand is addressed by companies such as Kärcher, the world market leader in cleaning technology with more than 11,000 employees and more than 12 million machines sold in 2014. The Kärcher product portfolio mainly includes high-pressure cleaners, vacuums, scrubber driers, sweepers, water dispensers, municipal equipment, vehicle cleaning systems, industrial cleaning systems, detergents, and several complimentary service contracts and services, such as software and consulting

Modern cleaning machines are powerful technologies, and facility management and cleaning service providers rely on large fleets of these types of tools to meet their efficiency and cost targets. For example, a banking customer with 3,000 branches recently awarded a cleaning contract to a large facility management company. The facility management company requires about 6,000 advanced cleaning machines to service this contract. The contract is renewed on a yearly basis. The facility management company will often try to pass some of its own risk on to the equipment provider by negotiating contract conditions that would require the equipment provider to take back its machines if the end customer contract is canceled. So it is in both companies' best interests to manage such a fleet of 6,000 machines as efficiently as possible.

These types of scenarios are the reason why Kärcher decided to develop a fleet management solution for cleaning machines that uses wireless connectivity to manage the equipment and provide fleet managers with a centralized, near real-time view of the fleet status, and provide additional functionalities like equipment utilization optimization and preventive maintenance.

KÄRCHER FLEET MANAGEMENT SOLUTION

Figure 4-9 uses the Ignite | IoT Solution Sketch template to illustrate the key elements of the Kärcher Fleet Management solution. The solution manages many different kinds of cleaning machines, from larger cleaning machines such as big scrubber driers to smaller vacuums, used in industries such as facility management, healthcare, retail, and others.

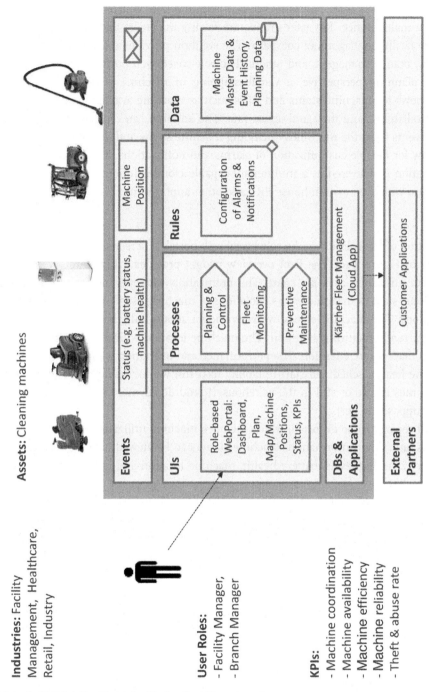

Industries: Facility Management, Healthcare, Retail, Industry

Assets: Cleaning machines

User Roles:
- Facility Manager,
- Branch Manager

KPIs:
- Machine coordination
- Machine availability
- Machine efficiency
- Machine reliability
- Theft & abuse rate

FIGURE 4-9. Ignite | IoT Solution Sketch for Kärcher Fleet Management

The solution supports processes such as planning and controlling, fleet monitoring, and preventive maintenance. Key user groups are facility managers and branch managers of the respective facility management company. The solution provides role-specific views for facility managers, branch managers, and others. The role-based web portal includes a dashboard, a machine planning perspective, a visual mapping of machine positions to locations, and detailed views for machine status and KPIs such as machine availability, machine efficiency, cleaning reliability, and theft and abuse rate. The solution can receive and process different types of events from the machines, including machine status and machine position. Business rules allow for flexible customization of alarms and notifications. The Kärcher Fleet Management solution is delivered as a multitenant-capable cloud solution. Customers can integrate the solution with their own in-house ERP and other applications.

PORTAL

A key feature of the solution is the role-based web portal. A screenshot of the main dashboard is shown in Figure 4-10. The fleet overview widget provides a high-level overview over the whole fleet utilization as a pie chart. The notification widget shows the most high-priority notifications, such as machine errors, violations of machine usage schedules, or use in invalid geo locations. The machine status overview widget shows only the status of those machines that are currently requiring attention. The machine location widget shows the location of the machines that require attention. The performance and utilization widget provides an overview of machine health, scheduled start reliability (last full week), machines assigned to facilities (are machines in use or still in the warehouse?), and deployment ratio (are machines where they are supposed to be?).

A full report can be exported, which includes machine utilization details, planned hours, deviations, and other information. Machine status can be viewed in full detail, including status, battery charging levels, battery health, machine location and last known address, as well as data timeliness.

One interesting lesson learned from the dashboard design was the machine status widget. The internal sales team naturally wanted to focus on "what is actually working." In the customer design workshops, it became clear that the customer assumes that most of the machines are working, and that he only wants to see the "machines requiring attention." This was important input for the design of this widget.

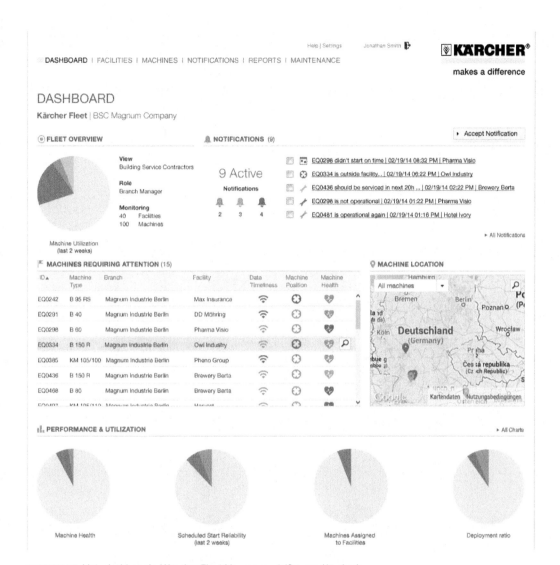

FIGURE 4-10. Main dashboard of Kärcher Fleet Management (Source: Kärcher)

ASSET INTEGRATION ARCHITECTURE

Figure 4-11 uses the Ignite Asset Integration Architecture (AIA) template to provide an overview of the main technical components of the fleet management solution.

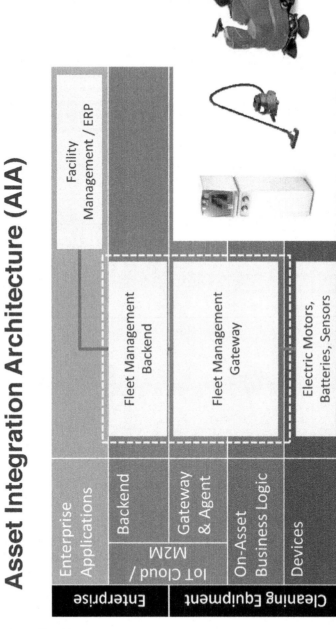

FIGURE 4-11. AIA for Kärcher Fleet Management

On the asset, a custom-made Fleet Management Gateway aggregates data from devices such as electric motors, batteries, and sensors, and makes this data available to the backend via a cellular network. In the backend, this data is received, processed, and stored in the central asset database, which also serves as the foundation for the portal. Customer-specific applications can be integrated through a set of specialized service interfaces.

LESSONS LEARNED

This section describes some key lessons learned and success factors from this project.

Project Organization

Management support

Having direct support from the Kärcher board of directors was vital for the success of this project, because of its transformative nature—after all, this project is a significant step from a pure product business toward a service model. See the discussion in Chapter 1 on servitization and "machine camp meets Internet camp"—this is exactly what is happening here.

Project management

A small, tightly knit project management team with direct communication channels and a clear focus on management of the interfaces to the various internal and external stakeholders.

Technology and partner selection

Selection "best of breed" components and suppliers based on a clear product vision and the results of the detailed stakeholder analysis.

Product Design

Customer stakeholder analysis

Detailed customer requirements analysis to ensure that this is not a technology-driven project.

Evolutionary product design

Small pilot that is developed and productized with lead customers, "design to time and budget" approach.

Focus on usability design

As we'll discuss in "User Interaction" on page 361, getting direct input from customers on key UIs such as the dashboard was important. For these key UI elements, custom UIs were implemented and externally designed by an UI company instead of using predefined widgets.

Data ownership

Another result of the stakeholder analysis was the reluctance of end customers to include certain sensitive data from their own ERP systems directly in the fleet management solution. Consequently, the solution now supports flexible segregation of data views.

Openness

A key decision that had to be made was if the hardware and software interfaces should also allow for integration of non-Kärcher equipment. The company eventually decided to do exactly this to provide customers with a comprehensive offering that fits their potentially heterogeneous environment.

TCO (total cost of ownership)

Cost for solution development and other costs must reflect the individual asset value, as well as the solution value add.

Technology

Adoption of new technologies

For a medium-sized business, openness for the adoption of new technologies cannot always be taken for granted. In this project, use of new technologies such as Amazon Cloud or Google Services was important.

Start of asset integration

The time and effort for integrating with the assets should not be underestimated. This is especially true if not all of the required hardware interfaces and sensors are already available and accessible. For example, the project found out that getting "battery health" data directly from the machines is not something that can be taken for granted. Devising and implementing a workaround for this took some time.

Localization

GPS positioning does not work well in closed buildings. Hence, the project team took to Google Services. At the end, this was more a cost than a technology question.

Telecom integration

Using a global carrier with a managed service helped ensure 96% availability for GPRS-based communication services.

Transfer from Project to Line Organization

Know-how

In-sourcing from external suppliers is important and takes time and resources.

Training and support

Creation and rollout of training concept, including train-the-trainer concept.

Sales enablement

Definition of pricing model, sales training, and marketing support are very important tasks and need to be planned for accordingly, including resource allocation on both sides of the organization.

Organizational change

Setup of a new competence center for these kinds of products in the organization is a key instrument to support successful change management.

We would like to thank Dr. Alexander Grohmann, Project Lead Fleet Management at Kärcher, for his support with this case study.

Case Study: Global Cold Chain Management

Perishable supply chain is the market for all commodities that require temperature cold chain management and a controlled environment to transport these products to market. Perishable products include frozen and fresh food, pharmaceuticals, chemicals, and many other specialty products such as flowers, root stock, and plants. The perishable supply chain consists of many forms of transportation such as trucks, trains, ocean vessels, and airplanes that are interconnected through distribution points such as ports and warehouse distribution centers (Figure 4-12).

FIGURE 4-12. Perishable supply chain

The market serves many constituents that work together in partnerships to move the commodities from the point of origin to the destination with performance determined by cost, time, integrity of the cold chain, freshness at destination, safety, and reliability. A perishable supply chain for blueberries from Chile to Europe, as an example, will start with the farmer or grower, who contracts with an ocean carrier to transport from Chile to Europe. The ocean carrier will arrange for a refrigerated cargo container (known by the trade name "reefer") to be loaded on a truck carriage at the port and driven to the farmer's location where the blueberries will be loaded into the reefer and the cold chain management will start. The condition of the blueberries after they are harvested (post-harvest food science) will influence the results of the trip, along with the type of packaging and other environmental effects along the route. The trucker then leaves the farm and transports the product to the port where it is checked in and put in inventory while it is staged for loading onto the vessel. During this inventory period and on the truck, the reefer must be powered so it can maintain temperature. The reefer is then unplugged and loaded on the vessel, with vessel turnaround times at port as short as possible to maximize the on-ocean utilization of the ship. The voyage to Rotterdam is about 30 days on ocean where the product is stored under temperature and atmosphere management. For fresh food, it is important, in addition to temperature management, to control the atmosphere in the container with a recipe that matches the commodity being transported. The controlled or modified atmosphere helps preserve the freshness of the product through reduction of the rate of respiration of the food, reduction or elimination of mold and other plant pathogens, and reduction or elimination of ethylene (a hormone that induces ripening). To stay fresh for this period of time, blueberries require a higher level of CO_2 along with other atmosphere modifications such as reduced oxygen levels or injection of ozone, scrubbing or oxidization of ethylene, and strict temperature control. Once the reefer arrives in Rotterdam, it is unloaded from the ship and placed back on a truck trailer for delivery to the importer. The the berries are unloaded, inspected, and then sorted and packaged for delivery to a retail outlet where the consumer can enjoy eating fresh blueberries in January six weeks after the berries were harvested. If there is a problem with the shipment, a process of claims will start where insurance and other parties determine what caused the issue and who is responsible for remuneration.

The market for perishable supply chain is a multibillion dollar global market. The number of refrigerated containers exceeds 1 million and is growing at 4%–5% per year. The demand for fresh and frozen food on a year-round basis is driving this market, as people around the world improve their lifestyles and demand a more nutritious, fresher diet. In addition, the market is shifting from designated reefer ships, which consisted of a few large refrigerated cargo holds, to ships that carry reefer containers. Post-harvest science and controlled atmosphere are also allowing a shift from the use of air cargo to ship fresh food to ocean reefer containers as a much more economical and environmentally friendly method of transportation.

FUNCTIONAL SOLUTION OVERVIEW

A high-performing perishable supply chain requires four elements:

Container resource planning (forecast, planning, tasks, and performance analytics)

Creates the ability to effectively utilize the fleet of refrigerated containers and provide the correct number of units at the right location at the right time for the commodities being shipped.

Equipment performance MRO (maintenance, repair, and operations)

Assures that the reefer container is operational and will perform for an entire trip to maintain the perishable supply chain. During the trip, the reefer and controller monitor and maintain the conditions required to assure that the highest quality commodity is delivered.

Cold chain management

The most critical factor in any perishable trip is consistent cold chain management, and the system must provide monitoring and control of temperature throughout the trip.

Fresh food atmosphere

A percentage of the perishable supply chain is the transportation of fresh food, which requires a controlled atmosphere managed to a recipe to assure the highest quality and freshest food is delivered.

This case study is based on the enterprise solution from Purfresh, which meets the requirements of perishable supply chain management through IntelliFleet™, an innovative SAAS enterprise application, and Intelli-Reefer™, a controller built on an Industrial Internet architecture. This solution provides all four elements for successful perishable supply chain control: fleet planning; forecasting and operations management; maintenance, repair, and operation (MRO); and intelligent cold chain management (ICCM). IntelliFleet provides the ocean and intermodal carriers an innovative technology for the transportation of perishable goods to market. The result is an economical and productive perishable supply chain solution that claims it will help solve the worldwide 50% food waste problem and allow ocean carriers increased productivity and margins.

One of the challenges for such a solution is that has to integrate with a complex logistics system which is already in operation and cannot be interrupted. Says Brian Westcott, PhD, CEO of Purfresh:

The way it works is a grower requests a trip with Purfresh through an ocean carrier. By forecasting demand and working with long-term contracts, Purfresh estimates demand and pre-positions controllers at the ports ready for installation. Once a booking is scheduled, a Purfresh agent installs the unit on a reefer (15-minute process) and presses a switch to start communication (through satellite or GPS) and synchronize with the IntelliFleet cloud software running in Amazon's Cloud infrastructure. The recipe is downloaded for the commodity set in the booking and real-time monitoring is initiated. During the trip, the reefer is monitored through the IntelliFleet software and alarms are triggered if setpoints or other events take place.

Figure 4-13 shows a screenshot of a trip.

FIGURE 4-13. Real-time trip monitoring

The system has complete functionality to perform all the functions needed for high-performing perishable trips using remote monitoring and control (Figure 4-14).

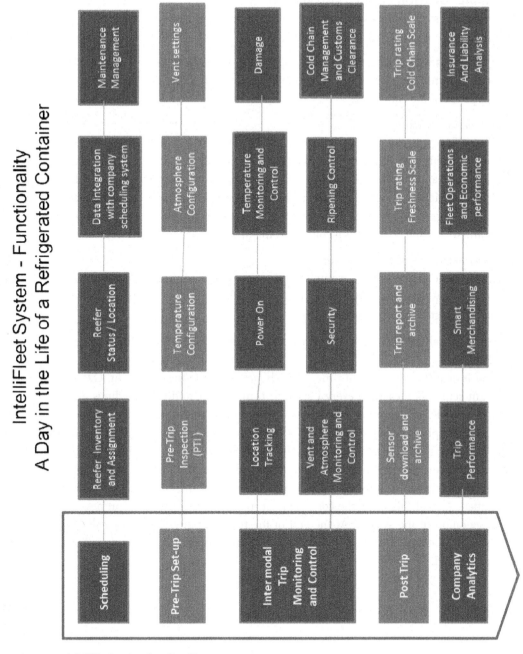

IntelliFleet System - Functionality
A Day in the Life of a Refrigerated Container

Scheduling	Pre-Trip Set-up	Inter modal Trip Monitoring and Control	Post Trip	Company Analytics
Reefer Inventory and Assignment	Pre-Trip Inspection (PTI)	Location Tracking / Vent and Atmosphere Monitoring and Control	Sensor download and archive	Trip Performance
Reefer Status / Location	Temperature Configuration	Power On / Security	Trip report and archive	Smart Merchandising
Data Integration with company scheduling system	Atmosphere Configuration	Temperature Monitoring and Control / Ripening Control	Trip rating Freshness Scale	Fleet Operations and Economic performance
Maintenance Management	Vent settings	Damage / Cold Chain Management and Customs Clearance	Trip rating Cold Chain Scale	Insurance And Liability Analysis

FIGURE 4-14. IntelliFleet system functionality

When implemented, the IntelliFleet solution turns a static reefer fleet into an automated remote control and monitored or intelligent reefer fleet.

TECHNICAL SOLUTION DETAILS AND AIA

The IntelliFleet system consists of three main components (shown in Figure 4-15):

Sensor network

    The sensors monitoring temperature, operating parameters, and atmosphere parameters are distributed throughout the container, embedded in the reefer ventilation system, and embedded in the controller.

Master reefer controller

    The reefer controller provides two-way communication to the IntelliFleet cloud application, and real-time control of the actuators for atmosphere control, including ozone generating units and venting valves. The controller also provides real-time data collection and storage, which it uploads through satellite every two hours. The controller also connects to the refrigeration controller and monitors, and can communicate and change operating parameters of the refrigeration controller, making it act as the master controller.

IntelliFleet Enterprise software application

    Provides the organization a complete monitoring and control application for individual reefers, as well as a complete fleet of reefers belonging to a company. IntelliFleet runs different instances for each company.

Figure 4-15 shows how these elements map to the Ignite | IoT Asset Integration Architecture (AIA).

Data is acquired in different time intervals based on the measurement. Ozone and door open light sensor is measured every 1 second. Temperature and CO_2 readings are measured every 10 seconds. Accelerometer and power off are measured on an interrupt basis and logged. The atmosphere data is filtered over a 10-minute period and then recorded as a filtered number for that interval. Data is stored in the controller. Communication with satellite is user selected but a normal interval that matches the dynamics of the reefer container is two hours. At two-hour intervals, a packet of information that reflects the current state of the system is transmitted. Also at this time, the controller can receive communication on new setpoints to adjust operation of the system. At the end of the trip or at any time during the trip when a GSM signal is acquired, the complete trip information to that point is downloaded to the cloud and stored.

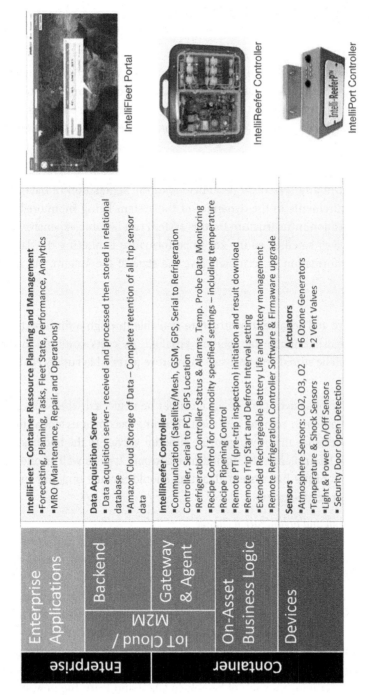

FIGURE 4-15. Asset Integration Architecture for Intellifleet

LESSONS LEARNED AND RECOMMENDATIONS

These are the key lessons learned by the Purfresh team in working with their customers:

Sensors and calibration

As in most control systems, the sensors are the most critical component, with significant cost and maintenance linked to these devices. Calibration and maintenance of the sensors occurs every few trips. There is constant review of more robust sensors as well as better, faster ways to self-calibrate the system for reduced operating costs and increased robustness.

Communication infrastructure

It is important in any system to be judicious in the acquisition of data, making sure to time the measurements to the dynamics of the system being monitored and controlled. The communication infrastructure for this system can become expensive if excessive data is transmitted over satellite, so the key to performance is filtering the data and transmitting enough information to accurately give the state of the system, but not transmitting excessive data.

Cloud computing

The inexpensive and reliable infrastructure available through a third-party cloud computing environment has made the solution possible. As costs continue to decrease, more information will be stored and analyzed to improve perishable supply chain performance.

Training

The human side of system performance cannot be neglected when converting to a more automated system with remote operation. Training becomes essential to the use of the system and confidence that it will provide superior service to the end customer. Layers of training should be implemented, including classroom type as well as one-on-one mentoring of operation of the live system. Training should include ongoing support through a strong customer service group.

Diffusion of innovation and organization change

The perishable supply chain is a complicated set of tasks requiring coordination of capital equipment. The system must be responsive to the variations caused by dealing with nature and biology. Schedules can easily become late due to weather or other natural events. The most difficult part of introducing any new innovation is changing the organization to work in a different way. At first, this will be uncomfortable and many people will find excuses on why the new system will not work correctly in this type of environment. Change is not easy, and most people resist change to some degree because they worry both that the customer will not receive the level of service that was previously delivered and that they as employees will not be able to adapt and learn the new skills necessary to operate a new system.

We would like to thank Brian J Westcott, CEO of Purfresh, for his contribution.

Case Study: LHCb Experiment at CERN

CERN, the European Organization for Nuclear Research, operates particle accelerators needed for high-energy physics research. Currently, CERN operates a network of six accelerators. Each accelerator increases the energy of particle beams before delivering them to the various experiments or to the next more powerful accelerator in the chain. The Large Hadron Collider (LHC) is the largest of these six accelerators. Located 100 meters underground, the LHC consists of a 27-km ring of superconducting magnets to control particle beams, as well as accelerating structures to boost the energy of the particles in the beams. Inside the LHC, two particle beams traveling in opposite directions at close to the speed of light are made to collide. This is comparable to firing two needles 10 kilometers apart with such precision that they collide in the middle. The machinery required to perform these kinds of experiments weighs tens of thousands of tons and must be capable of withstanding conditions similar to those that prevailed when life on the universe first began, such as high levels of radioactivity and extreme temperatures, for example.

There are currently four major experiments underway at the LHC. One of these—the LHCb experiment—is the main focus of this case study. It is installed in a huge underground cavern built around one of the collision points of the LHC beams. The purpose of the LHCb is to search for evidence of antimatter. This is done by searching for a particle called the "beauty quark" (hence the "b" in LHCb).

Like the other experiments, LHCb is designed to examine what happens when certain particles traveling at the speed of light collide. At the point of impact, many particles are generated. Some of these particles are very unstable and only exist for a fraction of a second before decaying into lighter particles. For more information on the physics theory behind all this, see [CERN09].

LHCB AND DATA MANAGEMENT

The LHC generates up to 600 million particle collisions per second (out of 40 million beam crossings = 40 MHz). A digitized summary of each collision is recorded as a "collision event." At the time of writing, CERN stores approximately 30 petabytes of data each year. This data needs to be analyzed by the physicists in order to determine if the collisions have yielded any evidence to prove their theories.

The LHCb experiment's more than 1,000,000 sensors generate colossal amounts of data. It will be some time yet before it is possible to store and analyze all of the analog data produced by these vast armies of sensors. According to Sverre Jarp, recently retired CTO of CERN openlab:

> Since it is impossible to manage and retain all of the massive amounts of analog data created by the LHC, we've had to devise a strategy for efficiently digitizing, compressing, filtering, and distributing this data for further analysis. Our solution to this problem is the Worldwide LHC Computing Grid (WLCG). The WLCG is a massive grid of low-cost computers used for pre-processing LHC data. We then use the World Wide Web—also invented at CERN—to give more than 8,000 physicists near real-time access to the data for post-processing.

As Andrzej Nowak, who worked closely with Sverre Jarp during his long-standing tenure at CERN openlabs, explains:

> Our challenge is to find one event in 10 trillion. Since we can't retain all of the analog data created by these 10 trillion events, we have to filter some of the data out. This upsets our physicists, because they are afraid we will throw away the one golden grain that will make it all worthwhile. So we need two things: Firstly, massive scale to ensure that we can keep as much data as possible. Secondly, intelligent filtering to ensure that we are really only throwing away the white noise, and keeping all the good data.

In order to address these challenges, the LHCb team has set up a multitiered approach to managing the data produced by these experiments (for an overview, see Figure 4-16):

- [A] Over 1,000,000 sensors are deployed inside the detector in the main LHCb cavern, right after the point of the primary particle collision (2). Once the collision has taken place, magnets are used to disperse the secondary particles, so that all sensors can capture parts of the now evenly distributed particles. Given the nature of the experiment, this area is highly radioactive when experiments are in progress. The sensors themselves are organized into different groups. For example, the main tracker contains sensors to help reconstruct the trajectories and measure the speed of charged particles. The electromagnetic and hadronic calorimeters measure the energy of electrons, photons, and hadrons.

These measurements are then used at trigger level to identify particles with so-called "large transverse momentum" (see [C]).

- **[B]** In order to protect the computer equipment from the high levels of radiation, the analog data from the sensors is transferred through a massive concrete wall via a glass-fiber network. The data transfer rate corresponds to 1 MHz. The first tier of this system for processing analog data comprises a grid of field-programmable gate arrays (FPGA) units tasked with running high-performance, real-time data compression algorithms on the incoming analog data.

- **[C]** The compressed sensor reading is then processed by a large grid of adjacent general-purpose servers (>1,500 servers) to create a preliminary "reconstruction" of the event. This processing tier uses detailed information about the sensors' 3D positions in order correlate the data from the different sensors. If this analysis yields a so-called "trigger," a snapshot is created. For each trigger event of this type, the event data (i.e., the snapshot of all sensor data at that point in time) is written to a file, which is then transferred via LAN to the external data center (i.e., above ground). On completion of this step, the data transfer rate drops from 1 MHz to 5 KHz.

- **[D]** The main CERN Data Center (shared with the other experiments) corresponds to Tier 0 of the system and consists of a grid of off-the-shelf computers for processing the data, as well as a farm of tape robots for permanent data storage. The input processing capacity of the data center for the LHCb is 300 MB per second. In addition to storage management, the main task of this data center is to ensure the "safe" offline reconstruction of events, which is something we will explain in more detail in the next section.

- **[E]** From Tier 0/CERN, the data is distributed to twelve Tier-1 sites in different countries. It is transferred via dedicated 10-GB network connections, which enable the creation of new copies of the experimental data.

- **[F]** About 200 Tier-2 sites receive selected data for further analysis and produce detector simulation data (to optimize and calibrate the detector and analysis.) Most of these sites are universities or other scientific institutions.

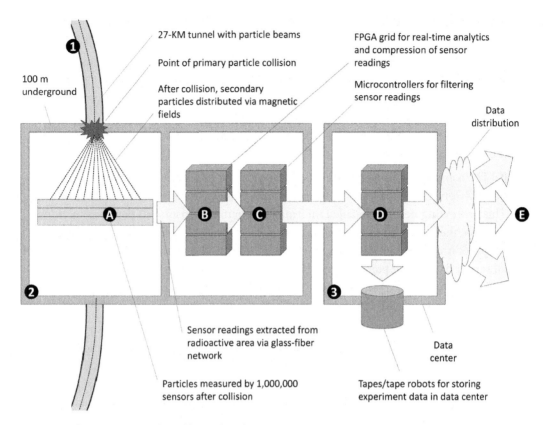

27-KM tunnel with particle beams

Point of primary particle collision

After collision, secondary
particles distributed via magnetic
fields

FPGA grid for real-time analytics
and compression of sensor
readings

Microcontrollers for filtering
sensor readings

Data
distribution

100 m
underground

Sensor readings extracted from
radioactive area via glass-fiber
network

Particles measured by 1,000,000
sensors after collision

Data
center

Tapes/tape robots for storing
experiment data in data center

FIGURE 4-16. Data management for LHCb experiment

The multitiered approach chosen by CERN for the management of its data has proven very efficient. CERN only has to provide 15% of the overall capacity required to process the data from the different experiments, with no need for a super computer. According to Massimo Lamanna, Section Leader of the Data Storage Services (DSS) group:

> *The data from each collision is relatively small—on the order of 1 to 10 MB. The challenge is the enormous numbers of collisions that require the collection of tens of petabytes every year. Because each collision is completely independent, we are able to distribute the reconstruction process across multiple nodes of the CERN computer center and WLCG grid. Surprisingly enough, the calculations we perform can be done very effectively using large farms of standard PC (x86) servers with two sockets, SATA drives, standard Ethernet network, and Linux operating systems. This approach has proved to be by far the most cost-effective solution to our problem.*

In order to increase processing capacity and ensure business continuity, CERN has recently opened a second data center in Budapest, Hungary. This data center acts as an extension of the main computer center at the Geneva site, and uses the same hardware and software architecture as the original data center. Budapest provides an additional 45 petabytes of disk storage, bringing the total number of processing cores to 100,000.

LHCB AND PHYSICAL DATA ANALYSIS

Without going into the physics theory underlying the LHCb experiment in too much detail, we will take a brief look at data analysis from a logical perspective. As we will see later, there is a lot we can learn here, even as nonphysicists.

Figure 4-17 illustrates the approach.

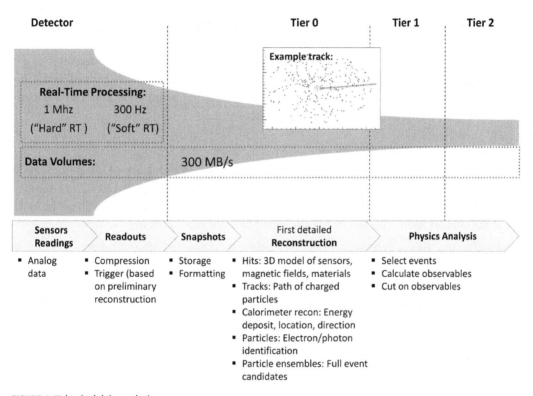

FIGURE 4-17. Logical data analysis

The collisions create numerous secondary particles that need to be detected. These secondary particles move through a 3D space based on a given trajectory, speed, and other factors. The raw analog data is delivered by sensors: a collection of points through which the particles pass. Because the amount of raw analog data is much too large to be processed by standard IT systems, a combination of FPGAs and microcontrollers work together to create "triggers," which initiate the generation of readouts (i.e., a collection of all sensor data existing at a given point in time).

These readouts are transferred to the data center, where they are stored and undergo basic formatting operations in order to create snapshots of the status of the detector.

One of the main processor-intensive tasks performed at the Tier-0 data center is the reconstruction process. Individual hits (detected by an individual sensor in a 3D space) are correlated and grouped to form trajectories (i.e., the path of a charged particle through the detector). Energy deposits from charged and neutral particles are detected via calorimeter reconstruction, which helps to determine exact energy deposit levels, location, and direction. Combined reconstruction looks at multiple particle trajectories, in order to identify related electrons and photons, for example. The final result is a complete reconstruction of particle ensembles.

These particle ensembles are then made available to physicists at Tier-1 and Tier-2 centers. The general goal of the physics analysis performed at the Tier-1 and Tier-2 level is to identify new particles or phenomena, and to perform consistency checks on underlying theories. Scientists working at this level often start with a simulation of the phenomenon they are examining. The output of the Tier-0 reconstruction phase is then further refined and compared with predictions from the simulation. When combined, simulation and Tier-0 experiment data often comprises tens of petabytes of data.

LHCb's Asset Integration Architecture

Figure 4-18 provides an overview of the Asset Integration Architecture (AIA) of the LHCb experiment.

For the purposes of our case study, the primary asset is the detector; we will not be looking at the collider itself. The detector is supported by three main systems:

Data Acquisition System (DAQ)
> The DAQ is a central part of the detector and responsible for crunching the massive amounts of analog data into manageable levels from a digital perspective. The devices are mainly radiation-hard sensors and chips. The Local Asset Control for the DAQ consists of a farm of FPGAs and microcontrollers that compress and filter the sensor readings, discussed previously.

Detector Control System (DCS)
> The DCS manages the LHCb experiment. It is mainly based on standard industry components—for example, a standard SCADA system is used for the DCS.

Detector Safety System and Infrastructure (DSS)
> The DSS runs critical components for cooling water, gas supplies, and so on. The DSS uses standard PLCs for managing these mainly industrial components.

With the exception of the DAQ, the LHCb is constructed like a normal industrial machine (admittedly a very big and complex one). Both the DCS and DSS use standard industry components. However, the device layer can only use radiation-hard components, while the DAQ makes the LHCb one of the best existing examples of "Big Data" at work.

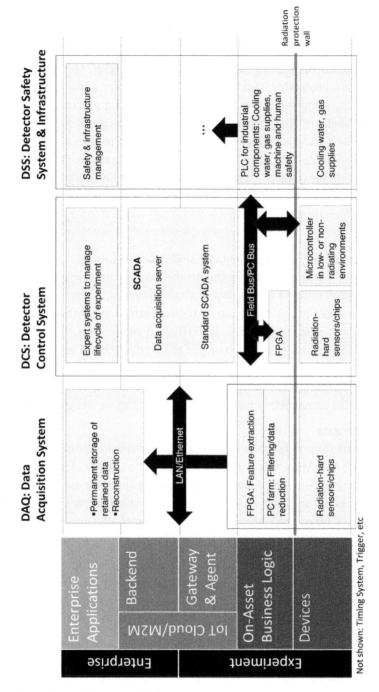

FIGURE 4-18. Asset Integration Architecture for LHCb

Lessons Learned and Outlook

This case study provides quite a few lessons that we believe can be applied to many IoT and Big Data projects in other domains.

Use of multitiered architectures for Big Data capturing and processing

The entire data processing cycle is based on multiple, highly specialized tiers that together act like a big funnel, with each tier performing specialized data filtering and enrichment functions. Tier 0 performs the basic data reconstruction and distribution tasks, while Tier 1 and Tier 2 focus on different types of physics analysis. CERN has succeeded in outsourcing 85% of its data processing resources to Tiers 1 and 2. And even between the detector itself and the Tier-0 data center, the data passes through multiple layers involving multiple steps, from high-performance compression, to initial filtering, through to reformatting and reconstruction. Each tier and layer performs an optimized function.

Use of specialized hardware for high-performance analog data processing

The LHCb uses a grid of high-performance field-programmable gate arrays (FPGAs) for the real-time processing of analog data and conversion into compressed digital data. The benefit of this FPGA grid is that it can be reprogrammed at a software level based on specialized hardware description language (HDL). In many cases, FPGAs are used as the "first frontier" in the real-time processing of analog data, before being passed on to a "second frontier" of even more flexible but less real-time microcontrollers. The "hard" real-time processing that occurs at this level is also a prerequisite for the use of time as a dimension in the correlation of data, which is something we will cover in the next point.

Correlation of sensor data

Correlating data from different sensors is a key prerequisite for making sense of the "big picture." At CERN LHCb, this is done using the 3D positions of all sensors in combination with timing information. Conceptually, tracking the movements of particles through a 3D detector is not so different from tracking the movements of customers through a shopping center, for example (except for scale and speed, of course).

Leverage grid computing

Because data structures and analytics patterns allow the division of processing tasks into different chunks, it is possible to use grids of inexpensive, standard hardware instead of more expensive, high-performance or even super computers.

And finally, another important lesson relates to the need to bring advanced filter logic as close to the data source as possible. As Niko Neufeld, LHCb Data Acquisition Specialist, explains:

The goal should be to enable the trigger system to perform a full data reconstruction close to the sensors. This should help us to dramatically improve the way we decide which data is to be kept as close as possible to the data source, thus minimizing the chances of critical data slipping through the net as a result of the initial data filtering step in the DAQ.

The authors would like to thank Sverre Jarp, Andrzej Nowak, Massimo Lamanna, and Niko Neufeld for their input in this case study. The work carried out at CERN has been associated with numerous Nobel Prizes, not least by helping to validate the work of Higgs-Engelman, recipient of the Nobel Prize for Physics in 2013, and provides a solid basis for the establishment of best practice in the area of IoT and Big Data.

CHAPTER 5

Connected Vehicle

According to many leading automotive industry experts, the future of mobility will be increasingly automated, electrified, and connected (see, for example, Keynote at Bosch ConnectedWorld 2014 (*http://bit.ly/connectedworld_2014_keynote*) by Dr. Denner, Chairman Bosch Group). These three trends are not independent of one another; as we will see throughout this chapter, connectivity is a key requirement and is at the very core of both automated driving and electric driving.

A good insight into the future of mobility was provided by major car manufacturers at the 2015 Consumer Electronics Show (CES) in Las Vegas. Instead of talking about the latest innovations in consumer gadgets or Internet TV as showcased at CES, most of the buzz centered on the connected, automated, and electrified vehicle. Automobile integration is being touted as the next great frontier in consumer electronics. In today's young urban circles especially, there is considerably more interest in connected services than there is in raw horsepower.

However, the market is still considered to be in its infancy. In this chapter, we will provide an overview of the most important use cases for the connected vehicle and the ways in which they relate to the IoT.

The connected dashboard and car infotainment are becoming increasingly important, not just in their own right but also as a data source for other advanced vehicle functions. Connectivity will pave the way for new services such as eCall and bCall, fleet management services for leasing and rental companies, and field data analysis for OEMs and suppliers. Another major IoT use case will be electric mobility, which encompasses connected charging services, roaming, and cross-energy management. Intermodal services will be central to the "smart city" of the future, and car sharing is already a reality today. Other services such as usage-based insurance (UBI) will create new business models for insurance companies.

The Holy Grail for those who follow developments in the connected vehicle space is, of course, automated driving. However, there is still some way to go before fully automated driving will be widely available. Until then, other topics such as automated parking and connected driving assistance will play an important role (Figure 5-1).

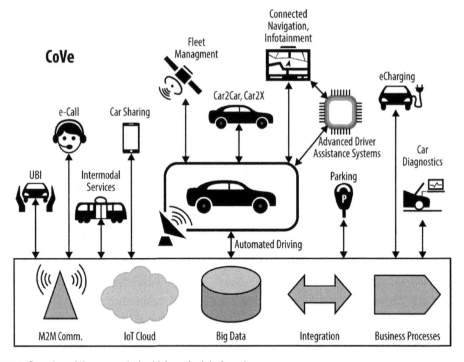

FIGURE 5-1. Overview of the connected vehicle and related services

One obstacle to these new business models is the level of heterogeneity found in car technology today. A modern mid-range car comes with approximately 60–70 embedded electronic control units (ECUs) that control the different subsystems of the car. Because there is no widely established method of sharing Internet connectivity with these different subsystems, many of today's connected services still rely on their own telematics control unit (TCU) for remote communication. The expectation in the future is that Internet connectivity will be an integral part of every vehicle's electronic architecture, and that greater standardization will be achieved in terms of the technical protocols required for data transmission and remote vehicle identification, authentication, and management. Obvious challenges along the way will include the issue of data security (i.e., who exactly will be permitted to access and use each type of data?).

Take the usage-based insurance example discussed earlier. Instead of the cumbersome process of having to install an additional piece of hardware, people expect to able to download the approved ACME insurance app onto a secure application sandbox in their car, and then follow a series of prompts in which they are asked if they want to allow ACME insurance to access their personal driving behavior profile. The initial recommendation to download the ACME insurance app will come from the cloud-based backend which, leveraging Big Data analytics, will have decided that it might be an interesting car app for the user based on their previous driving behavior.

But let's not get ahead of ourselves. Let's start at the beginning and address this fascinating application domain for the IoT step by step.

Car Dashboard and Infotainment

The car dashboard (Figure 5-2) is perhaps the most visible element of the emerging race to develop the ultimate connected vehicle—from a consumer perspective at least. Already accustomed to the ease of use and rich functionality of their smartphones, many consumers are now demanding the same from their car user interface. While Apple and Samsung deliver a new generation of smartphones almost every year, the automotive industry's release cycles for their infotainment solutions are typically much longer. Price is also an important factor.

FIGURE 5-2. TBD: Tesla Model S with 17-inch touchscreen

Naturally, it is not in the interest of the automotive vendor to hand over this critical piece of the car's user interface to the smartphone vendors. Ultimately, however, this is not just about direct revenue from the sale of infotainment systems—it is a much wider battlefield. After all, the dashboard offers a direct interface to the customer. It is not unlike the battle over which browser or search engine gets preinstalled on an operating system or smartphone. Establishing control over the applications and information that will be made available to the consumer via their car dashboard could be decisive in the achievement of billions in revenue in future years. For decades, the car industry has been struggling to build closer relationships with their customers, and the connected car represents a huge opportunity to close this gap. But equally, co-opetition with smartphone giants could pose a sizeable threat in this high-stakes space.

On the smartphone side, key initiatives include CarPlay by Apple and Android Auto by Google. The idea behind CarPlay is to connect your iPhone to a compatible touchscreen-enabled head unit. The iPhone then takes control and displays a set of approved apps on the car's touchscreen interface. This approach is sometimes referred to as "mirroring," because it converts the car's head unit into a display and charging service. Based on the Android ecosystem, Android Auto takes a similar approach, and has planned for functions such as GPS mapping/navigation, music playback, SMS, telephony, and web search.

For automotive OEMs, this is clearly a difficult proposition. "In terms of dashboard supremacy, OEMs face having to choose between lower costs and greater control. They can't have both," explains Volker Scholz, responsible for automotive strategy at mmi Consulting.

So it would seem that OEMs have just two options: either continue the costly development of their proprietary solutions (which are very unlikely to ever compete with the functional richness of the smartphone) or hand over control to the smartphone vendors. An interesting compromise between these two extremes could be what mmi terms an "app link"—a piece of middleware like the Bosch mySPIN app launcher that creates an improved link between the OEM's dashboard system and a smartphone via an OEM-defined API (Figure 5-3). Users can run selected apps on the smartphone and display an automotive-grade UI on the dashboard. They can then control the app using in-car controls. For example, Land Rover has taken this approach with its InControl solution, which is based on mySPIN.

A key advantage of the app link approach is that it enables new applications and can also leverage a number of the native car functions that are required for car-specific applications. To return to our usage-based insurance example, the UBI app needs to be able to access the driving profile so it can obtain data about mileage, average speed, abrupt braking, and more. The only way this information can be accessed is through the car's internal interfaces, via the CAN bus, for example [CAN1]. It seems highly unlikely that OEMs will open up these highly critical, native car interfaces to apps that can be downloaded from an app store outside the direct control of the OEM. Handing over this kind of control to Apple or Google would not only mean less business control for the OEMs—there is also a question of functional safety. Reading this type of data is one thing, but allowing active control over the vehicle (acceleration, steering, braking) is quite another. However, as we will see in "Digital Horizon" on page 149, the ability to converge car dashboard information such as map and route data with automated driving functions is perhaps one of the greatest opportunities presented by the IoT. This is where approaches like the app link could have a valuable role to play in building bridges between these different worlds, while also limiting the associated risk.

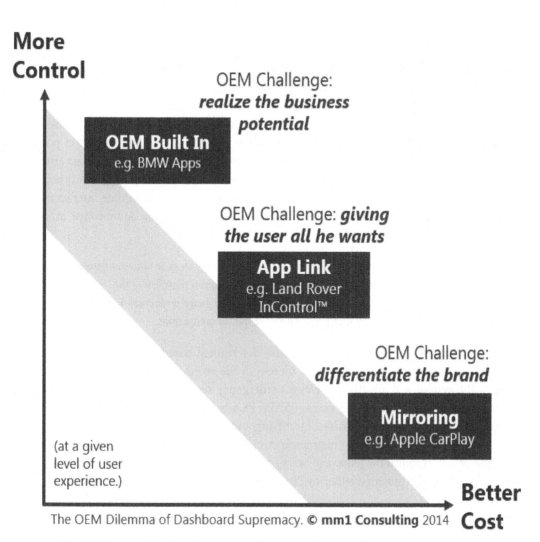

More Control

OEM Challenge: *realize the business potential*

OEM Built In
e.g. BMW Apps

OEM Challenge: *giving the user all he wants*

App Link
e.g. Land Rover InControl™

OEM Challenge: *differentiate the brand*

Mirroring
e.g. Apple CarPlay

(at a given level of user experience.)

Better Cost

The OEM Dilemma of Dashboard Supremacy. © **mm1 Consulting** 2014

FIGURE 5-3. The OEM dilemma of dashboard supremacy (Source: mm1 Consulting)

It is clear that this race for dashboard supremacy will remain an interesting space for the foreseeable future. According to Stella Löffler from mm1 Consulting, "There is no dominant solution yet. In the medium term, the right answer will vary from OEM to OEM. Probably from car segment to car segment."

Value-Added Services

Apart from the core vehicle functions already discussed, additional value-added services are also playing an important role in shaping the evolution of the connected vehicle. In the following section, we will discuss these services and also look at the various forms this generic platform is likely to take.

ECALL

eCall is an EU initiative aimed at leveraging vehicle connectivity in order to shorten the time required to direct emergency services to the scene of an accident. According to some estimates, eCall services could shorten emergency response times by 40% in urban areas and 50% in rural areas [EC1], potentially saving 2,500 lives a year [EC2].

Using various sensor inputs from embedded acceleration sensors, as well as devices such as airbags and belt tensioners (connected via the local CAN bus), eCall can detect potential crashes before they occur. It interacts with the backend using a combination of data and voice services. In the event of a crash, the GPS position and vehicle ID (VID) are transmitted to the backend via data service. The voice service is activated automatically to initiate interaction with the passengers. As Tim Kornherr, Head of Mobility Services for Automotive at Bosch, explains:

> For our customers, it is important that they can talk to an agent in their native language—particularly in a stressful situation like an accident. This has to happen regardless of the country they are traveling in. Our eCall solution has access to the driver's language preferences and can thus route incoming distress calls to a call center agent with the right language skills.

Following an assessment of the situation—determined based on feedback from the passengers via the voice service, or the lack thereof in the event that the passengers are unconscious—the system will inform the relevant emergency services. In the EU, this is managed through a public-safety answering point (PSAP). PSAPs are municipal call centers that handle local emergency calls and are capable of notifying and directing emergency services.

Figure 5-4 shows the Asset Integration Architecture for an eCall system. Note that the first line of communication (data and voice receivers) generally depends on telecom carrier interfaces and can be provided either by the OEM or by the eCall platform operator.

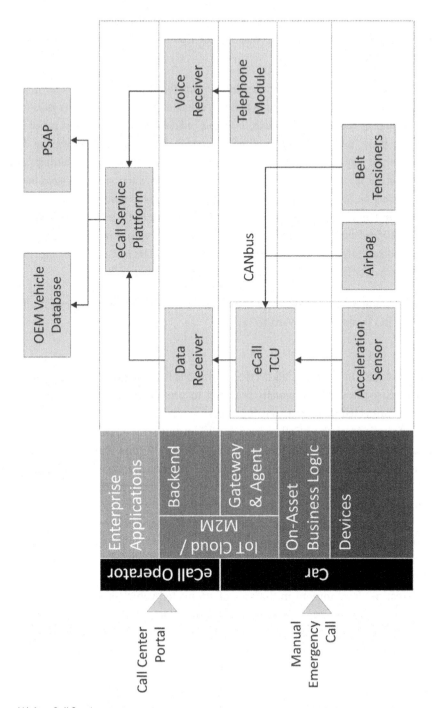

FIGURE 5-4. AIA for eCall Service

The introduction of eCall as a mandatory service within the EU has been postponed numerous times. Commenting on the reasons for this delay, Dr. Christoph Schillo, Peiker's Head of Product Strategy, explains:

"In our opinion, the main reason for this delay is that the complexity of the eCall service was underestimated. The eCall service requires technical standardization and legislative rules for a significant number of systems and interfaces, including onboard hardware, telecom carrier services, call center services, and PSAPs. And all of this applies across multiple countries in the EU. National interests play an important role, too. For example, France and the UK already had their own eCall systems. By the way, the French system is based on SMS text messages—good luck if you have an accident on New Year's Eve! Also, some carriers didn't see a business model in it for themselves. So what happened was that a number of OEMs, such as BMW and Mercedes, went ahead and simply defined their own systems. Mercedes started their rollout in 2012 with 9 countries, adding 10 more in 2013. This was only possible because these OEMs were able to manage the entire project themselves, or find the right partners for the required subsystems."

The EU has now finally agreed that the eCall system will be mandatory for all new vehicles sold in the EU from 2018 onward [EC2].

BCALL

An interesting variation of the eCall service is the bCall breakdown service. When a vehicle breakdown occurs, the driver is usually required to press a button to manually activate this service and be connected through to a call center.

Advanced versions of the bCall service don't just transmit basic data like vehicle ID and position, they also allow the call center agent to access real-time diagnostics data in the car. This is done using an onboard component of the bCall service that accesses the required data via an ODB II or similar interface [OB1]. Armed with this information, the call center's first-level support team can make a better initial assessment of the situation and decide on the next steps to be taken. For example, they may decide to send a service car with the right spare parts to the site of the breakdown.

STOLEN VEHICLE RECOVERY

Another interesting development in the area of connected vehicle services relates to recovery systems for stolen vehicles such as those provided by LoJack, Tracker, and OnStar.

These systems often use a small radio transceiver that is hidden within the car. The location of this transceiver is usually different for every car, in order to prevent it from being found easily by a potential hijacker. Once installed, the tracker ID and vehicle ID (VIN) are registered in a tracking system, together with additional information such as the vehicle make and model, license plate, and color. The car-tracking system can also integrate with the IT systems of law enforcement agencies, such as the National Crime Information Center (NCIC) system in the United States. In the event of theft, the vehicle owner reports the incident and the tracking system activates the tracking device, which will send out a signal to help locate the stolen vehicle.

USAGE-BASED INSURANCE

The last value-added service for connected vehicles that we will look at is usage-based insurance (UBI), also known as "pay-as-you-drive" or "pay-how-you-drive" schemes. The basic idea is that insurance companies get access to driving performance data, and in return offer customers insurance policies based on car usage (time), distance covered, areas visited, and driving behavior.

Conventional car insurance premiums are calculated using demographic metrics and are therefore not individualized. UBI is promising to change this. Current driving behavior is tracked using devices installed in the vehicle to capture behaviors, such as how far and how fast they drive, how often they brake hard or swerve, driving patterns like night driving/weekend driving, and more. Along with the conventional demographic metric, this data is then used to create a unique risk profile for each driver, which in turn forms the basis for calculating a customized premium for each insured driver. According to some studies, annual UBI premiums for "good drivers" can be up to 30% lower than with conventional policies [LN1].

For the highly competitive car insurance sector, UBI has the potential to become a market-changing differentiator for a number of different reasons:

- Lower premiums incentivize potential converts, particularly better drivers.
- Drivers are incentivized to drive safely in order to keep their premiums low.
- The degree of risk covered by the insurer is reduced.
- Claims should be lower, increasing profitability for the insurer.

Many insurance companies have started to add UBI offerings to their portfolio. In the United States, for example, Progressive, Allstate, State Farm, Travelers, Esurance, the Hartford, Safeco, and GMAC have all opted for this route [UBI1].

For several reasons—not least privacy and general availability issues—uptake on the consumer side was slow initially. However, this now seems to be changing. According to research firm Towers Watson, 8.5% of US drivers held a UBI policy as of July 2014, up from 4.5% in February 2013 [UBI2].

To support UBI on a large scale, specialized UBI management systems are required. One provider of such a solution is Tech Mahindra. The Tech Mahindra solution consists of three main components: the UBI vehicle tracking device, the connectivity and device manager, and the UBI insurance application. Figure 5-5 shows the Asset Integration Architecture (AIA) for the Tech Mahindra UBI solution.

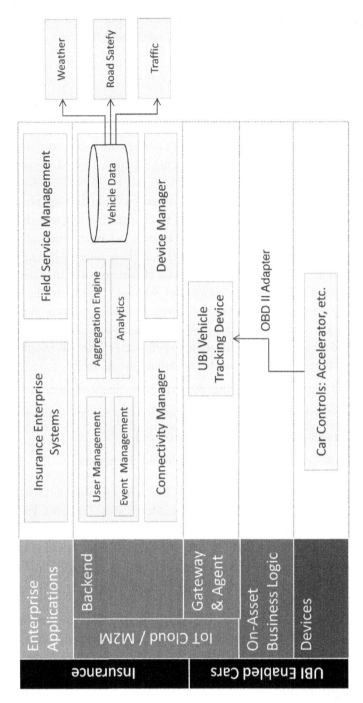

FIGURE 5-5. AIA for the UBI system

The UBI vehicle tracking device is installed in the customer's car. It connects to the car's controls via a standard OBD II adapter [OBD1]. Through this interface, the device can read data such as engine RPM, vehicle speed, positional information (latitude, longitude, and altitude), date, time, battery voltage, and engine parameters. It can also read data relating to driving events such as hard cornering, hard breaking, and aggressive acceleration which, from a UBI perspective, is particularly interesting. The GPRS/GSM modem within the device transfers the data to the backend. The OBD data is augmented with positional data acquired through the GPS receiver before being sent to the server.

The M2M application consists of two main components: the device management module and the UBI business application. The device management module manages device activation and connectivity. The devices themselves can be configured remotely through a web application or SMS interface.

The backend UBI application leverages this basic vehicle data and a Hadoop cluster is used to manage the large amounts of incoming vehicle data. The application provides business functionality such as user management, event management, advanced analytics, and driver scorecard features. The event-management module manages incoming notifications from the vehicle and can also initiate responses. Communication with users is handled through SMS and email-based notifications. Advanced analytics like moving averages for hard braking, cornering, acceleration, speeding, average speed by location, and driver scorecard trend analysis are useful for insurance companies. The application is also integrated with public data sources (to provide real-time contextual information) and backend systems, such as a GIS system and the insurance companies' existing record and claim management systems.

Data aggregation plays an important role in calculating UBI tariffs and managing contracts. Figure 5-6 provides an overview of the data aggregation model designed by Tech Mahindra. This model allows insurers to aggregate driver data in a structured way and use it to dynamically calculate a driver's insurance tariffs.

For many, the basic value proposition of UBI sounds interesting, at least at first glance. It's little wonder that UBI was picked out as an early poster child for M2M/IoT business cases. As with many innovations, uptake has been slower than anticipated. However, based on some of the research out there, it appears that UBI is finally gaining traction as a viable insurance model [LN1].

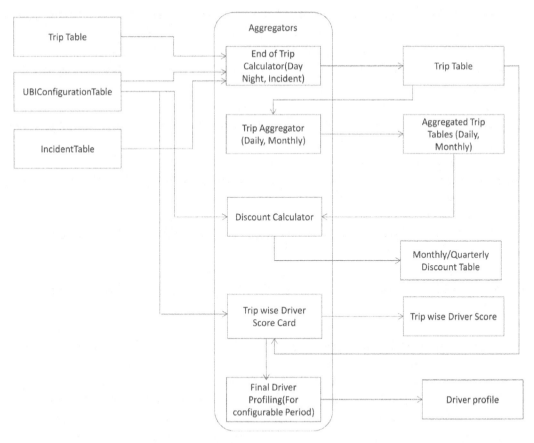

FIGURE 5-6. UBI data aggregation model (Source: Tech Mahindra)

SO, WHY NO OPEN CAR APP PLATFORM (YET)?

When you look at the examples of value-added car services previously discussed—from eCall to UBI—one question arises: Why is the development of value-added services so complex? It is complex because each solution provider has to install its own hardware in the car, establish its own telecommunications link to the backend, and implement its own data collection and event management systems in the backend before it can even begin to develop a single line of business logic!

The massive innovation potential of an open (or at least semi-open) app ecosystem has already been validated by smartphone players like Apple, Samsung, and Google. Most major app stores now feature tens of thousands of applications, many of which leverage sensors embedded in modern smartphones via controlled APIs offered by the smartphone OS.

Granted, if a smartphone app malfunctions or breaks the sandbox mechanisms used by the smartphone OS to secure the system, the worst that can happen is that the phone stops working or uses up more bandwidth than it's supposed to. A malfunctioning car app could actually endanger lives, which is a much bigger risk to take.

As we have already seen in our dashboard discussion, there are a number of ongoing initiatives aimed at combining smartphone apps with car infotainment systems. However, most of these initiatives focus on infotainment only, and do not look at achieving deeper levels of integration, as provided by the app link approach described earlier. Yet, apps such as UBI and eCall will require deeper integration with core car functionality, even if just at a read-only level. More advanced systems such as the Digital Horizon system, discussed in "Digital Horizon" on page 149, will require actual write access to the car's controls in order to function most efficiently. For OEMs, the act of handing over control to an external application understandably carries a huge risk, which is why most OEMs still require intensive and lengthy certification processes before allowing new applications into their car ecosystems.

Nevertheless, in order to generate the type of exponential growth seen in smartphone app ecosystems, OEMs will have to be much more open about how external applications can access core car functions.

Perhaps the first step in creating such an open car app ecosystem should focus less on what's inside the car, and more on what's outside the car (i.e., in the cloud).

Many car-related application services don't actually require an execution environment within the car itself. Take our eCall and UBI examples. Both could be easily built on a cloud-based application platform that provides access to the data they need. For these types of applications, there is little value-add to be gained from being directly embedded in the car, or from having to deal with backend car data management systems. A cloud-based, open car application platform with an efficient subscription mechanism for accessing car data would be fully sufficient here.

It will be interesting to see what this corner of the IoT will deliver in the coming decade. There are exciting times ahead!

Connected Enterprise Solutions

Leaving the end-consumer side of the connected car for a moment, we would like to turn now to the enterprise side of things. Many enterprises are also looking at ways to leverage the IoT and connected vehicles for enterprise solutions. Fleet management and telematics have been important topics for over 20 years now, and this whole area is getting increasingly sophisticated. Leveraging the new connectivity to learn about the performance of car components in the field is another interesting area, especially for car component manufacturers.

FLEET MANAGEMENT

Companies that operate fleets of cars, trucks, ships, railcars, and aircraft are often required to manage thousands of assets. For many fleet operators, the ability to have real-time data from these assets integrated into their fleet management systems is a very attractive proposition.

Airlines and logistics companies rely on this data to manage their transportation networks efficiently. Leasing companies can use real-time fleet data to optimize financial forecasting and planning.

In the early days of online fleet management, vehicle trackers and similar hardware devices were deployed within the vehicles as independent units—for example, GPS units for vehicle positioning. Communication between the vehicle and the backend can be terrestrial or satellite-based. Onboard bus systems like the CAN bus [CAN1] can be used by modern fleet management systems to access many different sources of data relating to the vehicle or asset (e.g., engine state, fuel level, driving behavior, etc.) This data can be used to provide functionally rich, connected fleet management solutions.

Figure 5-7 provides an overview of the main features of an advanced connected vehicle fleet management solution [BSI1]. Chapter 4 also looks at other forms of fleet management, such as container tracking (see "Case Study: Global Cold Chain Management" on page 99) and mobile work equipment (see "Case Study: Cleaning Service Industry and Technology" on page 92).

Basic fleet management functionality typically includes fleet master data management, as well as reporting and controlling features. Typically, a connected fleet management solution will need to integrate with other backend systems, such as an ERP or CRM system.

Vehicle state data can also be used for a variety of fleet management features. For example, mileage data can be used for proactive maintenance and to display the next service date to the driver. In this case, the system can also proactively guide the driver toward a suitable service station. Mileage reporting features can be used to compare projected final mileage against leasing contract data. Accident notification features notify the fleet manager when an accident is detected. Vehicle diagnostics features can store error codes from the vehicle and make them available in plain-text format. And finally, there are car theft warning features, which don't require an explanation.

The next set of fleet management features that we will look at relate to driving behavior. Fuel management features replace the requirement to manually record fueling operations and fuel levels. Driver behavior features allow the recording of data about the motorist's driving patterns such as speed, braking, and acceleration. Accident recorder features allow the storage of acceleration values, together with the status of relevant vehicle sensors both before and after an accident. When it comes to reconstructing an accident and determining the root cause, this information is invaluable. There are also features available for recording key data about routes traveled. This information is mainly used for tax purposes.

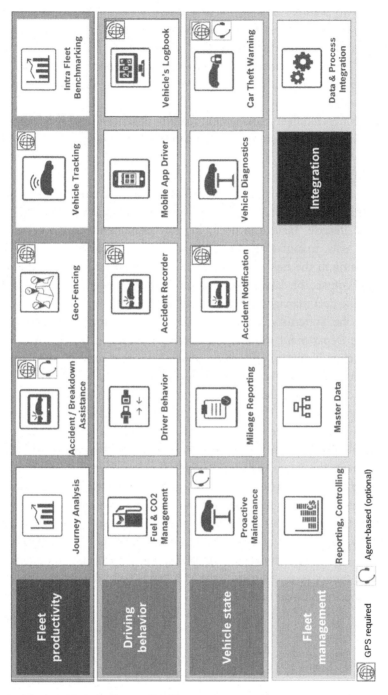

FIGURE 5-7. Fleet management features (Source: Bosch)

Fleet productivity features also rely on data analytics and related technologies. For example, journey analysis can help optimize transportation routes. Accident or breakdown assistance features provide support for drivers. Geofencing can be used to control vehicle usage and prevent theft. Intra-fleet benchmarking allows the optimization of fleet costs and availability by comparing parameters such as mileage, fuel consumption, driving behavior, and service intervals.

Some of the connected fleet management features described here also feed into other use cases such as the usage-based insurance model described previously.

SYSTEMATIC FIELD DATA

It's not just fleet operators who stand to benefit significantly from the ability to access real-time data from their vehicles. OEMs and car component manufacturers can benefit too, even mid-development lifecycle. Instead of designing car components on the basis of theoretical assumptions and tests, manufacturers can get access to detailed data on how their components are performing in the field. This provides an invaluable insight for product designers and engineers. Of course, the data required in this case is considerably more detailed than the data required for the fleet management solutions discussed before.

For example, the Systematic Field Data Collection and Analysis project (sFDA) led by Bosch's Corporate Department Automotive Systems Integration (C/AI) involves the deployment of data collection hardware units in millions of cars that connect up to various onboard car components such as car brakes or power steering units. The system can capture detailed usage patterns, including temperature, voltage curves, and more. Getting this data back from the individual vehicles and into the central system can be achieved in a number of ways. In some cases, cars are connected to the home WiFi, which is then used to transfer the field data back to the central sFDA system. However, the more common scenario is for the data to be downloaded whenever the car visits a participating car repair shop.

Data obtained in this way is invaluable for component developers. Two examples of the type of analytics results that can be obtained from field data are shown in Figure 5-8. The first example analyzes the usage patterns of individual pumps, the second shows driving behavior clusters. Naturally, data privacy plays an important role here too. In this particular case, the central system does not store the vehicle ID (VID), and instead uses an anonymized "hash value." This value cannot be traced back to the VID, but is helpful when it comes to linking all of the data for a specific car over time.

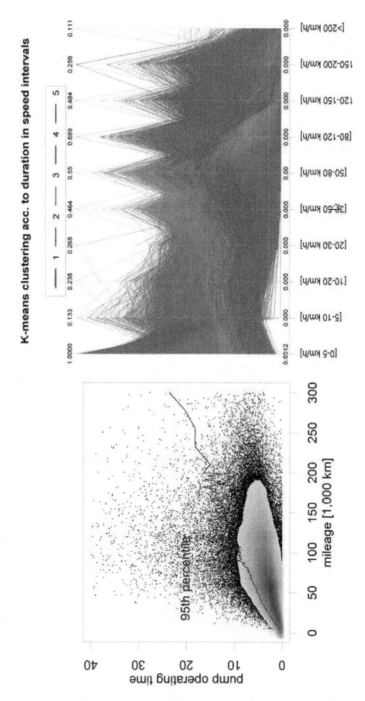

FIGURE 5-8. Two examples of field data analytics at work (Source: Bosch Software Innovations)

eMobility

More than 100 years ago, pioneers like Thomas Edison and Nikola Tesla laid the foundation for the electrified world we know today. Thanks to global electricity networks, electricity is now everywhere. Lights, household appliances, power tools, industrial equipment, computers, and trains—the world would grind to a halt if we didn't have electricity. The automotive industry is one of the few remaining industries that have thus far resisted electrification, relying for decades on fossil fuels instead.

And there is still uncertainty about whether the future of the automobile really is electric. There are some positive signs on the horizon: Toyota has successfully pioneered the hybrid car, and Tesla Motors is seen by many as the poster child for the eMobility movement. By early 2015, nearly every large OEM had unveiled an all-electric car, from the BMW i3, Chevrolet Spark EV, Fiat 500e, Ford Focus Electric, Mahindra Reva, Mercedes-Benz B-Class Electric Drive, Nissan Leaf, Renault Zoe, and Volkswagen e-Up! and e-Golf, to name just a few. With over 150,000 units sold by the end of 2014, the Nissan Leaf is leading the field by units sold. In total, approximately 350,000 all-electric cars and utility vans were sold by the end of 2014 [JC1]. However, when compared to the approximately 70,000,000 conventional cars sold worldwide in 2014 [ST4], this figure is still pretty insignificant.

Small (and even large) fortunes have also been lost in the race to develop next-generation energy sources and distribution systems for electric cars. Better Place spent approximately US $850 million of private capital on attempts to build up a network of battery recharging and swapping services for electric cars—without success. The stakes in this global game are high. OEMs that are too slow off the mark risk losing out on sizeable market share, while those who bet on the wrong technology run the risk of massive write-offs. For example, Tesla announced that it would invest US$5B in the construction of a vast battery plant with the goal of producing 500,000 car batteries annually by 2020 [AN2]—an investment viewed as very risky by some [WSJ1].

Despite these risks and the much-slower-than-predicted increase in the number of electric cars on the road, there is still a lot of movement and optimism in this space. The consensus from CES 2015 seems to be that the future is not just autonomous driving, it is electric driving.

Which brings us to our next discussion, in which we will look at some of the more important aspects of the electrification of automobile transport, such as charging, vehicle management, billing, and cross-energy management; all of which are primed to play a major role in the Internet of Things. For simplicity, we will also use the abbreviation EV for electric vehicle.

EV CHARGING SERVICES

The mileage that can be achieved by current car and battery technologies ranges between approximately 76 miles/122 kilometers (Ford Focus Electric) and 265 miles/426 kilometers (Tesla Model S 85 kWh) [WC1]. One of the main success factors for the widespread adoption of EVs will therefore be the development of widely available networks of EV battery recharging or swapping services. In some cases, vendors themselves have started building these recharging networks. For example, Tesla's supercharger network numbered almost 200 stations worldwide in 2014 [WI2]. Charging speed is an issue here too, because nobody wants to wait for hours before being able to continue their journey. One way to address this is to speed up the charging process (as Tesla has done); another is to look at physically swapping batteries. As we've seen, Better Place already failed to deliver this, and other companies like Tesla have made various U-turns in their plans to introduce battery-swapping stations.

From an IoT perspective, the integration of charging stations has multiple interesting angles. First of all, there is the question of integrating the charging station into the communication network. For example, the charging station must be able to identify the driver and their vehicle, and then validate the driver's credentials and account details via a backend system before the charging process can begin. In return, many different backend applications also require access to the charging stations, in order to access the station's status plus the battery load level of currently connected cars, for example. This means that the charging station acts as an intermediary between the car and the backend. One obvious use case that would require this kind of access is shown in Figure 5-9. This app can be used by EV drivers to easily locate charge spots across different charge point operators, directly start and stop the charging process—without the need for cumbersome RFID cards—and last but not least, process payment directly via PayPal.

According to Daniela Hartmann-Ege, Vice-President of Bosch Software Innovations:

Electric driving has huge potential to contribute to clean, hassle-free mobility, especially in urban areas. An interconnected public charging infrastructure based on the eRoaming initiative would be one way of overcoming range anxiety and increasing general acceptance of electromobility. This is a perfect example how IoT solutions can help enhance quality of life.

For more information about another, perhaps less obvious, use for this kind of information, see Chapter 3.

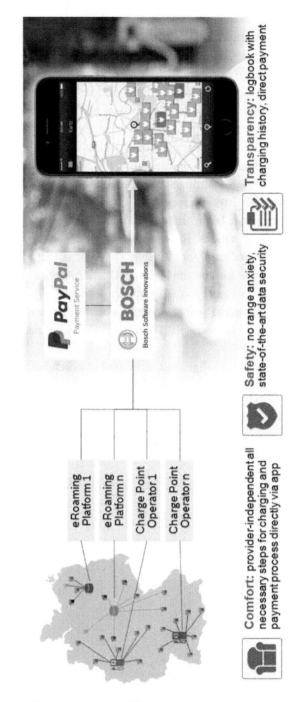

FIGURE 5-9. IoT solution "Public Charging Easy to Use" (Source: Bosch Software Innovations)

EROAMING

Another challenge in the area of EV charging is the fact that most EV networks are limited in geographic coverage. So it is very likely that EV drivers will have to use charging stations from different charge point operators, especially if traveling away from their hometowns. Similar to mobile phone networks, customers expect to be able to have one contract with one dedicated network operator, but the ability to use other networks if necessary—without having to register with multiple operators or deal with multiple invoices. In the telecommunications world, this is dealt with through roaming. In exactly the same way, establishing EV roaming for customers across multiple EV charging networks makes a lot of sense.

This is exactly what Hubject has set out to build—a roaming network called "intercharge everywhere" that supports roaming between charging station operators and eMobility service providers. The company is actually a joint venture between BMW, Bosch, Daimler, EnBW, RWE, and Siemens. Hubject's goal is to build an open platform that enables easy interconnection between the different stakeholders in these emerging mashup charging networks.

Figure 5-10 shows the main partners and stakeholders, and the interfaces between them. The eMobility provider makes a contract with the customer. The same provider also enters into a contract with Hubject, thereby simultaneously entering into a contract with all the various charging station operators. The Hubject platform then acts as a hub between the operator and the provider, ensuring smooth, secure integration between the various stakeholders.

From an Enterprise IoT point of view, this is an interesting scenario because it is an example of one of the advanced cases where the IoT solution integrates multiple different stakeholder organizations as well as the assets managed by these organizations (for more information, refer back to our discussion in Chapter 1 about M2M versus IoT versus Enterprise IoT).

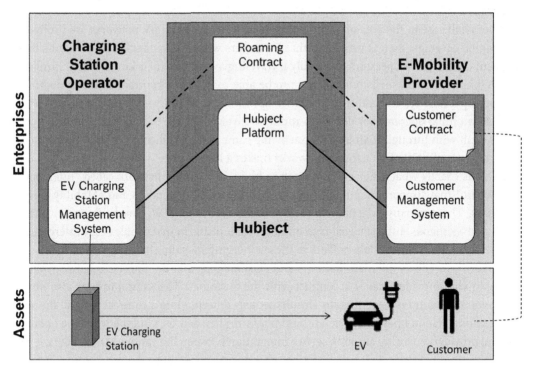

FIGURE 5-10. "Intercharge everywhere" partner network

EV REMOTE MANAGEMENT

The electrification of vehicles doesn't just have an impact on engine design and energy efficiency. Many see vehicle electrification as an opportunity to reinvent the architecture of the car as a whole. As a pioneer in this space, Tesla's cars have often been described as being more like a PC with added driving capabilities. One important point to note here is that connectivity in electric vehicles is simply assumed, and many features (e.g., the connected dashboard and remote management capabilities) are designed around this assumption.

Another interesting example in this space is the Mahindra Reva car. While Tesla addresses the high-end market for electric vehicles, the Mahindra Reva positions itself as an urban, electric micro-car. The Reva also comes with built-in connectivity, which provides customers, dealers, and operators with real-time insight into car status and performance. Figure 5-11 shows an example of Reva's web dashboard.

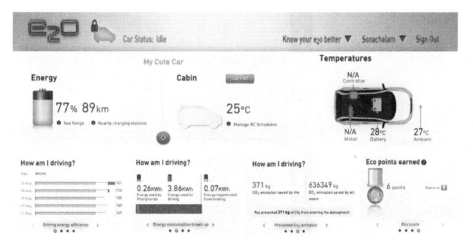

FIGURE 5-11. Reva customer portal (Source: Tech Mahindra)

This solution monitors the health of the electric vehicle and helps field support staff to identify the root cause of potential problems. It also enables customers to access information about the vehicle, as well as allowing remote access to certain parameters.

The solution is integrated with a number of different backend systems. An ERP system provides vehicle information such as the vehicle identification number (VIN) and battery information, for example. The dealer management system (DMS) provides customer information. A web application provides access to customer-specific information/operations in the vehicle such as its status, dealer locations, charging locations, remote charging, heating and ventilation, air conditioning, and climate system (HVAC).

It also provides status information about battery life, range, nearby charging stations, and remote vehicle operations like door locking and HVAC. It can also manage the vehicle's reserve charge. Key parameters for vehicle health are also provided (135 vehicle-level alerts handled) to support diagnostics and troubleshooting. Vehicle event replays provide complete transparency over the entire vehicle history. Figure 5-12 provides an overview of the system architecture.

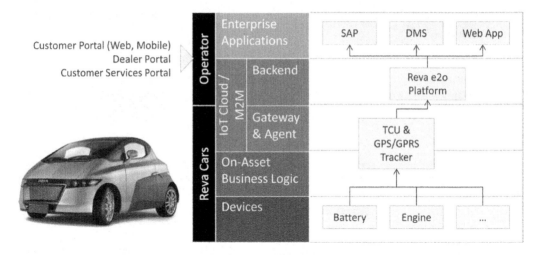

FIGURE 5-12. AIA for Reva Remote Management

EVS AND CROSS-ENERGY MANAGEMENT

One last point we'd like to mention in relation to EVs is their ability to provide energy storage capacity when not in use. Take Tesla's Gigafactory project, for example. Tesla is predicting annual battery production of approximately 50 GWh per year. This is a significant amount of energy storage capacity. Again, this is very interesting from a cross-energy management (CEM) perspective, which relies on energy storage mechanisms to help balance out supply and demand between energy consumers and different, mostly renewable energy sources. For a detailed discussion on CEM, see Chapter 3.

Car Sharing

Another excellent example of the opportunities presented by the connected vehicle concerns new car-sharing services such as Avis's ZipCar, Hertz on Demand, BMW's DriveNow, Daimler's Car2Go, and Volkswagen's Quicar.

Most of these services function in a similar way. They allow customers to use their smartphones to locate available cars and make a reservation. Once at the car, the customer can unlock it using an RFID chip, and then use an onboard computer (usually with touchscreen) to carry out further identification processes and other types of interactions. Once they have arrived at their destination (usually within a defined perimeter), the customer can simply lock and leave the car. The system will then automatically add the car back to the pool of available cars.

Let's take a look at the Asset Integration Architecture for such a system (shown in Figure 5-13). Within the car itself, an onboard computer (running Android or QNX, for example) provides local logic and generally assumes the role of gateway also. In many cases, an LED indicates the car's status to people outside. This is controlled by the onboard computer, which also integrates with an RFID reader to control access to the doors. Once inside, the driver usually has to enter a PIN number in order to complete the customer identification process. The computer can then use the car's CAN bus system to unlock the engine and send a message to the remote fleet management system to indicate that the rental process has started. The backend also provides a car-sharing application that manages customer accounts, billing, and so on.

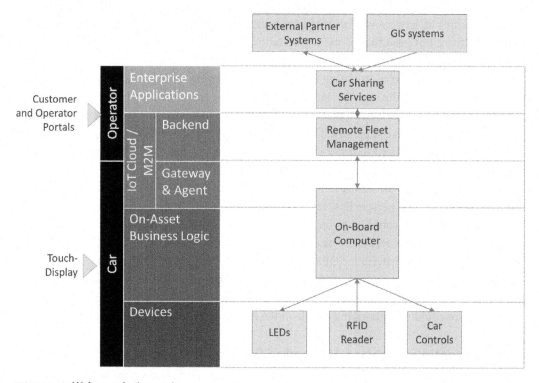

FIGURE 5-13. AIA for car-sharing service

This type of system combines many of the features of the other systems discussed. For example, much of the functionality of a traditional fleet management system, including advanced features such as geofencing, can also be found in a car-sharing system.

The car-sharing services described here have the potential to significantly disrupt the automotive industry in the coming decades. There are many interesting directions in which they can evolve. A logical next-step extension for the basic car-sharing concept would be the addition of usage-based insurance (UBI) as an extra feature for customers. Or take companies like RelayRides, which have introduced peer-to-peer car sharing: similar to Airbnb, but for cars. Overall, there is clearly significant potential for disruption in this space.

Intermodal Services

One last area of interest that we'd like to address is the area of intermodal services (i.e., services that combine several different means of transportation over the course of a single journey). One idea, for example, is to provide customers with a unified interface for their journey, even if this journey includes multiple different means of transport, such as using both a shared car and a train ride. This unified interface includes navigation and ticketing services. Extensions of the basic service include bonus systems aimed at integrating retail partners.

These kinds of services will become increasingly interesting, because they combine multiple perspectives, not least that of the connected vehicle and the smart city. What will also be interesting to observe is the way different stakeholders will position themselves in this space. For example, in addition to initiating the Car2Go car-sharing service, Daimler also launched an intermodal service through its Moovel platform that helps customers to optimize their route planning using different types of transport such as Car2Go car sharing, bike sharing, public transport, and taxi suppliers. The customer is given different smartphone apps and a web portal that allows them to quickly configure each step of their multistep journey, including reservation of Car2Go cars.

Naturally, the OEM's interest here is to get more customers to use their car-sharing service. From a smart city perspective, this might not always be the best approach. For a smart city, a better approach would be to optimize traffic flow, and avoid increasing inbound traffic during peak morning periods, for example. So, from a multimodal perspective, the expectations and optimization criteria for OEMs are completely different from those of the smart city. It will still be interesting to see how these kinds of multimodal services will evolve. The flexibility created by the emergence of the connected vehicle and new, connected car-sharing services especially, could well play a major role in the evolution of multimodal transportation.

Vehicle Functions (Toward Automated Driving)

This brings us directly to the discussion about the vehicle functionality of the future as enabled by the IoT. Naturally, the Holy Grail here is automated driving. Many publications also talk about the self-driving car or autonomous driving. We believe it involves much more than just vehicle autonomy—after all, the IoT will enable the connected car. In the following section, we use the term "automated driving" to refer to both autonomous driving and connected vehicles.

THE ROADMAP TOWARD AUTOMATED DRIVING

Although a lot has been written about the roadmap that will lead us to automated/autonomous driving, most people agree that "autonomous driving is not going to be a Big Bang, it's going to be a series of little steps" (Toscan Bennett, Volvo [LL1]).

Many different factors will have an impact on the evolution of automated driving; factors such as user acceptance, technology, legislation and, last but not least, insurance actuaries—the statisticians who calculate insurance risks and premiums.

Figure 5-14 shows a roadmap for automated driving, as developed by experts at Bosch. A key assumption in this roadmap is that the ability to efficiently combine data from different data sources in real time will be decisive. Single sensors are used for basic features such as adaptive cruise control applications like lane-keeping guidance. Sensor data fusion enables the merging of data from multiple sources to support advanced solutions like integrated cruise assist and highway assist. The addition of map data will support the highway pilot feature, which already provides highly automated driving functions. The biggest challenge for automated driving will be driving in densely populated urban areas, because of the many associated risks (e.g., crossing pedestrians, children at play).

Predicting future developments in this space is difficult. According to Wolf-Henning Scheider (member of the Bosch management board), Bosch has already received production orders to supply the radar, camera, control units, and other technology needed for semi-automated driving in 2017 and 2018. Based on this, he has laid out a four-stage roadmap [AN1]:

- In 2017, the first cars with integrated highway assist functionality will become available, with fully automated lane keeping for speeds of up to 75 mph.

- In 2018, the highway assist functionality will be extended to support higher speeds, as well as automatic lane changes based on driver approval. Drivers will still be required to keep their eyes on the road at all times.

- By 2020, the highway pilot functionality will support fully automated driving on highways. The driver will be notified if he is required to overtake a car, and if this doesn't happen quickly enough, the car will pull over and stop.

- By around 2025, Bosch believes that the auto pilot function will support fully automated door-to-door transportation without the need for any intervention on the part of the driver.

Given that in 2004, not one of the cars in the first DARPA self-driving contest made it past the first 7 of the planned 150 miles, these are clearly ambitious goals. Nevertheless, the market in general seems to agree, with many of the OEMs at CES 2015 confirming similar timelines [FC1].

Development steps – automated driving

Degree of automation

- Single sensor
- Sensor-data fusion
- Sensor-data fusion + map

ACC/lane keeping support
- Only longitudinal or lateral control

Integrated cruise assist
- Partially automated longitudinal and lateral guidance in driving lane
- Speed range 0-130 kph

Highway assist
- Partly automatic longitudinal and lateral guidance
- Lane change after driver confirmation
- Supervision of surrounding traffic (next lane, ahead, behind)

Highway pilot
- Highly automated longitudinal and lateral guidance with lane changing
- Reliable environment recognition, including in complex driving situations
- No permanent supervision by driver

Auto pilot
- Door-to-door commuting (e.g. to work) in urban traffic
- Strictest safety requirements
- No supervision by driver

FIGURE 5-14. Roadmap toward automated driving (Source: Bosch)

AUTOMATED DRIVING: TECHNOLOGIES

Naturally, sensors will play a key role in autonomous driving. Modern cars already use a number of different sensors, including tilt sensors (used by the light control system), high pressure sensors (used by the Electronic Stability Program [ESP]), torque sensors (steering system), steering wheel angle sensors (steering and ESP systems), acceleration sensors, seat occupation sensors (airbag control system), wheel rotation angle sensors (ESP system), and wheel angular velocity sensors (anti-locking braking system [ABS]) [LA11].

For automated driving, different sensors are generally combined to create a virtual image of the vehicle's surrounding environment. These include the following technologies (illustrated in Figure 5-15):

LIDAR

This technology uses laser to measure distances by analyzing reflected light. Used for adaptive cruise control (ACC), LIDAR devices are mounted on the front of the vehicle to monitor the distance between the vehicle and any car in front of it.

Radar

Millimeter-wave radars are commonly used. This involves various infrared and optical sensors being placed at the front, sides, and rear quarters of the vehicle.

Ultrasonic

Used for close obstacle detection, such as in automatic parking.

Cameras

Used to identify nearby hazards (pedestrians and cyclists), read road signs, and detect traffic lights.

Google is seen as one of the pioneers of autonomous driving. The central element of the Google car is a laser range finder (LIDAR) that is mounted onto the roof of the car [IE1]. The device generates a detailed 3D map of the environment. The system then combines these laser measurements with high-resolution maps of the surrounding area. Additional sensors include four radars to deal with fast-flowing traffic on freeways (mounted on the front and rear bumpers), as well as a camera close to the rearview mirror that detects traffic lights. For positioning, GPS is combined with an inertial measurement unit (IMU), which measures the actual movement of the car, thus complementing the GPS data.

Other concepts seen as important for automated driving are Car2Car and Car2Infrastructure, together also referred to as Car2X (or Vehicle2X). These technologies enable vehicles to communicate either with other vehicles (Car2Car), or with traffic infrastructure such as traffic lights (Car2Infrastructure). Car2Car technology should also enable predictive driving, because it allows cars to communicate with cars far ahead of them. Naturally, this would require all cars to support the same interfaces, which is a major obstacle in itself.

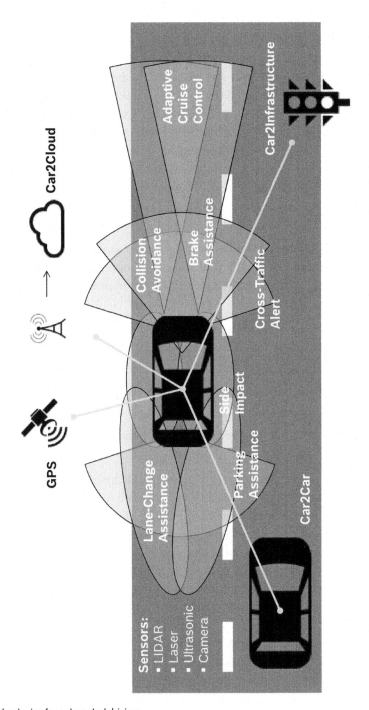

FIGURE 5-15. Technologies for automated driving

AUTOMATED DRIVING: SYSTEM ARCHITECTURE

The key challenge for any automated driving system is to manage and combine the significant amounts of data coming from the different sensors, and to create a consistent model from this data that can be used to make decisions about driving behavior.

A common solution to this problem is the creation of a hierarchical sensor fusion architecture [TI1], as shown in Figure 5-16 (again using our IoT AIA template).

Most sensors are equipped with a dedicated processing unit that creates a digital representation of the raw, often analog sensor data. For example, the output from a LIDAR sensor could be a 3D map of the vehicle's surroundings.

Sensor data fusion combines the outputs of multiple sensors. For example, the data from two cameras can be combined to extract depth information (also known as stereo vision). Similarly, data from different sensor types with overlapping fields of view can be merged to improve object detection and classification and to create a more precise model.

It is also possible to add data from external systems. For example, data from the car cloud will include detailed map data, traffic data, and weather data. The addition of data from a Car2X gateway is also possible.

The result is a detailed 3D map of the car's surrounding environment (Figure 5-17). This map is object-based and includes lane markers, other vehicles, pedestrians, cyclists, street signs, traffic lights, and so on. This detailed map is also positioned within a larger, less detailed map which is required for navigation. Both model perspectives are updated in real time, although at different intervals.

The entire process can also be described as a "reconstruction" of the real world in the virtual world based on sensor data. A similar approach can also be found in other case studies in this book; for example, the case study of CERN's Large Hadron Collider LHCb experiment. The term "reconstruction" is also used throughout Part II.

Leveraging the results of the reconstruction process, a central driving control engine can now use the model to make decisions about driving behavior, including speed, direction, emergency braking, and more. The engine interacts with the different car control elements such as the central VCU and different ECUs to achieve this.

Due to the highly heterogeneous environment found in most modern cars, as well as the complex nature of such a system, this type of highly centralized approach may prove risky in some cases. For example, it is very likely that, for security reasons, the autonomous emergency brake (AEB) feature will continue to be deployed as an autonomous system that is capable of overriding the central driving engine if need be.

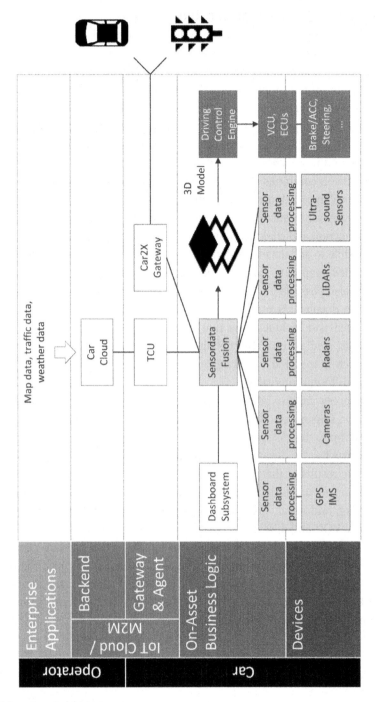

FIGURE 5-16. AIA for automated driving

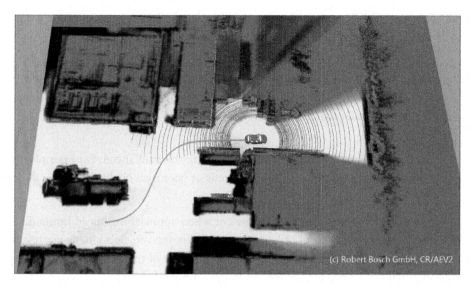

FIGURE 5-17. Google 3D data model (Source: [MI2])

DIGITAL HORIZON

Combining local sensor data with car cloud services will help optimize the driving experience even further while also supporting more economic driving. A good example of this is the Digital Horizon system developed by Bosch [ST2] (Figure 5-18).

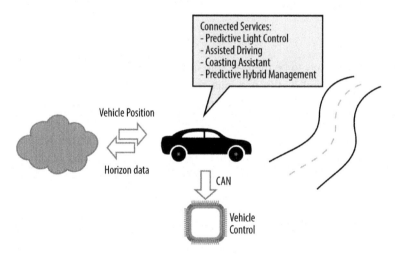

FIGURE 5-18. Digital Horizon

The Digital Horizon system combines a cloud-based backend with an onboard unit that also connects to the car's driving controls via the CAN bus [CAN1]. The cloud backend provides map data enriched with metadata relating to road conditions, speed limits, and other important information. The onboard unit takes this data and uses it to support a number of different services, including:

Predictive light control
By combining connected horizon data with sensor readings and camera image analysis, the system can adapt the lighting to the situation ahead. Features include headlamp beam height adjustment and predictive curve lighting.

Assisted driving
Speed can be regulated according to the condition of the road ahead. For example, the system can reduce the speed if there are tight bends or poor road quality ahead.

Coasting assistant (moving without propulsion)
Conventional braking on downhill stretches or when approaching speed limits dissipates the vehicle's energy in the form of heat. Coasting uses the vehicle's kinetic energy to overcome driving resistance. The system identifies stretches of road suitable for coasting and indicates when the driver should take her foot off the accelerator.

Predictive hybrid management
Hybrid electric vehicles can recuperate braking energy and store it in their batteries. In order to overcome limited battery capacity, the system uses topographical navigation data to determine the recuperation potential for the road section ahead. Based on this information, the system then discharges the battery sufficiently through increased use of the electric motor to ensure that the maximum amount of energy can be subsequently recuperated.

PARKING

Automated parking is likely to be the first step in the productization of fully automated vehicle controls (it is not included in the previous roadmap because technically it is not driving). Figure 5-19 shows a roadmap for automated parking technologies.

Initial production-ready parking support systems already provide parking steering control, where the car does the steering, and the driver controls the speed and the braking. This will be followed by parking maneuver control, where the braking step is also automated by the system. The next step will be remote parking assistance, which allows the driver to park his car from outside the vehicle. The final step is autopilot parking, which supports fully automated parking.

Because of the potential to easily convert multistory car parks into fully automated environments (at least in part), automated valet parking is another interesting area in which fully automated driving could be rolled out on a larger scale.

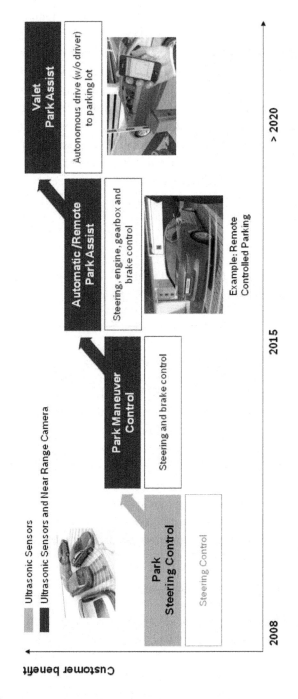

FIGURE 5-19. Roadmap for automated parking (Source: Bosch)

While some of these parking automation scenarios do not require connectivity between the car and external systems—and are thus perhaps not perfect examples of IoT solutions—they are still an important part of the overall picture. Moreover, there are other interesting scenarios in which IoT concepts can be deployed in combination with parking. The first example of this is automated valet parking (AVP), which connects the car with the parking deck, as well as the user with the AVP system (such as using smartphones for services like payment, booking times for drop-off and pick-up of a vehicle, etc.). Another good example would be community-based parking. In this case, sensors installed within the vehicle scan nearby streets for available parking spaces (even if the driver is not looking for one). This data is collated centrally and updated continuously. This means that any user of the system can get real-time information about available parking in the vicinity. This information can also be added to the map data in the driver's car navigation system.

Outlook

To wrap up our discussion on the connected vehicle, we have asked Dr. Rainer Kallenbach, CEO of Bosch Software Innovations, to share his views on what is happening in this space.

Dirk Slama: Rainer, how will you get to work in the year 2025?

Dr. Kallenbach: I'm quite positive that it will be by electric vehicle, and it will be highly automated. The first few meters, in my village, I will likely drive myself—but once on the freeway I will not need to intervene or monitor the way the car is driving. This means I'll be able to use the car's integrated screen to access my calendar and catch up on email—or Bosch social media posts—then I might send off some quick responses and make a few calls. As I also do a lot of commuting between various locations, the vehicle's navigation system will be already programmed with appointments from my calendar. While my car may have an electric range of 250 km, this won't be enough for all of my trips, so the system will also have reserved and scheduled recharging station stops and, if required, alternative public transportation.

Dirk Slama: What has to happen in order to make this work?

Dr. Kallenbach: For electric driving, the key challenges that need to be overcome are certainly related to electric energy storage and supply technology in terms of overall efficiency, energy density, and lifetime cost. A second important issue, which is probably still underestimated, is the availability of a reliable recharging infrastructure that is connected and managed via the Internet. For automated driving, we will need some further progress on vehicles' onboard sensors and algorithms, and more Internet-based information and the ability to stream near real-time map data directly to the car, which may call for some additional infrastructure. All in all, it will be a perfect IoT environment with seamless networking between cars, infrastructure, and environment. The technologies we need to achieve this are already becoming available right now.

Dirk Slama: What impact will this have on today's large OEMs and suppliers?

Dr. Kallenbach: This is hard to predict. Such profound changes in technology will create opportunities and risks. The opportunities can be seized by conventional large companies if—in addition to the highly specialized skills needed to manufacture cars and car components—they succeed in acquiring new competencies in new technologies (such as power electronics, IT and, in particular, the IoT) in time to secure a substantial piece of the newly developing value creation network. In any case, this implies huge and risky investments. The company's alternative (i.e., not to prepare for and embrace change) will almost certainly lead to obsolescence. This is the Bosch has been investing heavily, for a number of years now, in the electrification and automation of vehicles, as well as in IoT technology and its various applications.

Dirk Slama: What about Tesla and Google?

Dr. Kallenbach: Today they play an important role as forerunners in a new world of mobility, concretely demonstrating what is already possible. They have opened the eyes of many skeptics and conservatives. I see them mainly as our customers.

Dirk Slama: So all of this means exciting times ahead for end users?

Dr. Kallenbach: Yes...Well, maybe. I'm certainly looking forward to the commuting scenario discussed earlier. However, as an old-school member of Generation X, I think I'd miss the fun of driving. I'd like to be able to decide whether I drive myself or am driven. Personally, this is the reason why I'll be keeping a little sports car, complete with combustion engine and moving mechanical parts. No doubt it will have achieved vintage status by then...

CHAPTER 6

Smart City

THE SMART CITY IS A VERY INTERESTING POSSIBLE APPLICATION OF THE IoT. IN THIS CHAPTER, we will examine some of the key drivers of the smart city, as well as the corresponding relevance of the IoT. We will then take a look at a case study of the smart city in action.

Key Drivers

Global megatrends such as population growth, urbanization, climate change, and resource limitations are placing considerable pressure on cities around the world. Population growth and urbanization, in particular, threaten to aggravate existing problems like congestion, crime, smog, and aging public infrastructure.

Cities are becoming increasingly important in a global context. This is due to a trend toward urbanization, which means that, in the future, more and more people will live in urban areas. As a result, the majority of resources will be consumed in urban areas, giving cities the greatest potential to implement measures for the conservation of these resources.

Life in cities is becoming increasingly complex. This is because sectors such as mobility and energy are merging and becoming interconnected, a development that is partly driven by new communication technologies. Complex challenges faced by cities, such as reducing CO_2 emissions and securing energy supply, require integrated solutions that are aligned with the interdependencies that exist between individual sectors and silos.

Human behavior is also changing. This can be seen most clearly in areas such as mobility. The focus has shifted outward from owning a car to wider mobility opportunities. Innovative solutions like car-sharing services are seeing more widespread use, and intermodal transportation is becoming increasingly important.

Smart cities could be the answer to these transitions and challenges. Complete, integrated solutions are an essential part of managing this new urban model.

Every city has its own definition or ideas about what makes a smart city. What all of these different perspectives have in common is the intelligent use of integrated solutions. Speaking about the Smart City Wien framework strategy, Mayor of Vienna Michael Häupl describes it as "an umbrella strategy that aspires to create smart solutions to complex problems," while Wolfgang Volz of Bosch Software Innovations notes that "a smart city breaks down silos to create a web. It does this via a technological platform that interconnects systems to optimize performance and create new business models. Smart cities focus on the citizen, not only on the technology."

Smart City Examples

The first functioning smart cities are now emerging in North America, Europe, and Asia. For the most part, these start with intelligent solutions in one particular sector. In time, this is extended to include further intelligent solutions across other sectors. Few smart cities currently address all urban challenges. However, the number of smart cities out there is certainly growing...

SMART CITY PROJECTS IN CHICAGO: IMPLEMENTING LIVE PILOT TESTS

There are three main application areas for smart city and open data projects in Chicago, namely investment in infrastructure, focus on economic development, and promotion of community engagement:

Infrastructure investment

> The city plans to invest in a new fiber-optic ring to achieve gigabit speed over an open network. By combining this new network with a competitive price point, it hopes to create an incentive for digital technology companies to locate in, or relocate to, Chicago. The City of Chicago has run out of unlicensed radio spectrum. It is working, together with the Federal Communications Commission on Spectrum, on the concept of sharing spectrum allocated for public safety, so that, when available, it can be used for small cells, cell phones, and so on.

Economic development

> With a view to improving the existing Chicago health system, the city is investing in Chicago Health Atlas, a website used to display aggregate, map-based health information. It is also investing in Windy Grid, a program and platform for real-time, open data infrastructure investment. In collaboration with the Illinois Science and Technology Challenge, the Illinois Open Technology Challenge has been launched to bring government, developers, and communities together. The city also offers hosted web space to support people or organizations that want to create services that make Chicago better.

Community engagement

> Much of the community engagement work in Chicago is carried out by the Smart Chicago Collaborative. Initiatives include:

The City that NetWorks

A key positioning report on what steps the Smart Chicago Collaborative would like to take in the area of digital inclusion.

Digital Skills Initiative

A central hub for coordinating technology training across departments and delegate agencies that have received federal funding.

Connect Chicago

A loose network of more than 250 places in the city where Internet and computer access, digital skills training, and online learning resources are available free of charge.

Smart Health Centers

Trained health information specialists are placed in clinics in low-income areas to help patients connect to their own medical records and find reliable information about their conditions.

SMART CITY PROJECTS IN RIO DE JANEIRO: USING SAFETY TO ATTRACT NEW BUSINESS

Smart city initiatives in Rio de Janeiro largely center on safety and security, both in terms of disaster prevention and management, and freedom of information.

Originally planned for the Olympics in 2016, a fatal landslide in 2010 prompted Rio's mayor to bring forward the construction of a Center of Operations to tackle natural disasters and coordinate relevant emergency responses. The center was built in just eight months in partnership with IBM and Oracle, and is used by city decision makers to manage day-to-day city services, as well as for the aforementioned purposes. The center additionally allows these two types of service to be linked. For example, garbage trucks are coordinated via GPS so that, in an emergency, these trucks can be repurposed for other tasks, improving response times for the city.

To facilitate the flow of information, there is a press room located within the Center of Operations, where all media, television, and radio companies are accommodated also. In addition to enabling these more traditional information networks, the city has also made a significant amount of its data available to the public, including information on crime and mortality rates, as well as daily weather and congestion reports.

SMART CITY PROJECTS IN STOCKHOLM: STRUCTURING A DIALOG WITH CITIZENS AND PRIVATE COMPANIES

The main focus for Stockholm as a smart city has been to bring its citizens, government, and other constituent parts together, enabling simple, effective communication, and an open flow of information.

One such example is the city's investment of €70 million in high-quality, accessible e-government services since 2007, which has created over 50 new digital services and cut management costs substantially.

The city's fiber network is managed by a public company named Stokab. Formed in 1994 to create a forward-looking fiber-optic infrastructure, the company is also charged with fostering a growth environment, one which favors competition and development throughout the Stockholm region.

Another major communications development in Stockholm is the establishment of the Kista Science City, an innovation cluster specializing in ICT. Companies such as Ericsson, Microsoft, and IBM are among those with a presence in Kista, while 6,800 students are now studying ICT courses at Stockholm University and the Royal Institute of Technology in Kista Science City.

The city of Stockholm is working toward energy and transport efficiency via a number of initiatives, such as the Royal Seaport smart district, which aims to be CO_2 neutral by 2030, using the smart grid to enable electricity in different houses at different times of day.

It is also exploring ways to make better use of existing traffic monitoring and congestion mechanisms, and has implemented a Green IT initiative to reduce environmental impact through the use of IT, as well as to limit the impact of the IT sector itself.

SMART CITY PROJECTS IN BOSTON: CONNECTING CITIZENS WITH CITY SERVICES

The Mayor's Office of New Urban Mechanics in Boston (MONUM) is responsible for the three core programs that make up the city's smart masterplan: "Participatory Urbanism," "Clicks and Bricks," and "21st Century Learning."

Participatory Urbanism

Participatory Urbanism describes how smart technologies are fostering a new wave of citizen involvement in their community. The projects that form part of this program are intended to support the creation of new, citizen-centric products and services. Initiatives include:

Citizens Connect

This smartphone application enables members of the population to make their neighborhoods better by giving them an easy tool to report service problems, starting with a pilot SMS version called "citizens connect txt."

Community PlanIt

A platform to explore how online platforms can complement in-person community meetings, as well as trying to reach audiences that might not attend community meetings.

Innovation District Welcome Home Challenge

A competition focused on attracting and growing businesses in Boston's Innovation District.

Participatory Chinatown

Participatory Chinatown is a video-game-like platform that aims to engage a broader range of people in informative and deliberative planning and development conversations.

Clicks and Bricks

Clicks and Bricks is a program of projects that investigates how new technologies are linking the building of the city to how it is managed and experienced. Most specifically, Clicks and Bricks focuses on how to link designers and technology specialists outside of City Hall with leaders and staff from the city's Public Works and Transportation departments. Initiatives include:

Redesigning the Trash System

The city is partnering with IDEO to tackle this challenge by means of human-centered design.

Street Bump

Street Bump is a mobile app that helps residents to improve their street. As they drive, the mobile app collects data about the smoothness of the ride. That data provides the city with real-time information that it can then use to fix problems and plan long-term investments.

City Worker

To help city staff better manage infrastructure and respond to citizen requests, the city has developed a smartphone application that allows workers to easily check their daily work list and access and record information about the condition of city infrastructure such as street lights, trees, and roads.

Adopt-A-Hydrant

A pilot project that encourages Boston residents to shovel out snowed-in hydrants during the winter. Through the app, residents can claim hydrants they intend to shovel out after storms.

Complete Streets

A project led by the Boston Transportation Department, Complete Streets is an effort to improve the flow of people and goods through Boston.

21st-Century Learning

21st-Century Learning is a series of e-education projects that aim to deliver convenient, integrated, and life-long learning to the citizens of Boston. It also aims to facilitate relationships between educators, students, and parents to improve both the in-school and out-of-school educational experience. Initiatives include:

Boston One Card

As part of the city's effort to have its schools, community centers, and libraries provide a seamless system of educational opportunities for young people, the city is piloting a single card that provides access to all these resources for Boston Public School students.

Discover BPS

This web app helps parents navigate the public school options available to their children.

Where's My School Bus

This app allows parents to view the real-time location of their child's school bus on their computer or smartphone.

Autism App/Assistive Technologies

The city is working with two local companies and an international robotics company to develop new learning applications for children with autism.

Classtalk

Classtalk is designed to help teachers send text message reminders to students about homework and tests.

MONUM is also considering education from an open data perspective. It believes that opening up school-related data such as student behavior, grades, and disciplinary records would create massive opportunities for value-added education services and after-school programs.

SMART CITY PROJECTS IN HONG KONG: FOCUSING IN ON ICT

Hong Kong's approach to becoming a smart city has been to focus intensively on ICT and what it can bring to the life of the city. This is most clearly visible in their approach to information and data management, improvements to WiFi networks, and development of e-government solutions.

Electronic Information Management was central to Hong Kong's 2008 Digital 21 Strategy, the aim being to ensure that information is better managed and more readily available. The approach focuses on three key areas, namely content management, records management, and knowledge management.

The Office of the Chief Information Officer is responsible for the city's main web portal. Their aim is to satisfy 80% of citizen requests via e-government services. As of December 2012, there were 49 government mobile applications and 38 mobile sites. By placing WiFi facilities at designated government premises, the GovWiFi program aims to transform Hong Kong into a wireless city, providing free wireless Internet to all citizens.

In terms of open data, the government holds a significant amount of data that could be of significant value to the public (e.g., demographic, economic, geographical, and meteorological data, historical documents, and archives). However, this information has not historically been in a format that facilitated value-added reuse by third parties.

In order to combat this, Hong Kong's government has launched a data portal entitled Data One. This 18-month pilot scheme has made geo-referenced public facilities data and real-time traffic data available for free. A competition held to find the best applications of this data was won by an app that located the nearest doctor and tracked patient appointments. Following the success of this trial, and support from citizens and industry, the government plans to continue with the portal, and gradually add more datasets.

Business Models and KPIs for Smart Cities

A smart city project must be financially sustainable. It is not enough to think about funding for just the initial stages of the project, as any project must live long enough to change the life of the city. As such, once the city's most specific pain point has been identified (this will be the initial focus of the project), other use cases must also be defined to ensure life-long sustainability for the project. These uses cases should generally either increase city income or reduce city expenditure to a degree that enables the project to be funded as a whole.

The concrete benefits of the smart city can be classified into three main categories, namely financial savings, creation of new revenue, or resolution of a pain point:

New revenue
> Barcelona has reduced its parking costs by 22% while increasing its parking revenue by between 20%–30%. With the implementation of smart parking solutions, cities can increase efficiency, reduce time wasted in traffic congestion, and introduce simple automatic billing, to name a few examples.

Savings
> In France, 20% of drinkable water is spoiled by leakage attributable to aging pipes. By implementing smart water grid solutions, a city can reduce consumption and thus save money.

Pain point
> On French public transport, 1 in 2 passengers feel unsafe (47%). By increasing visible security on transportation, those responsible for France's public systems would help to resolve a major pain point. In the long term, the increase in security should also be beneficial in terms of passenger numbers.

When measuring the success of a smart city initiative, relevant KPIs could be simple, quantitative ones (the number of 0-emission buildings for example, or a measurable increase in parking revenue), or they could be more complex, qualitative improvements (such as an increase in the city's attractiveness, or greater happiness among citizens). The difficulty lies in agreeing on feasible, concrete KPIs when the customer is a city. Cities generally do not have a global picture when it comes to the improvements made available by the Internet of Things. The role of a supplier is to smoothly translate the city's needs into smart solutions, with adapted KPIs.

Keynote Contribution: Wim Elfrink, EVP at Cisco

Wim Elfrink is Executive Vice President for Industry Solutions and Chief Globalization Officer at Cisco, and is a leading expert on the subject of smart cities. In the following interview with Wolfgang Volz, Project Manager (Smart City) at Bosch Software Innovations, he talks about his vision for the smart city, as well as how it can best be measured in terms of drivers, criteria, and success.

Wolfgang Volz: What first attracted you to the subject of smart cities?

Wim Elfrink: My initial interest in the subject came about eight or nine years ago, as I traveled through China, India, and Africa. The Western world is aging. As the United States grows older and Europe shrinks, the populations of India, Africa, and the Middle East are increasing by more than 40% to 50%!

The 21st century will therefore be dominated by shifting dynamics and massive demographic change, as the world grows more and more heterogeneous. One of the principal trends will be in global urbanization. 50% of the world's population now lives in cities and urban areas for the first time in history. This figure is set to reach 70% by 2050. We're talking transformation on a huge scale!

For example, I used to live in Bangalore, where I built Cisco's second headquarters. Six hundred new people join that city every day. That means you need a new school every quarter, or a new hospital for each new year! Obviously, this is not a demand that can physically be met. So I started to think about what technology could do, how it could help. And that's how Cisco's IoT initiative came about. At Cisco, we now call this the Internet of Everything—the connection of people, processes, data, and things.

My father was an architect in Rotterdam. He was a physical architect; I became a digital architect.

We can now put a digital overlay on top of anything physical and say, "What can this enable?" This opens the way for unprecedented opportunities, increased productivity, and new revenue. We think that, in total, the IoE can create $19 trillion of economic value over the next decade, and one of the biggest areas is in urban services of smart cities, which can capture €3 trillion in value. To realize this IoT/IoE opportunity, information and communications technology (ICT) must become the new essential infrastructure along with water, gas, and electricity.

Wolfgang Volz: Can you tell us more about the concept of "urban services"—more specifically, what the major drivers are?

Wim Elfrink: Back in 2000, the IoT was associated almost exclusively with RFID. Nowadays, about 15 billion devices are connected to the Internet, which is still just 1% of what's possible. We estimate that this figure will be closer to 50 billion by 2020. This translates to 300,000 devices, from mobile devices to industrial sensors, being connected each hour. It's happening as we speak—this is the smart revolution, right now. One of the major drivers for this, as ever, is financial. The price of devices and sensors is no longer prohibitive, and the lifetime of batteries is increasing. The explosion of smartphones, tablets, and apps has led to the generation of large amounts of data, as well as opening up new opportunities to monetize this data. We're in a new era of digitization. We also have IP version 6 now, which enables us to handle data from a massive number of devices. All of these considerations, plus the emergence of new standards, are the tipping point for new services.

Wolfgang Volz: In your experience, which use cases are most attractive for smart cities? And what exactly does "smart" mean to you?

Wim Elfrink: Over the past few years, the definition of the smart city has evolved to mean many things to many people. Yet, one thing remains constant—an essential part of being "smart" is knowing how to utilize ICT and the Internet to address urban challenges. To use the example of India again, where new cities are in the planning stage, one of the fundamental questions being raised well upstream of breaking any ground is: do we build a road structure first or a digital infrastructure? There is a paradigm shift occurring here—at a basic level, what does connectivity mean in this day and age: is it physical or digital?

I have two boys, 15 and 17. They have two physical states: they are asleep or they are online. They work differently, study differently. When I arrive in a city, I look around; I am educated physically. While I look up, they look down—at their phones. They get all of their information online. The next decade will be the decade of data. All these devices (or "things") generate massive amounts of data. According to IDC, only 0.5% of this data is currently being used or analyzed. The challenge for the smart city is to determine how to turn this data into information, this information into knowledge, and this knowledge into wisdom, by proposing the kind of *what-if* scenarios that lead to the creation of urban services.

Every city has its own specific pain points. For example, if you're in Mumbai, it may be sewage systems, in San Francisco it may be parking, in Hamburg it may be dockside services. The main use cases we have seen to date have been in the areas of parking, lighting, and water. In Hamburg, for example, we have managed to massively reduce traffic through the introduction of smart parking. But the really exciting thing is when we can mash up these services to move away from a traditional stovepipe system and create a truly horizontal infrastructure. Think about the possibilities—if you combine, say, street lighting services and public video monitoring systems—you can remotely monitor the number of people in a given square on a given evening and adjust the level of street lighting in that area accordingly. Barcelona is one of the best smart city examples I can think of. They have created an entirely new governance model, mashed up services to create a horizontal infrastructure, and embraced technology as an integral part of their urban infrastructure.

Wolfgang Volz: You publish a lot about the smart city. In some of your recent publications, you offered some excellent examples of how the IoT/IoE can contribute to the urban environment. Can you give us a brief summary?

Wim Elfrink: Yes, of course.

As I mentioned previously, Barcelona is an excellent example. Mayor Xavier Trias has developed a showcase smart city that anticipates the creation of $3.6 billion in economic, social, and environmental value over the next decade through the use of the IoE. Citizens in Barcelona can interact with government officials via kiosks or mobile devices, alert one another to accidents or potholes, find parking spaces or store discounts on their cell phones, or have their sensor-equipped garbage cans picked up when they're full—not just on Tuesday mornings.

The IoE is real and is functioning in real-life environments—not only in Barcelona, but in numerous other smart cities around the world, including Copenhagen, Amsterdam, Chicago, Hamburg, Songdo, Abu Dhabi, and Brisbane, to name just a few.

Cisco has been working with the city of Barcelona for a while now to tackle its messy parking problems. The local government has installed a network of light and metal detectors to sense whether or not parking spots are occupied. Drivers get information on which spots are free through a combination of apps and digital signs linked to the Internet. The city also collects valuable information on parking and driving patterns that can improve traffic management, and drivers can use the app to pay for their spots. The city says these new urban services boost parking revenue by $50 million.

Wolfgang Volz: What do you see as the main success criteria for smart cities?

Wim Elfrink: I think four main criteria need to be satisfied:

Visionary approaches and thought leadership
You need to have a smart city master plan that addresses the question of what ICT can add. Without a master plan, it's not going to work—it will remain a set of fragmented and disjointed ideas.

Global open standards and smart regulations
The city needs to provide protocols, standards, and regulations that enable the use of free data. Existing regulations will need to be rethought with a view to removing old-world barriers; looking to the future rather than the past.

Openness to public-private partnerships and participation

Cities need to create a business model that allows for investment and carefully consider what the best model for a public-private partnership may be. (Pay as you go? A one-off investment?)

Balanced ecosystems integrating global, international, and local facets

The creation of innovation centers for local urban services will be an important element of this.

Wolfgang Volz: How do we measure the success of a smart city? What are the key performance indicators?

Wim Elfrink: To my mind, there are five clear indicators of a smart city's success:

Investments

Can you attract investors and create jobs by marketing yourself as a smart city?

Energy savings

70% of the world's energy consumption is by cities. A large proportion of this usage is waste! We project that it is possible to reduce consumption by 30%–50% using smart approaches.

Reduction in water consumption

30% of water is lost through leakage. A simple sensor-based warning system could generate massive savings and reduce waste by up to 50%.

Traffic improvement

30% of traffic is caused by people looking for a parking space. That's 30% of traffic, which is total redundancy, and easily fixable.

Reduction in crime rates

Put simply, if the social environment improves in a city, people are happier, and the crime rate goes down.

Wolfgang Volz: Thank you for this great insight into the Internet of Everything and the potential of smart cities for our future.

Relevance for IoT

New developments in software, IT, and the Internet have made it possible to reach out to any member of an urban population in seconds, whether on a one-to-one, one-to-many, or many-to-many basis. Smartphones, social media, and blogs provide a direct way for members of the public to share their interaction with the city. Open data like city maps, parking guidance, and public transport timetables further feed into this bank of information. Once both the people and the things in the city connect to one another, as is envisioned, it should quickly become possible to make more intelligent use of the city infrastructure, particularly where this may currently be limited during peak times.

Connecting things like cars, homes, and public or private systems via sensors opens up multiple opportunities to meet such challenges. However, it is important to understand that the connection alone is not enough; the connected things and associated data have to be utilized in a meaningful way. They must become an active part of the stakeholder's daily interaction with the city—for example, informing both the family and the fire service in the event of a fire in the family home. This is the essence of the emerging "Internet of Things and Services": to connect physical and virtual worlds, users, and business entities, thereby enabling new possibilities and synergies. For the first time in history, we can create a connected city that directly improves our quality of life.

The key technological challenge is to link all systems via an open platform that can be used as broadly as possible, as the cross-pollination of data is integral to success. What we need is a city platform capable of integrating data from all services in the city, including power plants, transportation, buildings, traffic, industrial machinery, security systems, and more. A solution like the Bosch Smart City suite should have the capability to collect, process, and analyze enormous data flows from the complete spectrum of smart city layers. By leveraging such capabilities and data, these technologies would be able to help city administrators make informed key decisions and support citizens in their day-to-day lives.

The smart city is closely linked to ICT, and benefits from the expertise that has been built up over time. The smart city is not only about huge projects, but also about minor improvements. Innovation-led projects are the best way to explore the smart city's possibilities. Public-private collaboration should create many business cases, with a smart city system leveraging various layers of existing ICT investment, such as infrastructure, operations, data, processes, and so on.

The following key architectural principles, standards, and integration requirements should be considered when designing smart city ICT architecture:

- Open standards and capacity for integration—by hardware providers, city service providers, city administration and citizens, and third-party solution providers.

- Reusability of data, availability of data, provision for multidimensional data.

- User-driven, flexible, and user-friendly upper-layer solution implementation.

Monaco Case Study

On July 10, 2012, the Principality of Monaco and the Bosch Group signed an agreement targeting Monaco 3.0, a connected city. Since then, initial feasibility studies have been conducted with the Principality in order to jointly explore the connected city concept, including the following application areas: communications, mobility, energy, security, and health. As a first direct result, an operational on-site demonstration has been developed to illustrate the capabilities of Bosch's technology platform, as well as its implementation as part of a connected city approach. In this approach, Monaco's existing services, systems, and data are integrated into the platform while new and innovative services are developed in parallel. The four examples we will look at here are use cases of the demo and were defined around the topic of mobility together with Monaco's Public Works, Environment, and Urban Development department.

The essential goals to be achieved were as follows:

- Operational on-site connected city demo
- Seamless and secure data exchange between different departments for faster decision making and creation of new services
- Improvements to mobility, security, and quality of life in Monaco
- Better interaction with citizens and visitors
- Reduction of operational costs while introducing new and better services

THE CITY PLATFORM

The City Platform serves as a central communication and integration platform for existing and new systems. It allows the implementation of new processes and services by managing captured data, with existing systems remaining sovereign in terms of internal data and functionalities. In the event of direct access to existing department systems not being possible for reasons of security or privacy, data that is relevant for other attached systems can be explicitly pushed to the City Platform. The Bosch City Platform allows the interconnection of data and services from various sources, which facilitates the creation of new services and enables greater visibility of available data. Data reporting, statistics, and analytics can be viewed via one common tool. This means participating departments can easily create additional services, or adjust and model rules and processes. Basing cross-departmental communication on a single platform and sharing common data significantly reduces IT costs and enables easier information flow.

Figure 6-1 shows the Asset Integration Architecture (AIA) for the Monaco City Platform.

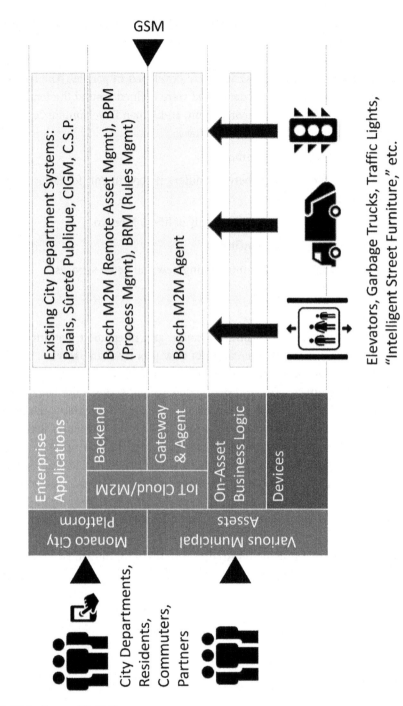

FIGURE 6-1. AIA for Monaco City Platform

CROWD MANAGEMENT AT AND AROUND THE MONACO TRAIN STATION

Bosch cameras will be mounted in defined areas of the Monaco train station to monitor entrances and exits, as well as points of interest (such as elevators). The cameras are intelligent; the integrated Intelligent Video Analysis (IVA) module analyzes a permanent video stream recorded by each camera and reports the number of people present. This data is added to the actual video stream to form a separate metadata stream, which is securely transferred into the backend via a virtual private network. Crowd management is integrated with camera intelligence. This sends alerts to the platform, which allows better management of crowding at elevators. It also means traffic control can be redirected immediately to avoid a buildup of congestion as people leave the station. As a result, pedestrian traffic flows in and around the train station will be much smoother. Long-term data collection enables statistical analysis for the purposes of urban planning and city development. Easier information sharing between different parties (e.g., ambulances and fire brigades) enables public service departments to deliver a higher level of security and service.

FLEET MANAGEMENT BY GEOLOCALIZATION

Everybody loves a clean city, but nobody wants to be stuck in traffic behind a garbage truck. Three of Monaco's garbage trucks will be equipped with Bosch geolocalization sensors to provide information on their current locations. These sensors are capable of capturing geolocation data, which will be transmitted via GSM networks to the City Platform. Sensor data contains a limited number of data fields (e.g., sensor ID, timestamp, data type, data value) and will be enriched with further meta and master data before being processed in backend systems. This data allows a dynamic presentation of the truck ID and current location on a map for better resource allocation, route planning, avoiding downtime, or preventing traffic jams. In a subsequent step, current vehicle routes and positions will be added to the mobility app for smartphones to assist citizens, commuters, and tourists in their choice of travel route through the Principality.

Geolocalization of garbage trucks offers the following benefits:

- Information about current truck location
- Reduction of traffic congestion
- Improved traffic flow for a given infrastructure
- Optimization of necessary service time per house and street
- Better resource planning, including reassignment of available capacity, and quick replacement of broken trucks

MONACO 3.0 MOBILITY APP

The Bosch Connected City is a win-win for public services, residents, commuters, and tourists. Within the demonstration platform, a smartphone app is provided to selected test users.

This mobility app brings connected technology together with public services, such as bus networks, parking lot management, waste collection, and roadwork information. It also provides up-to-date information to users and helps various city departments to operate more efficiently. Furthermore, the app has a crowdsourcing function that allows people to actively participate in and improve city life. In addition to the existing fault recognition system, users will be able to log relevant visual and status information about the condition of public services such as elevators or escalators.

The bidirectional smartphone app offers the following benefits:

- Route assistance for users with reduced mobility
- Simplified use of public transport to reduce traffic flows and CO_2 emissions
- Involvement of citizens and visitors in city life and development
- Receipt of up-to-date feedback on conditions and quality of public services and infrastructure
- Significant reduction of downtimes due to quicker awareness

Lessons Learned and Outlook

Didier Manning, Bosch Software Innovations, summarizes his experience with smart city projects as follows [DB1]:

> As cities evolve, they bring new challenges for technology developers and manufacturers alike. It used to be enough just to deliver a good product. But the city of tomorrow demands more. Take cameras, for example. In the past, camera manufacturers simply weren't concerned with what the city was planning, or what exactly the cameras would be used for. Today, the technology must offer a solution; city administrators expect to see not just a sophisticated camera, but a business plan as well. That business plan should ideally be carefully tailored to the customer city and its needs. For companies, this means they have to work more closely with their customers and put themselves in the customer's shoes. The customer-supplier relationship will change as a result. One challenge that applies particularly to software is the timely processing and analysis of data; after all, a connected city generates at least 100,000 events per second. When it comes to getting connected, a city has two basic options. One calls for equipping things (sensors/actuators) with local intelligence. The advantage of this option is that the system can collect data where the data is generated, and will forward it only as dictated by the logic in place. However, the downside is a loss in flexibility should the city choose to install a new or overarching system. The second option is central control: a central platform receives all data and then routes it as needed.
>
> The reality will probably lie somewhere between these two options. Targeted application and the cost-benefit effect will ultimately decide what makes more sense: a centralized or decentralized system.

All of this is still quite a way off, since, in most cases, cities lack a strategic structure. What's needed is a kind of authority, someone to take the lead and shape the city of tomorrow. This way of thinking is strange to most cities, but if they want to get connected, they have to change how they do things—they need to get out of their silos and into a network.

PART I CONCLUSIONS AND OUTLOOK

A large part of the M2M and emerging IoT solutions rely on wireless connectivity, and this is a trend that we see increasing in the future. The GSMA is the global trade association of mobile operators and related companies, and is responsible, among many other activities, for the development and promotion of new business opportunities and ecosystems. Naturally, the GSMA is very close to the pulse of the IoT market and an ideal candidate to discuss with us the current state of the cellular IoT space and also future developments. The following Interview with Alex Sinclair, CTO of GSMA, provides an interesting outlook.

Jim Morrish: What are the leading cellular M2M/IoT applications right now?

Alex Sinclair: Machine-to-machine (M2M) connections accounted for 2.8% of all global mobile connections, or 189 million, at the end of 2013, according to GSMA Intelligence (GSMAi), so it is still very much a nascent technology at a relatively early stage in its development. We believe that with the right standards and regulation in place, it will have a fundamental impact on the way we live and work, reducing waste and inefficiencies and delivering major social and environmental benefits in security, healthcare, transportation and logistics, education, and energy, among many other sectors of the economy. However, it is also having an impact right now.

Regulation

Advances in the M2M market have often been underpinned by regulation, on a national level, as well as in verticals such as automotive and utilities.

Scalable Opportunities for MNOs in Automotive

The car automotive sector is by far the largest scalable opportunity in M2M for a number of reasons:

- Long production and in-use cycles for connected vehicles present the need to future-proof connected cars, and consequently OEMs are fitting LTE modules into vehicles.

- Additional revenue-related streams are presented by the connected car, such as the insurance market, which has introduced pay-as-you-drive usage-based plans for consumers that have helped to lower costs significantly.

- Both OEMs and infotainment designers have seen the potential to develop in-car entertainment services within connected cars.

- The opportunity to implement multibilling mechanisms and combine multiservices via a single connection (e.g., the connected car). AT&T, for example, has introduced its AT&T Drive service which aims to package connectivity, data analytics, and info-tainment for both automakers and developers specialized in providing live linear TV and video-on-demand streaming services within automotive vehicles.

Fleet Management Tracking Services

Real-time GPS tracking used in fleet management represents a huge segment for a range of global operators. Fleet management enables companies to track both individual vehicles and shipped cargoes, including vehicles that need to be serviced. Fleet management also helps to ensure that drivers are obeying speed limits and following the best routes.

Government Mandates

Other initiatives such as Emergency Call (eCall), a road accident alert system that requires an embedded in-vehicle SIM using satellite positioning and mobile connectivity, is scheduled to be integrated into all new vehicles in Europe over the next few years. Russia is also in the process of deploying an accident notification system called ERA-GLONASS, and Brazil has introduced another regulation-driven telematics project tracking stolen vehicles called SIMRAV, which allows all new vehicles to be fitted with a capability to be tracked and disabled in the event of theft.

Implementing Legislation: Smart Metering

Smart metering is also an area where we are seeing huge growth driven in part by legislation in the European Union. The systematic use of embedded mobile connectivity to create smart utility grids and smart energy environments can improve suppliers' ability to effectively manage demand for energy, and enable consumers and businesses to use energy and water more efficiently. Mobile connectivity can give both utility companies and their customers' real-time information about energy and water usage, enabling them to spread demand across the day and take action to reduce wastage. Millions of residential electricity, gas, water, and heating meters are becoming "smart," meaning they can be monitored, controlled, and managed at preset intervals, be it hourly or daily. To date, EU member states have committed to rolling out close to 200 million smart meters for electricity and 45 million for gas by 2020, at a total potential investment of 45 billion.

Implementing Legislation: Healthcare

The healthcare sector is another vertical that is seeing positive traction in development terms and has the potential to see huge growth if provided with a positive regulatory environment. It is a challenging area, where mobile operators need to work closely with government and other regulatory stakeholders at a national level. We have already seen government-led projects in this sector in markets such as Singapore, France, and the United Arab Emirates—countries that have instigated initiatives on mobile health, while in the United States, government policies are in place to incentivize mHealth (e.g., ePrescriptions and incentives for hospitals to administer in order to reduce readmissions).

B2B2C mHealth services are also a big opportunity with some operators, such as Telefónica and Orange, seeing good traction with mHealth offerings. Many operators have dedicated health divisions in their operational structure. Such a setup has been established in order to seek the best way to provide sufficient healthcare support via a multitude of technologies, including Bluetooth and cellular.

Jim Morrish: Are there any specific industry initiatives that we should know about?

Alex Sinclair: The GSMA recently issued guidelines for the IoT market that outline how devices and applications should communicate via mobile networks in the most intelligent and efficient way. You should also be aware of the GSMA Embedded SIM Specification for remote SIM provisioning, which is now being deployed by operators around the world.

The guidelines called "IoT Device Connection Efficiency Guidelines," are designed to support device and application developers as the IoT market develops and are intended for use by all players in the mobile ecosystem, ensuring that mobile networks can efficiently accommodate the increased number of connected devices and services resulting from the rapid growth of M2M. The guidelines will help IoT device and application developers expand the number of devices connecting to mobile networks, whilst preventing service outages and ensuring optimal performance that will ultimately enable the market to scale across a diverse range of sectors, including automotive, transportation, utilities, and health. The guidelines include a number of best practice areas such as data aggregation within devices, nonsynchronous network access, application scalability, and guidance on how to manage signalling traffic from deactivated or out-of-subscription SIMs. They have received the backing of leading mobile operators, including AT&T, China Mobile, China Telecom, China Unicom, Deutsche Telekom, Etisalat, KT Corporation, Orange, NTT DOCOMO, Tata Teleservices Ltd., Telefónica, Telenor Connexion, and VimpelCom.

The GSMA's Embedded SIM specification allows mobile network operators to provide scalable, reliable, and secure connectivity for M2M connected devices that are often hermetically sealed, such as in the connected car or smart meters. It also facilitates over-the-air operator provisioning and management, which provides service flexibility to end customers. The GSMA's Embedded SIM specification promotes a common global architecture that will reduce costs, drive efficiencies, and further accelerate the rapidly growing

M2M market, which is set to reach 244 million global connections this year according to GSMA Intelligence. A number of organizations have launched compliant solutions, including AT&T, Etisalat, NTT DOCOMO, and Telefónica; as well as Gemalto, Giesecke & Devrient, Morpho (Safran), Oberthur Technologies, Sierra Wireless, and Telit. The GSMA also commissioned independent research from Beecham Research that estimated that the immediate industry-wide adoption and deployment of the GSMA Embedded SIM Specification will deliver 34% higher market growth by 2020.

Jim Morrish: Mobile industry has been waiting for the M2M hockey stick for 5–10 years, do you still see this happening?

Alex Sinclair: GSMA Intelligence recently released its latest figures that show that global cellular M2M connections are currently set to reach close to one billion by 2020. At the current rate of trajectory, global cellular M2M connections will reach 974 million by 2020, growing at 26% per year (CAGR) in the period between 2014 and 2020. We believe that this growth rate could go above 40% a year if a number of favorable market conditions are achieved, leading to a potential two billion cellular M2M connections globally by 2020. These could include the introduction of additional government policies enabling a wider deployment of cellular M2M in key sectors such as utilities, smart cities, automotive, and healthcare, in addition to increased standardization on remote provisioning and APIs, and significant M2M module cost reduction enabling a wider range of connected products and services.

Jim Morrish: What are the biggest opportunities for the mobile industry in the Internet of Things?

Alex Sinclair: Recent research commissioned by the GSMA highlighted that the two biggest opportunities lie in the connected car and consumer electronics markets. A number of these we have already highlighted, but others such as the wearables market, for example, will also be a significant area of development. It currently has the perception as an extension of the smartphone, but this will change. It also has a diverse use potential across business and consumer sectors.

Jim Morrish: Can you give some examples of where mobile connectivity has proven key to unlocking value?

Alex Sinclair: Mobile operators' M2M revenues are dependent on application type, scale, and on the approach to service delivery. For example, connectivity-only deals reap far less revenue than end-to-end (E2E) solutions. So it is important for the mobile operator to be able to provide a more value-added offering, either via acquiring expertise or by partnering with other companies, in order to increase revenues from M2M. For example, KT

Corporation achieved this by launching a Taxicall solution generating higher revenue, increasing customer stickiness, and reducing churn. We are still only at the beginning, but Vodafone, for example, recently revealed that its M2M revenue as of end of June 2014 was up 30.7% year-on-year "driven by increased innovation and a widening range of vertical markets."

PART II

Ignite | IoT Methodology

Efficiently managing the transition toward IoT-based business models is becoming increasingly important for many companies. The strategy for this transition needs to be defined and managed at the enterprise level, while the implementation of new IoT solutions and the enabling of existing products for IoT usually happens at the project level.

Based on our own experience, the analysis of the case studies presented in Part I of this book, and many expert interviews, we have collected a set of best practices for both IoT strategy management and project execution. The Ignite | IoT Methodology is based on these best practices and consists of two parts (Figure II-1):

Chapter 7

Helps enterprises to define their IoT strategy and prepare the organization for IoT adoption. Supports the creation and management of a portfolio of IoT projects to support the IoT strategy. Mainly relevant for COOs, CTOs, corporate strategy, and product portfolio management.

Chapter 8

Supports product managers and project managers in the planning and execution of IoT-solution projects. Covers the plan, build, and run phases of IoT projects.

Ignite | IoT Strategy Execution

Define IoT strategy and prepare
organization for IoT adoption.
Create and manage a portfolio of IoT
projects to support IoT strategy.

Ignite | IoT Solution Delivery

Plan, build and run IoT solutions.

FIGURE II-1. Ignite | IoT Methodology overview

CHAPTER 7

Ignite | IoT Strategy Execution

MANY LARGE COMPANIES FIND IT EXTREMELY DIFFICULT TO DEAL WITH DISRUPTIVE PARADIGM shifts. This is not a new observation. In 1942, Joseph Schumpeter coined the seemingly paradoxical term "creative destruction" as a way to describe "the free market's messy way of delivering progress" [EC1] (actually, it can be traced back to the works of Karl Marx, but let's not go there...). Probably the most cited example of a company that was unable to deal with disruptive technologies is Kodak. Although Kodak was one of the inventors of digital photography, the company failed to transform itself from a leader in film-based photography to the new, digital business models. Schumpeter's gale seems like a perfect summary of the dilemma many large companies face—the inability to reinvent themselves from the inside, and the extremely fast pace at which startup companies are creating new digital businesses on the green field.

In our view, there was never a distinct, defining moment in the history of Kodak that initiated its decline—the company's decline took more than a decade and had multiple different causes. In the context of the IoT, every company has to ask itself how much of a potentially disruptive paradigm shift the IoT represents, and how long this shift will take in its respective vertical markets. These are exactly the issues that the Ignite | IoT Strategy Execution methodology aims to address: create a better understanding of what the transformative IoT roadmap should look like for an individual company, learn how a portfolio of IoT opportunities should be managed, and establish how individual IoT initiatives can be identified, approved, and executed.

Now, we don't expect many CEOs to read this book and then directly apply the Ignite methodology to their IoT strategy. However, many managers will get ideas from this chapter that they should be able to apply to their own situation and maybe use them to influence top management. And possibly even more importantly, we have been asked by many people working at the project level how they can better sell their ideas, get resource commitments, or generally ensure management buy-in for their IoT projects. In this kind of situation, it is not only important to understand how you can structure your own IoT business case; you will also need to look at how this business case is seen by management in the context of other business opportunities—and how you should develop your own business case in order to sell it successfully.

Most of what we discuss in this chapter will be more interesting for those in the "machine camp" who work for large industrial companies with complex product portfolios. However, people in the "Internet camp" working for the large incumbents in this space may also be very interested.

Figure 7-1 summarizes the key elements of the Ignite | IoT Strategy Execution framework, which is divided into six areas: IoT Strategy, IoT Opportunity Identification, IoT Opportunity Management, Initiation, IoT Center of Excellence, and IoT Platform.

A company's *IoT Strategy* needs to reflect the extent and speed at which it should shift toward the IoT: Should the company become a pioneer and attempt to gain rapid market share but at the risk of failure? Or should it become a follower that will only implement a new IoT solution if there is certainty that the customer will accept it and buy? Some companies consider the IoT as just one of many important paradigm shifts happening at the moment, and invest only limited resources into IoT adoption. Other companies see the IoT as the fundamental paradigm shift of the next decade, and have made large investments in IoT programs alongside the establishment of far-reaching internal change management programs. The IoT strategy needs to provide vision, goals, and guiding principles. It should also provide a high-level description of how strategic alliances and partner ecosystems in IoT-related business areas should be developed. Finally, it needs to manage the portfolio of IoT opportunities and projects, as well as budget planning and management of the IoT roadmap.

IoT Opportunity Identification, the generation of innovation ideas for IoT solutions, can either happen as an open process, which draws on the innovation potential of employees, customers, and developers, or as part of a more structured approach, where ideas are derived from a given context, such as the company's value chain, for example. Ideas that show the most promise need to be elaborated in more detail, using templates for idea refinement, for example.

Having made it through the first quality gate, the most promising ideas are then refined as part of the *IoT Opportunity Management* phase. A more detailed business model has to be prepared in order to assess feasibility and the business case. The following Impact & Risk Assessment phase ensures that all possible outcomes of the business model are given sufficient consideration.

Once an IoT opportunity has been approved, it can be moved into the *Initiation* stage. In this stage, management has to decide on the best way to set up the initiative: as a dedicated internal project, as a spin-off, or even as an M&A project, for example. For internal projects, these activities interface with the *Ignite | IoT Solution Delivery* methodology.

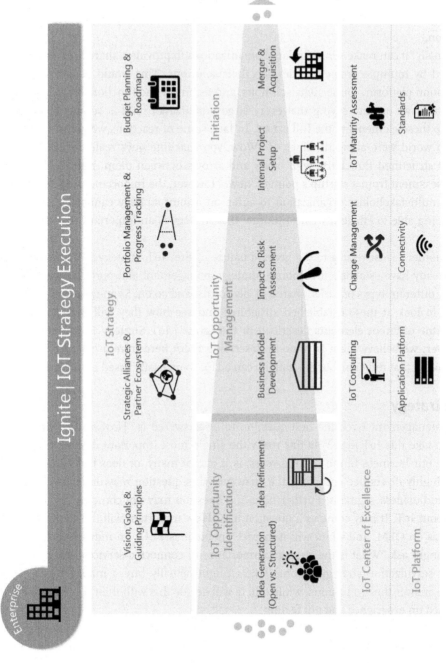

FIGURE 7-1. Ignite | IoT Strategy Execution

An *IoT Center of Excellence (CoE) can help new* projects gain momentum faster, by providing IoT consulting and change management support, for example. IoT maturity assessments can help an organization to better understand where it currently stands with respect to IoT adoption.

Finally, it can make sense for large organizations to provide a shared *IoT Platform* that can be used by multiple projects to develop their solutions. This would usually include an IoT application platform, connectivity solutions, and technical and functional standards.

Again, we are not saying that every large organization that is serious about IoT has to develop these elements to the full extent. In fact, some of reactions we got from people in the startup world were along the lines of "Wow, you machine guys really feel better if you can look at structured flowcharts with boxes and arrows between them, right?" This might be a fair assessment from a startup's point of view. However, the importance of getting people in a large, multistakeholder organization to agree on a joint strategy cannot be underestimated. And being able to efficiently communicate this strategy is an important first step toward this goal.

Another caveat relates to the generic nature of the "IoT Strategy." Large companies usually already have established corporate strategy management and portfolio management processes, different types of CoEs, shared IT platforms, and so on. So in most cases it will be necessary to look at these established structures and see how they will need to be adapted to reflect the different elements described in the Ignite | IoT Strategy Execution methodology. However, we believe there is value in describing them here from a generic, IoT-centric perspective, so that individual organizations can adapt them easily based on their own needs.

IoT Strategy

On a management level, the first question to be answered is "How seriously do we actually have to take this IoT hype?" Is this really the single most important disruptive force that will change our business in the coming years, is it one of many, or does it not matter at all? In a large, highly diversified company, the answer to this question may differ from business segment to business segment. Furthermore, the question may not come in the form of a question about IoT. It may come as a question like "How important will the connected vehicle be to me as an OEM, and when will it impact my business?" Or an industrial equipment company might ask "What is the strategic importance of connected services in the context of our overall servitization strategy?" Some CEOs might actually hire a management consultancy firm to answer these questions, while others will decide this with their inner management circle based on experience and gut feeling.

What seems important is that the questions, and the answers to these questions, are explicitly articulated, and form a solid basis from which the management team can derive a vision, goals, and guiding principles.

This vision could include things like:

- ACME Industries will transform itself from a pure product business into a market-leading provider of connected industrial services.
- ACME Automotive will establish itself as the leading provider of an open, connected vehicle application platform.

This should be accompanied by a set of more concrete goals and business objectives, for example:

- In the product areas of X, Y, and Z, we will generate X% of annual revenue from connected services.
- In the product areas P, Q, and R, we will reduce maintenance costs by X% based on connected services.

A set of key strategies and guidelines should support the following:

- ACME Corp will establish an internal, IoT-focused, open innovation program in combination with a strategic value chain analysis to identify key opportunities.
- ACME Corp will earmark $X million in funding for the top 10 IoT opportunities.
- The split between internal and external projects and M&A focused activities should be roughly X% to Y%, subject to analysis of individual cases.
- In the area of XYZ, we should build an open partner ecosystem, while in the area of PQR, we should aim to control the platform and only allow for selected partners, such as A, B, and C, for example.

Senior management should also take on personal responsibility for a list of strategic tasks, for example:

- The CEO will change the annual budget process to reflect IoT priorities.
- The CEO will contact partners A, B, and C to initiate partnership discussions.
- The CFO will work with the M&A team to allocate X% of the M&A budget to the new IoT strategy.

IoT Opportunity Identification

Once the overall strategic framework has been defined, the next question to be asked is: How can we break this all down into concrete opportunities? Say an OEM has agreed that they want to pursue the connected vehicle as a key strategy, and have allocated a set amount of resources to the strategy in general. As we saw in Part I, the connected vehicle is a very broad concept, with many different related opportunities, from connected horizon initiatives to community-based parking. And most likely, there are further promising opportunities in this area that have not even been identified yet. So how can an OEM that has identified the connected vehicle as a strategic area ensure that the best opportunities are identified and eventually funded?

IOT OPPORTUNITY CATEGORIES

The first thing that is helpful is to come to an agreement within the organization on what types of opportunities are to be looked for in the context of IoT. Questions like "Let's see what kind of things we can connect up and maybe add some services to" are not going to be a helpful approach. Instead, it can be helpful to provide an overview of the most likely categories or opportunities that should be identified.

For example, Figure 7-2 differentiates between new business and internal improvements on the top level. For each of these two areas, a number of general categories like maintenance improvements or data-centric business models are defined, together with some typical KPIs and examples.

	Category	KPIs	Examples
Internal Improvements	Maintenance Improvements	• Improved OEE (Overall Equipment Effectiveness)	• Remote Condition Monitoring • Preventive Maintenance • Predictive Maintenance
	Logistics Process Improvements	• Improved Stock-Level Management • Reduced Transportation Overhead • Reduced Loss and Theft	• Remote Stock Level Monitoring • Fleet Management • Container/Freight Tracking
	Quality Improvements	• Improved Product Quality • Improved Service Quality	• Freight Monitoring, e.g. Farm2Fork
New Business	New Product-Centric Business Models	• Product Revenue • Profit Margin	• Real-Time Car Sharing (DriveNow, Zipcar) • Health Buddy Appliance
	New Data-Centric Business Models	• Data-Generated Revenue • Profit Margin	• Nest
	New Service-Centric Revenue Models	• Service Subscription Revenues • Profit Margin	• eCall Service

FIGURE 7-2. IoT opportunity categories

Applying this example to your own business domain can be helpful in structuring the search for the best IoT opportunities.

IOT IDEA GENERATION PROCESS

The next step is to understand the different options that are available for managing the idea generation process in a large company, and how to best apply these options to the generation of IoT business opportunities. There are usually two main ways to generate ideas in a large company: either open idea generation (green field approach), or a more structured idea generation approach, where ideas evolve in a given context, such as how they relate to the company's current value proposition, for example. The latter approach is usually organized as a top-down process. It typically involves an internal strategy team or external consulting firm that performs a thorough analysis of the market, including the partner ecosystem, and the potential impact of the IoT on the company's and even the industry's value chain.

Open idea generation typically produces more disruptive ideas. Companies should therefore have multiple channels in place to gather these ideas—channels such as employees, customers, and even developers.

Example: Bosch Web 3.0 Platform

Bosch has implemented a web-based ideation platform called "Web 3.0 Platform," that allows Bosch employees (or distinct communities) to input and vote for ideas. Quick Scan is an input and filter method (evaluating market, revenue, and feasibility) that provides an initial rating of the idea when it is first input. The core team (employees of Bosch Corporate and business units) conducts dedicated workshops with subject matter experts to assess the ideas in more detail. Usually, the Osterwalder canvas is used to draft the business model for the selected ideas. Having passed another quality gate, projects are set up. For more details on this process, see "Business Model Development" on page 189.

So far, there are more than 600 ideas related to connected vehicles in the database (collected within a timeframe of 18 months), and the first concrete project launches, such as "360 degree parking," for example. We asked Bosch representatives responsible for the Web 3.0 Platform about their experiences with the platform. Peter Busch, Senior Expert at Bosch Corporate Research, spoke about the challenges facing project teams when the company's business plan has already become obsolete by the time an idea has reached a certain quality gate. The "window of opportunity" for IoT ideas cannot be aligned with company business plans defined in earlier years. Because Internet-based product lifecycles (including development phase) are much shorter than those applicable for traditional products in the mobility area, this alignment issue becomes even more challenging. On the one hand, there is huge pressure to produce IoT ideas quickly, while on the other hand, large companies especially have a very lengthy planning and development phase. He added that there are further IoT-specific aspects causing issues: the IoT opens up a transversal context, touching on several domains; something that contradicts the vertical focus of Bosch business units. "Since IoT ideas are often relating to multiple business units, it is difficult to get all right people on board," explains Sven Kappel, Senior Expert for Embedded Software & Connected Services at Bosch. A key factor in the success of the project is to identify the business units' common interests in order to align their involvement, in spite of their differing strategies.

Another issue identified by Sven relates to the fact that the organization does not always have the capacity to identify ideas and develop them in a timely manner. It therefore requires new ways of finding resources, such as open source communities, or the Bosch Startup Platform (BOSP), the company's own business incubator established in 2014.

Employee Incentives

Another important point to consider is the question of how you want to encourage continuous innovation among your employees, with the aim of improving the company's processes and coming up with new solutions.

There are good reasons to involve employees in the innovation process: They might be closer to end users and the customers they serve, accumulating more knowledge of their needs. Furthermore, they usually represent multiple functions, ranks, and locations, reducing the risk of "silo mentality."

There are established programs offering incentives to employees at large organizations. The Siemens 3i Program (the 3 i's stand for "Ideas, Impulses, and Initiatives," the name given to a system for submitting suggestions established in 1997) is such an example: employees can submit their ideas for new services or process improvements and receive monetary reward in case of success, such as, for example, a reward of 10% of the annual cost savings. In Germany, more than 100,000 ideas are brought to life per year within the 3i Program [SI1].

According to Peter Fürst, Managing Partner at five i's innovation consulting GmbH, money is definitely not the only incentive and should be handled with care. Especially for new product and new business ideas, appreciation and visibility of ideas and accomplishments support motivation.

Peter Fürst believes that it is not only the submitter of an idea who should benefit from an incentive- or appreciation-based system: many ideas grow from the impetus of more than one person, so the achievements of all these creators of an idea should be honored. Otherwise people will cease discussing their ideas, fearing the other person might steal the idea and submit it first. Within such a climate, creativity is deadened rather than supported.

One possible way of addressing this could be to establish an "innovators club" that offers its members attractive benefits in terms of continuing education and social networking, such as giving them the opportunity to visit interesting trade fairs and conferences, for example.

IDEA REFINEMENT

Many good ideas do not look too pretty when first conceived. They need care to grow and mature before they can really convince possible stakeholders. Fortunately, there is no shortage of ideation methodologies that offer support for idea refinement. At this point, we would like to highlight two approaches that we found helpful.

The first approach is the St. Gallen Business Model Navigator™ [BM1]. The University of St. Gallen (USG) has done extensive research into different types of business models and the reasons why they are successful. Based on an analysis of more than 250 business models, USG has identified a set of repetitive business model patterns that can be applied to construct new business models. The USG now offers a set of cards detailing the different business model patterns that can be used to refine new business ideas, offered during regular workshops held by the university. This, in combination with the research USG has done on IoT-specific business models, is now a powerful tool for creating and refining IoT business models.

Another interesting tool for idea refinement is the Innovation Project Canvas developed by five i's innovation management GmbH [IPi]. The Innovation Project Canvas is an extension of the original Osterwalder Business Model Canvas and has already been proven to be applicable for IoT concepts, such as in the field of smart home appliances, for example. Figure 7-3 provides an overview.

What is particularly useful about the Innovation Project Canvas is that it works in three phases. In the first, the interdisciplinary team focuses on possible customer groups, and on developing a compelling value proposition. The team refines the idea until convinced that it can offer significant benefit to the target group(s). In the second phase, the team discusses possible solutions that can deliver the value proposition and business model. Again, the result of this phase is revised and further improved.

Finally, in the third phase, an Agile development strategy is planned. The team identifies the most critical unknowns, or risks, and focuses on addressing these in the next phases of development.

The Innovation Project Canvas brings together all of the key members of a future project team in order to promote a common understanding of the project's aims and content. The unified development of an attractive value proposition with a profitable business model quickly reveals the true potential of an idea, wins over enthused customers, and increases the commitment of the individual team members.

The output of the idea-refinement phase, the detailed idea sketch, can be used for presentations at the next quality gate level. After approval, it can be used to develop the business model.

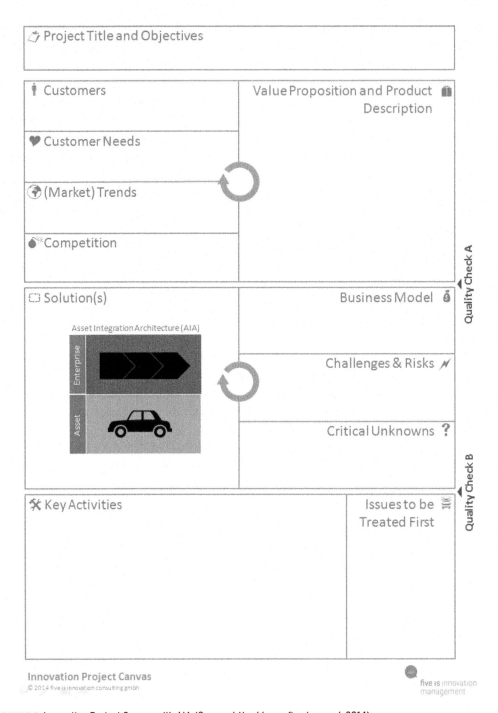

FIGURE 7-3. Innovation Project Canvas with AIA (Source: http://www.five-is.com/, 2014)

OPPORTUNITY QUALIFICATION

At Bosch, the QuickScan method is used to qualify and select opportunities. Silke Vogel, Strategic Marketing Manager at Bosch Corporate, describes this method as follows:

> *The QuickScan method has been developed by the Web 3.0 core team members as means of quickly identifying promising business ideas leading to "the pot of gold." The method focuses on three main criteria that are key in our view to creating success stories: market attractiveness, technological feasibility, and profitability. For all three main criteria, a specific set of subcriteria have been identified using five-point scales and detailed descriptions. In this way, all core team members evaluate the business ideas bilaterally, based on a common understanding, making the final scores of each business idea comparable to one other.*

IoT Opportunity Management

Usually, after an idea has passed the first quality gate, a small team is assembled to further refine and validate the idea, with the goal of creating a concrete business case document that can attract funding. Typically, a small team works on an IoT business model for a couple of weeks or even months, before it is presented to the investment committee to decide on. If all IoT initiatives follow a similar IoT business model approach, it makes it easier to compare and prioritize the different proposals.

At Bosch, the project teams developing IoT business models include employees with multiple competencies, such as domain experts, business model coaches, and marketing consultants. Having both this organizational embedding, and a leader who is passionate about the idea from the start, is crucial. Another success factor is the structure of "podular" organizations. Silke Vogel explains what this means:

> *Highly motivated and energized team members join autonomous units. They have more decisive powers, can act in an "intrapreneurial" way, close to the customer, while also benefiting from the established structures and competencies of a large company. This makes them faster and more efficient.*

BUSINESS MODEL DEVELOPMENT

As established business model canvases don't really address the specifics of IoT business models, a team at Bosch has worked on developing an IoT-specific approach to business model development. Veronika Brandt, manager of this team at Bosch Software Innovations:

> *Addressing IoT-specific aspects, like the intricacy of a partner ecosystem with complex value chains, is extremely important in the IoT. This means that the business model needs a clearly articulated partner value proposition. Another IoT-specific aspect is the use of data derived from connected things, and the services built on top of this information. Because of this, we have developed the IoT Business Model Builder—an extension of the Osterwalder canvas. In the Opportunity*

Management phase, it serves as a guide through the process of defining the components of the business model. Usually, the input is the formulated idea and the output is a business case.

Figure 7-4 outlines the main components of the *IoT Business Model Builder*.

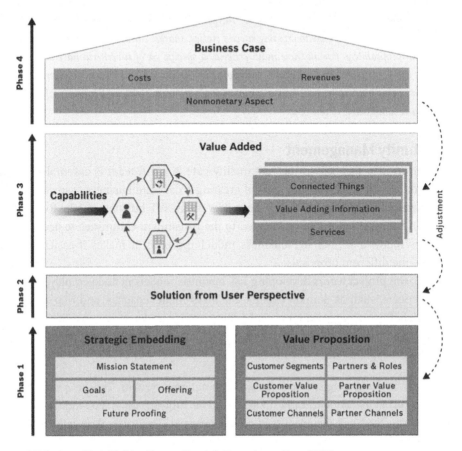

FIGURE 7-4. IoT Business Model Builder (Source: Bosch Software Innovations, 2015)

Just like when building a house, we start at the bottom:

Strategic embedding

This phase sets the foundation of the business model and ensures alignment with the IoT strategy, or the IoT vision of the enterprise. It defines the purpose of the business model in the mission statement and outlines its mid- and short-term goals. Performing "future proofing" should indicate how the business model intends to deal with future challenges. This includes thoughts on how to foster the development of differentiators, such as core competencies (making it harder for the business model to be imitated) and responsiveness to future change. The strategic embedding also contains a brief description of the offering.

Value proposition

To enhance the attractiveness of the offer for customers, the tried-and-trusted approach of segmenting target groups, formulating a value proposition, and defining customer channels (interfaces to the customer at all touch points in the customer journey, from awareness to after sales) can be employed. Because IoT solutions often depend on a strong partner ecosystem, the value proposition has to respect partners in the same way as customers. First, unless partners are not already named (e.g., by existing strategic partnerships or relations), their roles must be defined (e.g., information provider, broker, operator). Then, we need to define "what's in it for them," outlining the partner value proposition for each partner role (or candidate). Finally, the partner channels can be defined, as "other partners," for example (it's even possible for the customer to be defined as a channel).

Customer journey

Describing the end-to-end solution from the customer's point of view helps to emphasize the features of the offering that the customer finds relevant. Here, it is relevant to focus on the actual user/consumer of the offering, irrespective if this is your customer or the customer's customer (in B2B2C solutions). Defining the customer journey has another positive side-effect: it makes sure all relevant channels to the customer have been identified, and these serve as customer touchpoints at every stage of the journey, from awareness to after sales.

Value added

Once the solution has been defined, the value added can be illustrated. Core element of the value added is the stakeholder network, usually illustrated in a flowchart that visualizes relevant parties (own enterprise, partners, customers) as nodes, and value and service streams between these nodes. Constituting elements of the network are the capabilities of the parties: they are a mix of technology, resources, and know-how they can bring in to support the solution. The capability assessment helps define which nodes are best suited to deliver certain services. Once the network has been defined, it should be captured for each node what connected things this node is managing, which value-adding information it delivers (or derives from connected things), and which services it delivers.

Business case

Once the value added has been defined, it is easy to calculate the business case: the most cost-relevant aspects are indicated in the value-added phase and the estimated revenue should be taken from the customer and partner value proposition. A relevant and fair approach is to calculate the total costs of ownership (TCO) for the solution across all parties involved in the network, and to then define the return model by allocating the returns among the stakeholders in a fair manner. This requires cost transparency across all parties involved, once again underlining the importance of trust and strategic partnerships in the IoT ecosystem. There are several techniques and templates that can be used for the business case calculation, but we recommend harmonizing one across all IoT initiatives, as this makes the business models easier to compare.

Strategic impact and subsequent business models

The chimneys of the house in our diagram indicate two nonmonetary effects of a business model that should be looked at in conjunction with the business case. For example, if the business case does not look promising, but the company needs to implement the business model in order to enter a new market, or to access a new technology, these strategic aspects have to be documented. The second chimney, "subsequent business models," is very specific to the IoT: when defining the business model and capturing all the data associated with connected devices, it is very common that the teams come up with interesting new ideas on how to leverage the data (e.g., by combining them to new value-adding information) and create new services. Some ideas are not leveraged within the same business model, but rather developed in separate business models. However, they need to refer to the business model that they are built upon.

Partner Ecosystem

The following advice on IoT partner ecosystem development comes from Anuj Jain, Director Partner Management by Bosch Software Innovations.

The IoT value chain is long and wide, encompassing physical assets, operational services, and digital services. Key considerations for IoT initiatives are:

- What are the elements of the value chain that one can realistically deliver given the current capabilities?
- How much of the control does one require on the IoT value chain ecosystem?

Practically, it is neither possible, nor reasonable, for any single player to specialize in all the aspects of the IoT value chain. For IoT initiatives, the right strategy is a partner ecosystem with a shared vision, passion, and objective. This allows ready access to specialist know-how and expertise at reasonable costs—an essential factor in the success of IoT projects. A well-crafted partner ecosystem accelerates the time to market, improves return on investment (ROI) for each stakeholder, and enhances the customer experience. It also assures customers that their investment will have continued support and innovation across the entire value chain.

Historically, only large, established behemoths like Daimler, Airbus, Microsoft, and IBM worked on building a partner ecosystem. In those cases, the "behemoth" was at the center of the ecosystem, typically wielding enormous influence and often defining the character of the ecosystem. IoT is popularizing an ecosystem of a value-adding network of partners and collaborative organizations that leads to competitive advantage. Both large companies and smaller players are successfully working on more diffused, less centralized ecosystems that arise organically and that lead to more equal and collaborative partners.

Let's look at some popular examples of successful ecosystems:

- Top of the mind is the example of Apple and the music industry. The music industry owned assets (music rights). Steve Jobs spotted the opportunity to provide a legal, affordable, and easy way to provide music to fans. Apple created a platform, and operated it well (operations services and digital services). Apple succeeded and controlled the ecosystem.

- An exciting example is DriveNow. BMW manufactures great cars (physical assets). Sixt has extensive experience and competency in fleet operations and customer management (operational services). A concept to offer the cars on a more flexible basis was generated. Both organizations joined hands to develop a platform—DriveNow (digital services) to offer an innovative car-sharing service. Both partners are working at an eye level and significantly contributing to the partnership.

- Another interesting ecosystem battle being played out at the moment concerns car infotainment. This is high-cost, high-margin equipment, traditionally controlled by OEMs. It allows a direct link to the customers that OEMs don't want to lose. It's about challenge and opportunity. Google and Apple enter with their connected services, disturbing the balance. Alignments are shaping up and the final stable ecosystem is yet to be established.

Customers are now looking for end-to-end solutions, not a collection of building blocks that they have to stick together. Customers expect open standards and interoperability. Customers require products and solutions that evolve with their operational needs. Currently we are just scratching the surface when it comes to possible uses of IoT technologies. It is expected that IoT solutions will continue to expand both horizontally and vertically to deliver even more value to the end customer. A partner ecosystem provides customers with access to a deep well of industry-specific knowledge and industry applications to address increasingly complex problems.

We encountered this situation recently, while working on a project to enhance digital and operational services for handheld industrial power tools (physical assets). Options were to keep this closed or confined, or to make it open standard and allow integration of any handheld power tools from any manufacturers. We opted for the latter and opened the platform further by successfully proposing to the Industrial Internet Consortium to make this a testbed for handheld industrial power tools. Bosch established an ecosystem together with Tech Mahindra, Cisco, Mongo DB, and Dassault Systems to bring the best of competencies to the overall solution.

The critical part of the ecosystem development journey is to identify the right partners. Such an ecosystem may work best if it's based on revenue share vis-à-vis subcontractors. This is easier said than done, as each stakeholder carries a different perception of its contribution to the ecosystem. Mutual trust in ecosystem partners is very important. The ability to collaborate at the customer level (the most sacred thing in the business world) is a sign of a most valued partnership. The trust required for a joint go-to-market is significant as it not only demonstrates belief in each other's products and expertise, but also that both parties trust the other to work toward a mutually beneficial outcome.

To return to our "clash of two worlds" discussion (which you'll recall from Chapter 1), it's important to identify what camp you belong to: the manufacturing camp or the Internet camp. How does this translate realistically into delivery capabilities and market access? Should we focus on core capabilities and allow organic development of an ecosystem? Or aim to play a significant (perhaps controlling) role in shaping the ecosystem? Where should we start here? Should we:

- Define precise roles?
- Establish a legal basis or a strategic partnership agreement?
- Jointly develop new products?
- Initiate joint marketing activities (press releases, thought leadership events, webinars, etc.)?

The IoT is still in its initial phase, it requires upfront investment, and cannot deliver immediate returns (in the next quarters or so), but instead lays the foundation for good long-term returns. For the most part, middle management (with short-term number orientation) find it difficult to manage this mismatch in expectations. Further, IoT project spans multiple verticals and horizontals. There is still lack of clarity about the group best suited to lead such initiatives, and many teams and individuals start politicking. Such partnerships require a significant involvement and commitment from the C level (and sometimes the board) in order to manage these complexities and provide direction.

Organizations don't have enough time or money to waste on signing a bunch of agreements that just say "I love you; you love me." Successful ecosystems involve high levels of trust, matching communication styles, and complementary skills. Extreme prudence is required for establishing such ecosystems.

Developing the IoT Business Case

While it is important to understand all of the strategic aspects of the business model, many senior executives pay particular attention to the quantitative perspective—that is, the concrete business case (Figure 7-5).

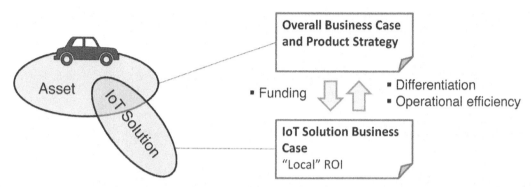

FIGURE 7-5. Business case context

Because business cases are always forward-looking, some managers take a cynical view of employees performing Excel-based exercises. However, most managers agree that these exercises are a good way to force the team to really think every aspect of the business model through in detail. Many budget discussions have been decided based not on the quality of the detailed business case calculation, but simply on the single number presented by the team as the result of this calculation. In this context, it is particularly important to understand the scope of the business case that is developed. Recall from Chapter 1 our differentiation between the asset and IoT solution: it is absolutely critical to understand and communicate whether or not the business case relates to the overall asset or to the IoT solution only. Take the eCall example that we have used numerous times already: it is important to understand whether you are calculating a business case that says how much money you can make on the eCall service alone, or whether you are calculating how many more (or fewer) cars you will sell by being able to offer (or not offer) an eCall service. Keep in mind that the ROI of the "local IoT" solution will not always be positive. In many cases, the additional funding will be the "cost to compete" from the asset's perspective.

Let's start by taking a more detailed look at the local ROI of an IoT solution. Figure 7-6 provides an overview of a generic IoT business case model. This model is based on the simple assumption that every IoT solution consists of a combination of asset enhancements (e.g., the on-asset hardware) and services that are implemented by leveraging the new connectivity to the asset. This service can be a fully automated IT service, or a human-operated service like a call center service (or both). So naturally, asset enhancement and service show up both on the cost and on the revenue side. On the cost side, we usually have to differentiate between capital expenditure (CAPEX) and operating expenditure (OPEX), while on the revenue side, we differentiate between up-front revenues (e.g., through hardware sales or a service sign-up fee) and recurring revenues (e.g., service subscriptions). Taking all of this together helps to calculate the "local" IoT solution ROI. It is really not rocket science, but in our experience it can be quite helpful when selling an IoT business case to visualize its key elements in a way similar to Figure 7-6.

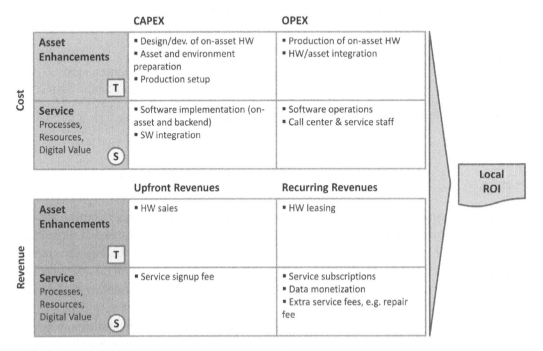

FIGURE 7-6. Local IoT solution ROI

The next perspective is the overall business case, as shown in Figure 7-7. Again, this has to look at both asset enhancements and services. However, in this perspective we can also look at cost savings and operational efficiency on the one side, and differentiation and strategic benefits on the other.

In some cases, it will be possible to quantify this; in other cases, the case will have to be argued qualitatively. In either case, it is usually very useful to present these different aspects of the overall business case in a structured manner.

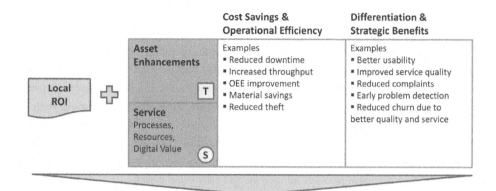

	Cost Savings & Operational Efficiency	Differentiation & Strategic Benefits
Asset Enhancements	Examples • Reduced downtime • Increased throughput • OEE improvement • Material savings • Reduced theft	Examples • Better usability • Improved service quality • Reduced complaints • Early problem detection • Reduced churn due to better quality and service
Service Processes, Resources, Digital Value		

Local ROI ➕

Contribution to overall business case

FIGURE 7-7. Overall IoT business case

Business Case Challenges

Of course there are many challenges in the development of an IoT business case that are not obvious at first glance. Based on his experience, Felix Wortmann from the University of St. Gallen points out two major IoT business case challenges:

> First of all, fixed costs for IoT hardware development should not be underestimated. While this is certainly not new to the traditional hardware community, people with a software background often think that new development methodologies and the latest advances in the context of Arduino and Raspberry Pi have fundamentally changed the laws and economics of hardware development. And yes, today first prototypes can often be realized on low budget hardware, for example, Arduino sets are available for less than $50. However, creating reliable hardware that can actually be deployed in the field still has very high associated costs. It is not only a question of initial design and proto-typing. The investments required for testing and certification, and the cost for actually integrating IoT capabilities into existing hardware have to be taken into account as well. This means that from the very beginning, significant fixed costs that occur even before first revenue can be generated have to be considered. For this reason, there are significant risks involved. In addition, business models often rely on economies of scale to cope with fix costs and facilitate acceptable unit costs. To illustrate these thoughts, let's take the example of a business case for a security solution for elec-tronic bicycles. The initial assumption was that a sensor could simply be attached externally to the bicycle. However, digging deeper into the overall business case, it turned out that in order to provide a compelling use case, and also to achieve acceptable unit costs, this sensor has to be designed directly into the power train of the bike. This dramatically increases the initial investment and fun-damentally affects the overall business case.

Secondly, IoT-enabled connected products require a backend infrastructure that generates operat-ing costs on an ongoing basis. This is a fundamental difference compared to nonconnected products that do not generate costs after they have been sold. Thus, the operating costs of connected products have to be tackled. Either, they are calculated into the one-time sales price, or ongoing payments are introduced. However, pay-per-use or subscription-based models usually face severe customer acceptance challenges, specifically if hardware comes into play. Especially in the consumer context, people are often not willing to pay money for a physical object, connected or not, on an ongoing basis. This means that operating costs have to be calculated into the sales price. As a kind of risk insurance, companies use a variety of tactics, planned obsolescence, for example. Also, companies try to ensure that IoT-based products can still operate even if the provider shuts down its central infrastructure. Take, for example, the Philips Hue. This connected light bulb is designed to also work on the basis of a controlling local gateway, without the Philips backend. This effectively gives Philips the opportunity for a "graceful" exit strategy: If it would should down its own backend serv-ices, the customer has less functionality but the product still works.

These are just some examples for the complexity of IoT business cases, yet they illustrate why a structured process for their development can be helpful, and why they also take time to reach a certain level of maturity.

IMPACT AND RISK ANALYSIS

Business models, and especially business cases, deal with future value streams, so they are subject to uncertainty. It is important to highlight the degree of uncertainty within the busi-ness model to increase transparency for decision makers, and in order to deduce the tasks necessary to address these uncertain factors (e.g., if certain cost assumptions are very vague, it will be helpful to request proposals in the next step of the process to validate these estimations).

A helpful tool for reducing risk is scenario planning. Based on defined parameters (e.g., target group, time frame, etc., as assumed for the business model), different future scenarios are sketched out. This can be done based on trends or cause-and-effect relationships. In the next step, a plan has to be worked out to determine how the business model can best respond to the future scenario. It is important to explore those elements of the business model that generate impact and value in the context of a strategy. By acting out different future opportunities, weak points and strong elements can be revealed, which allows for the develop-ment of a future-proof business model.

Putting It All Together: The Business Plan

Having developed the business model, which can be based on the IoT Business Model Builder, the team needs to put together an actionable business plan. Of course, this will reuse many of the elements in the business model, but will have a stronger focus on execution planning. Sequoia Capital, one of the most respected venture capital firms in Silicon Valley, recommends the following approach for startups [SC1]:

Purpose

Define the business in a single, declarative sentence.

Problem

Describe the customer's pain, and how he is coping with it today.

Solution

Provide use cases to demonstrate how your solution addresses the customer's problem. Describe where the product physically sits.

Why now

Describe the historical evolution of your solution category. Describe factors that enable disruption today.

Market size

Describe the total available market and the segment targeted by your solution based on a precise customer profile.

Competition

Describe key competitors and compare competitive advantages.

Solution

Describe form factor, functionality features, architecture and development roadmap, as well as key intellectual property.

Business model

Revenue and pricing models, average account size and/or lifetime value, sales and distribution model, and description of current customer pipeline (if any).

Team

Proposed organizational and management structure for the new business.

Financials

Forward-looking (e.g., three years) profit and loss plan, balance sheet and cash flow plan, and funding requirements.

We have made some small changes to the original list from Sequoia Capital to ensure it fits the needs of an internal project. But in general, it seems to us like a good idea to follow the guidance of the "Internet camp" and apply it to an internal project proposal. Many companies will already have a standard template for project proposals that should at least be cross-checked with this structure.

OPPORTUNITY SELECTION

For the steering committee that will be presented with the business plans for the various IoT investment opportunities, the key question is: How should these different opportunities be evaluated and prioritized? In a corporate environment, there will always be a certain amount of political behind-the-scenes influencing, but it can be really helpful to map out the different opportunities and make them comparable, ideally on a single chart. It is important that the evaluation criteria be aligned with the overall IoT strategy, as defined at the beginning of this chapter.

In the light of our previous discussion on the "local" business case versus the contribution of the new IoT solution to the overall competitiveness of the related asset, it would seem natural to pick these two perspectives as the key dimensions for an IoT portfolio evaluation chart, (Figure 7-8). Assuming that one would want to strike a good balance between these two dimensions, the chart should also define an "IoT investment corridor" that defines the area within which the investments should ideally be located. While the "ROI over a defined time period" (or some other economic measure, like economic value added, EVA) is usually easily quantifiable, the overall strategic contribution is usually harder to quantify.

Also, this needs to incorporate the overall value of the particular asset class to the company. A small strategic increase in value for the main asset that contributes 50% of the company's revenues easily outweighs a huge strategic increase in value for a niche asset with low overall revenue contribution. Another important factor that is not included in this approach is market pressure—in other words, how critical is the timing of this investment?

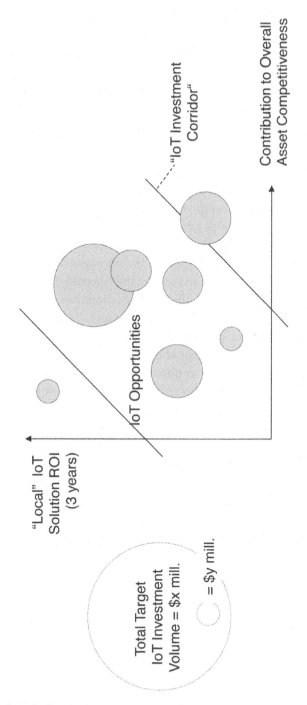

FIGURE 7-8. IoT opportunity evaluation chart

It will always be difficult to create hard, reliable quantifications of these factors. Also, one should not underestimate the importance of the political power-plays and other factors that typically go along with corporate decision processes. However, the approach described here should help at least to create a certain level of transparency and objectification of the IoT investment decision process. And again, the end result might not be called "IoT investment evaluation chart" but something more vertically specific, like "Connected vehicle opportunity evaluation chart," or some such. But the basic principles should apply.

Project Initiation

What usually happens in parallel to the development of the detailed business plan is an evaluation of the ideal organizational setup and execution strategy. In addition to the important time-to-market factor, one has to look critically at internal execution capabilities (Figure 7-9). Again, this comes back to the "machine camp" versus "Internet camp" discussion from Chapter 1. Which direction are we coming at this from? And where do we need to end up? Will we be able to develop the required culture and capabilities internally?

Based on these kinds of questions, the steering committee will have to make a decision about the best way of managing each IoT opportunity. Typical options include internal projects, external acquisitions, or spin-offs. Also quite common is a mixture of these—that is, to set up an entity that consists in one part of people with strong roots in the larger enterprise, and another part of people that came in through acquisitions. Also, the term "acqui-hiring" has become popular recently, describing a strategy of acquiring companies, less for their products and customer base than for their team and talent.

Careful attention must be paid to organizational setup, especially for IoT opportunities that are developed by leveraging existing internal organization. In particular, the interfaces and relationships between the solution team and the existing asset organization are essential.

At Bosch, there are more and more cases where "podular" organizations are set up on the business unit level as well. "It is easier, if there is already a home port for the ideas within the organization," says Ms. Silke Vogel. "This way, the employees, who have worked on the idea refinement and business model development, can drive the projects in the execution phase as well."

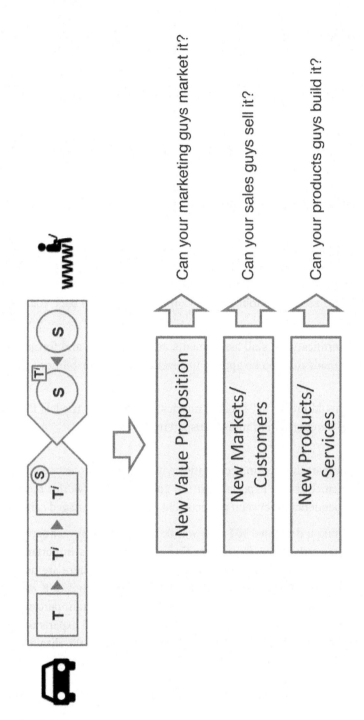

FIGURE 7-9. Organizational challenges

IOT CENTER OF EXCELLENCE

If the company sees IoT as a long-term transformation, then setting up an IoT Center of Excellence (CoE) should be considered to guide and expedite this transformation. Based on the description of the typical functions of a CoE [AE1], an IoT CoE could look as follows:

Support

An IoT CoE should support business lines to realize IoT opportunities through the provision of IoT consulting services. These services can include IoT business case creation, IoT project setup, and IoT project execution coaching. As authors of this book, we are slightly biased, but we would naturally recommend the Ignite | IoT Methodology as one possible foundation for such services.

Guidance

An IoT CoE should help to define the necessary standards, methodologies, tools, and knowledge repositories. Some of these will be highly vertical-specific. However, best practices for setting up things like a remote communication infrastructure for mobile assets could be standardized (see "Mobile M2M Communication" on page 302 for examples).

Shared learning

Training and certifications, skill assessments, team building, and formalized roles are all established methods that can be applied to developing IoT capabilities.

Measurements

An IoT CoE should create IoT-specific metrics and maturity models that help make the progress of the transformation more transparent.

Governance

They should support the steering committee with the cross-project coordination and other detailed governance tasks. Especially in the connected IoT world, there will always be many cross-dependencies between projects that need to be managed carefully.

Naturally, running a dedicated IoT CoE will be a significant investment, and many companies report mixed results from their other CoE initiatives. It is important that the CoE is seen by the projects as value-adding, and not as a disturbance. There are usually two options for the setting up of the CoE: a dedicated CoE resource, or a virtual CoE with members who are embedded in operational teams but are allowed to spend a certain percentage of their time in supporting the CoE. The latter has the advantage that the CoE experts are coming from a hands-on project background with a lot of experience, but has the disadvantage that these highly respected experts are often drowned in project work and can't really fulfill their part-time CoE role as much as needed.

IOT PLATFORM

Finally, enterprises embarking on the IoT journey should consider investing in the setup and operation of an IoT platform that can be shared by the different IoT projects. Such a platform could be comprised of the following:

- Remote asset connectivity—for example, based on the M2M platform of a telecommunications carrier or a mobile virtual network operator (MVNO; see "M2M/IoT Communication Services" on page 298)

- IoT application development and runtime (see "Platforms and Enablement" on page 371)

- IoT data management infrastructure (see "[Big] Data and Process Management" on page 320)

- IoT security infrastructure—for example, central identity and certificate management (see "Security" on page 363)

- Standards—for example, for communication protocols and the like

- Asset interface repository—for example, a central wiki to describe the functional and technical interfaces of different device and asset types that play an important role in the organization

Theoretically, providing such an IoT platform should be seen as a blessing by everybody needing to get a project off the ground quickly. However, we should definitely be aware of the inherent risks of such a central platform approach. One of these is that the platform might actually not work (e.g., because it is over-architected and not field-tested). Or it might not be ready on time. Or it might be inefficient and too difficult to operate. These are just some of the real risks involved in developing a central platform. On the other hand, if this needs to be done for each individual project, there is also a real risk that the project team won't get it right half the time. So the sensible thing to do would be to observe those initial projects that seem to be developing the best platform approach, and then identify the parts of these projects that can be generalized. So it really is a question of maturity and timing.

SUMMARY AND CONCLUSIONS

As we explained at the start, some of the processes and methods described here are very generic and need to be adapted to the vertical needs and specific circumstances of the individual organization. For some companies, the elaborate way of developing a detailed business model as described here may seem like overkill. However, we have seen many examples where such business model development took significant time and many iterations—especially for solutions that need to be embedded into existing, large-scale, complex ecosystems.

Particular attention needs to be paid to the organizational structure of the project. IoT projects almost always require multiskilled and multicultural teams. Aligning the "machine camp" with the "Internet camp" is a challenging task. One possible approach is described as follows by Joe Drumgoole, Director at MongoDB, Inc.:

> *The Internet of Things provides a framework for both these communities to interact. If [large players] can create a bridge between those worlds, they will be successful, but I think success will come in the context of early wins with a small number of partners. Lead with the Internet people and use them as a foil to provoke the manufacturing people into action.*

Another important thing to consider is that business plans for early-stage startups or projects rarely survive the first year without major modifications. So supporting an Agile (this does not mean unstructured or uncontrolled!) development approach will be a key success factor for most IoT initiatives. We will address this in more detail in the next chapter, the Ignite | IoT Solution Delivery methodology. This methodology is designed to support the next phase for those IoT projects that have managed to come through the strategy selection process with sufficient funding to start implementing their ideas and vision.

CHAPTER 8

Ignite | IoT Solution Delivery

Ignite | IoT Solution Delivery is the part of the Ignite | IoT Methodology aimed at IoT product managers, project managers, solution architects, and other IoT stakeholders. The goal is to make IoT best practice available in the form of a technology-independent, reusable, open source methodology that supports IoT solution design as well as IoT project setup and management by providing project templates, checklists, and solution architecture blueprints.

A key characteristic of IoT projects is that they tend to combine multiple, very different disciplines within a single project that incorporates product design and manufacturing, embedded hardware and software, local and remote communication, enterprise application development and integration, cross-domain security, and more. (Figure 8-1).

Take, for example, the eCall solution presented in Part I. From an asset perspective, this is only a tiny part of the hugely complex bill of material (BOM) of a modern car. Nevertheless, from the eCall project manager's perspective, it is important that they manage the asset interface and ensure that on-asset components are properly integrated, which means finding the right place to install the eCall telematics control unit (TCU) in the car, incorporating the TCU into both the BOM and the manufacturing process, and so on. The TCU and its software represent a traditional embedded project, with very specific skills required for development and testing. Integrating the solution with a mobile carrier network that covers all required regions and then managing this carrier integration is more like a small telecommunications project, requiring a different skill set. Finally, implementing the backend software to enable the call center to manage incoming calls, route them to an agent with the appropriate skills, and forward them to the public-safety answering point (PSAP) is more reminiscent of a traditional enterprise software project. As we can see, even a project of moderate complexity like the eCall project requires the combination of multiple skills.

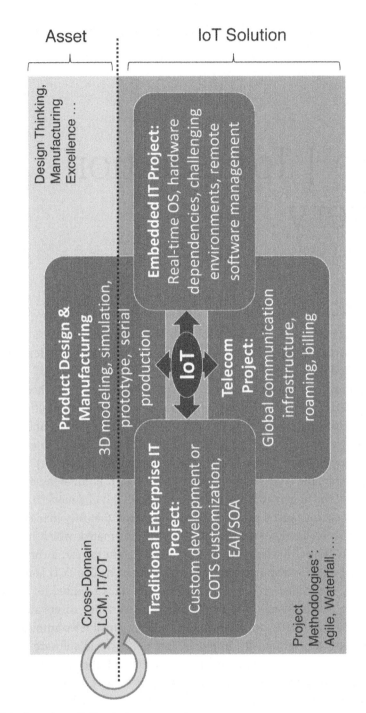

FIGURE 8-1. Multiple dimensions of IoT project management

At present, there are only a limited number of experts available with the required level of in-depth experience in this kind of multidisciplinary project management—for example, those who have successfully managed telematics and M2M projects and are now starting to apply these skills to IoT projects. However, in order for the IoT to gain more widespread acceptance, it will be necessary to make this experience available to a broader audience. This is the goal of Ignite | IoT Solution Delivery. We aim to provide a high-level methodology that integrates all the various skills and disciplines required for IoT projects, and then collaborate with experts from the different disciplines to record their experiences and best practices and incorporate them into the methodology.

Ignite | IoT Solution Delivery (Figure 8-2) can be broken down as follows:

IoT Solution Lifecycle
This perspective focuses on planning, building, and running IoT solutions.

IoT Building Blocks
This perspective contains reusable artifacts from successful projects, in the form of IoT Project Dimensions, IoT Architecture Blueprints, and IoT Technology Profiles.

IoT Project DB
This is a database of reference projects that have been analyzed in order to derive best practices for the IoT Solution Lifecycle and Building Blocks.

The IoT Solution Lifecycle (Plan/Build/Run) contains the following elements:

Initial Project Design
This design blueprint builds on the elements defined as part of the generic IoT Building Blocks, including project self-assessment using IoT Project Dimensions, solution architecture using IoT Architecture Blueprints, and technology selection using IoT Technology Profiles.

Project workstreams and project organization
This blueprint defines the top-level organization and workstreams typically found in an IoT solution project. A checklist for each workstream is provided, along with a list of common dependencies between the workstreams.

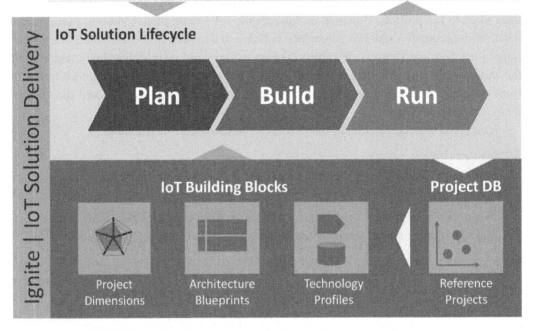

FIGURE 8-2. Ignite | IoT Solution Delivery (Source: www.enterprise-iot.org)

The IoT Building Blocks consist of the following elements:

Project Dimensions

This is a precursor of formal project requirements. Project dimensions are used for project self-assessment, project comparisons, architecture and technology selection, and so on.

Architecture Blueprints

Building on existing architecture blueprints (such as service-oriented architecture, or SOA), these add new architectural perspectives necessary for IoT projects and provide a superstructure for integrating the various architectural perspectives that are required.

Technology Profiles

These profiles identify and describe the most important technologies usually required for IoT projects. This leverages IoT architecture perspectives to describe where these different technologies fit into the overall IoT architecture. Finally, this attempts to link back to the project dimensions in order to support the technology selection process.

The remainder of this chapter describes the IoT Solution Lifecycle. Chapter 9 discusses the IoT Building Blocks, with a focus on Technology Profiles.

IoT Solution Lifecycle: Plan/Build/Run

Planning, building, and running an IoT solution will, of course, be different from solution to solution. However, we believe that there are some commonalities between IoT solutions that allow us to make certain assumptions in terms of what a generic, methodological approach should look like. We will first discuss some of these assumptions before discussing our approach in detail.

ASSUMPTIONS

Ignite does not make any assumptions about the general project management approach taken (e.g., Agile or Waterfall). Of course an Agile approach will usually better fit the innovative and often explorative nature of many IoT projects. However, as we will discuss in more detail later, there can be situations that will not allow a fully Agile approach, such as when it comes to custom hardware development or fixed-price development contracts. Also, there are currently different competing approaches for scaling Agile to support multiple or large teams, which usually is a key prerequisite for IoT. Consequently, Ignite is limiting the assumptions that it is making about the structure of IoT projects. The main assumption that Ignite makes is that most IoT projects will follow a basic Plan/Build/Run pattern (Figure 8-3). This is, of course, a strong simplification, but it helps with the discussion in the following chapters. The Plan/Build/Run phases for an IoT project are described as follows:

Plan

> The project planning phase starts after the funding decision (see Ignite | IoT Strategy Execution). Usually, a small but dedicated team takes the ideas and requirements from the business planning phase to create an initial project plan, including a solution definition. This could include, for example, a (usually lightweight) RFP document (Request for Proposal), or (in a more Agile environment) the initial set of high-level epics which would have to be broken down to more detailed user stories later in the build phase. During the plan phase, the initial team will also usually be responsible for sourcing (internally or externally) the larger team that will later build the solution.

Build

> The build phase is usually executed by a larger team or teams. Recall that especially in IoT we often have to deal with multiple, multidisciplinary teams. It is important to notice that because of the usually very dynamic nature of IoT projects, the planning continues during the build phase. Especially with an Agile approach, detailed planning will be done for each sprint. In many cases, the higher-level documents created in the planning phase will have to be continually adapted to reflect new or changing requirements, or lessons learned from previous sprints.

Run

Sometime around the Start of Production (SOP) of the IoT solution, the project team is usually disbanded and the solution is handed over to a line organization. In modern organizations, this line organization will set up an integrated DevOps organization that deals with both continued development and operations of the solution. Notice that due to the potentially highly distributed nature of IoT solutions, DevOps for IoT can be more complex than normal DevOps.

Scope and Relationships

Ignite is always assuming that the asset itself is managed in a different organization than the IoT solution. Nevertheless, there are usually strong dependencies between these two organizations.

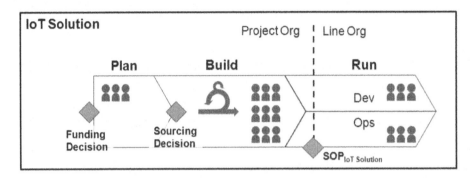

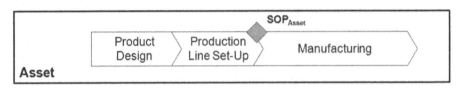

FIGURE 8-3. Plan/Build/Run of IoT solutions

APPROACH TAKEN

Given the need to support different approaches to project management, the Ignite methodology focuses on what we believe is specific to an IoT solution, leaving it to the project manager to combine it with the project management model of choice.

In terms of project structure, the Ignite approach builds on the high-level structure illustrated in Figure 8-4. The first thing we can see is that there is a distinction between the assets themselves and the IoT solution. Design and manufacturing of the assets is not typically within the scope of the IoT-solution project. However, it is essential to recognize that the interface between the organization responsible for the asset and the IoT-solution project is extremely important. This is true in situations where the IoT solution is integrated with the asset after the initial design of the asset ("retrofit"), as well as in situations where the asset is designed from the ground up to support one or more IoT solutions. In either case, the IoT solution is likely to depend on certain "on-asset" hardware and software which define the solution's interface to the backend services.

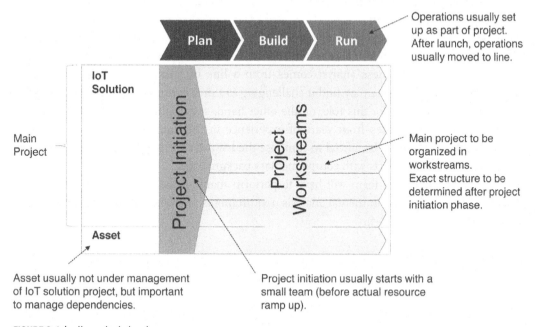

FIGURE 8-4. Ignite project structure

Another key element of the Ignite | IoT Solution Delivery is the assumption that a typical project has an initiation phase and a main implementation phase. The initiation phase starts after the business case has been approved and the organization has given the go-ahead for the project in principle. During this phase, there is usually a relatively small team working on the project (i.e., this is before the ramp-up of resources).

This phase is followed by the main implementation phase. The Ignite approach for this phase is based on a concept that we call "workstreams." This is a top-level structure that applies across the main project. In PMI terms, the workstreams would be the top-level work items in the work breakdown structure (WBS). In our experience, the term "workstream" better reflects the usually highly dynamic nature of IoT project management with all its different stakeholders and dependencies.

IoT Project Initiation

An important aspect of the Ignite | IoT Project Initiation phase is a requirements analysis, which is more in-depth than the analysis performed during the business model creation phase. In comparison, this requirements analysis takes a deeper look at specific user requirements, with the goal of reaching a level of detail that is capable of supporting an initial solution design. The project initiation is usually performed by a small team of subject matter experts. In particular, the team should have a dedicated solution architect (who may not have been as deeply involved in the business model creation phase). In addition, the team should include a business analyst with extensive domain knowledge and a clear vision for the functional aspects of the solution.

If we remember our previous discussion on the "clash of two worlds," it becomes clear that finding suitable business analysts and solution architects is both critical and challenging. For example, if the business analyst comes from a line of business that was traditionally responsible for the asset, he may find it challenging to think in terms of services. If a service-centric person is chosen for this role, on the other hand, she might lack the in-depth domain knowledge that only comes from years of experience in the domain of the asset. In some cases, therefore, it may be beneficial to compose the team for the IoT Project Initiation phase by selecting multiple experts with complementary backgrounds.

The project initiation team will have to perform many of the usual tasks in this phase: stakeholder analysis, environmental analysis, requirements analysis, risk and resource assessment, and so on. (Figure 8-5).

FIGURE 8-5. Project initiation

In the following sections, we will describe which additional IoT-specific aspects will be added to these standard project tasks. The final outcomes of the Ignite | IoT Project Initiation phase are the initial solution design and the project structure, based on the workstream structure described previously.

INITIAL SOLUTION DESIGN

Ignite | IoT Solution Delivery defines a set of key artifacts for the Initial Solution Design, which are shown in Figure 8-6. We differentiate between artifacts that cover analysis, projections and planning, functional design artifacts, and technical design artifacts. Although they may be created in parallel, it often makes sense to group them as described in this section.

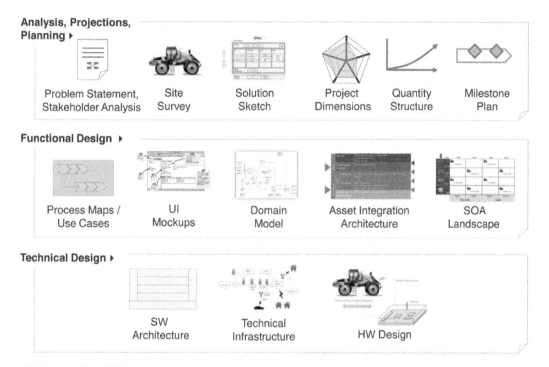

Analysis, Projections, Planning ▶

| Problem Statement, Stakeholder Analysis | Site Survey | Solution Sketch | Project Dimensions | Quantity Structure | Milestone Plan |

Functional Design ▶

| Process Maps / Use Cases | UI Mockups | Domain Model | Asset Integration Architecture | SOA Landscape |

Technical Design ▶

| SW Architecture | Technical Infrastructure | HW Design |

FIGURE 8-6. Initial IoT Solution Design

Some of the artifacts that Ignite | IoT Solution Delivery proposes are not IoT-specific at all, such as the milestone plan. Some artifacts have IoT-specific extensions, such as the proposed quantity structure or the SOA landscape for IoT solutions. And some artifacts have been created specifically for IoT solution design, such as the IoT project dimensions, the IoT Solution Sketch, or the Asset Integration Architecture. In this section of the book, we want to focus more on how a project team can work with these artifacts in the design phase. For this reason, we will only offer examples here and then provide more formal definitions later in "Building Blocks" on page 255.

Specialized design artifacts have a long history in software design. Most notably, the Rational Unified Process (RUP) is based on an exhaustive set of specialized software design artifacts for the different perspectives and phases of a software project. RUP drew some criticism for being too artifact heavy in the past. Agile approaches such as SCRUM often rely on very basic artifacts like user stories, rather than architecture artifacts. From an Agile perspective, "the code is the truth." Ignite | IoT Solution Delivery tries to strike a balance here between these two extremes. In our experience, it can be very helpful to rely on certain standardized architecture and design artifacts to ensure common understanding between the different project stakeholders. In order to ensure this, Ignite | IoT Solution Delivery has to ensure that the artifacts are sufficiently lightweight, yet sufficiently expressive, and that the different artifact types integrate well with one another while minimizing redundancies.

Analysis, Projections, Planning

The first set of Ignite | IoT design artifacts is intended to support analysis, projections, and planning. The initial problem statement or executive summary is often taken from the business model (see Chapter 7). The detailed analysis ideally includes a site survey, which provides further insight into the asset and its environment. The IoT Solution Sketch is a one-page, high-level overview of the proposed solution design. The IoT Project Dimensions support project self-assessment. The quantity structure looks at the planned growth of key entities such as users and assets. Finally, the milestone plan defines the key milestones of the project.

Problem Statement/Executive Summary

As stated before, the problem statement and/or executive summary often comes from the business model phase. Ideally, it contains a one-page description of the problem domain and vision for the IoT solution using language that can be easily understood by business stakeholders. It also provides a simple and intuitive graphical overview of the key solution elements. See Figure 8-7 for an example.

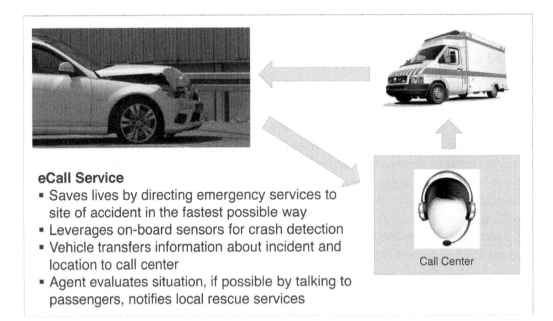

eCall Service
- Saves lives by directing emergency services to site of accident in the fastest possible way
- Leverages on-board sensors for crash detection
- Vehicle transfers information about incident and location to call center
- Agent evaluates situation, if possible by talking to passengers, notifies local rescue services

Call Center

FIGURE 8-7. Executive summary

Stakeholder Analysis

There are many best practice frameworks for stakeholder analysis in a project context (e.g., see *http://stakeholdermap.com/*). Ignite | IoT builds on an IoT-specific framework for stakeholder analysis that was originally devised by Dr. Heinz Derenbach (former CEO of Bosch Software Innovations) and his team. One key lesson learned from this team is that most IoT solutions are made up of four central elements, each with associated stakeholders: the assets and corresponding devices, the related enterprise services, the solution users, and the partners. Figure 8-8 provides an overview of these four key elements of an IoT solution.

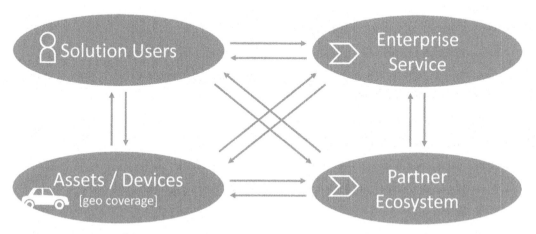

FIGURE 8-8. Four key elements of an IoT solution

In our experience, identifying and defining these four key elements and the interdependencies between them is a very good starting point for analyzing the key aspects and stakeholders of an IoT solution. In certain cases, some of these elements may have already been included in the business model analysis, but generally without examining the interdependencies between them in any great detail.

Site Survey

As part of the IoT Initial Solution Design, we strongly recommend that a site survey is carried out. This would ideally start with a physical visit to associated sites, such as the factory where the assets are manufactured or a site where they are used. To complement this, interviews can be conducted with experts on different aspects of the assets and the sites where they are typically deployed (if applicable).

The site survey document should cover all asset- and site-specific aspects, such as the following:

- Type of asset (e.g., stationary or moving).
- Category of asset, including the industry segment (e.g., manufacturing or CPG).
- Behavior of asset—is it a dumb asset (e.g., a beer keg or pallet) or an intelligent asset (e.g., vending machine, PLC, vehicle)?
- Business operations and asset lifecycle.
- Solution integration (native or retrofit).
- Asset interfaces (ModBus, CAN bus, MDB, serial bus, GPIO, etc.).
- Internet connectivity around asset (e.g., a cellular, Ethernet, or WiFi network).
- GPS options around asset.
- Environmental conditions around asset, including operating temperature or asset location (e.g., in a moving container/vehicle, factory, retail store, outdoors, etc.).
- Power supply requirements and/or sensor installation requirements.

Some of the survey results can later be incorporated into the IoT Project Dimensions, described momentarily.

Solution Sketch

Based on the results of the analysis, Ignite | IoT recommends creating a high-level solution sketch using the format outlined in Figure 8-9. This can often be created during a workshop attended by the key stakeholders, with the outcome captured in a structured format.

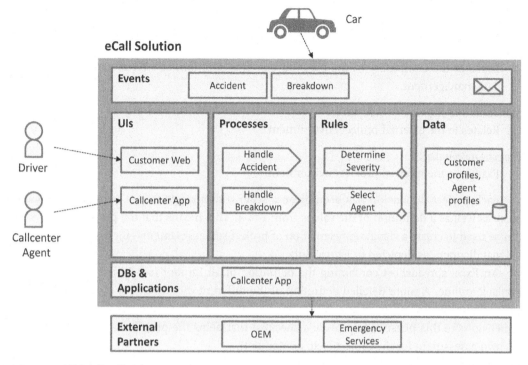

FIGURE 8-9. IoT Solution Sketch

The IoT Solution Sketch covers all four solution elements identified in "Stakeholder Analysis" on page 217 and adds a number of important details. For example, the solution sketch attempts to identify or define the key events (or any other key communications) submitted from the asset to the backend. In addition, it captures key UIs, business processes, rules, and data entities (all in list form). Furthermore, databases and applications are shown, as well as external partners to be integrated.

The solution sketch is more detailed than the executive summary. However, it focuses on key entities only, and does not provide a formal and complete list of these entities. The main purpose of the solution sketch is to start narrowing down the solution scope and create a common basis for communication between business and technical project stakeholders.

Project Dimensions

Ignite | IoT defines a set of IoT Project Dimensions that help to capture all important aspects of an IoT solution. There are currently 5 main dimensions, with a total of approximately 40 subdimensions. The five main dimensions are:

Assets and Devices

Covers aspects like number and value of assets, asset complexity, required on-asset processing power, hardware requirements, and lifecycle management.

Communications and Connectivity
Focuses on technology, bandwidth, and latency for both local and remote communication.

Backend Services
Looks at the complexity of the backend business solution, as well as aspects specific to data management.

Standards and Regulatory Compliance
Relates to the external project environment.

Project Environment
Examines the internal project environment.

Each project dimension has been given a scale with a range from 1 (simple) to 4 (complex), as well as a definition of the values from 1 to 4. This means that the project dimensions can be used to create a visual representation of project self-assessment—for instance, by using a Kiviat diagram, as depicted in Figure 8-10.

An Excel spreadsheet containing the definition of all Ignite | IoT Project Dimensions is available online. A more detailed definition of the different dimensions is also provided later in "Building Blocks" on page 255. As shown in Figure 8-10, the main purpose of the project dimensions in this phase is to provide a checklist that helps the project manager to carry out his own assessment for the project (self-assessment).

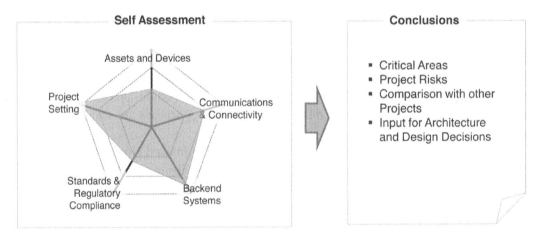

FIGURE 8-10. IoT Project Dimensions

The results can be used to identify critical areas and project risks, as well as input for the solution architecture and design decisions. In addition, the Ignite | IoT team is currently building up a database of various projects that have provided us with the results of their self-assessments. This allows project managers to compare their project with others, and to benefit from the lessons learned.

Quantity Structure

Like every solution design, an IoT project also requires a quantity structure. The quantity structure must be closely aligned with the requirements of the business stakeholders and should show projected growth in key areas (Figure 8-11).

		2015	2016	2017
	# Assets	...	...	...
	# Events	...	...	...
	# Users	...	...	...
	# Processes	...	...	...

FIGURE 8-11. IoT quantity structure

From an IoT point of view, these areas should include the following: number of assets over time, number of events sent from assets to the backend, number of users (total and concurrent), and number of process instances per year (for key processes such as asset activation, incidents, etc.) This information will be of vital importance to the solution architect.

Milestone Plan

Finally, as with normal projects, the Initial Solution Design for an IoT-solution project should include a milestone plan. The milestone plan should ideally be structured around the workstream structure of the project, and also highlight key dependencies from different workstreams, as shown in Figure 8-12. Typical milestones in an IoT project include:

System demo
Often a first important technical milestone, which helps to validate key functional and architectural assumptions. This will often focus on basic on-asset and backend functionality, not including things like security, field-level communication services, and so on.

First integrated release
This release will add field-level communication services and other key cross-functional capabilities, including a first cut of the operation environment.

Minimum viable product (MVP)

The intention is to use the MVP for tests with a small group of early adopters: "The minimum viable product is that version of a new product which allows a team to collect the maximum amount of validated learning about customers with the least effort." In an IoT project, the scope of the MVP is often much harder to define than in a pure software project because of the high overheads of custom hardware development and field communications.

Field tests

The importance of field tests in an IoT project is another key difference from a pure software project. Field tests are mandatory to learn about the behavior of the solution in a realistic environment, including field-level communication, dealing with potential communication failures or communication delays, and so on. Since field tests usually have to be performed with real assets under realistic conditions, they can be more time- and resource-consuming than any pure software test.

Release candidate

In an IoT environment, it is often much more difficult to update individual components after the initial release (because of the distributed nature of IoT solutions, as well as the often high levels of validation requirements). Consequently, a release candidate for an IoT solution usually has higher requirements with respect to functional completeness and quality than a release candidate in a nonregulated, pure-software environment.

Extended field tests

Many IoT projects perform extended field tests which might include thousands of test users over a longer period of time.

Homologation/Validation

Many IoT solutions are deployed in highly regulated industries, such as transportation, energy, and healthcare. Each IoT project has to ensure sufficient planning of time and resources for the required validation processes.

Start of Production (SOP)

The SOP of an IoT solution can often be seen as a "point of no return." Once the hardware production starts and the first customers get online, even minor changes to system components are somewhere between very painful to virtually impossible.

As we can see, milestone plans for IoT projects are very different from nonregulated, pure-software type of projects. This is a challenge for any IoT project manager who is coming from the Internet world.

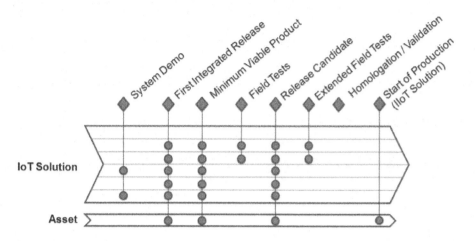

FIGURE 8-12. Example Milestone Plan

Functional Design

The level of detail of the functional design proposed by the Ignite | IoT Methodology in this phase is typical of what would be found in a lightweight response to an RFP (Request for Proposal). This should be sufficient to start the implementation phase of a project, especially if using an Agile approach in which a product backlog is groomed in order to capture and manage detailed requirements. The functional design described here is not intended to meet the more detailed requirements of a fixed-price offer, for example.

Getting Started: Use Cases and UI/HMI Mock-Ups

A good first step toward creating a functional design is to establish a high-level catalog of the most important use cases (strictly speaking, the initial use case catalog should be created as part of the original analysis, but because it is an important design artifact, we have included it here). For an IoT solution, these use cases can often be identified by looking more closely at the asset lifecycle (see "Manufacturer Perspective: Connected Asset Lifecycle Management" on page 3). Each use case definition should follow established best practices for use case design (see "Use Case 2.0: The Guide to Succeeding with Use Cases" (*http://www.ivarjacob son.com/download.ashx?id=1282*)), and provide a high-level description of the stakeholders/roles and activities involved.

Alternatively, in a more process-oriented organization, a process-centric approach can be used. In this case, instead of a use case catalog, a process value chain can be created for the solution (again, most likely based on the asset lifecycle). For selected processes, it is also possible to use a process flow diagram, using ePC or BPMN, for example. However, in this case, we recommend sticking to a fairly high level, focusing on the "happy path" process flow.

Regardless of the approach taken, this work is usually carried out by the team's business analysts, with support from the solution architect. Many business analysts and solution architects are highly structured in their thinking and like to start the functional design process using a structured approach. However, a key aspect of functional design is close interaction with end users and business stakeholders. And within this group, we often find people who are less structured in their thinking. Often, these people don't like abstract thinking, and prefer simple visualizations, as provided by UI mock-ups, for example. Because many in this group think in terms of applications, it is important to ensure effective communication by speaking to them in these terms.

This is why Ignite | IoT recommends creating initial mock-ups for the solution's key user interfaces (UIs) and human–machine interfaces (HMIs). These mock-ups should be lightweight and focus on the key interface identified as part of the use case or value chain analysis mentioned previously. Mock-ups provide an ideal basis for discussing ideas and validating requirements with end users and business stakeholders. They can also help identify and capture the full picture in terms of important data entities, use cases, processes, events, and so on. For an IoT solution, the following mock-ups are typically relevant:

HMI
Asset user and asset administrator interfaces (e.g., machine HMI displays, remote web interfaces, onboard displays in cars, etc.).

End user self-service interfaces
User account management, personal usage statistics, and so on.

Process support interfaces
UI for call center agents, for example.

Partner interfaces
UIs for solution partners and incident management for external support providers, for example.

Adding Some Structure
Most likely, the mock-up approach described in the previous section will not be very structured in the initial stages. It focuses heavily on the user point of view and sees processes, algorithms, and the like from a black box perspective. For this reason, Ignite | IoT recommends taking a more structured, IoT-specific design approach in parallel (again, the boundary between analysis and design is not black and white here).

Most IoT projects have developed certain theories that have become a fundamental part of their business model. For example, the people at CERN have built the Large Hadron Collider (LHC) based on physical theories that date back to Einstein and others. Or take Google and Nest: it's quite likely that Google have made assumptions about the kind of analytics they'll be able to run with the data gained through their acquisition of smart home technology provider Nest.

One problem with these theories is that until they have been proven, nobody knows for sure if they are right. And especially in an IoT world driven by sensor data/Big Data, many theories and business model assumptions will evolve over time as people learn from the data they have collected.

For many IoT projects, the creation of a digital model of the physical world based on sensor data forms the basis on which these theories and assumptions will be proven. Which is why the process of carefully designing this digital model is a key part of the solution design process. The assumptions made in the business model will have to drive the granularity of the digital model. It needs to be able to answer important questions:

- What data entities will have to be collected?

- How often?

- To what level of accuracy?

Take the example of a soccer game: if, in terms of a business model, we are a betting agency, then capturing the results of each game should be sufficient, unless we also need the information about each individual goal (i.e., who scored the goal and when). If we are the coach of a soccer team, our business model demands that we continuously optimize team performance. So in this case, our digital model would be closer to a heat map that tracks the positions of each player for the duration of the game. Some teams have already started tracking the detailed movements of individual players using high-accuracy positioning systems and motion capturing technology to allow for performance improvements in individual players. When visualized in 3D, these models already look very close to the real game.

Keep in mind that the creation of a more detailed digital model can dramatically increase the cost of project implementation, data transfer, and operation. In many cases, you will be surprised at how even very simple digital models can produce powerful business models.

The next question in the design process concerns the inception points that can be used to capture data. What types of sensors can be used? Where can they be positioned? How can they be accessed remotely? What's the best way of ensuring adequate power supply? And so on. To stay with the simple soccer example, how can you actually capture the fact that a goal was scored? Up until recently, very few soccer leagues allowed or required goal-line technology. So what are your options if there is no direct way of capturing the required information? Can you deploy a microphone system in the soccer stadium to measure the applause, working on the assumption that loud applause or protest indicates a goal?

This brings us to the next phase, the "Reconstruction" phase (Figure 8-13). We will see that the data collected from sensors doesn't always map directly to the required digital model. In this case, we need to implement a process that takes available sensor readings, events, and the like, and then uses this data to create the digital model we need in order to support our business model.

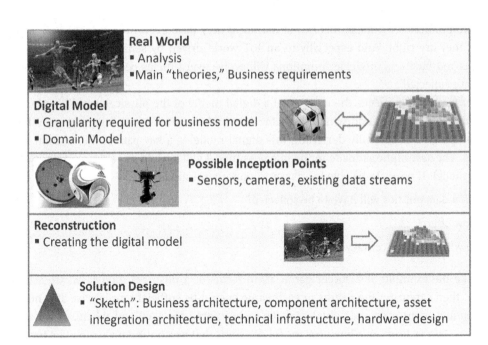

Real World
- Analysis
- Main "theories," Business requirements

Digital Model
- Granularity required for business model
- Domain Model

Possible Inception Points
- Sensors, cameras, existing data streams

Reconstruction
- Creating the digital model

Solution Design
- "Sketch": Business architecture, component architecture, asset integration architecture, technical infrastructure, hardware design

FIGURE 8-13. Structured IoT analysis and design approach

To take a more realistic example of a reconstruction process, let's look an IoT solution that uses beacons to track movements of customers in a retail store in order to make location-based shopping recommendations. In this example, the first part of the reconstruction process is to map beacon-specific information (distance, positions of beacons, etc.) to customers' actual 3D coordinates. The next step is to map customer positions to potential areas of interest, so that the recommendation engine can do its work.

One example that takes the concept of reconstruction to the extreme (and actually inspired our use of this concept) is the CERN/LHCb case study described in Part I:

- LHCb deploys more than one million sensors to get low-level, analog data

- A highly complex, multitiered reconstruction process is triggered for each particle collision by combining these analog events with the 3D coordinates of each individual sensor

- The result is a 3D model of the trajectories of each individual particle after the collision

- Based on this digital model of the collision, physicists can validate their physics theories about particle collisions

This example shows how important the concept of reconstruction is in the IoT world (apparently if you do it right, you can win a Nobel Prize). Especially for IoT solutions that rely on more complex digital models and sensor data, the Ignite | IoT Methodology recommends investing sufficient time and resources in defining the digital model and the corresponding reconstruction process.

If the solution architect is convinced that there is a good match between the digital model design and the reconstruction process, he can use this digital model as an abstraction in the next steps of the design process. As we will see, the digital model for an IoT solution can have multiple facets. At its core, we recommend creating a Domain Model (described in the following section) to provide a consolidated, business data-centric, technology-independent version of the digital model. Over time, the model will need to be updated to include events, components, processes, and so on. Let's start with the Domain Model.

Domain Model

Domain models are neither new nor IoT-specific. However, they can be a powerful tool in helping to create a business-oriented, consolidated view of the key data entities of an IoT solution.

We recommend using very basic Unified Modeling Language (*https://en.wikipedia.org/wiki/Unified_Modeling_Language*) (UML) elements for the Domain Model, such as:

- Classes
- Attributes
- Associations
- Aggregations
- Inheritance/specialization

A good starting point for identifying the key entities in your IoT solution are the four key elements from the stakeholder analysis discussed earlier:

Assets and devices
Identify between one and five key entities. What attributes of the assets and devices are particularly important?

End user
Users and specializations (e.g., asset owner, back office staff, etc.).

Enterprise
"Lease" as the key entity that defines the relationship between the asset and user, for example.

Partner
Assignment of incidents, for example.

On a broad level, the Domain Model should focus on the key entities and their most important relationships. Knowing what to omit can sometimes be as tricky as identifying the key entities. Some advice:

- Avoid "1980s entity/relationship wallpapers." A Domain Model usually has between 15 and 30 entities, no more.

- Use simple UML, as described earlier.

- Allow for a certain level of "vagueness." This is especially important in this age of NoSQL databases and an environment like the IoT where not all data types will be known in advance.

As we will see, one key advantage of the Domain Model is the ability to create a visual representation of the data distribution across the different solution layers. Leveraging service-oriented architecture (SOA), we can map the entities from the Domain Model to the different components (Figure 8-14).

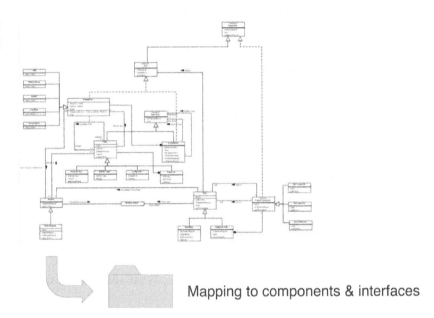

High-level
Domain Model

Mapping to components & interfaces

FIGURE 8-14. IoT Domain Model

Asset Integration Architecture (AIA)

The Asset Integration Architecture (AIA) is an architectural approach that has been specifically developed for IoT solutions. A description of the high-level concept has already been provided in Chapter 1. Two main tiers are introduced here: asset and enterprise. These two tiers are integrated through an IoT Cloud (or an M2M Platform). In the asset, the local gateway and agent software allow integration with the different devices that form part of the asset. The gateway also ensures connectivity with the backend. In the backend, the IoT Cloud usually has an integrated database containing information about all of the assets that have been registered with the system. The IoT Cloud ensures that this information is synchronized with the actual data from the asset. The IoT Cloud backend typically contains very asset- and device-specific data and functionality and is integrated with backend applications to provide additional business services.

Figure 8-15 shows an AIA for the eCall service. The eCall solution consists of a call center application in the backend, which integrates with the so-called public-safety answering point (PSAP). The backend also contains the eCall Event Processing subsystem, which receives events from vehicles in a potential crash situation. These events are submitted from a telematics control unit (TCU) in the car. The main purpose of the TCU is to act as a gateway, but it also has some limited business logic running locally, as well as an acceleration sensor which forms part of the solution. Also, the TCU integrates with the airbag via a CAN bus.

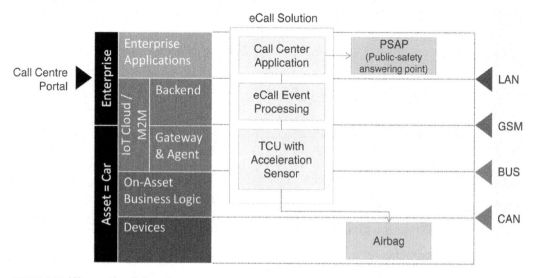

FIGURE 8-15. AIA example: eCall service

The main purpose of the AIA is to provide a canvas that can be used to present the different architectural elements of an IoT solution in a standardized way, and to provide information about the distribution of the different architecture elements in the IoT solution.

Data Distribution

Now that we are familiar with the concepts of the Domain Model and Asset Integration Architecture, we can combine these two concepts to address data distribution (Figure 8-16). This is a very important aspect of any IoT Solution. A naive data distribution design can lead to significant performance problems and unnecessary communication costs.

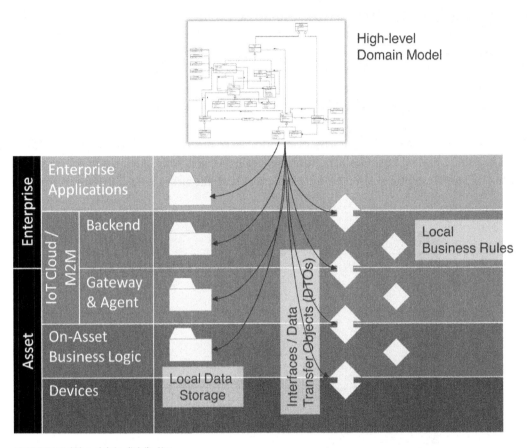

FIGURE 8-16. AIA and data distribution

For each of the entities identified in the Domain Model, the task is to identify where in the AIA these entities might exist—either by design (green-field), or because they already do (brown-field). Closely related to the distribution of data is the distribution of key business rules.

An experienced solution architect will typically have a good overview of the key restrictions that apply to data and business rule distribution, such as latencies and bandwidths between the different tiers of the AIA, local storage restrictions, and processing limitations. By combining these restrictions with quantity structure information from the original analysis (e.g., expected number of assets, etc.), she can create an initial proposal for the data distribution design by mapping data entities and rules to the AIA.

For example, say that a smart home solution requires an important business rule that makes a decision based on room temperature and weather forecast. In this case, the solution architect has two options:

Option A: local rule

Push weather forecast data to the smart home appliance on a regular basis and run the rule locally.

Option B: backend rule

Send the current room temperature to the backend and run the rule in the backend each time a decision is needed.

The tradeoff is clear: how much data traffic will option A generate as a result of pushing weather forecasts from the backend to the appliances versus how much traffic will option B generate as a result of pushing data from the appliances to the backend? There are a number of factors to consider here, such as the number of appliances, required update frequency and data volumes for weather forecasts, average number of rule executions per appliance, and more.

This relatively simple example and the resulting complex analysis clearly demonstrates why an efficient distribution design for data and business rules is so important to the success of an IoT solution.

SOA Landscape

Closely related to the preceding discussion is the topic of software componentization. Once hyped, service-oriented architecture (SOA) has come through a lengthy learning curve and is now seen by many as an unsexy but necessary approach to addressing the problems associated with distributed, heterogeneous software systems.

An SOA typically has two perspectives: a technical protocol perspective (REST versus web services) and a functional perspective. The whole area of standardizing technical protocols for the IoT is still very dynamic, so our focus here will be on the latter—the functional perspective. As described in [EBPM], the functional perspective defines the four key layers of an SOA that can be applied across application silos independently of the underlying technology: UI, process logic, orchestration, and basic/data-centric services. The advantage of looking at a heterogeneous application landscape through an SOA perspective is that it becomes quickly transparent which application silo owns which data and which processes. This is important information, which is usually hard to come by. Also, this perspective is helpful in identifying the software components and their dependencies on a nontechnical level. This can be interesting for the data and logic distribution discussion, for example. In the later stages of the design process, the provision of technology-independent documentation for the key software components and their interfaces also becomes important. In many cases, a wiki-based approach is preferable over a technical SOA repository because of the associated overheads.

In a distributed system with network latencies and bandwidth limitations, the design of the component interfaces must be as efficient as possible. The experience from distributed object computing (CORBA, DCOM, J2EE) has shown that complex object interaction patterns are not suitable for most distributed systems. Instead, simpler, RESTful services have been introduced. The same patterns and restrictions also apply to the design of software compo-nents in the IoT—if anything, they apply more, given that aspects such as high latencies, net-work service disruptions, and other problems are even more of a factor due to the open nature of the IoT.

Consequently, Ignite | IoT proposes to build on existing best practices for SOA architec-ture design and extend these to the IoT. From an SOA point of view, the applications running on an asset are no different from any other application. Because SOA takes a technology-agnostic perspective, adding embedded applications and real-time operating systems to the already heterogeneous SOA world of Java, COBOL, and PL/1 code shouldn't make a difference.

As shown in Figure 8-17, Ignite | IoT proposes to extend the familiar SOA map diagram by adding a section for assets to the right and extending the UI layer to include human–machine interaction (HMI).

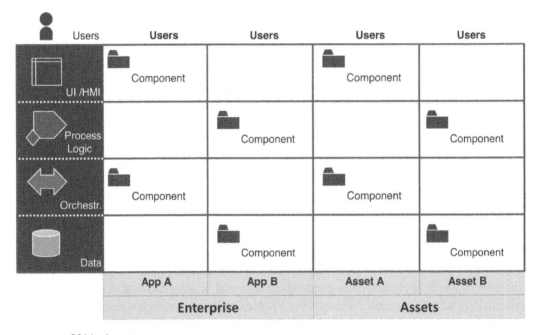

FIGURE 8-17. SOA landscape

This type of SOA map can be of great value in helping to identify the key software components that need to be integrated or developed as part of the IoT solution. The SOA perspective is different from the Asset Integration Architecture (AIA) perspective described earlier in that the main focus of the SOA is to make the key software components and their main business functions transparent. The SOA perspective proposed here is technology-agnostic and really focuses on business functions, while an AIA takes more of a systems perspective, possibly containing references to concrete technologies used.

Technical Design
Finally, the technical design should provide an overview of the solution's software architecture, hardware design, and technical infrastructure.

Software Architecture
The software architecture should define the key software components and their dependencies:

- On-asset OS/firmware, application container, and middleware
- Backend OS, application container, and middleware (e.g., messaging, BPM, or BRM)
- Database technologies and libraries
- Identity management, security technologies, certificate management, etc.
- Important software libraries and open source components
- Infrastructure for software updates on the assets
- Development tools

Hardware Design
The hardware design should focus on those elements that are specific to the IoT solution—usually the on-asset hardware (Figure 8-18). The typical level of detail in this stage should cover:

- On-asset hardware, such as a gateway consisting of the following elements: CPU, memory, local interfaces, cellular modem, local wireless connectivity, antenna, casing, distributed sensor nodes, etc.
- Position and mounting on the asset
- If distributed sensor nodes are deployed, the position and mounting of these nodes on the asset

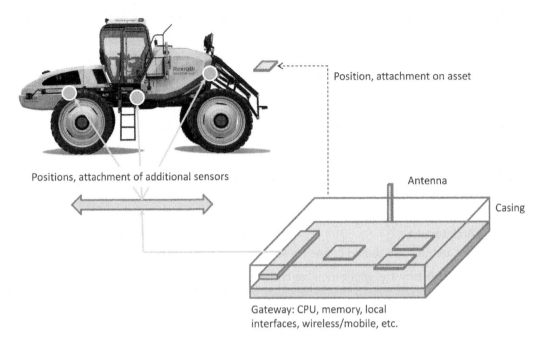

Position, attachment on asset

Positions, attachment of additional sensors

Antenna

Casing

Gateway: CPU, memory, local
interfaces, wireless/mobile, etc.

FIGURE 8-18. Hardware design

In case of custom hardware development, the next level of detail in the hardware design would address the main components (e.g., CPU, memory, power supply, digital I/O, communication modules, etc.). Figure 8-19 shows an example for the design of the main board of a telematics unit for the eCall service, as described in Chapter 1.

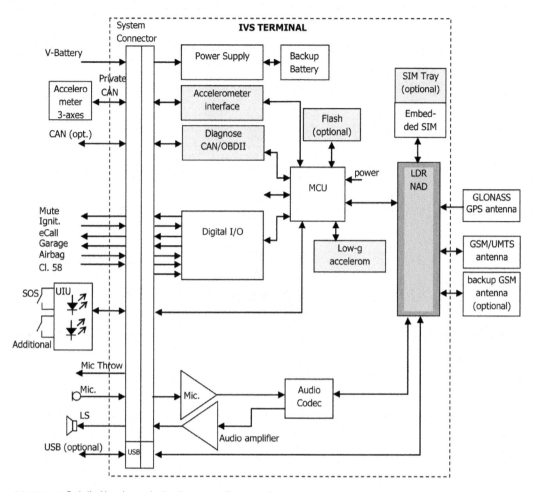

FIGURE 8-19. Detailed hardware design (source: peiker group)

Technical Infrastructure

The design of the technical infrastructure will be highly specific to the individual solution and, in particular, to the network infrastructure used. Figure 8-20 shows an example from Alcatel-Lucent (*http://bit.ly/mobile_service_role*).

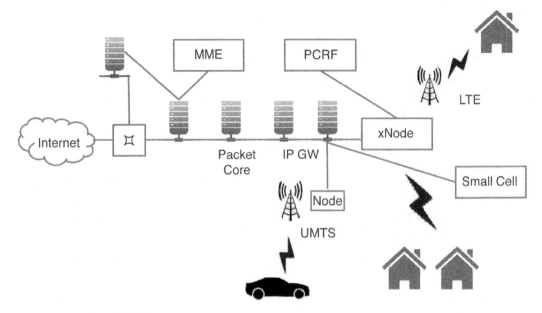

FIGURE 8-20. Technical infrastructure

MAKE-OR-BUY DECISION

Based on the outcome of the Initial Solution Design, the project team has to make an important decision: make or buy. This is a decision that will have a huge impact on the project. One important factor here concerns corporate guidelines and policies. Another relates to strategic project goals and the availability of required solution components. Typical make-or-buy questions in an IoT project include:

Common off-the-shelf (COTS) solutions
    Are COTS solutions available for aspects such as fleet management, vehicle tracking, smart metering, and so on?

On-asset hardware
    Should custom hardware or standard hardware be used?

On-asset software
    Should we use a preintegrated OS, firmware, application container, and development tools? Or should we choose a custom solution?

IoT cloud/M2M middleware
    What are the benefits of using a lightweight, often open source framework versus full-blown, commercial IoT cloud/M2M middleware?

Wireless communication

Should we rely on a single telecom operator or work with a mobile virtual network operator (MVNO) to ensure better global coverage?

Depending on the outcome, another related question concerns who should take on the role of general contractor—the enterprise itself, a system integrator, or the M2M division of a telecommunications company, for example.

IoT Project Structure

Once the initial solution design has been completed, the final task in the project initiation phase of an IoT project is usually to set up the organizational structure of the project. This is what we will discuss here.

CONWAY'S LAW

IT is governed by numerous laws, many of which are important for the IoT—not least Moore's and Metcalfe's laws. A less widely known law—yet extremely important in our experience—was put forward by Melvin Conway in 1968. According to this law, the structure of a software system will reflect the structure of the organization that produced it. For example, if three development teams are working on an IT project, chances are that the resulting architecture will have three main components. Consequently, if the goal is to create an architecture with three components, the organizational structure of the project should be made up of three development teams.

With this in mind, the organizational structure of the project must take into account the results of the initial solution design as well as the results of the make-or-buy decision. Figure 8-21) shows an example for an IoT project organization derived from an Ignite-based Solution Design, including dedicated teams for backend services, communication services, on-asset components, cross-cutting concerns, solution infrastructure, operations environment, and asset preparation.

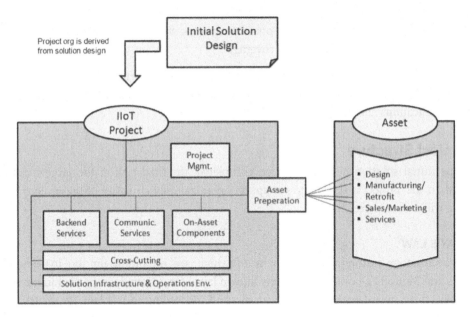

FIGURE 8-21. Mapping solution design to organization

IOT PROJECT WORKSTREAMS

The Ignite |IoT Methodology uses the concept of workstreams as the top-most project structure. Furthermore, we believe that for a complex project with as many dependencies as an IoT project, it is not possible to come up with a complete and fully stable work breakdown structure (WBS) during the Initiation Phase—even if using a more traditional Waterfall approach. The concept of workstreams better reflects the dynamics of these projects. Each workstream should be mapped to a set of key deliverables (defined as work packages, according to PMI [PMI], for example) from the Initial Solution Design (Conway's law!), and needs a team and a team/workstream manager.

Although making generalizations is difficult, our analysis has shown that for many IoT projects it makes sense to define the workstreams illustrated in Figure 8-22:

Project management
> Well-defined in the PMI PMBOK [PMI], but also needs to incorporate solution architecture management across the first six workstreams.

Cross-cutting tasks
> Inclusion of tasks that have dependencies right across the subsequent workstreams, including security, asset lifecycle management, solution integration, and testing.

Solution infrastructure and operations
> Setup and management of the hardware and software infrastructure required for developing and operating the solution, including a solution for application lifecycle management.

Backend services

Implementation and operation of backend services; integration with existing applications.

Communication services

Setup and management of communication infrastructure.

On-asset components

Design and manufacture or purchase of on-asset hardware and implementation of on-asset hardware.

Asset preparation

Preparation of the asset and/or environment for the new solution.

FIGURE 8-22. Proposed IoT project workstreams

In the following sections, we will look at each workstream independently, taking into account key tasks and dependencies with other workstreams.

Project Management

Whether based on a Waterfall or Agile approach, each project needs an efficient project management process. PMI, the Project Management Institute, defines the key elements of project management. In "A Guide to the Project Management Body of Knowledge (PMBOK)" [PMI], it identifies initiating, planning, executing, monitoring and controlling, and closing as the five key project management processes. The same applies for an IoT solution project; for further details on standard processes, refer to the PMBOK guide. At this point, we would like to highlight certain project management tasks that we believe to be at least partially specific to IoT. For project planning, these include the following:

Procurement planning

The complexity of the process of procuring the components and services required for an IoT solution (e.g., for on-asset hardware and communication services) should not be underestimated. These processes therefore need to be started early and planned for accordingly.

Resource planning

We already know that one of the key characteristics of an IoT project is the diversity of skills required, from embedded software to communications to enterprise software. This makes the resource mobilization process challenging, and sufficient time and resources need to be planned for this task.

Quality management

The QM reports for the solution should include solution-specific reporting items (e.g., communication service quality, average asset status, etc.).

Solution architecture management

The solution architect who was ideally already responsible for the initial solution design will be required to continuously review the detailed designs created by the individual workstreams, and ensure that all of the different designs add up to one consistent solution. This requires the establishment of an architecture review process to ensure the architectural alignment of each of the different workstreams.

Interface management

Efficient managment of the technical interfaces (software, communication protocols, and hardware) between the different solution components and workstreams is one of the most important success factors of any distributed systems project. We highly recommend the following:

- Establishing a dedicated role with responsibility for coordinating all of the cross-component interfaces and continuously liaising with the different workstreams.

- Establishing a central repository for capturing all cross-component interfaces, including a technical and a functional description of each interface. However, avoid tool overkill: use a wiki as a flexible and lightweight mechanism for creating and maintaining this central interface repository. This is especially relevant given that there is a good chance that the interfaces will be highly heterogeneous, from REST and OPC, to MQTT and CoAP, to very device-specific protocols.

Cross-Cutting Tasks

True to its name, the cross-cutting workstream is responsible for tasks that cut across all the other workstreams, such as the security, asset lifecycle management, solution integration, and testing workstreams.

Security

Given the importance of security to any IoT solution, there is a strong argument for making it a top-level workstream in its own right. However, because security impacts each of the other workstreams, we believe that it should actually be treated as a cross-cutting workstream.

For a detailed discussion of the technical aspects of IoT security and how they concern the other workstreams—on-asset components, communication services, backend services, and infrastructure—refer to "Security" on page 363.

In terms of the security workstream, it is important to understand that security is not just about technologies; it also requires security policies and processes, all of which need to be defined here. Also, the project must define a strategy for ensuring and validating the security of the solution, including:

Risk assessment
This should help to identify the highest-priority threats and the profiles of the most likely attackers. For an IoT solution, this obviously has to include attacks on assets and asset-related communications, as well as an asset-specific impact analysis.

Security architecture
Specialized architectural perspective that shows how different security mechanisms will be integrated into the solution architecture.

Security implementation
Detailed plan including work packages for implementing the security architecture, which usually is cross-cutting and involves all other workstreams.

Security testing and validation
Dedicated test strategy to help identify potential flaws in the security architecture and implementation. This could require outside experts.

Asset Lifecycle Management

As per our discussion in Chapter 1, many IoT solutions have a huge impact on the asset's lifecycle, touching as they do on integrated product/service design, product manufacturing, service development, marketing and sales, distribution and activation, service operations, remote condition monitoring, solution support and product maintenance (including remote maintenance and predictive maintenance), digital services, and resale and retirement.

We recommend creating a dedicated role in the project with responsibility for looking at the solution from an asset lifecycle management perspective across all workstreams, thereby ensuring that this important perspective is addressed end-to-end.

Take asset activation, for example. This important part of the lifecycle usually has an impact on the on-asset software, the communication services, and the backend services. So it makes sense to look at it from a centralized perspective in order to ensure that the best solution is implemented across all workstreams.

Solution Integration and Testing

Finally, solution integration and testing is also another important cross-cutting task. The person or team responsible will be required to liaise with all the other workstreams in order to agree on key release milestones, interface versions, staging mechanisms, processes, end-to-end test plans, and more. Again, not too different from any large enterprise IT project, but with the added complexity of having to integrate the on-asset components into the test plan.

It is not always possible to create a test environment that fully reflects the field environment. If you have an IoT solution tasked with managing 1,000,000 devices, testing this solution with 1,000,000 test devices is not going to be feasible. Instead, pragmatic mechanisms will have to be found to allow completion of an initial integration test using a limited number of actual devices. Load generators can then be used to simulate a system with 1,000,000 devices and thereby test the scalability of the backend systems.

Similarly, efficient test strategies will have to be devised for communication services. If planning a global rollout, testing all locations is not always going to be possible. In this case, the test team will be required to closely work with the service provider in order to define a joint test plan.

Again, because these kinds of integration tests usually have an impact on all other workstreams, it makes sense to centralize these tasks under the cross-cutting tasks workstream.

Solution Infrastructure and Operations

This workstream is responsible for setting up the overall infrastructure that will be used to build, test, and operate the solution. In particular, it includes the standard infrastructure setup tasks found in any enterprise software project. However, in addition to these standard tasks, there are a number of tasks that are specific to IoT solutions.

For a standard enterprise application, this workstream would require members of the development project and members of the operations team to work closely together in order to agree on the different environments required—usually development, testing/integration, and production. They would also need to agree on the related staging processes required for integrating multiple development updates into a new release and ultimately making the new release available in the production environment.

Configuration management and release planning, as well as steady-state and operations planning, also form part of this workstream. Tasks such as hardware sizing and acquisition, backup management, security infrastructure (firewalls, DMZ, etc.), systems monitoring, alarm management, scalability planning, availability management (e.g., primary/disaster site, each with local resilience), customer help desk functions, and more need to be taken into account also. If the solution is cloud based, cloud instance health monitoring, cloud SLA management, and cloud-2-enterprise application integration need to be taken into account as well.

Even for a standard project, the diversity of technologies, tools, concepts, and people involved here makes for a complex scenario. For an IoT solution, you have all this, and more, due to the highly distributed nature of such solutions.

This workstream will have to ensure that application lifecycle management (ALM) in all its complexity is applied consistently from the backend to the asset. This includes providing the required software update infrastructure for the assets, asset monitoring, management of errors and alarms issued by assets, and so on.

Another key issue concerns the customer support infrastructure. For example, most telecommunications companies provide their support teams with specialized tools that allow them to perform basic equipment tests—such as "pinging" a DSL modem to test whether it is online, for example. This functionality is usually built into the core call center application, which provides additional information such as the customer contact history. Many IoT solutions will require similar support capabilities, which will need to be addressed in this workstream.

If the IoT solution is designed to support an existing field service team—by providing remote condition monitoring (RCM) or predictive maintenance capabilities, for example—the provision of technical training to this team is also going to be very important.

Backend Services

Typical work items in the backend services workstream include creation of a solution for the management of assets and asset data, implementation of solution-specific processes, and integration with existing applications via enterprise application integration (EAI) or SOA service-oriented architecture (SOA).

If you are using a specialized M2M/IoT application platform (for details, see "IoT Technology Profiles" on page 268), you will have to select, acquire, and install this platform—a process which, if started from scratch, can take weeks, if not months, especially if it is a strategic technology decision.

The goal is usually to build a dedicated tier in the backend containing a central representation of all field assets. It includes up-to-date asset status data and a detailed asset event history, as well as management functions for individual assets or groups of assets. An M2M/IoT application platform will generally provide out-of-the-box features for implementing these functions, such as a method for communicating with remote assets and managing asset data locally. These platforms often come with an administration console that provides an overview of all deployed assets and their corresponding status.

The backend service workstream will be required to create suitable profiles for each asset and for the devices deployed on these assets. The profiles will then need to be implemented on the platform. This can be done using the tools provided by the platform, for example.

In most cases, the administration console will not be suitable for end users, so a solution-specific UI will have to be implemented. This could be part of a specialized application in which solution-specific processes have been implemented. These processes will generally have to be integrated with a number of existing enterprise applications.

For a car-sharing service, for example, the first step involves creating a central model of the remote assets (the vehicles in this case) in the backend. This is followed by the implementation of UIs and applications for car-sharing customers. A mobile application then accesses the central asset repository to get data on current car locations so they can be visualized on a map. The application also needs to support a car reservation function. For the billing process, an existing application is integrated. The web UI provides users and call center agents with a detailed car usage history. This data is pulled from events received from the car's onboard unit, such as events that signal the beginning and end of a car rental process.

Another key task generally involves integration of the solution with a user management system. In the simplest case, this requires a web-based solution for user registration and login. In many examples—such as the car-sharing service case—this might be more complex, and involve setting up a more elaborate registration process to validate the user's driver's license and issue a chip card for opening the car, for example.

Communication Services

The structure of the workstream for setting up and managing communication services between the assets and the backend will depend on many factors, not least the required global coverage, maximum latency and bandwidth, cost, and so on. "M2M/IoT Communication Services" on page 298 provides guidelines for selecting the right technology and provider.

Based on the initial solution design, this workstream is concerned with completing a more in-depth analysis in order to determine the best possible setup for the communication service. This can involve tasks such as the following:

- Collecting detailed requirements on scope/services, including expected traffic profiles and backend connectivity and locations

- Analyzing hardware capabilities, available support for hardware selection based on communication services supported, and interaction with mobile network and roaming

- Determining the regulatory situation in the launch markets, including communication regulations and vertical-specific regulations (e.g., country-specific regulations for the eCall service)

- Monitoring communication behavior and potential impact on network, such as data volumes, required resilience, and exception handling

This information will provide the basis for selecting the right technology and communication service provider. The time needed to select a provider and negotiate service contracts should not be underestimated.

During the build phase, it is important that the service provider makes a test environment available. The overall solution will then need to be integrated with the communication service provider's infrastructure and tested. This can be done using the operator's dedicated portal for managing connectivity, for example.

During runtime, the same portal will be used to monitor and manage the communication network, including provisioning status, device data usage, SIM status, networks errors, and so on.

The following interview with Stephen Blackburn, Director of Sales Engineering at Aeris, provides more valuable insights into these topics.

Jim Morrish: What are the key points on the project manager's checklist with respect to planning and implementing the mobile communication part of his solution?

Stephen Blackburn: This project manager must have the understanding and insight to shepherd the development of a mobile communications solution from start to finish and have the scope to understand the widely differing elements that come into play. He must oversee the following considerations:

- Go-to-market business model: how the company will charge their customer?
- Application communication call flow: how the device will interact with the network?
- Definition of expected usage patterns, including normal operating patterns and over-the-air upgrades.
- Supply chain planning, taking into consideration device manufacture, device provisioning in carrier network as well as testing the communications link at the end of manufacture, and channel-to-market goals.
- Cellular carrier selection.
- Carrier integration (API integration).
- End-to-end application test plan incorporating testing of the communication link across different RF conditions.
- Device carrier certification.
- Carrier support SLA understood and in place.
- Customer support process definition and support team training.

Jim Morrish: What are the key interfaces between the mobile communication workstream and the other workstreams (i.e., on-asset hardware, security, etc.?)

Stephen Blackburn: The PM should be aware of how the mobile communication planning impacts other parts of the business so that these other groups are able to provide

---

input to planning and execution, as well as ensure that their own requirements are met. The key crossover areas include:

- Regulatory approvals
- Manufacturing and supply chain
- Security
- IT systems
- Operations and support
- Finance

Jim Morrish: Can you give advice on solution testing, specifically the mobile communication part? How does testing change in this type of environment?

Stephen Blackburn: Comprehensive testing is key. It is not only important to test the core functionality of the product, it is also essential to ensure the solution operates correctly over a cellular network, which has different characteristics to a LAN, for instance.

In addition to solution testing, if the device is going to go through carrier certification to be permitted onto a specific carrier's network, then the carrier will want to check that your device is a "good citizen" on the network. An example of this might be the behavior of the retry algorithm used by the device if it fails to connect to the application server in your data center. At this point, the reader might wonder, "Why would a carrier care?" The thing is that carriers design for network capacity, assuming user access to their network follows a random distribution. If all users tried to access the network at the same time, congestion may result and block other users' access to service. So imagine you are planning a massive rollout of hundreds of thousands or even millions of devices. If your data center experiences an outage resulting in all of your deployed devices losing contact with the network at the same time and they all try to retry immediately and fail, and retry immediately again and continue to fail, this will put a synchronized load on local towers and the carrier network infrastructure, which could impact other users if it were to cause congestion. So designing a random back-off algorithm and testing it prior to certification is a good idea.

Solution testing usually includes lab testing in a controlled environment, but it is important to include a field testing phase to test the solution in the environment in which it will later be deployed. During the lab testing phase, engineers typically ensure that the device has a good signal level which will provide a good quality cellular connection and achieve consistent data rates across the air interface. This is fine for basic functional testing, but negative test cases should be introduced to force poor signal quality conditions that are sometimes present in the field and lead to low bandwidth and long latency conditions. Applications requiring near real-time communication may not operate correctly under these conditions, so it is critical to consider this when designing the application, selecting the technology (e.g., 2G, 3G, LTE all have different latency characteristics), and when testing the application.

After the lab testing is completed, and assuming everything operates as expected, there will be a high level of confidence that the device will operate as expected for a majority of its operation. However, there are those 5% of test cases that cannot be contrived in a lab and only the confluence of events found in a field environment can expose those cases. So it is important to think about all of the use cases that describe the solutions deployment, and then think of a few more and plan a limited pilot deployment to test those use cases. Test locations should include environments with poor and good quality cellular signals. Field testing a small device population will provide an indication of how the population of devices will behave after launch. Providing you select the appropriate sample size and deployment environments, if you see a problem with 1% of your devices then, within a margin of error, you are likely to see the same problem in 1% of your devices after launch. If you can address the problem and get the problem device count to an acceptable margin, then there is a high level of confidence that after launch, the percentage of devices with problems remain manageable.

Jim Morrish: Are there any pitfalls to be avoided during solution deployment and commissioning?

Stephen Blackburn: Issues that can occur during deployment depend on both the application and the deployment model. For instance, if the device is sold to consumers for a solution that is deployed in their home, it is a certainty that a percentage of homeowners will place the device in the area of the home with the worst cellular coverage (i.e., their basement). It is important to provide simple instructions that explain how to place the device. If it is within budget, it is often worth putting some indicator on the device which lets the user know when they have placed it in an area with sufficient coverage.

Other applications may require the device to be placed in an area that isn't optimal for cell tower coverage (e.g., a manhole). These types of applications are typically installed by field technicians and it is important to equip them with a network scanning tool that can provide signal quality measurements for the networks covering an area. The technicians can use this to determine the signal quality in the location and determine the best placement.

Jim Morrish: How about after going live—what are the key things to plan for?

Stephen Blackburn: If the solution completed a pilot field test phase, the risk of major problems after launch has been greatly reduced. However, even if during testing you are confident there are no issues, it is likely that some of the end users will experience problems, including "operator error" type problems. So it is essential to set up appropriate support processes and train the support team to handle the inevitable calls from customers.

Support personnel will generally be trained on the product features and how to operate them, but it is also very important for the support team (usually tier 2) to receive training on how to diagnose connectivity issues. This is where a rich set of diagnostic tools from the carrier, if available, become a huge benefit. If your tier 2 engineer can log into a portal and check if the device in question has registered on the carrier network, started a data session, and she can observe the recent behavior, she can immediately focus the investigation to the root of the problem and provide quick feedback to the customer. If these tools are not available, then a call to the carrier helps but is generally a lot slower.

On-Asset Components

Based on the input from the Initial Solution Design phase, this workstream is concerned with finalizing the design for the on-asset hardware and software. This can involve hardware manufacturing, local communication, selection and implementation of firmware and software, as well as integration and testing.

On-Asset Hardware

Ideally, the required sensors and actuators, as well as gateways and other on-asset hardware, will have already been identified as part of the Initial Solution Design phase. As part of this workstream, further testing and evaluation will generally need to be carried out in order to ensure that all elements are working together properly.

Depending on the outcome of the make-or-buy decision, a sourcing process may have to be initiated for external procurement of the required hardware components. Alternatively, it may be necessary to initiate a hardware design and prototyping process, followed by a hardware manufacturing and testing process.

On-Asset Operating System and Application Container

Selection of the operating system and application platform or container usually goes hand in hand with selection of the hardware. A number of M2M/IoT hardware providers offer integrated solutions, some of which even offer a backend management service that allows for remote management and remote firmware upgrades. Although we have grouped all tasks relating to application lifecycle management under the solution infrastructure workstream, there is a strong dependency between these two workstreams. The same also applies to lifecycle management of the application software running on the application platform. Finally, implementation of backup and restore functionality for local data should also be addressed at this point.

On-Asset Middleware

If you are using M2M or IoT middleware, the on-asset-specific elements of this middleware will have to be preinstalled and configured.

You will also need to set up and configure the communication protocols and ensure security certificate management for this middleware. These tasks can have strong dependencies with the cross-cutting tasks and solution infrastructure workstreams.

Similarly, local processes for distributing and updating application software will have to be tested and integrated with the backend solution provided by the solution infrastructure workstream.

Device Integration

In many cases, the on-asset middleware will require the implementation of hardware-specific drivers, so that data and services offered by different devices can be made available to the backend in homogeneous format. The design and implementation of these local drivers and protocols should not be underestimated.

Also, assumptions made during the initial solution design phase about the accessibility of certain interfaces may not be correct. If it turns out that the asset needs to provide a certain interface, this information will need to be passed back to the asset preparation workstream. For example, we saw in one of our case studies that the initial design was based on the assumption that the asset would provide access to battery health data, which did not turn out to be the case. In this particular situation, it took quite some time to upgrade the asset so that it was capable of providing this interface, which in turn had an impact on the rollout of the entire solution.

On-Asset Business Logic

Implementation of on-asset business logic is another key task of this workstream. This can range from low-level embedded software to complex business logic, including local business rules and data management. Companies such as Cisco are promoting the concept of "fog computing" with powerful gateways that can store significant amounts of data on the gateway and process significant volumes of data locally. This can be related to our discussion of the functional design phase, specifically data and logic distribution between the on-asset software and the backend. While the functional design provides an initial proposal, the details will have to be decided in this workstream. Because data and logic distribution has an impact on the backend workstream as well, close interaction is required between both workstreams. Also, we recommend implementing a central interface management as part of the project management process (see "An Open Letter to the Ignite Team" on page 251).

Backend Integration

For integrating the asset with the backend, the required protocols must be available locally on the asset. For some gateways, for example, this is not always a given. Another important task involves defining the relevant authentication and authorization procedures. As a rule, user management will also need to be synchronized with a central backend function.

Asset Preparation

As discussed in Chapter 1, the Ignite | IoT methodology assumes that the IoT project is implemented independently of the main organization responsible for the asset the solution is built on. Because it represents the organizational interface between the asset and the IoT solution, the asset preparation workstream is extremely important. It is important to make it an explicit workstream, and to clearly identify who it is owned by, and who has to contribute to it. Contributions generally come from both the asset team and the solution team. Overall ownership should be assigned to one of the two teams.

The asset preparation workstream is required to look at the entire lifecycle of the asset and the solution, including analysis, (potentially integrated) design, asset manufacturing, solution implementation, support, and operation.

During the analysis phase, the asset (and potentially its environment) will need to be analyzed in order to determine the best way of mounting the solution's on-asset hardware components (e.g., antennas, sensors, beacons, gateways, etc.). This will involve consideration of aspects such as access to local bus connections and power supply.

If the solution requires a specialized network, the requirements for setting up this network will have to be examined. If the solution relies on beacons (or similar) for indoor positioning, the Cartesian coordinates of the exact positions of the beacons will have to be captured.

If the asset was designed from the ground up, or modified to accommodate the IoT solution, there will need to be close alignment between both teams during the design phase, as well as clearly defined technical interfaces (on the hardware and/or software level).

In terms of integration between the asset and the IoT solution, it is worth considering the asset's EBOM (engineering bill of material). An asset will generally have a full EBOM stored in a PLM (or similar) system. For an IoT solution, the BOM may well consist of different sections: the onboard hardware, the onboard software, and the backend software, for example. The EBOM for the asset should include a reference to the onboard hardware at least.

Decisions will also need to be made in relation to the asset's manufacturing process. Are the on-asset hardware components attached to the asset as part of the asset's manufacturing process? Or will these be retrofitted afterward? In either case, provisioning of the on-asset components will have to be taken into account in the supply chain process. Also, special assembly skills may be required and provision will need to be made to secure these.

In terms of a retrofitting approach, the Purfresh case study provides an interesting example. In this case, a set of specialized devices (gateway and sensors) had to be retrofitted onto containers' onboard cargo ships. Purfresh set up a process whereby specialized handling agents perform this task in the short timeframe in which the container ships are docked at the harbor where the solution is to be installed. Note that this process not only includes local assembly, but also activation and testing.

Finally, many IoT solutions are designed to improve after-sales processes. This can involve remote condition monitoring, predictive maintenance, and even digital after-sales services (see Chapter 1). The asset preparation workstream needs to be responsible for training the organizational teams involved in the new capabilities and ensuring seamless adoption—to the point of building up new organizational units, if required.

IoT and Agile

In the beginning of this chapter, we argued that Ignite should be independent of the underlying project methodology (e.g., Agile or Waterfall). However, in our interaction with different experts, many people felt very strongly about IoT and Agile, so we will dig a little bit deeper, starting with a direct reaction to Ignite from the Agile community.

AN OPEN LETTER TO THE IGNITE TEAM

This open letter was written to us by Christian Weiss, Managing Consultant at Holisticon AG. We think this is a very good contribution in the category "Clash of Two Worlds":

Dear authors of the Ignite | IoT methodology,

Before I start my rant, let me congratulate you on the first publicly available IoT methodology. The increasing importance of IoT requires such a methodology. Your book and website are an extremely valuable contribution.

However, I do have one major issue with your approach—and this is very close to my heart. As you are correctly saying, IoT projects are multidisciplinary and thus an IoT methodology has to combine multiple skills and disciplines. Most experienced project managers will agree that this alone represents a huge risk. In addition, current IoT projects usually have to deal with a lot of new and (b)leading edge technologies, which further increases the project risks. Of course these big risks are coming with huge opportunities; but these risks will have to be managed effectively, nevertheless.

The issue is that in my opinion your simplified Plan/Build/Run methaphor implies a Waterfall approach to IoT project management. To be fair, you are also stating in your introduction that Agile is one of the different options for the IoT project manager. However, you don't seem to be making a strong case for it.

The Plan/Build/Run metaphor might work on an abstract management level, and it is not wrong in principle. However, I do think that it is an oversimplification, and a very dangerous one as such. The danger here is that management can easily get the impression that it would be possible to create a complete and detailed plan for such a high-risk undertaking like an IoT project—and that the only challenge then is to execute this plan step by step. If this is built into a methodology, then I am not surprised that I am still finding projects which follow this approach.

The summary of your Plan/Build/Run approach describes that an IoT project is like any other project, starting with an initial planning phase, followed by a phase that results in the initial release, followed by rollout and maintenance.

NO! PLEASE STOP THIS! A phase always relates to a period in time. Consequently, a planning phase has to be understood as a period in time during which all you do is planning, but no building. And the build phase implies that all you do is building, but no planning. I really do hope that this is not what you are implying!!! Plan/Build/Run should not be seen as phases, but rather as disciplines. Because in reality you have to actively plan until the very end. And the build process should hopefully also start from the very beginning.

Of course, the Agile approach also knows phases. However, the phases (i.e., periods in time) are not so much defined by the tasks which are to be executed. Instead, these phases are defined through other characteristics, e.g., goals and priorities, types of artifacts, team structure, etc. This is why these phases are called differently in an Agile approach.

Also, there was one other statement in your introduction which made me nearly angry: "fixed price projects are often using a Waterfall approach." Unfortunately, this equation "fixed price = Waterfall" is supporting those laggards who still claim that you can't do fixed price with Agile. Which in my opinion and experience is complete nonsense!

Don't get me wrong: Design-to-budget is a completely legitimate requirement. However, fixed price is not a question of finalizing the detailed design upfront, but rather a question of stringent prioritization throughout the project. And this is exactly what Agile was invented for. I would claim the exact opposite: using an Agile approach for fixed price projects significantly increases the chances for success!

Fair enough. There are still some (especially large) companies out there that frequently use the Waterfall approach. However, in my opinion a new methodology should aim to improve the world. So why not make Agile the standard for IoT projects? My well-meant criticism is that instead of stating a clear position in favor of Agile for IoT, you are trying to be open for everything. And you shouldn't. The Agile approach aims to make risks manageable. The strength of Agile is exactly in highly dynamic situations with many unknowns—so where if not in the IoT should it be the default?

My recommendation: Make Agile the default for Ignite. And add a footnote for nostalgics that the traditional approach is also supported, but not recommended for IoT.

Best regards,

Christian Weiss

LIMITATIONS OF AGILE IN THE IOT

We decided to include the letter from Christian Weiss because we think this is an important controversy, and that Agile can provide many benefits to IoT projects. However, we also think that there are still some unresolved issues when it comes to applying Agile to IoT projects, including the following:

Scaling Agile to large, distributed project organizations

Many basic Agile methods like Scrum were initially not designed to support large, highly distributed projects which span multiple organizational silos. Over time, different approaches have emerged to address this problem, including Scaled Professional Scrum [SPS], Large-Scale Scrum [LeSS], and Scaled Agile Framework [SAFe]. However, it seems yet unclear which approach will prevail.

Cultural differences

While many software development organizations have adopted Agile for a couple of years, many IT hardware or asset engineering organizations are still used to working with more traditional, sequential or long-term planning-oriented approaches. Again, this comes back to our "clash of two worlds" discussion.

Hardware is not virtual

As Michael Thompson from Huawei points out in [AS], all resources required in hardware development are physical: "the amount and type of memory needed, the number and type of interfaces, the amount of logic to perform tasks—all of this is fixed and is not easily changed." This is very different from software development, where all resources such as memory allocation and so on—are virtual and can be easily changed. Furthermore, software is compiled or interpreted. With today's build environments, this means that changes to software can be applied and tested virtually immediately. Physical hardware design, on the other hand, takes longer and requires longer-term planning. Finally, the virtual nature of software makes it so much easier to define self-contained increments that can be delivered and tested as the result of a sprint.

Challenging release management

The often highly distributed nature of assets, as well as the difficulty in applying remote software updates, (not to mention hardware updates) makes change and release management for IoT solutions extremely challenging. We are not saying that this makes Agile development impossible, but it certainly changes some basic assumptions found in typical Agile software development, especially compared to Internet-style applications which frequently apply a "Perpetual Beta" philosophy, which cannot be applied to most IoT solutions.

Long planning and validation cycles for physical assets

Many IoT projects require alignment of different, often highly siloed organizations, such as the asset manufacturing and after-sales services organizations. Especially in enterprise environments, this often requires a long-term planning horizon. Furthermore, many, if not most, IoT solutions will have to undergo long validation phases, again requiring a long-term planning perspective. Furthermore, in many industries, such as the healthcare industry, it is virtually impossible to apply changes to a validated environment without a complete updated project, including a new validation.

We don't think that any of these points should prevent an organization with a high level of experience in an Agile, multidisciplinary development to apply a full-scale Agile approach to IoT, as described in the following sections, but we also think it is important to be aware of these potentially challenging issues.

AN AGILE APPROACH TO IOT

Leveraging some of the established approaches for scaled Agile development like [SPS] or [SAFe], we think that a full-scale Agile approach to an IoT project organization should look as described in Figure 8-23.

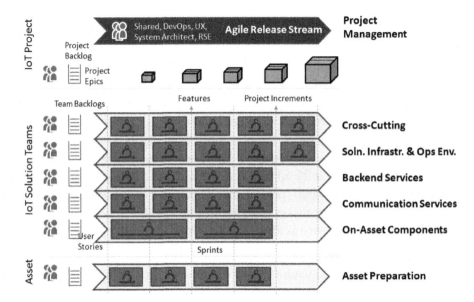

FIGURE 8-23. An Agile approach to IoT

The key elements of this Agile IoT organization include:

- A central project organization which provides project management, shared resources, DevOps, UX, system architecture, and RSE (release stream engineering). The release stream has its own backlog of higher-level epics, which are more coarse-grained than features and user stories.

- Each team or workstream has a team backlog which includes user stories that can be implemented in the scope of a single iteration. Notice that in IoT, a "user" in the user stories is not limited to a human user but could also relate to an asset, for example.

- A basic iteration frequency is defined (e.g., three-week sprints). The basic iteration grid defines the standard beginning or end of iterations across all workstreams. However, there can be some IoT-specific exceptions:

  — In order to cater to the typically longer development cycles on the hardware side, it might be a good idea to use longer iteration cycles for the on-asset hardware workstream. These should be multiples of the standard, e.g., six weeks.

  — Given the strong dependencies between the on-asset software and the backend application, consider moving the sprint start of one of these workstreams, for example, by one week. This way, it can be easier to manage the dependencies between these workstreams.

- Deliverables of the workstreams are features or full project increments. The scheduling of these deliverables needs to be synchronized with the overall milestone plan.

- The asset preparation workstream can also be run as an Agile sequence of iterations. It might have to be synchronized with a more Waterfall-oriented approach that is often found on the side of the asset organization.

As we can see, leveraging Agile for IoT requires a scalable approach. Many organizations will have to learn and find out for themselves how agile they can or want to go about their IoT projects. The specific nature of IoT projects might sometimes lead to hybrid approaches, which are a combination of Agile and Waterfall (also sometimes referred to as "Wagile"). This must not necessarily be a bad thing if it is a better fit for the Agile maturity level of an organization.

Building Blocks

Having discussed the Plan/Build/Run perspective of the IoT Solution Lifecycle, we would now like to introduce what we call the IoT Building Blocks (Figure 8-24). In essence, these are formal definitions of some of the artifact types that we have already presented as part of the Plan/Build/Run perspective.

The first building block is named IoT Project Dimensions. This is a precursor of formal project requirements. Project dimensions are used for project self-assessment, project comparisons, architecture and technology selection, and so on.

The next building block consists of the IoT Architecture Blueprints. Building on existing architecture blueprints (such as service-oriented architecture), these add new architectural perspectives necessary for IoT projects and provide a superstructure for integrating the various architectural perspectives that are required.

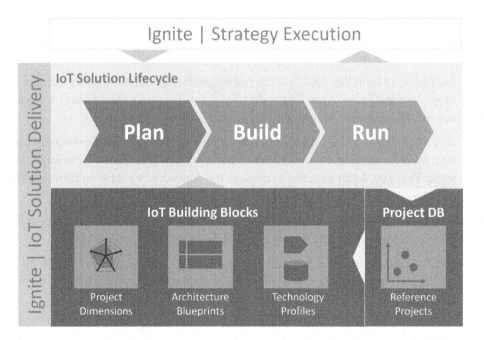

FIGURE 8-24. Ignite | IoT building blocks

Third, the IoT Technology Profiles identify and describe the most important technologies usually required for IoT projects. They leverage IoT architecture perspectives to describe where these different technologies fit into the overall IoT architecture, and link back to the project dimensions in order to support technology selection.

Finally, the IoT Project DB is an initiative that aims to record IoT case studies in a structured way. It uses the project dimensions to capture the essence of the different projects, make them comparable, and learn from each individual project.

IOT PROJECT DIMENSIONS

In order to be able to capture information about IoT projects in a structured way, the Ignite | IoT Methodology defines a group of five IoT Project Dimensions with 5–10 subdimensions per group (approximately 40 subdimensions in total). For each dimension, Ignite | IoT defines a scale from 1 to 4, with definitions for each scale level.

The five main groups are Asset and Devices, Communications and Connectivity, Backend Services, Standards and Regulatory Compliance, and Project Environment. Figure 8-25 provides an overview of the five groups and the associated dimensions.

Each IoT Project Dimension defines a scale from 1 to 4. A 1 indicates "Low/Simple" from the perspective of the project manager, while 4 means "Complex/Challenging." For some dimensions, it is possible to quantify the different scale levels, while for others we have to use a qualitative definition. Figure 8-26 provides some examples.

The basic idea is that the IoT Project Dimensions should be used to conduct project self-assessments, compare different IoT projects, and select the solution architecture and technologies to be used in a project (Figure 8-27).

For project self-assessment, an Excel template containing the IoT Project Dimensions can be downloaded from the Ignite | IoT website. Project managers can use this template like a questionnaire to go through the project dimensions. The end result is a Kiviat diagram (or "spider diagram") that provides a visualization of the input. This process will help project managers to obtain a better understanding of the risks and challenges involved in their projects.

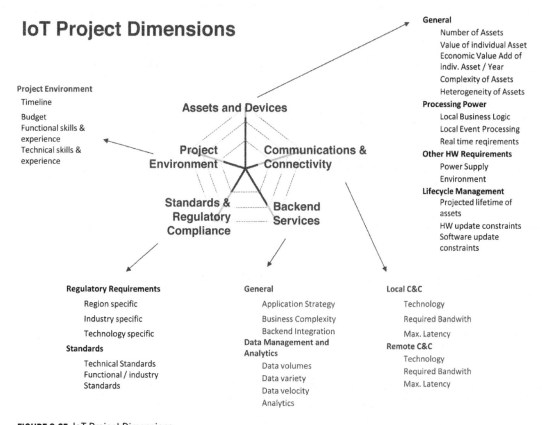

FIGURE 8-25. IoT Project Dimensions

For project comparison purposes, we are currently building up a database of IoT projects that we have analyzed using the Project Dimension template. This database will also be made available on the Ignite | IoT website.

To provide support for the technology selection phase, our goal is to end each IoT Technology Profile with a discussion of the suitability of the technology with respect to the different IoT Project Dimensions.

Assets and Devices

Project Dimensions	1: Low/Simple	2	3	4: Complex/Challengi...
General				
Number of Assets	100s	10.000s	100.000s	Millions
Value of individual Asset	<100€	<1.000€	<100.000€	>= 100.000€
Economic Value Add of indiv. Asset / Year	<100€	<1.000€	<100.000€	>= 100.000€
Asset Complexity - Integration Perspective	Zero integration	Simple interface semantics	Moderately complex inteface	Very complex interface sema...
Asset Heterogeneity - Integration Perspective	0-1 interface types	2-3 different interface types (inc...	Ve 4-10 different interface types	>10 different interface types
Processing Power				
Local Business Logic	Proxy functions only	Basic store and forward logic to ad...	Simple business logic, e.g. rul...	Complex business logic, e.g...
Local Event Processing	1 event / day	1 event / minute	1 event / second	10.000 events / sec
Real time requirements	Daily batch synch	Response within seconds	Response within sub-second	Deterministic response in na...
Other HW Requirements				
Power Supply	„220V Wall Plug"	Automatically recharged battery (e...	Large battery with moderate r...	Small battery with very long
Environment	In-door	Rough In-door, e.g. factory	Outdoor, moving (e.g. car in w...	Extreme conditions, e.g. air...
Lifecycle Management				
Projected lifetime of assets	<1 year	~5 years	~10 years	>20 years
HW update constraints	All assets can be accessed by spe...	E.g. Drive Now – technician can acc...	Asset configuration must be u...	impossible to update HW
Software update constraints	Central access mgmt, assets alwa...	normal distributed system constra...	very difficult - long times betw...	impossible to update SW

Communications & Connectivity

	1: Low/Simple	2	3	4: Complex/Challengi...
Local C&C				
Technology	Standard Bus System	Standard Wireless	Advanced Wireless, e.g. Facto...	Very Advanced wireless, e.g. s...
Required Bandwidth	100 bytes / sec	100 Kbits / sec (e.g. RS 485, RS 232,	1-10 Mbit / Sec (e.g. video dat...	>100 Mbit / Sec (e.g. sensor o...
Max. Latency	>10 ms (e.g. RS 232)	1-10 milli seconds (e.g. WLAN, Blue...	micro seconds (e.g. EtherCAT,	nano seconds (e.g. ASIC, FP...
Remote C&C				
Technology	LAN	WLAN	Global Telecom Network (e.g...	Spezialized global telecom ne...
Required Bandwidth	100 bytes / month	100-500 Kbit / Sec (e.g. GPRS)	0.5-10 Mbit / Sec (e.g. UMTS/L...	>100 Kbit / Sec
Max. Latency	90 Min (LEO, e.g. OrbComm; text n...	seconds (GPRS)	milli seconds (WAN)	micro seconds (e.g. LAN)

Backend Services

General

FIGURE 8-26. Project dimension scales

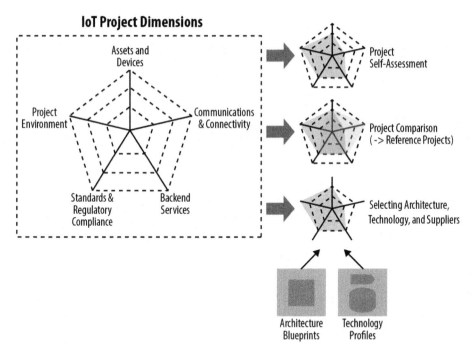

IoT Project Dimensions

Assets and Devices

Project Environment

Communications & Connectivity

Standards & Regulatory Compliance

Backend Services

Project Self-Assessment

Project Comparison (-> Reference Projects)

Selecting Architecture, Technology, and Suppliers

Architecture Blueprints

Technology Profiles

FIGURE 8-27. Use cases for project dimensions

IOT ARCHITECTURE BLUEPRINTS

As already introduced in the "Plan/Build/Run" section, Ignite | IoT relies on a set of artifacts that are used to describe the solution architecture from different architectural perspectives. Figure 8-28 provides an overview of the different artifacts—in particular, for the functional and technical design.

While some of these artifact types are well-known standard artifacts from normal IT projects, others are specialized artifact types that have been specifically developed for use in IoT projects. In particular, the Asset Integration Architecture (AIA) has been defined as part of the Ignite | IoT Methodology to help describe the relationships between assets and devices ("things") and the backend. This will be our focus in the following section.

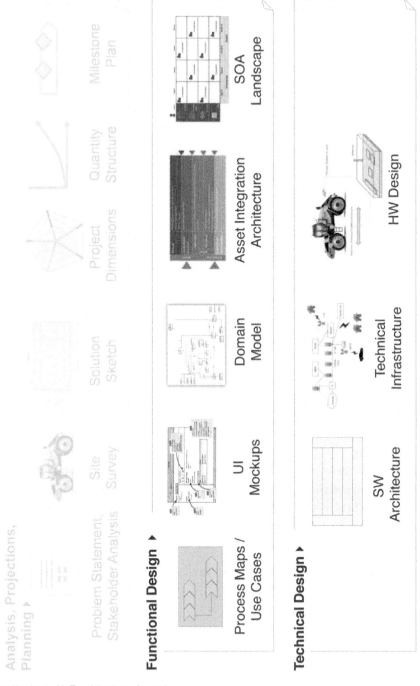

Analysis, Projections, Planning ▸

Problem Statement, Stakeholder Analysis

Site Survey

Solution Sketch

Project Dimensions

Quantity Structure

Milestone Plan

Functional Design ▸

Process Maps / Use Cases

UI Mockups

Domain Model

Asset Integration Architecture

SOA Landscape

Technical Design ▸

SW Architecture

Technical Infrastructure

HW Design

FIGURE 8-28. Key Ignite | IoT architecture elements

Asset Integration Architecture

We have already provided a high-level overview of the Asset Integration Architecture (AIA) in Chapter 1. The basic idea of the AIA is that in an Enterprise IoT context, most solutions involve connecting assets with backend services provided by enterprise applications. According to our definition, an asset is an entity that is usually of primary economic interest to the enterprise, such as a vehicle, a machine, or a building. On the asset, we find different kinds of devices, such as sensors, actuators (like an electric motor to open a window), and so on. Usually, these devices would also have some kind of onboard power management and device control—for instance, to operate a motor at different speeds. Many assets also have multiple onboard computer systems for various tasks. For example, a modern car has between 50 and 80 engine control units (ECUs) and similar, specialized microcontrollers for managing the different elements of the power train (engine, transmission, drive shafts, differentials, etc.). This is what we call the "on-asset business logic."

In Enterprise IoT solutions, one typical challenge is managing large fleets of fixed or mobile assets. This is usually achieved using a specialized tier that creates a logical link between the asset and the enterprise. We call this the IoT cloud or M2M tier (Figure 8-29). On the asset, this tier usually deploys a gateway and a software agent. The gateway can physically connect with the different on-asset hardware components on the one hand, and enable remote connectivity with the enterprise backend through mobile or satellite communication, for example. The software agent performs software-based local integration tasks. Often, the agent creates local objects (known as "device proxy objects") that encapsulate the different connected heterogeneous devices, thus providing one homogeneous remote interface with the backend. The agent can also provide additional functionalities like event management, local event management, security, and local software lifecycle management.

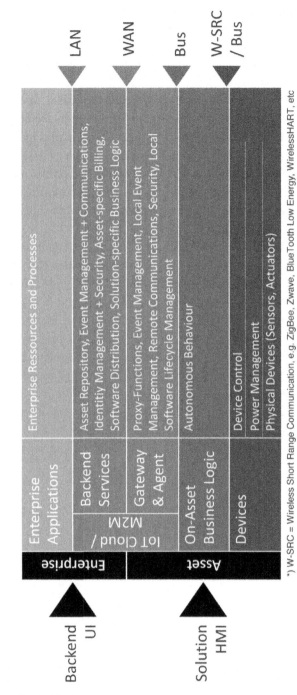

FIGURE 8-29. Asset Integration Architecture

The counterpart is the IoT or M2M backend on the enterprise side. The IoT/M2M backend typically implements a database to manage information about the remote assets and devices, including device status information and event history. This asset repository is a central function of the IoT/M2M backend, and is usually combined with event management or stream processing, identity management and security, asset-specific billing functionality, and remote software distribution.

In addition, the IoT/M2M backend uses different kinds of middleware technologies to integrate with existing backend applications, such as enterprise resource planning (ERP), customer relation management (CRM), and product lifecycle management (PLM).

An important architectural decision is whether the new backend application logic should be implemented as part of the IoT/M2M backend or as part of an existing backend application. Later, in "IoT Technology Profiles" on page 268, we propose an approach in which business process management (BPM) can be implemented as an integration layer between the IoT/M2M backend and the enterprise applications to make end-to-end IoT processes more transparent (see "On-Asset Middleware" on page 249 in "IoT Technology Profiles" on page 268.

Mapping the AIA to Different Industries

One important benefit of the AIA is that it provides a structural blueprint for the large number of highly heterogeneous approaches that can be found across different industries. Figure 8-30 provides an overview of how the AIA maps to the various industry-specific approaches.

For example, in the automotive industry, you will usually find an architectural approach in which multiple, highly specialized engine control units (ECUs) are distributed around the power train. A vehicle control unit (VCU) acts as the head unit and provides a central integration point for other systems—for example, the entertainment system. Because the ECU and the remote control telematics control unit (TCU) are explicitly separated in most cars, we have mapped the TCU to the gateway function in our AIA. A sample use for a TCU would be a vehicle fleet management solution in the backend.

Take, as another example, the area of smart homes. Here it is common to find a central smart-home controller that combines gateway functionality with more advanced local business logic in a single device, which can use Bluetooth, Z-Wave, EnOcean, or WiFi to connect to different local nodes such as a thermostat or window control unit.

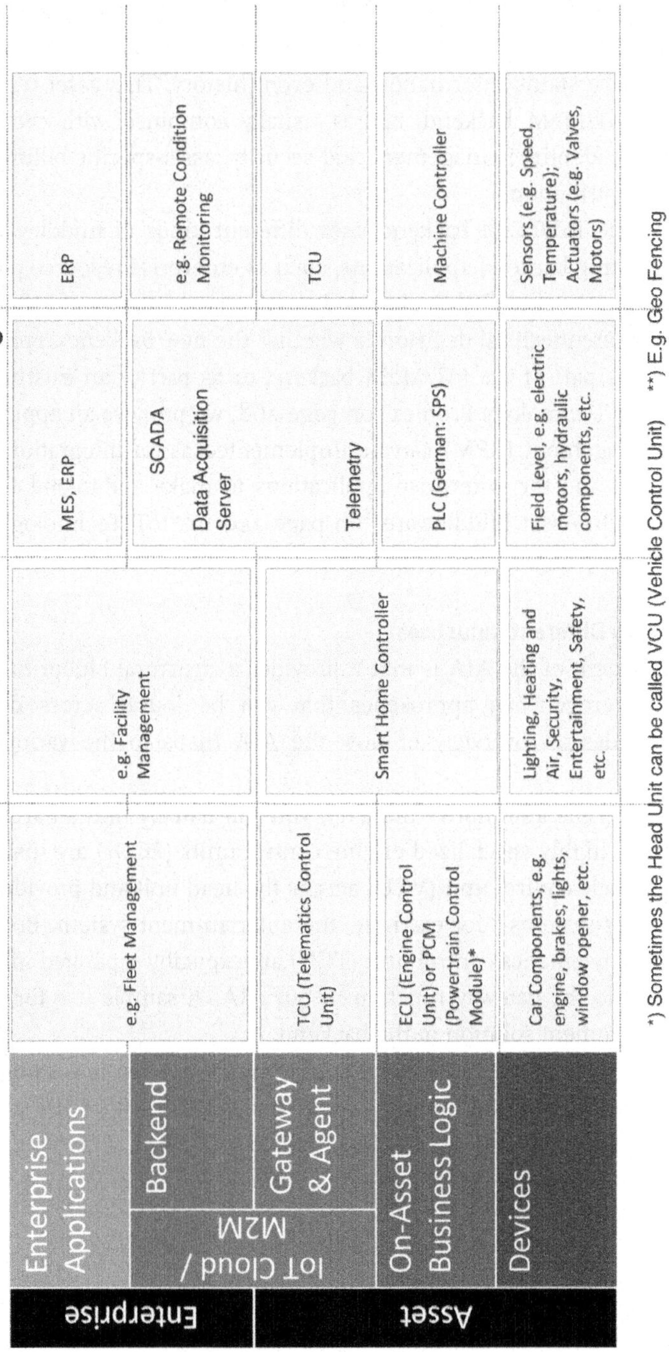

	Automotive	Smart Home	Manufacturing	Mobile Industrial Assets
Enterprise — Enterprise Applications	e.g. Fleet Management	e.g. Facility Management	MES, ERP	ERP
Enterprise — Backend (IoT Cloud / M2M)			SCADA Data Acquisition Server	e.g. Remote Condition Monitoring
Asset — Gateway & Agent	TCU (Telematics Control Unit)		Telemetry	TCU
Asset — On-Asset Business Logic	ECU (Engine Control Unit) or PCM (Powertrain Control Module)*	Smart Home Controller	PLC (German: SPS)	Machine Controller
Asset — Devices	Car Components, e.g. engine, brakes, lights, window opener, etc.	Lighting, Heating and Air, Security, Entertainment, Safety, etc.	Field Level, e.g. electric motors, hydraulic components, etc.	Sensors (e.g. Speed, Temperature); Actuators (e.g. Valves, Motors)

*) Sometimes the Head Unit can be called VCU (Vehicle Control Unit)   **) E.g. Geo Fencing

FIGURE 8-30. AIA mapped to different industries

Another example that can be easily mapped to the AIA is manufacturing. In the manufacturing sector, you will generally find programmable logic controllers (PLCs), which are specialized microcomputers used to control and automate industrial electromechanical processes —for instance, to control machinery on factory assembly lines. The PLC would therefore be the on-asset logic deployed on or close to the machine. Supervisory control and data acquisition (SCADA systems) leverage telemetry technology to remotely manage a network of PLCs and provide a central data-acquisition server in the backend.

As we can see, the Asset Integration Architecture defined by the Ignite | IoT Methodology serves as an integrating perspective that can be used regardless of industry-specific standards. We will see how this can be used in the next section.

AIA-Based IoT Architecture Patterns

Strictly speaking, the AIA is not an architecture in itself but rather an architectural lens through which different IoT architecture patterns can be observed. Figure 8-31 presents some examples for concrete IoT architecture patterns.

On the right side of Figure 8-31, we can see a simple pattern, "Device2Backend," in which the device itself is directly connected to a backend (e.g., a mobile phone). Next to that, "Peer2Peer" (or "Device2Device") describes a pattern where devices interact with each other directly. Next, the "Local Hub" pattern describes connectivity for multiple devices through a central local hub, such as a smart home controller. The "M2M" architecture pattern describes a more hierarchical management of multiple assets that are connected to a central backend. In keeping with our definition of M2M, this type of solution is limited to applications like remote condition monitoring (RCM) and does not provide advanced services. Such services are added in the "Enterprise IoT" architecture pattern.

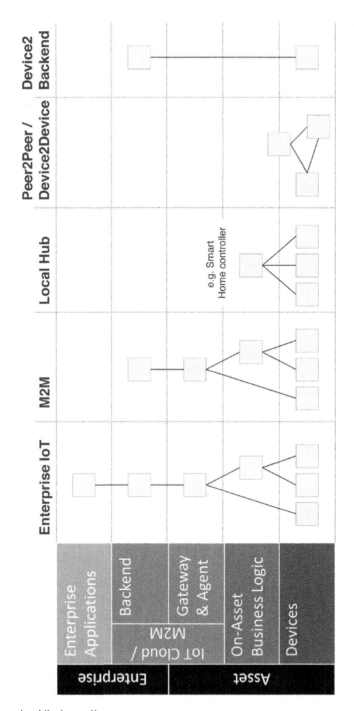

FIGURE 8-31. AIA-based architecture patterns

Cross-Domain Integration: Subnets of Things (Again)

As discussed in Chapter 1, many IoT solutions will start as more self-contained solutions—or, as we dubbed them, Subnets of Things (SoTs). In order to integrate multiple SoTs, such as a fleet management and an energy management solution, it is important to understand the architecture options, which are described in Figure 8-32.

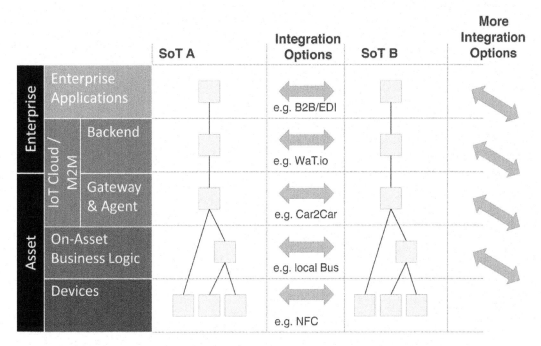

FIGURE 8-32. Cross-domain integration options

In principle, integration can take place on any of the layers of the AIA. On the device level, integration can happen through any kind of (usually wireless) near-field type of communication, an example being Bluetooth. Between different on-asset microcomputers, a local bus system can be used for integration. Gateways may also interact with each other directly—for instance, in a Car2Car type of integration scenario. Specialized integration middleware providers such as wot.io can integrate multiple different IoT/M2M backend platforms. Alternatively, integration might actually take place on the application level in the backend—either by integrating backends with each other (and yes, this means that EDI or Electronic Data Interchange is not going to go away in the near future), or by having devices interact with other backends (e.g., a cloud-based smart home type of integration).

IOT TECHNOLOGY PROFILES

This section looks at different technologies that are often used for IoT solutions. The technology profiles we have identified have been clustered into six groups, including Gateways and Sensor Networks, M2M/IoT Communication Services, [Big] Dataa and Process Management, User Interaction, Security, and Platforms and Enablement (Figure 8-33).

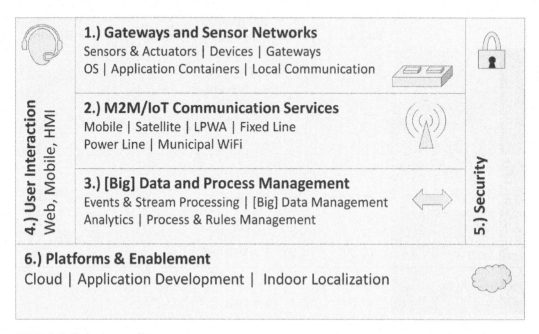

FIGURE 8-33. Technology profiles

Our aim is to provide an overview of the key technologies and how they relate to the other concepts described in the Ignite | IoT Methodology, in order to provide project managers, product managers, and solution architects with an overview of the different technologies and a better understanding of when to use them and when not, depending on the profile of their project. We have attempted to follow the template presented in Figure 8-34.

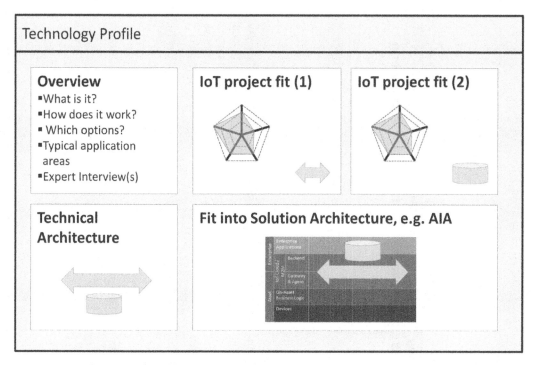

FIGURE 8-34. Technology profile template

In practice, however, it proved impossible to describe all of the technology profiles using exactly the same template, because the technologies are simply too diverse. Nevertheless, the general idea is to provide a high-level overview of the technology, the underlying technical architecture, and how it fits into the AIA, before discussing how the project dimensions of a particular project can help to indicate whether or not the technology is a good fit.

IoT Gateways and Sensor Networks

This section deals with on-asset hardware—which enables local and backend integration—with an emphasis on IoT gateways and related concepts. Because this is such a broad area with few widely accepted standards, we have tried to define a couple of common scenarios first, as shown in Figure 8-35.

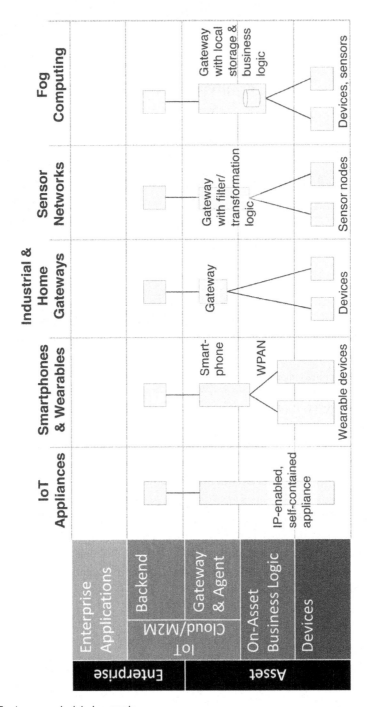

FIGURE 8-35. IoT gateways and related concepts

Common on-asset integration topologies include:

IoT appliances

IP-enabled, intelligent, self-contained appliances like security cameras or intelligent power tools (see Part III). These kinds of IoT appliances can be integrated into any IP network directly, and generally don't rely on specialized external gateways.

Smartphones and wearables

A smartphone or wearable (in this case, "deployed" on a person, not an asset) that provides backend connectivity via a mobile carrier network, as well as local processing power and wireless connectivity to a network of nearby wearable devices. This is sometimes also referred to as a wireless personal area network (WPAN).

Industrial and home gateways

These deliver either wireless or fixed-line connectivity to a backend. They also provide local integration logic (such as bindings/adaptors) and wireless or wired connectivity to local devices. Local devices can be household appliances (in the case of a smart home gateway) or sensors (in the case of a sensor network).

Fog computing

Fog computing (a term coined by Cisco) is an extension of the basic gateway concept, where the gateway adds significant local storage and compute capabilities.

M2M/IOT GATEWAYS. Many M2M and IoT solutions rely on gateways. A gateway is a specialized computer that is typically deployed on or close to an asset (at least in our Enterprise IoT context). Gateways provide connectivity to different devices, to the Internet, or to enterprise networks. In addition, gateways usually run local logic, from simple routing logic and more complex data collection and filtering to highly complex automation, analytics, and application logic, depending on the solution.

Working with an M2M/IoT gateway-centric architecture has many advantages:

- Multiple, heterogeneous devices can be more easily integrated by utilizing gateways for protocol mappings and local connectivity.

- Gateways enable more semantically rich applications by providing abstractions.

- Execution of local business logic enables real-time behavior and helps to reduce response times.

- Gateways help to implement a level of autonomy that ensures stability (e.g., in the event of network problems).

- Local data analysis and filtering helps to reduce network traffic.

- Gateways can deploy local security solutions that help to improve overall solution security.

- Gateways can ensure consistent enterprise policies across a field of work.

- Decoupling gateway functionality from the hardware for onboard business logic facilitates individual lifecycles.

There are many different types of M2M/IoT gateways in use today. Consumer gateways are used in home automation and security, as well as in home energy management. Specialized commercial gateways are employed in a wide range of verticals, including transportation, connected vehicles, manufacturing, and energy.

Adi Reschenhofer, CEO of Wyconn, says:

> Most M2M/IoT gateways share some common features like wireless and/or wired connectivity for integration with local devices, local compute and storage capacities, as well as backend connectivity. Our M2M/IoT gateway matrix (see Figure 8-36) provides an overview of the most common gateway types and their key features.

In the following section, we will take a look at the main features of M2M/IoT gateways before discussing current trends and recommendations for gateway selection.

LOCAL COMPUTE AND STORAGE. Not only are chips getting smaller and more powerful with every generation, but today we have complete computer systems available in incredibly small sizes and at very low cost. Modern smartphones have the processing power and storage capacity of yesterday's high-end servers. Astonishingly powerful, credit card–sized, single-board computers like the Raspberry Pi are now available at minimal cost.

At a Gartner conference in 2014, the savvy IT research firm presented its predictions for IoT processors. We have summarized our learnings in Figure 8-37. In the presentation, Gartner focused on predicting unit shipments for IoT-enabling processors. The interesting message was that they actually foresaw a steep increase in more powerful, 32-bit microcontrollers, with slower growth predicted for 8-bit and 16-bit microcontrollers. According to Gartner, embedded processors and application processors will only represent a fraction of the processing power of the IoT.

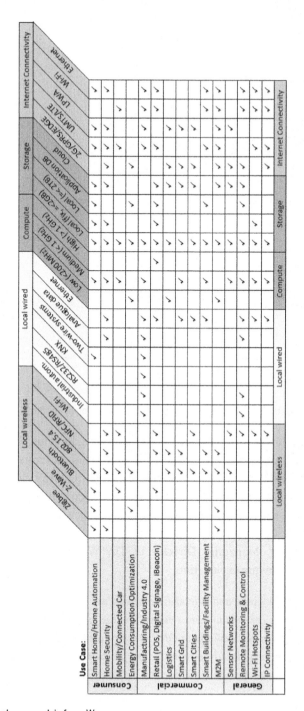

FIGURE 8-36. M2M/IoT gateway matrix from Wyconn

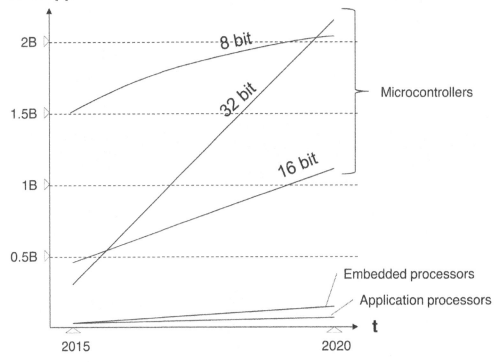

Units Shipped

2B — 8-bit

1.5B — 32 bit

1B — 16 bit — Microcontrollers

0.5B

Embedded processors

Application processors

2015   2020   t

FIGURE 8-37. Shipment predictions for IoT processors (based on presentation by Gartner)

In general, it is interesting to note that more and more domains of traditional embedded systems are now being replaced by higher-level systems, such as Linux-based platforms. This is driven by the need for functionally rich solutions, which require rich middleware functionality (e.g., for communication). Higher-level solutions are extremely expensive to develop for low-level embedded systems. Figure 8-38 provides an overview of the most common IoT platforms, their main technical characteristics, and typical use cases.

Roman Wambacher, Managing Director of Dr. Wehner, Jungmann & Wambacher GmbH, provides the following explanation:

Full OS systems such as Linux and Windows Embedded are now used as IoT gateways, but also for applications such as car infotainment systems. Smaller footprint systems like Intel Galileo or full embedded OS systems like VxWorks or QNX are often used for complex applications with heterogeneous devices and specialized requirements (i.e., functional safety, real-time requirements, or mission criticality), and/or because of the need to support a broad range of embedded processors and microcontrollers.

	Memory & Storage:	CPU:	IoT Use Cases:
Full OS • Linux, Windows Embedded	Memory: > 512 MB Storage: > 1 GB	32 B/64 B	IoT gateways, car infotainment
Small Footprint/ Embedded OS • VxWorks, QNX, Galileo	Memory: > 8 MB Storage: ~32 MB flash	32 B	Mission-critical, real-time apps
Minimal emb. OS • TinyOS, Contiki, RIOT, ArdOS	Memory: 5-50 KB Storage: ~10 KB	16 B	Single-purpose applications
Microkernel	Memory: 512 B Storage: 0.1 KB	8 B	Sensor nodes

FIGURE 8-38. IoT application platforms

Minimal embedded systems like TinyOS, Contiki, and RIOT are often used for single-purpose applications in homogeneous environments with limited local computing resources. They are also employed for sensor nodes in sensor networks. Finally, microkernel architecture—often implemented as a custom solution—is used for simple sensor nodes, and is typically optimized for size, cost, or energy consumption.

LOCAL WIRELESS CONNECTIVITY. A key feature of many gateways is that they enable local wireless connectivity to distributed devices and sensor nodes. There are many different standards and technologies, most of which deal with bridging distances below 100 meters. The key differentiators are distance/range, bandwidth and latency, power consumption, and cost. Figure 8-39 provides an overview of some of the key local wireless technologies.

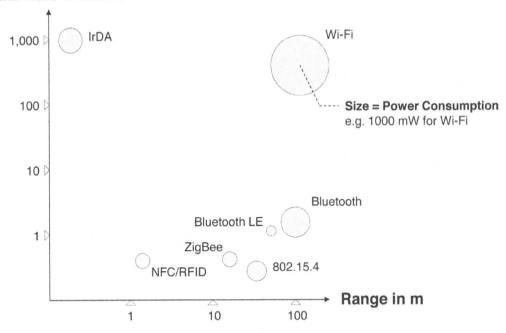

FIGURE 8-39. Overview of key local wireless technologies

Here is a brief outline of the different technologies:

Bluetooth Low Energy
Probably the technology with the largest ecosystem (smartphones, tablets, etc.). Low power, good range, moderate data rates.

15.4
Low-level standard used in closed ecosystems like smart energy. Foundation for higher-level standards like ZigBee and WirelessHART.

ZigBee
Strong focus on low power consumption. Targeted toward smart meters, home automation, sensor networks, remote control units, and the like. Especially useful for battery-operated devices.

WiFi
Widely adopted, high data transfer rates. But also high power consumption and relatively complex infrastructure requirements.

NFC
Low power, but also very short range.

IrDA

Good data transfer rates, but requires line of sight.

BACKEND CONNECTIVITY. In order to integrate the gateway with a remote backend over a long distance, gateways usually have to rely on technologies such as satellite communication; carrier networks (2G, 3G, 4G); low-power, wide-area networks (LPWA); metropolitan area networks (MANs); or fixed-line/power-line communication. Because this is an important and complex area in itself, we have dedicated the next technology profile in this section to this topic ("M2M/IoT Communication Services" on page 298).

SENSOR NETWORKS. Sensor networks will play an important role in many IoT solutions. As shown in Figure 8-40, sensor networks usually rely on intelligent gateways (1, 4) to ensure backend communication (7) and to integrate local networks of sensors or sensor nodes. Multiple sensors can either be integrated into a multisensor device or physically distributed as sensor nodes that use local wireless communication to send data back to a local gateway for further processing. A multisensor device would typically use a specialized board for sensor integration (2), such as Arduino or FPGAs. Multiple sensors can be directly connected through one or multiple local bus systems (3). The wireless sensor network connects multiple sensor nodes (6) via local wireless communication (5).

So as we can see, most sensor networks are built around a local component that combines the features of an IoT gateway (as described earlier) with local business logic. Table 8-1 provides an overview of the key components of this type of intelligent sensor gateway.

The selection of technologies depends primarily on the concrete requirements, some of which might even contradict each other. For example, the requirements for system accuracy might lead to the selection of an expensive sensor element, but the budget may not allow for this. In this case, either the best possible compromise must be found or the requirements must be adjusted accordingly. Depending on the task at hand, a one-off investment (especially in software development) could help to reduce the production cost per unit—for instance, by working around the limitations of sensor elements chosen on cost grounds by means of data fusion and very good algorithms.

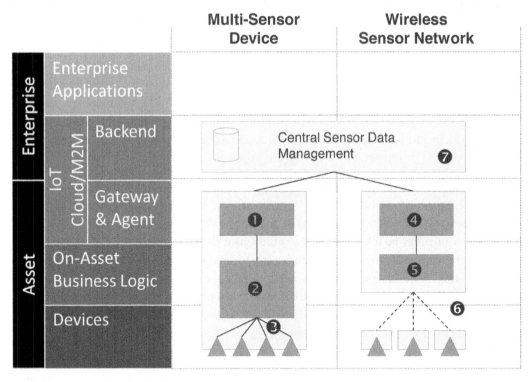

FIGURE 8-40. AIA for sensor networks

TABLE 8-1. Key features of an intelligent sensor gateway (Source: Bosch Connected Devices and Solutions)

Component	Criteria	Examples (this list is not exhaustive)
Power supply	Flexibility (input), performance, efficiency, costs, space requirements	LDO, pulsed
Sensor elements	Measurements, measuring range, resolution, drift, cross-influences, size, energy requirements	Acceleration sensors, gyroscopes, temperature sensors, humidity sensors, magnetic field sensors, light sensors, pressure sensors, microphones
Microcontroller	Memory (flash, RAM), processing power, energy saving modes, special functional units (DSP, communication, etc.)	Cortex M3, M4, Atmel family
Local communications/ radio	Range, technology, and frequency range (important for national regulations), performance (coverage, availability, bandwidth), safety, interoperability, technology lifespan, operating costs	ZigBee, Bluetooth (LE), WiFi, 6LowPan, etc.

Component	Criteria	Examples (this list is not exhaustive)
Local communications/ fixed line	Cost for installation, interoperability, bandwidth, topology (bus vs. point-to-point)	2-wire, CAN, RS-232, RS-485
Protocols	Interoperability, layers covered (e.g., ISO/OSI model), overhead, security, safety, communication	LWM2M, ZigBee profiles, MQTT, etc.
Basic software	Memory requirements, real-time capability, standard support, event-based vs. task-based, performance overhead, communication middleware	RTOS, time-slice operating systems, embedded Linux, etc.
Algorithms	Memory requirements, accuracy, energy efficient	Calculation of position in space, motion, status of objects (open/ closed, on/off)

Naturally, sensor connectivity plays an important role. We have already discussed and compared the general details of close-range wireless technologies in "M2M/IoT Gateways" on page 271. Table 8-2 provides an overview of the connectivity technologies that are typically used for wireless sensor networks, grouped by area.

TABLE 8-2. Sensor connectivity (Source: Bosch Connected Devices and Solutions)

Area	Sensor connectivity (typically)
Smart home	BLE, ZigBee (esp. USA), Z-Wave, DECT ULE, WiFi (without battery operation) Trend: LoRa, LPWA (in definition)
Smart wearables	BLE (because of interoperability with phones + low range need)
Industry 4.0	BLE, ZigBee (no real-time capability), proprietary (2.4 GHz, 868 MHz) Trend: Wi-Fi (5.8 GHz), DECT ULE (good range, no 2.4 GHz competition), Pico LTE Cable-based—field buses (ProfiNet, CAN, Modbus, etc.), RS-232/RS-485, Ethernet
Transport and logistics	GPRS (= 2.5g), 3G = (UMTS), LTE, (Transport: LPWA = low power wide area network = LoRa, Sigfox) Trend (for usage with gateway: BLE, Wi-Fi, RFID (logistics very near))

SENSORS AND SENSOR CATEGORIES. Most sensors comprise one or more sensor elements (depending on the metrics required). For large production volumes (>10,000), application-specific integrated circuits (ASICs) are used. Both parts are housed in a package with electrical and electronic interfaces to the outside. This package is used for mounting (usually by means of soldering to a circuit board).

In large-volume production environments like the automotive industry, the ASIC controls the sensor element in accordance with the configuration provided by the surrounding system (the sensor node). It also preprocesses the data from the sensor element, for example by linearizing measured values, correcting deviations, and so on. The sensor usually communicates outward (with the surrounding system) using digital interfaces such as I2C or SPI. The ASIC often supports different operating modes for different applications. For example, modern acceleration sensors support modes in which the sensor runs using very little power and waits for a movement. If motion is detected (because acceleration occurs), the sensor sends a message to inform the surrounding system. As a result, the surrounding system can remain in sleep mode for as long as possible, and only becomes active when an interesting event occurs.

Modern sensors contain an increasing number of sensor elements. Sensors that can measure rotation, acceleration, and magnetic fields on all three spatial axes are standard today. Each axis and each type of measurement has a corresponding Degree of Freedom (DoF). Thus, a highly integrated sensor would be a 9DoF sensor.

Stefan Schuster, Sensor Network expert from Bosch Connected Devices and Solutions, describes the key sensor categories like this:

Many IoT applications require motion and orientation sensors, in particular gyroscopes and acceleration sensors. Gyroscopes measure the rotation (gyration) of a system along the three spatial axes. Unlike highly specialized sensors, which only measure a single axis, sensors in consumer devices usually measure all three axes. Typical measurement ranges for sensors in consumer devices are up to several 100°/s. Smartphones represent one field of application for these sensors. The information obtained can be used to run games, for example. In the automotive industry, gyroscopes are used to identify the yaw of a vehicle and correct it if necessary (ESP). Information about the rotation is merged with information about the gravitational acceleration (cf. acceleration sensors) to determine the position of a device in space.

Acceleration sensors measure acceleration along the three spatial axes. This includes gravitational acceleration (1g in the direction of the center of the earth). Because this metric is also determined, acceleration sensors on three axes can also identify which way is "down." This is used in smartphones and tablets, for example, to set the display orientation. Typical measurement ranges for this type of sensor in consumer devices are +/- 16 G on all three axes. One example of an industrial application is accident detection (shock sensors). Furthermore, acceleration sensors are often used for positioning applications. They are usually installed in consumer devices in the form of a MEMS element. Although vibrations can distort measurements, they can also be detected (within the limits of sensor capabilities).

Another important category of sensors relates to magnetic field sensors. These sensors measure the magnetic field in all three spatial axes, depending on the design. Typical measurement ranges go from a few uTesla up to 1000 uTesla. By way of comparison, consider the following scenario. The geomagnetic field in the Stuttgart region is around 50 uTesla. Based on magnetic field data, a compass can be implemented. To achieve greater precision, however, this data is combined with data about gravitational acceleration and the rotation of the device.

Possible applications for these sensors include compass function, the detection of magnetic fields that arise due to electrical current flow (e.g., to determine if a device is switched on or off), or the registration of magnetic fingerprints to detect a change in direction or position.

The next category concerns environmental sensors. These sensors detect temperature, air humidity and pressure, illumination level, or noise. Gases or substances in the air can also be detected. To increase accuracy, the different sensor data is often merged and compared. For example, a precise temperature reading is a prerequisite for calculating precise relative air humidity.

These sensors are used in the area of smart homes, for instance, to determine the conditions in a home. Light sensors can also be used as proximity sensors. If a sensor is suddenly obscured, for example, this can indicate that a smartphone is being held up to an ear.

The microphone can register more than just noise: it can also be used as a simple sensor to determine the sound levels in a particular location. However, with increasing demands on the information provided by the metrics, increased processing power or corresponding functional units in the microprocessor will soon be required for frequency analysis.

Microphones and light sensors can still frequently be found as analog sensors, with no digital interfaces. The data must then be processed elsewhere accordingly.

SENSOR FUSION. Modern sensor networks often rely on a technique known as sensor fusion, which fuses inputs from multiple sensors into a single digital model. One example of advanced sensor fusion discussed in this book is autonomous driving (see Chapter 5). In this use case, data from multiple sensors like cameras, radar, and LIDAR is combined to create a 3D model of a vehicle's close surroundings, including objects like other vehicles, pedestrians, and cyclists.

SENSOR NETWORK APPLICATION AREAS. Stefan Schuster, Sensor Network expert from Bosch Connected Devices and Solutions, has compiled the following short overview of the typical usage profiles of sensor networks in the areas of smart homes, smart wearables, transport and logistics, and Industry 4.0. These usage profiles can be used as a starting point for a development that is typical to a particular area. It is important to point out that these usage profiles are constantly evolving because of new technologies or new requirements. In addition, the manufacturer's platform strategy can often lead to sensor nodes being built from predefined components, although the requirements may allow for further optimization in individual cases. Reasons for this include economies of scale for purchasing, manufacture, and reuse of know-how or software parts, which help to reduce development time, risk, and cost.

SENSOR NODES IN SMART HOMES. The area of *smart homes* includes solutions that monitor the condition of doors, windows, or even lights and heating, and that control them accordingly. Information is also forwarded to the user, who can intervene as required by configuring the system or using direct control commands.

The requirements that sensor nodes must meet in this area can be roughly classified as follows:

- In the consumer sector, which is our focus here, cost targets are very tight, and the number of units is medium to high. Product lifecycles are short, which means it must be possible to update the software. The sensor nodes must be integrated into the home as unobtrusively as possible, so they must often be small. Users generally expect them to be easy to install, so communication must be wireless. Customers do not want heavy maintenance requirements, so battery life must be long (usually two years). Batteries must also be readily available, so a standard battery type should be used. Depending on the manufacturer's strategy, interoperability with systems from other manufacturers may be important, so standard connectivity may be required.

- The system must work as promised; however, the imperative for functional reliability is not comparable to that of automotive components, for example. "Good enough" performance is often the goal.

Based on these requirements, the following profile can be defined as a starting point:

- The data the sensor elements must record is determined by the intended use of the sensor node. It is often a good idea to provide additional sensors that may not be needed just yet, but that will allow for future functionality enhancements. One example would be to include acceleration sensors in a sensor node that measures temperature. In a future software enhancement, the customer may then implement a function to have the sensor react to shaking—for instance, by taking a measurement outside of an otherwise active cycle. The main priority for the sensors is to maintain the required level of accuracy with minimal power consumption. Software can often be used to compensate for reductions in accuracy.

- Minimal power consumption does not necessarily mean low consumption during active operation. Instead, this often involves a supporting operation that allows the sensor to remain in sleep mode for as long as possible, only becoming fully active when changes occur to the physical metrics being registered (e.g., motion-activated wake-up mode in gyroscopes and acceleration sensors).

- The microprocessor must meet low to medium demands for processing power and memory. Typical processors are based on a Cortex M3 or M4 core. The M4 has a Digital Signal Processing (DSP) unit and is therefore the preferred choice for tasks that involve signal processing—for example, analyzing audio signals from a microphone. Typical memory sizes are 16-128 KB RAM and 64-512 KB flash memory. Energy efficiency is also important in this context. This is generally achieved not only through low power consumption during operation, but also by supporting modes in which only very small parts of the microprocessor are operational. These parts preprocess data and signals and then bring the entire microprocessor into active mode when required. Modern microprocessors with Cortex M3 have three, four, or more of these modes. The time during which the microprocessor must be fully active to complete its tasks should be kept as low as possible. The wake-up time of the microprocessor must also be considered. This should be as short as possible to ensure short cycle times.

- The algorithm must of course meet the functional requirements, but must also be optimized for energy efficiency (to allow the electronic components to remain switched off for as long and as often as possible), enabling the microprocessor selected to be as small and as cost-efficient as possible.

- Power supply to the system is determined on the basis of the target costs for manufacture and the required battery life. DC/DC transformers are typically used, which are very efficient. If the budget is very tight, linear regulators can be used. These are not as efficient, but are much cheaper—at the expense of the battery life of the system. Batteries are usually selected from the types readily available on the market (i.e., AA, AAA) and are limited by the space available.

The wireless technologies used in the smart home sector vary widely. Typical technologies are presented in Table 8-2. Data transfer rates are generally low. For energy efficiency reasons, as little data as possible is sent as seldom as possible. This has repercussions for the algorithm, which must evaluate the sensor data as far as possible in the device, and then send high-level information only. (Consider the following example: the algorithm receives data about the acceleration and rotation of a door at one-second intervals. However, it only transmits the event "door open," which it extracts from the data. This event occurs much less frequently and can even be transmitted in a single bit.)

WiFi is not really feasible for battery operation if a battery life of two years is required, and is used only in exceptional cases. Connection to the sensor node is often via Bluetooth (particularly the low-energy "LE" variant) or ZigBee. With ZigBee, the standard is sufficient to specify events such as "door open/closed" (cf. ZigBee Home Automation), whereas with Bluetooth LE, the specification does not reach this high level. Range is usually not critical, but problems may arise in large houses, or houses with very thick concrete (or similar) walls. In this case, an alternative technology can be selected or intermediate stations can be used. (ZigBee supports mesh networking, in which each node communicates data between other nodes, thus increasing overall coverage.)

Depending on the interoperability requirements, the protocol used can either be LWM2M, proprietary protocols, or the higher layers specified by ZigBee. LWM2M and end-to-end IP connectivity are particularly suitable for ensuring maximum independence from individual transfer technologies.

SMART WEARABLES. This area includes sensor nodes that are built into sports devices, for example, or worn directly on the body.

Demand for these devices comes from the consumer sector, just like in the area of smart homes. The cost targets per item are very tight, and the number of units ranges from medium to very high. The space requirements of the components are a critical factor. Because devices usually run on a battery, energy requirements are also very important. However, users often accept the fact that battery life is limited, and this is compensated for by using rechargeable batteries. Communication requirements are usually characterized by short transfer paths (to a smartphone); similarly, connectivity is also characterized by connection to a smartphone, and to the wireless standards and protocols available in the phone. From a functional point of view, requirements are often prioritized so that minor inaccuracies in data capture are accepted in favor of very small size and low costs (e.g., tolerance in recording movements with a wristband during the day). Update capabilities are often limited; new functions are not implemented in the sensor nodes, but rather are added in the smartphone (as an app) or in the backend. However, there is a growing trend toward over-the-air updates for sensor nodes.

Available space and power requirements are important criteria for selecting sensor elements. As a rule, the only sensors included are those that are necessary for capturing the required data. Because of space limitations, it can be a good idea to use very highly integrated sensor elements (9 DoF), even though these are more difficult to evaluate due to cross-coupling effects, and despite the fact that higher tolerances may arise in data capturing.

The processing power requirements that the microprocessor must meet are low to medium. Available space and battery requirements are decisive factors. System-on-chip (SoC) systems offer significant advantages in this case, as they combine microprocessor and wireless connectivity in one integrated circuit (IC). Typical memory sizes are 4-64 KB RAM and 16-256 KB flash memory.

Because the microprocessor selected is often very small due to space, cost, and energy usage requirements, the algorithm can be designed in such a way that large amounts of data are transferred in cycles. (The power consumption of the radio transmission range is not particularly critical, as the required range is generally low and batteries can be recharged.) Data is then evaluated in the smartphone or the backend. The more data is transferred with little pre-processing, the more new functions can be implemented in the smartphone or backend via updates. However, this depends to a large extent on the specific use case. For example, a step counter will reliably identify steps in the sensor node, and only report the event "step" to the smartphone.

Recall that the Asset Integration Architecture defines several IoT architecture patterns. In the AIA, most cases in this area can be covered by the M2M pattern, with the smartphone playing the role of the gateway and mapping the business logic. If there are multiple sensors, they can be linked to each other (body area network), in which case the architecture would be based on the Device2Device pattern.

The battery is often very small and peak current is limited, so power requirements over time and peak currents both must be considered for all components during the design phase. The power supply may need to provide for appropriate buffers.

Bluetooth LE is currently the dominant wireless connectivity technology in use, thanks to its interoperability with a wide range of smartphones, its low power requirements, and its sufficient range.

TRANSPORT AND LOGISTICS. This area encompasses sensor nodes that are used to monitor assets like containers and crates while they are being transported or stored. It includes the monitoring of location (indoor/outdoor), vibrations, temperature, and so on. Depending on the use case, the recorded data is either transferred wirelessly upon request or cyclically, or else it is recorded persistently and read directly (in a data logger use case). If the data is read directly (via USB or similar), then a wireless connection is not necessary. Power is usually provided by a battery. Reliability requirements are generally high. Depending on the asset to be monitored, a decision will be made in favor of either a low cost per unit with a high number of units, or a medium cost per unit with a low number of units. Service life using a battery depends greatly on the use case and especially on the length of time for which the asset must be monitored. Space requirements are also highly dependent on the relevant asset to be monitored, but are usually of medium importance. Requirements due to environmental influences can be high, depending on the specific environment (e.g., one with extreme temperatures).

The selection of sensor elements is dependent on the data to be monitored—it is not possible to make a general statement about necessary accuracy levels or other requirements. Depending on the asset to be monitored, measurement ranges usually extend beyond those found in typical consumer applications (e.g., monitoring goods in a cooling chamber).

The requirements the microprocessor must meet are low to medium—these are usually applications for recording and transferring data. For designs in which data is recorded for a long time before being read, the memory requirements are higher. Additional memory is often used in these cases. Depending on how long the asset needs to be monitored, the power requirements are a decisive factor and also influence the choice of microprocessor.

In many cases, the algorithms are comparatively simple threshold triggers. For example, if a monitored asset exceeds a certain temperature for a specific length of time, an alarm is triggered. However, depending on the use case (such as motion detection), the algorithms can also be complex.

Data transfer is highly dependent on the use case. Three general cases can be distinguished:

- If the device needs to be monitored within a large area (such as outdoors) and if data transfer during monitoring is a priority, technologies such as GSM-based data transfer are useful. These make sensor nodes very expensive, consume a large amount of energy, and have high peak currents, resulting in high demands on the power supply. In the AIA, this would be the Device2Backend pattern.

- If the asset is in a controlled, manageable space, and if data is transferred during monitoring, technologies such as WiFi (which has low energy efficiency), BLE, LoRa, or proprietary wireless standards can be used—usually depending on the existing infrastructure. A gateway is also frequently used. In the AIA, this would be the Enterprise IoT pattern.

- If data is not transferred during monitoring, but rather is read as required, one option would be to use cable technologies (e.g., USB, which can also be used to simultaneously recharge the sensor node). Alternatively, short-range wireless technologies can also be a good option. BLE is particularly suitable where tablets, smartphones, or PCs are used to read the data, as it is widely supported by these devices.

EXAMPLE: SENSOR SELECTION AND INTEGRATION. Stefan Schuster and Julian Bartholomeyczik both work for Bosch Connected Devices and Solutions (BCDS). BCDS is a Bosch division that develops and markets innovative connected devices and tailor-made solutions for the IoT. The following discussion provides an example of the creation of a solution sketch for an IoT sensor network.

Dirk Slama: Could you talk us through your sample solution sketch for an IoT sensor network?

Stefan Schuster and Julian Bartholomeyczik: Sure. A solution sketch includes both the problem space (the task set for the project) and the solution space (the technical solution that resolves this task). There are two different approaches for creating a solution sketch: top-down and bottom-up.

Let's take a brief look at the terminology and typical approaches. We speak of a top-down procedure if a specific task has been set—for example, in the form of a question: How can we identify wear and tear on machines at an early stage? A technical solution that accomplishes this task is created and components are designed and created accordingly.

In a bottom-up procedure, components for the technical solution already exist—for example, in the form of existing platforms, sensors, or algorithms. These projects are often exploratory in nature. A typical opening question in this case would be: "What can we detect in a machine using these sensors/this data?"

To help speed up projects, BCDS has created a platform construction kit that includes a development kit for sensor networks. The kit contains a wide range of sensors for all sorts of different applications.

In reality, projects are created using a combination of these two procedures. Platforms, for instance, can be approached from both directions. A platform can be designed either from the top down as a superset of application projects, or from the bottom up as a collection of existing technical components. Application projects rarely define a solution entirely from the top down; instead, they use existing components—for example, from a platform.

Let's use a concrete example: say we want to enable early identification of wear and tear on a machine with rotating parts in order to plan maintenance periods efficiently.

First, the project must be defined as precisely and as independently of the implementation as possible. Committing too soon to one implementation possibility can narrow the solution space prematurely and should be avoided.

In addition to the functional requirements, system requirements that define the framework of the solution must also be adhered to. These include cost limits, the environment in which the system must work, and set interfaces to existing systems.

Dirk Slama: So, what would you describe as good requirements?

Stefan Schuster and Julian Bartholomeyczik: The core questions are as follows: What does the user want to learn from the system? What actions must the system perform and when, and/or under what conditions? What are the basic economic conditions, and what environment must the system work in?

In this example, the user wants the system to inform them in good time about wear and tear on a machine. The machine is operated in an industrial setting. We assume that a process control system already exists and can be contacted via TCP/IP. We establish the price that potential customers are willing to pay for monitoring a machine, which results in a target price of €30 for manufacturing a sensor node. The system should be connected without cables and should have a battery life of one year.

For the functional part, a theory is established, from which we can derive the data required for the system to fulfill the task. In this example, the theory states that wear and tear on a machine can be identified through increased vibrations in the machine bed. This kind of theory is usually defined by a domain expert (i.e., an engineer who is familiar with the machine).

Ideally, the theory should be validated first. In our example, this is done by taking measurements at two machines: one in proper working condition, and one in the condition that you need the system to identify (i.e., parts are worn). This type of validation process can be used both to check the theory (vibrations increase when parts are worn) and to select suitable sensors (by using them to run tests). It also enables a mounting position or a series of suitable mounting positions to be determined at this stage. From these positions, other variables can be determined, such as available space and resistance to liquids and temperatures.

When the theory is validated, it is converted to a digital model. In our example, the measurements taken provide information on the extent of the vibrations, the frequency, and the changes to these parameters depending on the degree of wear and tear. Ideally, measurements are taken at multiple machines to determine the variance between machines.

Sensors are selected on the basis of the digital model, the nonfunctional requirements, and the experience gained from the validation process. Existing data might also be utilized (e.g., does the process control system already know the rotation speed of the engines?). Data collection points are therefore specified precisely. And in a final step, the system can now be represented in a "solution sketch." Note that our focus is on the sensor perspective here, and not on the backend.

In this example, the sensor system designed is fitted close to the axle-bearing points in the machine. It is powered by a battery and transfers data wirelessly. An important decision here relates to where the digital model should be implemented. The following are two possible scenarios: In the first scenario, the model is implemented in the sensor node. This means that a simple message is sent to the superordinate system when the machine reaches a certain level of wear and tear. In the second scenario, the digital model is implemented in the central control system, which means that the sensor data is transferred and wear and tear is calculated in the superordinate system.

This decision is driven by the following considerations in particular:

Energy requirements of the sensor node
Sending data requires a lot of energy. Preprocessing on the sensor node reduces the data transfer requirements.

Available processing power and available data
Data processing can require processing power that is not feasible on a sensor node within the specified economic limits. If additional data from other sources is required to ensure correct calculations, then calculation can only be performed where all necessary data is available.

The protection of know-how and the division of supply
If the algorithm needs to be protected, and if it was created by the sensor manufacturer, then implementation in the node makes sense.

In our example, the algorithm is implemented on the sensor node, as all required data is available, processing power is low, and battery life is essential.

Dirk Slama: Thanks! Finally, let's talk briefly about the main components of the solution sketch.

Stefan Schuster and Julian Bartholomeyczik: The main components are the actual sensor element, a microprocessor, and an element for radio communication. Following tests with a microphone and an acceleration sensor, and after determining the frequency range and amplitudes, an acceleration sensor is chosen. The microprocessor is selected from the manufacturer's construction kit (platform strategy, cf. bottom-up procedure) and the dimensions are such that the algorithm can run and there is still some space for enhancements. The radio connectivity is selected on the basis of the range requirements and battery usage requirements. A Bluetooth LE (BLE) connection is selected. A gateway is implemented which receives the data via BLE and then converts to WiFi to enable connection with the process control system.

INDUSTRY 4.0. This area is linked to the field of transport and logistics. It concerns the monitoring of machines and equipment as well as the materials and components used. Reliability requirements are high. Cost pressure per number of units is not as high as for consumer products in the areas of smart homes and smart wearables. The need for minimal installation space depends on the location in which the sensor node will be installed, but we will classify the space requirements as medium here. Depending on the application, power may be available via cable. However, a battery is commonly used to minimize the effort required to retrofit a sensor node of this type. Requirements due to environmental influences can be high, depending on the specific environment (extreme temperatures, oil mist, vibrations, etc.).

When selecting a sensor, high levels of reliability and accuracy are usually the main deciding factors. Machines have a wide range of in-built sensors. Depending on the use case and the connectivity of these sensors, the data they capture can be tapped into so that the entire solution can be achieved without dedicated sensor nodes. For retrofitting solutions, however, a sensor node to be installed later would be useful.

The microprocessor must meet medium to high requirements—algorithms may become quite complex, and high reliability requires complex software with correspondingly high memory and processing power requirements. As with the sensor element, cost pressure is not as important a consideration with a low number of units as in consumer applications with a high number of units.

Energy efficiency is important if the solution (especially a retrofit solution) needs to be completely wireless. If sensors are installed in concealed locations, changing a battery is a high cost factor due to the required downtime and impact on working times. Depending on where the sensor is installed, a long service life can be achieved by choosing large batteries.

In terms of the algorithms, a lot depends on the energy efficiency requirements and available energy. If these requirements are very tight, it is a good idea to process data on the sensor node so that little communication with the superordinate system is required. For example, an event is only transferred when a specific level of wear and tear has been reached. If flexibility in data evaluation is a priority, and if other information, such as vibration data, must be sent to the backend, data transfer must take place more often—at the expense of battery life.

Wireless connection is critical in the industrial sector, because in many cases, the environment does not offer favorable conditions for wireless communication. Technologies such as LoRa can be useful here, but a wireless standard has not yet been established. Most machine operators and manufacturers would like a connection to the field bus systems used, which are usually proprietary. This can be done using appropriate gateways, which are then developed specifically for the application.

TRENDS AND OUTLOOK. The entire area of IoT gateways, sensor networks, and so on is a fast-moving field of the IoT. In the following interview with Mitko Vasilev, CTO of openBerlin Cisco IoT Innovation Center in Berlin, we discuss some of the current trends in gateway technologies.

Dirk Slama: Mitko, Cisco is making a big push in the direction of fog computing. What developments can we expect in this area?

Mitko Vasilev: We are digitizing our environment to optimize our business processes, our social communities, and our personal lives. The exponential data growth and requirements for real-time digitization will require an additional intelligence layer with complete cloud functionality that will be distributed at the edge of the network, where the Internet ends and the real world begins. A number of major companies have adopted an open IoT architecture incorporating a new intelligence layer at the edge known as "fog."

The fog layer will lead to a paradigm shift in distributed compute, storage, and analytics. Today, businesses typically deploy separate devices and multiple software controllers for different services. The fog concept combines services, orchestration, manageability, and programmability in a single distributed platform.

Fog-based architectures will change how devices are connected and data is processed, both for Enterprise IoT and Home IoT gateways. Today, data is sent to, processed, and stored in public or private clouds. There the data is analyzed and commands are sent back to the devices to act upon that information, and operators are then notified. Fog computing helps to overcome the costly need to constantly move data to a single Data Lake, and enables both stream analytics and the transformation of plain data into actionable data close to data points in near real-time analytics. The new methodologies are opening up new business models and also help to meet modern compliance and regulation policies. This is critical for accelerating the mass adoption of the IoT today, and will provide the cost-effective, scalable, and stable infrastructure that is required for future growth.

Dirk Slama: Let's focus on home gateways for a moment. What's happening in this space?

Mitko Vasilev: Home IoT gateways are merging and will continue to merge into several common hardware platforms that differ in terms of the software and services used. The underlying operating system is typically based on open source Linux implementations (predominantly Debian variations, Busy Box, or Yocto) combined with a number of open community-supported tools for orchestration and device management. The current trend in the area of entertainment-enabled gateways will continue with a big emphasis on video streaming to any device, home media services, and integrated home monitoring and management capabilities. Gateways will need to interact with appliances and control systems in the home by using radios and IoT communication stacks (such as Bluetooth low energy or variations of 802.15.4 on 868 MHz/902 MHz ISM bands, like ZigBee and Z-Wave). IoT middleware systems will use gateways to expand environment-sensing capabilities, either with in-built sensors or sensors connected mainly via wireless technology. This will provide the necessary data and platforms for IoT applications to offer a completely personalized home experience. Open source hardware platforms based on general-purpose CPUs are making these applications more attractive in terms of cost and ease of use, paving the way for the mass adoption of personalized services like control devices for temperature, light, and security systems.

Most gateways will provide connectivity over multiple ISM (Industrial, Scientific, and Medical) radio bands simultaneously (i.e., 169/433/868/902 MHz, 2.4 GHz, and 5 GHz). This is in response both to the dense environment of connected things and to requirements for higher data rates in the gigabit range. The radios integrated in the gateways have already begun to combine BLE, wireless, and new standard-based 802.15.4 radios into a single embedded chip, and this trend is set to continue to an even greater extent. Multiple industry alliances will enable local area connectivity and interoperability between IoT gateways and home appliances, both on a networking and a software communication level. However, interoperability still remains a major challenge to be overcome in the near future.

The application-hosting capabilities of home IoT gateways will open up a new "platform-as-a-service" (PaaS)-style application delivery to connected homes for an improved end-user experience. The combination of gateways, IoT PaaS, and IoT middleware software layers in the cloud will create an open end-to-end vertical architecture.

The cybersecurity mechanisms aligned with IEEE standards (e.g., 802.1x for device authentication, 802.11i for securing wireless transmissions, etc.) will be auto-enabled on the majority of home IoT gateways as well on the devices they will connect.

SoC circuits combining general-purpose CPUs and DSPs for offloading multimedia processing and accelerating protocol translations will become increasingly common in home IoT gateways.

Dirk Slama: Thanks! And what about the enterprise side of things?

Mitko Vasilev: The hardware architecture of Enterprise IoT gateways will fall into two major CPU architectures: ARM-based CPUs for low-end (and, in some specific cases, mid-range) gateways, and x86-based CPUs for certain mid-level and all high-level product lines. The unification of CPU architectures will facilitate cross-platform deployment of business applications and simplify native services as well as virtualization integration. Most gateways will provide combined hardware and software stacks that will already be highly optimized for end-to-end secure IoT architecture.

Monolithic operating systems will be virtualized to achieve increased optimization of the underlying hardware. In modern Enterprise IoT gateways, different hypervisor technologies (e.g., KVM, WR, etc.) will be used in order to optimize the prevailing multicore architectures. Linux-/UNIX-based operating systems with enterprise-level support will be predominant due to their flexibility and business applications ecosystem. Most modern gateway-operating systems will be componentized into dynamic micro-services (i.e., routing, security, content delivery, application container hosting, etc.), which will enable optimized use of the constrained embedded environment. For the enterprise market, the hardware refresh cycle is generally in the range of 20+ years, which will introduce more purpose-built IoT hardware with extended hardware lifecycles. The mainstream availability of new gateways and services is driving the demand for purpose-built gateways for specific verticals that will clone a single flexible architecture. Reference designs will be structured into groups, mainly due to different certification, compliance, and business requirements. Gateway modularity will be significant for flexible IoT deployment and, due to the need for different interfaces, IEEE 802.11, IEEE 802.15.4, Modbus, RS485/232—and many other open and proprietary connections—will continue to play an important role in the coming decades.

Fog computing will enable middleware services as well as distributed compute and storage capacities across all gateway ranges. More advanced orchestration and management mechanisms will optimize resources across the entire edge of the enterprise domain. Pure connectivity gateways for IoT enterprise applications will not be able to provide the new business model infrastructure required by industry-disruptive trends like the Internet of Things.

Local wireless connectivity will be based on more standardized ISM bands, IEEE 802.11, and IEEE 802.15.4. Strong enterprise-level cybersecurity policy mechanisms will be enforced on all communication in order to ensure industry-certified compliance (802.1x, 802.11i, and others).

Local wired connectivity is shifting toward the predominant Gigabit Ethernet in low- and mid-level IoT gateways, with higher adoption of multigigabit interfaces (2.5 Gbps, 5 Gbps, 10 Gbps) in high-end gateways. Multigigabit speeds will be needed on gateways combining high-speed IEEE 802.11ac wireless interfaces, business requirements for high-speed throughput, and bandwidth-demanding applications. Speed is nothing without control, and this principle also applies to the enterprise networking domain. Deterministic networking provides guaranteed networking services and, once based on IEEE Time-Sensitive Networking (TSN), the technology will enable Enterprise IoT gateways for new use cases and cybersecurity mechanisms for industry verticals such as manufacturing, automotive, and so on. Proprietary deterministic networks will disappear over the next decade as the refresh cycle of industrial customers becomes aligned with open TSN architecture based on IEEE standards.

Enterprise IoT gateways are based on multicore compute-efficient hardware architecture that provides the necessary performance capabilities for complex analytics and programmability functions on the gateway itself. A greater number of protocol translation and data normalization functions will be hardware-accelerated by purpose-built CPUs and software stacks for IoT purposes. Hypervisors will provide the necessary abstraction layer for the cost-optimized use of the underlying hardware, as well as for the secure isolation and execution of multiple microservices in the fog layer.

Permanent storage capacity will grow to terabytes of SSD storage, allowing the distributed storage layer to optimize data allocation and storage operations. The majority of process-specific data will be stream processed at the edge of the enterprise domain and stored in a distributed manner between the fog and cloud layers. Stream analytics provides the mechanisms for acting on data close to the data source and mitigating the latency between line-of-business and the cloud.

IoT middleware will scale from fog gateways to the cloud layer, thus providing data, applications, policies, analytics, and an improved user experience across the business. Lightweight analytics engines will be built inside the gateway stack and will be programmed and controlled by centralized business intelligence applications via REST APIs.

Element management functionality will be tied to virtualization in a true software-defined networking architecture, with most functions abstracted in network and device controllers. Open protocols for communication will become predominant, with wider adoption of industry-based standards MQTT, XMPP, AMQP, and dozens of others that will serve specific business and operational needs.

The Internet of Things is disrupting the design and operation of enterprise and home networks at an unprecedented rate. The importance of starting with open, standard-based architecture today is rapidly becoming a key factor for ensuring business success in the future.

RECOMMENDATIONS. To conclude this section on IoT gateways with a set of actionable recommendations for project managers, we spoke with two experts about their experiences on the implementation side. We will start with the gateway vendor perspective: Adi Reschenhofer is CEO of Wyconn, a vendor of managed M2M/Industrial Internet gateways.

Dirk Slama: Adi, why do gateways play such an important role in IoT projects?

Adi Reschenhofer: A gateway-based architecture is the key approach for future IoT projects. Implementing a gateway-based architecture will allow you to update key project elements such as security, edge device functionality, and protocols via the gateway itself.

Dirk Slama: What is the best way to implement custom features on the gateway?

Adi Reschenhofer: If you need a certain feature on your smartphone, you simply download an app from an app store. This is what IoT platforms will be able to offer in the near future. IoT projects currently involve custom software and hardware development, but the idea here is to commoditize as much as possible. This means that hardware will soon be available as a standard off-the-shelf product. Software features will be packaged in apps that can be purchased in the marketplace and distributed to the designated gateways.

Dirk Slama: How is security implemented?

Adi Reschenhofer: One challenging issue regarding security in IoT projects is the fact that gateways and devices ("things") need to be authenticated without user interaction. This means that the identity of a gateway or device needs to be set up either during manufacturing or later in a commissioning process. Having gateways implemented on the edge of the network provides you with the possibility of updating security policies or exchanging entire security algorithms, if necessary.

Dirk Slama: What are the other benefits of having a gateway in place?

Adi Reschenhofer: Further advantages of gateway-based architecture include resources that can be used to process or store data close to its source and avoid sending large amounts of data to the backend systems. In addition, having the possibility to adapt to future requirements simply by deploying an app is a huge benefit that accelerates time to market.

Dirk Slama: How do you select the right gateway category for your project?

Adi Reschenhofer: Finding the right fit is the key challenge. The proper sizing of the gateway is determined by the use case. Computer and Internet connectivity are cost and energy consumption drivers. Putting effort into estimating the compute and connectivity needs is the key to implementing a sustainable solution.

Dirk Slama: How do you decide between a custom gateway and an off-the-shelf gateway?

Adi Reschenhofer: The make-or-buy decision is based on the availability of a standard product for a specific requirement. In cases where a standard gateway can offer you the features required for your IoT project, it is valid to use it. This will help save time, which is what is needed to design, develop, test, certify, and produce a custom device. In some cases, minor adaptations to existing products—such as adding hardware modules via serial, USB, Ethernet, or other ports—can also deliver the required solution.

In certain cases, nontechnical factors can influence the decision-making process. If the gateway is needed for a consumer solution, brand design is very important and will most probably result in the development of custom enclosures. If you are retrofitting gateways in existing machines, a redesign might be necessary as well.

Dirk Slama: What are the key aspects to watch out for in terms of manageability?

Adi Reschenhofer: You basically have to ensure that your solution supports the complete solution lifecycle (i.e., Plan/Build/Run). In all phases, the management system must provide full visibility and control. It is also important to monitor a gateway's vital parameters like CPU utilization, memory, and storage usage to ensure faultless operation. The management platform is also used to distribute the firmware and specific apps.

Building on these insights from the vendor perspective, we also spoke to Roman Wambacher, Managing Director of Dr. Wehner, Jungmann & Wambacher GmbH, a highly specialized boutique software company with strong roots in telematics and M2M. In the following interview, Roman provides us with the typical project manager perspective.

Dirk Slama: Roman, from a gateway perspective, what are the key challenges involved in an M2M/IoT project with complex and widely deployed assets?

Roman Wambacher: The first thing that comes to mind is heterogeneity. Many of our customers have deployed tens of thousands of assets in the field over several years, if not decades. Numerous projects that we get involved in have to retrofit gateways to existing product lines. Very often, there are multiple generations of complex asset classes or product types, each with different product variants, which have all been rolled out globally. This means that interfaces to the different devices on these products are also highly heterogeneous. We often have to deal with a multitude of interfaces, and backward compatibility is critical, even for new solutions. Many customers start solutions by focusing on the assets that are already in the field. This way, they can access a large base of connected assets very quickly.

Dirk Slama: So how do you deal with this heterogeneity?

Roman Wambacher: Well, one thing we recommend is that our customers establish a dedicated interface management system for their product portfolio. This system must address hardware and software interfaces, both on the protocol level as well as on the functional level. It also has to take versioning, product variants, and backward compatibility into account. A closely related issue concerns product variant management. Only by addressing this centrally can you manage global M2M and IoT solutions on a large scale. For example, you need a central mechanism that controls how you deal with different configurations for specific products. If you don't manage this properly—ideally in an automated manner—it will hit you hard on the cost side later.

Dirk Slama: What about data availability?

Roman Wambacher: Yes, that is an important issue as well—as is data quality. Most products that were designed and deployed in a pre-IoT world simply didn't have to pay much attention to these issues. The products live an isolated life in the field. Take battery fill level as an example. In all likelihood, a nonconnected product will not have put a lot of effort into providing a high-quality interface to this function. In the IoT world, the situation is very different. Interfaces to things like fuel consumption or operating hours suddenly become very important. In many projects, the people on the solution side are astonished that such basic asset functions are not available at all, or not in the required quality. There is a good chance that an embedded software developer will not have given much thought to the fact that in a connected world, it could be a problem if an asset temporarily sets the operating hours to zero during startup. In the IoT world, this is exposed immediately.

Alternatively, take something like product identification. Very few existing product lines will actually have a consistent way of uniquely identifying assets in the field through automated interfaces or an electronic identification plate. So you will probably have to get creative and move this problem to the solution level, for example, by using a pairing approach based on QR codes or something similar.

Dirk Slama: How do you deal with this kind of situation?

Roman Wambacher: You have to address this systematically, product type by product type, and version by version. All data from the products has to be validated per product type and version. You will be surprised by the many different meanings of basic things like "product health" that different product versions might have. Integration tests are extremely important—you can't start early enough. And, of course, you have to perform field tests. Finally, your project plan has to provide for the unexpected. Don't underestimate the complexity of fixing interface problems in such an environment, especially if they require changes on the asset side.

Dirk Slama: And how do you select a gateway?

Roman Wambacher: Well, using an off-the-shelf gateway always sounds attractive, because of the cost of custom gateway development. In many cases, however, it will be hard to avoid. Generic gateways are often too feature-rich and hence too expensive. Or else they lack certain critical interfaces you need in your project. In our experience, if you need 10,000 or more gateways, there is a good chance that you will end up opting for a custom solution.

Dirk Slama: What do you have to take into consideration for global rollouts?

Roman Wambacher: Well, ideally you want a single type of gateway for all countries to reduce complexity and TCO. However, in many cases this will not be possible, for several reasons. Most notably, there are country-specific technical requirements—different frequencies used for LTE, for example, or CDMA versus GSM. Modems that support multiple options do exist, but this will add to the cost side. You should not underestimate the extra costs you will incur by supporting multiple gateway types. Just think of the government approval processes you will have to go through for each gateway type—and each new version!

Dirk Slama: What other cost drivers are involved in this type of project?

Roman Wambacher: Many people think that the main cost driver is communication costs for mobile data exchange. However, this is usually not the problem, at least in our experience. The bigger problem comes from manual and inefficient management processes for gateways and related issues, such as SIM card activation/deactivation or asset configuration. Asset configuration in particular is something that could be automated, but this would add to the development cost—even though from a TCO point of view it would make a lot of sense.

Another cost driver is feature creep. For many assets, the lifecycle of the gateway will be much shorter than that of the asset itself. So it should be OK to just focus on a minimum set of features for the gateway and trust that a next-generation gateway will be developed sometime in the future.

Finally, many companies don't plan for additional development budgets after the initial release. However, in our experience, most M2M/IoT projects are never-ending stories. And this should be seen as a positive thing. If a project is successful, there will be a constant demand for new, value-adding features.

M2M/IoT Communication Services

The Enterprise IoT project manager will face many uncertainties, and no two Enterprise IoT solutions are likely to be the same, or even similar. However, there is one concept that is fundamental to any analysis of our connected future, and that is the need for connectivity. At some point, all Enterprise IoT project managers will need to consider how remote assets can be connected to a wider enterprise backend. In some cases, appropriate communications connections will already be in place, but, more often than not, the Enterprise IoT project manager will need to consider new options.

In this section, we consider alternative approaches to providing connectivity for remote assets, so that these assets can be integrated into an Enterprise IoT solution. Fundamentally, there are two types of connectivity that can be considered: managed connectivity and unmanaged connectivity. We devote the bulk of this section to managed connectivity, that is, connectivity provided as a service by a third party. An Enterprise IoT project manager may of course choose to deploy analogous technologies and operate their own networks, but the technology selection and management considerations are similar.

SERVICE OVERVIEW. We have defined six key M2M/IoT communication services:

- Cellular (2G, 3G, 4G)
- Low-power, wide-area (LPWA)
- Metropolitan area networks (MANs)
- Satellite
- Fixed line
- Power line communications

These technologies differ significantly in terms of the reach of connectivity, the ability to support mobile assets, and also the levels of data throughput that can be supported. Figure 8-41 summarizes these key considerations.

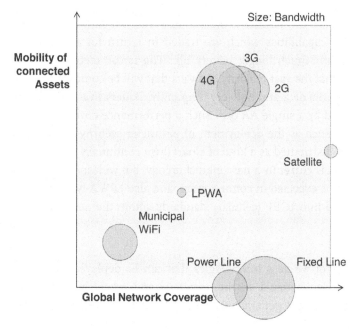

Services:
1. Satellite
2. Mobile: 2G, 3G, 4G
3. LPWA (Low Power Wide Area, e.g. SigFox)
4. Municipal WiFi
5. Fixed Line
6. Powerline Communications (e.g. for Smart Metering)

FIGURE 8-41. Key technical considerations of managed communications services

Of all these connectivity options, probably the most interesting are the wireless technologies. In general, wireless technologies have the potential to support a relatively homogenous connectivity environment (so that all remote assets of a particular type can be connected using the same technological solution). In turn, this allows for relatively simple monitoring and fault resolution of remote devices from a central location.

Fundamentally, wireless communications technologies are always a compromise between a relatively limited set of constraints such as data throughput rates, battery life, remote device cost, network cost, and the laws of physics. The main difference between the various wireless technologies is that they have been "optimized" in different ways:

Cellular (2G, 3G, 4G, 5G)

"Mobile" is the technology that currently dominates the IoT in terms of wide area connectivity. Realistically, it is the only technology that can support a range of intrinsically mobile applications (such as vehicle platforms and eCall). This group of technologies also benefits from very wide-ranging geographic coverage and a reasonable level of homogeneity across national borders (potentially allowing for international "roaming" of connected devices). Data throughput rates are reasonable (240 kbit/s for 2G, 42Mbit/s for 3G,

326Mbit/s for 4G, and faster for 5G), and this group of technologies is well established in the M2M/IoT space. Given their importance, we have dedicated much of the remainder of this chapter to a detailed discussion of cellular M2M communications.

Low-power, wide-area (LPWA)

In many ways, LPWA networks are very similar to mobile networks, but with significantly compromised data throughput capabilities which are traded in return for significantly lower price points and potentially much longer battery life. The raison d'être for these kinds of technology is the fact that the vast majority of assets that will be connected to the IoT will, in fact, generate very little data and not very frequently. Battery lives can extend to 10 years and beyond, powered by a single AA cell. Such a performance envelope opens the door to many possibilities, such as the deployment of perimeter security sensors for industrial locations that can be distributed as a kind of smart dust, continually monitoring events for up to 10 years. LPWA is currently a nascent technology, but widespread deployment of such technologies can be expected in coming years, and also LPWA-type capabilities are likely to be incorporated into 3GPP (cellular) standards within the next couple of years.

Metropolitan area networks (MANs)

This category includes a range of wireless technologies that can be deployed within an urban environment. Typically deployments are homogenous and relatively ubiquitous within a single urban conurbation, but generally vary between different urban conurbations. This makes MAN-type solutions particularly suitable for smart cities solutions (e.g., controlled street lighting, traffic signage, and refuse collection), but less suitable for solutions that extend beyond the limits of a single (or limited number of) urban conurbation(s). Wireless MAN technologies can vary considerably in terms of technical capabilities, ranging from technologies that are equivalent to LPWA to technologies that are equivalent to WiFi.

Satellite

Satellite is the most flexible of all wireless connectivity solutions, but at a price. Although it is possible to support multiple MB streams over a satellite link to a moving "connected" asset, the cost is likely to be prohibitive for the vast majority of potential IoT applications. At the other end of the scale, there are satellite solutions currently under development that will potentially match current 2G (cellular) modem capabilities and price points. As a general rule, satellite tends to be the "best option" for connecting IoT devices when it is the "only option." Use cases include the monitoring of refrigerated shipping containers ("reefers") on the high seas, although even then it is likely that that container ship has deployed some kind of local onboard connectivity (e.g., 2G cellular), so that the cost of satellite communications can be shared between multiple containers.

As mentioned earlier, fixed connectivity options are, in general, significantly less interesting:

Fixed line

If available, fixed-line solutions can be very good options for connecting a remote asset. However, if fixed-line connections are not available, the cost of deploying such connections specifically to connect an IoT asset is likely to be prohibitive. In cases where assets are connected using fixed-line infrastructure, the actual final connection to a remote device is likely to be an Ethernet connection, and so potentially extremely high connectivity speeds can be supported.

Power line

This is a niche communications solution, generally only suitable for electricity smart metering. The technology works by multiplexing a "signal" onto a "carrier" which is, in fact, an electrical power cable. This works well for electricity metering, as the electricity utilities deploying the solution generally have access to both "ends" of the power supply to a building (i.e., the smart meter and the corresponding electricity distribution substation), but few other potential users of power-line communications enjoy such access.

Focusing once more on the key cellular (2G, 3G, 4G) technologies, it is worth highlighting a fundamental market structure consideration. Established mobile communications markets are highly evolved, and include players with many different market positionings. Two key such positionings are that of the mobile network operator (MNO) and the mobile virtual network operator (MVNO).

From a (human) customer perspective, these entities are pretty similar, in that they can both provide mobile communications services, including voice and data. In traditional telecoms markets, there really is very little to differentiate between the products and services offered by an MNO and an MVNO, other than brand considerations (and perhaps a niche market positioning for MVNOs).

From a technical perspective, however, an MNO and an MVNO are quite different; an MNO owns and operates its own radio access network (RAN), whereas an MVNO "piggybacks" on a RAN that is owned by an MNO. In both cases, it's the MNO that actually provides the radio access network and carries the calls and data, although in the case of an MVNO, the entity that actually faces the customer is something other than an MNO. Essentially, an MVNO focuses on marketing, customer acquisition, and billing, and wholesales MNO-provided connectivity. There are different "flavors" of MVNO too, ranging from "light" (these MVNOs do little other than marketing, customer acquisition, and billing) to "heavy" (these MVNOs also build and own some core network infrastructure elements).

This market structure has been carried forward into the M2M world, with both MNOs and MVNOs offering to connect machines. The key distinction in the M2M space, however, is that an M2M MVNO can establish wholesale relationships with more than one MNO in each territory in which it operates. There are two main consequences of this potentially one-to-many relationship. The first is that MVNOs can, to some extent, select different MNO carriers for each connection that they manage, potentially selecting the MNO that offers the best signal strength in a specific location. The second consequence is that MVNO-provided M2M connections can potentially be a little more footloose in terms of migrating to a MNO network that offers better rates. In fact, leading-edge MVNOs can now offer a level of flexibility in terms of association of a single connection with different partner MNO networks, so that the overall solution could almost be characterized as a virtual-shared RAN. The price to be paid for that flexibility, however, lies in the cost, and in the flexibility and homogeneity of interfaces to partner MNOs. For some M2M applications, this will be a trade-off worth making. For others, it won't.

MOBILE M2M COMMUNICATION. Having discussed different M2M/IoT communication services, we will now take a more detailed look at mobile M2M communication, as this is one of the most widely used and complex technologies for remote connectivity today, and will continue to be so for the foreseeable future.

We start by introducing some basic concepts of mobile M2M communication. We will then discuss common challenges, followed by an example for an M2M communication platform that can help address many of these challenges.

For the remainder of this section, we will use the term M2M to refer to mobile M2M communication. See also the discussion on M2M versus IoT in Chapter 1.

BASIC ELEMENTS. For mobile M2M, some of the most important elements are the M2M SIM cards, the communication modules that use these SIM cards, and the M2M devices that use the communication modules:

M2M SIM Card
> The Subscriber Identity Module, or SIM card, identifies the subscription through which a mobile device can attach to a network and access services. SIM cards are available in a variety of physical form factors, including the standard plastic UICC mini (2FF), micro (3FF), and now nano (4FF) SIMs familiar to smartphone users and the more specialized SON-8-chip form factor, which is an electronic component that can be soldered into circuit boards. The choice of SIM type for M2M use depends on the specific application. Key considerations include the lifetime needed and the environment in which the SIM must operate. The service life of many M2M applications exceeds the rated lifespan of standard SIM cards. Ruggedized SIMs intended for the M2M market support more read-write cycles and longer data retention periods in order to extend their useful lives. In addition, the SON-8 form factor typically offers greater resilience against temperature and vibration.

M2M Communication Module

The Communication Module is essentially a mobile phone. In the early days of M2M, actual phones were used. Today, it is a small circuit board containing all the pieces needed to communicate with a mobile network using the subscription provided by the SIM. In effect, it is a specialist modem, designed to be easy to integrate into an M2M device and provide it with a complete communication service. Communication modules must be compatible with the types of mobile network that the M2M service will use, taking into account regional standards, radio frequencies, and the generations of mobile technology to be supported. This is a critical decision affecting the cost of the module, network coverage, and the longevity of the service.

M2M Device

The M2M Device processes data from the real world and exchanges it with the backend application via the services provided by the Communication Module. M2M devices are generally specific to individual types of application, such as the smart meters used in utilities or the telematics units in the automotive industry. In some cases, the M2M device contains the sensors and actuators that carry out measurement and control while, in others they communicate with them by means of a local connection and specialist communications protocol such as the controller area network (CAN) developed for automotive.

The M2M communication network enables communication between M2M devices and the backend. Important elements include the radio access network (RAN), mobile core network, access point name (APN), and backhaul connectivity:

Radio access network

The radio access network consists of the base stations owned by the local mobile network to which the M2M device attaches in order to get service. Its purpose is to provide the radio connection to the device and pass traffic back to the mobile core network belonging to the M2M service's communication service provider. Several generations of radio access network such as GeRAN (2G), UTRAN (3G), and E-UTRA (4G) are in common use.

Mobile core network

The core network is in the "home" network of the M2M Communication Service Provider (CSP) and acts as a hub between the customer's backend systems and the local mobile radio access networks to which their devices attach. The core network consolidates traffic and generates usage records, allowing the CSP to carry out billing. It is also the location at which the mobile subscriptions are registered. It allows individual devices access to specific services such as voice or data, and also controls the radio networks that they can attach to. When a device attempts to attach to a radio access network, the RAN contacts the device's home mobile core network in order to verify the identity of the device and check the services to which it should be granted access.

Access Point Name (APN)

The APN can be thought of as a virtual data network that the M2M device joins when it sets up a mobile data connection. Important aspects of APNs include IP addressing schemes, authentication mechanisms, and whether the APN is public or private. The APN is hosted by the mobile core network and may be associated with a particular backhaul connection. Shared APNs, such as Internet APNs, are used by devices belonging to many different M2M businesses, and typically offer quick access and minimal setup in return for limited functionality and security. Private APNs are purpose-built for individual services and offer additional functionality such as private IP addressing, greater security, and separation from other traffic.

Backhaul

Backhaul connectivity moves traffic between the mobile core network and the backend system. While not technically part of the mobile core network, such connectivity is usually provided by the CSP as one element of a complete end-to-end solution. A variety of types of backhaul are in common use, ranging from private leased lines to secure tunnels over the Internet. If a SIM is roaming the RAN and core networks are provided by different mobile network operators, the RAN is part of the "serving network," while the core is part of the "home network."

CHALLENGES. According to Mike Prince, Principal Product Manager for M2M Platforms at Vodafone:

> *M2M communication has very different characteristics to those of traditional mobile communication. M2M businesses and Communications Service Providers alike must deal with issues such as new commercial models, global service management, SIM logistics, system operation on a very large scale, and management of different traffic patterns. M2M is distinct from both IT and traditional mobile communication and requires its own specialist methodology and solutions.*

In the early days of M2M, many MNOs assumed that M2M connections were simply data connections, and that little needed to be done to serve this new market other than issue what were then regarded as "standard" data SIMs and contracts. As Mike's quote highlights, the reality of the M2M market proved to be somewhat more complex. Here are some of the more immediate and significant differences between M2M connections and human-centric voice and data connections:

Commercials

With long periods of device inactivity, unique traffic patterns, and very narrow margins in many M2M businesses, it is clear that standard mobile tariffs are unsuitable for M2M. International services, where the distribution of devices across countries is variable, introduce particular uncertainty over roaming costs.

SIM logistics

SIMs are commonly inserted into M2M devices during production of the device itself, often using a chip-based form factor rather than the more familiar plastic component. After initial testing, the SIM lies dormant for an extended time as the device travels through its supply chain before finally being activated. Certain types of M2M device, may later be recycled between users, leading to further periods of inactivity. This creates difficulties for mobile operators who must carefully manage and optimize their return on the use of scarce resources. M2M businesses attempting to use standard SIMs in this way face significant complexity and cost in order to maintain their subscriptions.

Scale

Some M2M businesses deploy devices in volumes that are otherwise unheard of, with single services running to millions of devices. Large-scale M2M requires a high degree of automation.

Operations

Unlike a smartphone, whose owner may bring it back to the shop or call a service desk if something isn't working, machines must operate independently. Installation and activation must be highly automated and any subsequent troubleshooting carried out remotely in order to minimize costs due to site visits.

Traffic patterns

Machines work in different locations and at different times of day than human beings. They may be static or highly mobile. Each machine "conversation" may involve smaller amounts of data, but when things go wrong, they can keep trying. As a result, the M2M traffic on a network follows a very different pattern to that generated by other types of mobile device. Close supervision is necessary to make sure that networks are not hit with excessive traffic volumes and customers are not faced with expensive bills should devices malfunction.

Device-originated communication

Connections for mobile data communication are originated by the device rather than from the network. This serves consumer mobile needs, but in M2M it means that a back-end system is reliant on devices to initiate connections before it can exchange data with them.

Security

Enterprises use M2M to support their critical business processes. M2M applications frequently deal with sensitive data or control important infrastructure. It is essential that M2M communication has an appropriate level of security, bearing in mind that the level of threat is likely to rise over the lifetime of a service as awareness of the role played by M2M increases and attackers become more sophisticated.

Beyond these items, the potentially global (or multicountry) nature of M2M solutions can drive significant complexity in tariffing, service management, and "customer" support. As Mike highlights:

Whereas traditional mobile services are strongly associated with an individual home country, M2M services can be required to operate across regions or even globally. At the time that a SIM is installed in a device its destination is often not known.

SIM LIFECYCLE. Because the SIM plays such a central role in M2M, understanding the M2M SIM lifecycle (shown in Figure 8-42) is helpful in addressing some of the challenges outlined in the previous section.

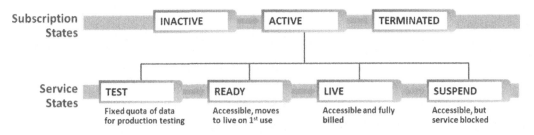

FIGURE 8-42. M2M SIM lifecycle (Source: Vodafone)

The lifecycle of an M2M SIM is very different to that used in traditional mobile services. In addition to the standard states relating to basic activation and deactivation, a number of other states are needed in order to provide greater granularity of control during the active stage of the SIM's life. These states help automate control over connectivity during the process of building, testing, shipping, and using M2M devices. By varying the tariff according to SIM state, it is possible to match commercials to the customer's situation. For example, a given amount of usage or time can be offered for testing.

M2M CONNECTIVITY MANAGEMENT PLATFORMS. In order to address the M2M challenges outlined previously, carriers must deploy M2M connectivity management platforms. Such platforms are highly scalable multitenanted systems, typically delivered as cloud services. They enable a high degree of self-service and are optimized for management by exception of large volumes of SIMs and devices.

The connectivity management platform plays a central role in reducing the risk for an enterprise in adopting M2M. Figure 8-43 provides an overview of the basic M2M elements and connectivity management platform interaction.

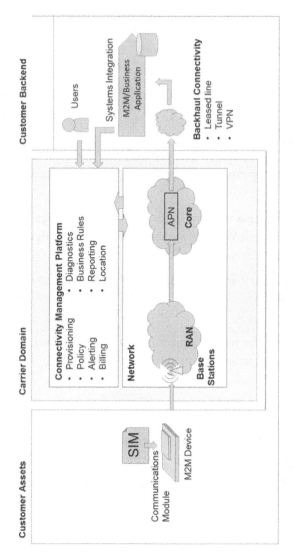

FIGURE 8-43. Overview of key M2M elements and M2M platform

Key features of an M2M connectivity platform include:

Online graphical user interface
Allows users to administer and manage their service. Accounts with clear roles and permissions give users access to the functions they need in order to carry out their own tasks while avoiding unnecessary complexity.

APIs

Allow the integration of customer systems in order to support end-to-end business processes that depend on M2M communication.

Ordering and provisioning

Efficient generation of high-volume SIM orders, and bulk provisioning of subscriptions onto the system.

Device wake-up

SMS triggers that can be invoked by a backend system that needs to communicate with a device. The device's response to a trigger should be to initiate a data connection.

Security

Measures to restrict access to network resources and guard against fraudulent use. Deep integration with dedicated M2M networks platforms should offer in-depth security.

Session management

Detailed real-time control over data sessions including access controls, address assignment, and usage quotas.

Analysis and reporting

Broad examination of the records concerning one or more devices in order to build up a picture of service characteristics or produce specific datasets.

Diagnostics

Detailed drill-down on the behavior of a specific device in order to identify the cause of faults. May examine live data or historic records (e.g., protocol trace for voice, data, and SMS communications) or the outcomes of proactive tests.

Notifications

Proactive notifications of events of significance to different users in the customer or service provider organizations (e.g., usage alerts).

Business rules

Configurable toolkit of measures, rules, and actions that can be used to automate processes and deal with exceptions.

Audit trail

Historical record of events and changes that serves to provide a full audit trail.

Rating and billing

M2M specific tariffs that can be applied to services as required and which take into account the full platform feature set.

Revenue assurance

Detailed usage records to allow verification of bills.

Online support

Ticketing, documentation, help, and user forums.

Figure 8-44 shows the portal Dashboard provided by Vodafone to its customers for managing M2M connectivity.

FIGURE 8-44. Vodafone M2M Portal (Source: Vodafone)

MCS AND IGNITE ASSET INTEGRATION ARCHITECTURE. Figure 8-45 describes the AIA for MCS.

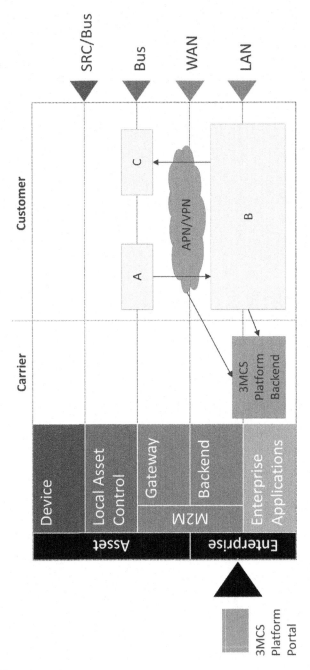

FIGURE 8-45. AIA for MCS

Recommendations and Outlook

Building on the discussion so far, this section focuses on the future development trajectory for M2M/IoT communication services. We start by summarizing the role of (M2M) platforms, to date. We then define "best practice" for (IoT) connectivity platforms and discuss new and emerging technologies in the IoT connectivity space. We will end with a set of recommendations for providers of connectivity platform services.

THE ROLE OF (M2M) PLATFORMS TO DATE. Mike Prince, Principal Product Manager for M2M Platforms at Vodafone, says:

> *The key role for M2M and IoT platforms is to reduce the levels of friction that exist in today's IoT markets. This friction is generated by a wide range of factors, including high entry costs, lack of standardization in specific segments, limited skills and awareness, different and varying market conditions between countries and geographies, and regulatory policies. As a consequence, CM platforms play a central role in reducing the risk for an enterprise in adopting M2M.*

Thus far focused almost exclusively on cellular-based technologies, connectivity support platforms have made significant contributions to the growth of many M2M and IoT solutions. This is the case particularly where different types of connections are required at different stages of the lifecycle of a cellular connected solution. For example, in the automotive industry, a significant market for cellular connections, the ability to activate and deactivate SIM connections is necessitated as a result of various production, test, and launch stages.

In addressing the M2M requirements of industry verticals, the design, development, and building of M2M solutions can be compared to complex IT solutions. The use of connectivity support platforms allows enterprises to standardize connectivity management, and extend the functionality within solutions. The current limitation is that very few connectivity support platforms have been designed to be flexible or adaptable in terms of different connection technologies. Once applications have been developed, it requires significant time, effort, and money to change devices, add connectivity technologies, or adopt and integrate new application requirements with new data models. This generally leads to multiple, specifically designed solutions with limited reuse, or the integration of connectivity support platform capabilities.

With M2M applications becoming ever more advanced and complex, coupled with the emergence of the IoT, connectivity platforms will need to evolve. Where previously connectivity support platforms allowed connection to a narrow set of devices and primarily cellular connectivity options, future requirements can be characterized by increasing agility and flexibility.

We have already seen a similar trend in application development where abstraction has become a preferred approach for the emerging range of M2M/IoT application platforms. We expect similar developments in the connectivity support platform space, characterized by an ever-increasing technology agnosticism. This combination of abstraction and agnosticism allows for the scale and heterogeneity (of devices and protocols) to be managed through fewer platforms. It also enables developers to focus more on application development rather than specific communications technologies or device characteristics.

But the simple idea of a "technology-agnostic" connectivity support platform belies the complex and challenging task involved in managing the characteristics of multiple connectivity options. For example, an M2M solution for container freight tracking might require some combination of satellite, cellular, and short-range connected devices. The ability to support these different connectivity technologies with a single platform solution could be a significant benefit and differentiator for enterprises and operators, system integrators, and providers of M2M/IoT application platforms alike.

Managing different connectivity technologies is a complex task. Providers of multitechnology connectivity platforms face the challenge of working across different protocols; managing multiple billing, real-time data, and reconciliation functions; and ensuring secure and resilient communications across a range of communications technologies. Each connectivity technology will behave differently when it is "working properly," and may require different actions when an error status occurs. Accordingly, the ability to offer a well-defined and managed connectivity solution drawing in multiple connectivity technologies can be a significant competitive differentiator. For enterprises, such a solution removes much of the difficulty of integrating new connectivity options, and opens the door to new tariffing and billing options.

DEFINING "BEST PRACTICE" FOR (IOT) CONNECTIVITY PLATFORMS. Twelve technical and commercial capabilities and features, as illustrated in Figure 8-46, define the "best practice" elements for connectivity support platforms. Delivering these capabilities and features will ultimately reduce friction in the marketplace, enabling significant growth in connected devices, and providing improved ROI, which in turn will open new markets and application development opportunities. In this space, technical and commercial capabilities and features are closely related, and are now converging to bring about a single and comprehensive connectivity proposition.

However, it is clear that the "best practice" capabilities and features listed are not the same as those typically cited for cellular connectivity support platforms. Such capabilities would typically include connection provisioning, usage monitoring, and some level of support for network fault resolution. By contrast, the best practices listed here typically address higher-level commercial application development, application management, and implementation considerations. Ultimately, the pursuit of best practice for a connectivity support platform will result in its being repositioned as a "connectivity platform" that provides actual multitechnology connectivity.

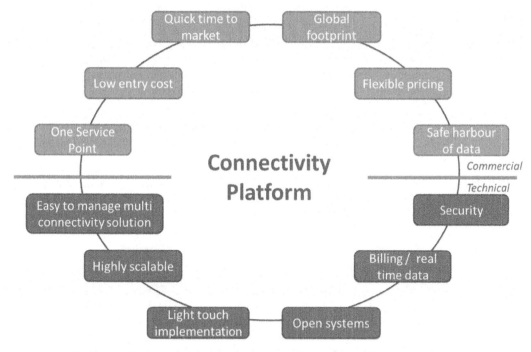

FIGURE 8-46. "Best practice" elements of connectivity platforms (Source: Machina Research 2014)

Table 8-3 and Table 8-4 describe these "best practices" in more detail. Table 8-3 details commercial best practices, while Table 8-4 expands on technical best practices.

TABLE 8-3. Six commercial best practices for connectivity platforms (Source: Machina Research)

Best Practice element— Commercial	Description
One service point	Enterprises may potentially need to manage multiple connectivity technology options to support their M2M and IoT applications. Providing flexibility and opportunity to create and select between multiple service connectivity providers (e.g., mobile operators in a given geography) and connection technologies (satellite, cellular, low-power wide area networks, etc.) through a single connectivity platform delivers an efficient and compelling proposition for enterprises.
Low entry cost	Deployment costs for complex connectivity solutions remain a challenge for many enterprises. Platform providers should ideally deliver solutions that allow for a combination of light touch implementation approach, unit- and/or usage-based charging models, and also allow enterprises differentiated service-level options, all to encourage market entry at lower cost levels.
Quick time to market	Reducing time to market for M2M and IoT solutions is a competitive benefit for enterprises. Connectivity platforms will ideally provide the tools and options to support this, enabling quick-to-launch connected solutions.

Best Practice element—Commercial	Description
Global footprint	More and more enterprises are engaged in multiple geographical markets, and ideally connectivity platforms will provide connectivity solutions with a homogeneous global footprint and multiple service provider options per country.
Flexible pricing	Having access to multiple connectivity technologies on one platform enables enterprises to review and select different pricing options from different providers. This function should ideally remain as flexible and easy-to-use as possible and offer enterprises a competitive range of available services providers.
Safe harbor of data	Observant of national regulations relating to the management of data, a connectivity platform will ideally be able to deliver and manage safe harbors for data in a way that complies with local regulations.

TABLE 8-4. Six technical best practices for connectivity platforms (Source: Machina Research)

Best Practice element—Technical	Description
Easy-to-manage multiconnectivity platform	The platform should ideally be easy to manage and able to support multiple connectivity technologies. This will involve managing and initiating different communication protocols based on rules and policies; managing a variety of billing, real-time data, and reconciliation structures; and providing secure and resilient networks. This capability should also include key elements of connection provisioning, usage monitoring, and fault resolution.
Highly scalable	The platform will need to be highly scalable to include additional connectivity technology options, and meet increasing requirements of applications both in terms of scale and functionality. The platform will most likely be structured around an abstracted approach to connectivity management, and increasing the number of connectivity options should ideally be a core capability of the platform.
Light touch implementation	The platform will need to enable a quicker and less complex integration process through APIs and provide modular software components to design customized dashboards.
Open systems	Closely linked to the capability of managing scalability, software environments should remain as open as possible, allowing for extensibility and further development where required by enterprises. In markets where an increasing number of connections and applications are predicted, highly proprietary solutions would be a significant limitation.
Billing/real-time data	Being able to manage different billing models and forms (such as retail, wholesale, and agency), and enabling a wide range of reporting and traffic and usage analysis tools is key.
Security	Delivering and embedding security throughout the M2M or IoT solution will emerge as a critical factor in a range of solutions, and connectivity platforms will need to be able to address these security requirements across the various connectivity technologies and form part of a seamless end-to-end security solution.

OUTLOOK. The outlook for the connectivity space is dynamic and diverse. There is a wide range of developments expected, including the enhancement and evolution of existing technologies, the introduction of new technologies, and the blurring of technologies at the periphery. We will briefly discuss these trends in the market in the following paragraphs.

The highest-profile change in existing technologies is the introduction of the soft SIM. Specifically, this development represents the evolution of the physical removable SIM card toward an "embedded," "component," or "M2M-Form Factor" (MFF) SIM that is more robust, less sensitive to heat or vibration, and more secure, not least because it cannot be removed and used in another device. These embedded SIMs should also be cheaper and ultimately help to simplify the supply chain.

Such "soft SIMs" are managed by cellular operators over the air (OTA) and are shipped with a "bootstrap" mobile operator configuration (the IMSI number) that allows for initial connectivity (via inter-carrier roaming.) Once such devices connect to a local network in the country in which they are activated, it is possible to implement a new IMSI, automatically and over the air, which "re-homes" the device onto a new (local) carrier network. Ultimately, it is the soft SIM that will allow you to buy cellular airtime for your iPad from the App Store.

Clearly, today's technologies are also evolving. The inevitable "5G" cellular technology is in the works already, and new capabilities are being developed for 4G. However, for once, it seems that "faster is not necessarily better" for some of the latest iterations of today's cellular technologies. Currently, one of the key thrusts for 4G and 5G is the development of cheap, low-bandwidth connectivity that is very light in terms of power consumption (potentially enabling very long battery life).

This development has been driven particularly by mobile operators in response to the perceived competitive threat from new technologies such as SIGFOX. These technologies offer nationwide, out-of-the-box connectivity as a service (such as as you might expect from a mobile operator), at minimal cost (cost of hardware device), and with up to 10 years battery life from a single AA cell. The price paid for this extreme battery life is in bandwidth: SIGFOX can only support 144 (short) messages per device per day, but that's more than adequate for many M2M applications. A host of other players are currently emerging in this space, often with very different go-to-market strategies. Emerging players include the likes of M2M Spectrum, NWave, SemTech, and many more. Generically, these new providers are referred to as low-power, wide-area (LPWA) network providers. Huawei has also muscled in on the act through its acquisition of Neul, and these companies are now jointly developing a "clean slate" Cellular IoT ("CIoT") solution aimed at deploying an LPWA service in old GSM spectrum that has been freed up by the migration of data traffic to 3G and 4G networks.

As ever, there is also a range of innovative technologies waiting in the wings, pining for recognition as accepted (de facto) standards, at least within specific niches. These include the likes of Zigbee, ZWave, and visual light communications (VLC), or Li-Fi, and a perennial favorite: high altitude, low orbit (HALO) platforms. And many more.

And, of course, more and more things will become connected to the IoT, leading to the widespread adoption of home area networks (HANs), vehicle area networks (VANs), and personal area networks (PANs). And no doubt many other yet-to-be imagined area networks, which we could potentially term "xANs." Ultimately though, the "things" at the very periphery of the IoT will be only intermittently connected, or even simply "sensed" as opposed to communicating in any meaningful way. This will result in a blurring of technologies at the periphery, particularly where near-field communications (NFC) can be substituted by a range of other technologies (e.g., 2D barcodes, RFID, and WiFi direct) which could be termed near-field communications technologies.

This type of market development is further illustrated by the following interview with Nigel Chadwick, CEO of Stream Technologies.

Jim Morrish: Can you describe the approach that you take to providing connectivity for IoT?

Nigel Chadwick: It has long been popularly, but wrongly, perceived that the connectivity layer pertaining to a connected "thing" is a generic commodity. The reality is that this connectivity layer is highly differentiated in terms of technical parameters such as resilience, as well as fragmented in terms of footprint and communications protocol "type."

Ultimately, we think that the IoT will be best supported by what we term a *"Unified Access Connectivity Environment" (U-ACE)*. Such a platform should be adaptive to multiple connectivity protocols—including cellular (2G, 3G, LTE, CDMA), satellite, WiFi, low-power, wide-area radio networks (e.g., LoRa), and others. This is particularly valuable to established wireless carriers, evolving LPWA network operators and enterprises, since such a solution can provide third parties with a powerful yet simple, low cost—fast deployment solution to monitoring, managing, and monetizing connected Things.

Jim Morrish: What's the key difference between this approach and the typical approach that might feature in the market today?

Nigel Chadwick: To date, connectivity "platforms" designed for the IoT have tended to evolve and be deployed as proprietary or closed to specific network operators and service providers. They are also largely designed and built to manage a singular wireless layer (largely cellular but also some satellite).

With this in mind, there are several key differences when compared to the unified connectivity environment that I described earlier:

- A U-ACE should be technology-agnostic and be designed to work with any type of wireless protocol. In turn, this means that multiple network connectivity layers can be fully managed from a single platform. The U-ACE therefore becomes a one-stop

---

solution that provides a full range of connectivity types and geographic coverage, and can support the extension of powerful connectivity management tools outside of the "on-net" reach of existing carriers—for example, extending management capability of cellular carriers into LPWA, or satellite operator capabilities into cellular. It also ensures that connectivity management is effectively "future-proofed."

- A U-ACE should be what we term "technically light and noninvasive." Through a simple set of APIs, a "virtual state" of the host network connection can be created, relying on the underlying integral but external infrastructure, to provide real-time and granular monitoring and management of each connection. This enables a fast and low-cost deployment, resulting in minimal time to market for both network operators and client organizations.

- The use of APIs is important for another reason. A U-ACE should be able to coexist with any existing platform used to manage connections—either above or below in the vertical chain of connectivity management. This enables extension of wireless connectivity and presentation of a single user interface for those interacting with the platform, thereby avoiding the multiple platform view and engagement with all the inherent complexity and duplication, and associated risk and resource cost.

Stream Technologies has developed such a U-ACE. It's a platform that we call IoT-X. IoT-X has fast evolved into an IoT connectivity-based ecosystem, reflecting Stream's vision of the kind of Unified Access Connectivity Environment that I described earlier. IoT-X is about much more than just connectivity. There is a growing number of integrations into IoT-X, including other platforms that enable device management, data exchange management, and other aspects that are often critical to the successful implementation of an end-to-end IoT solution. Examples of integrations completed so far include ARM's Mbed, ThingWorx, and wot.io. This means that enterprises and wireless carriers (and their end customers) can "plug into" the already extensive and growing ecosystem inherent within IoT-X.

Jim Morrish: Isn't managing all those technology choices a huge task, just in and of itself?

Nigel Chadwick: Stream has continuously evolved IoT-X in a Darwinian way over a 10-year development timeframe. Given the scaling requirement, as well as the breadth of the platform capability, there has been a focus on how best to remove "friction" in the process of integrating into third-party wireless networks, and also from end user perspectives in terms of ease of use and functionality. The company has evolved to a situation whereby it is pretty much a software development house, with a fully developed platform that automates connectivity monitoring, management, and billing. We also have in-house specialists in each of the core wireless technologies and infrastructure we deal with—

cellular, satellite, LPWA, backhaul infrastructures, and coding. We have provided connectivity to end customers since 2000, so carriers and enterprise organizations engaging with us to adopt IoT-X are increasingly relying upon the technical expertise vested in the company to help them figure out how to deploy vertical solutions, thereby moving up the value chain.

Jim Morrish: How should a U-ACE cope with intermediating between the limitations of any specific device connection and customer needs and demands?

Nigel Chadwick: A U-ACE should be agnostic and capable of accepting data via any connectivity protocol. Off-the-shelf adaptors for most of the current common (and not so common) protocols should be readily available. Given the U-ACE is purely dedicated to management of the communication layer, there is essentially very limited intermediation necessary.

Data is data regardless of where it comes from. At Stream Technologies, we've always tried to keep everything as simple as possible to reduce complexity and chances of failure. Our approach has been to make all networks comply with a defined structure rather than trying to make each individual network work together. What we've created is an abstract concept of how a network should function, and we adapt networks in to this. One of the benefits to this is that as soon as a new network is configured in, it instantly gets access to all our other services and integrations.

Jim Morrish: Who do you see as your ideal customers (and partners) within the overall IoT ecosystem?

Nigel Chadwick: We believe IoT-X and U-ACE have the potential to unlock substantial value for a range of customers and partners through enabling connectivity income on a large-scale basis and/or reducing the total cost of ownership (TCO). This means that system integrators and solution providers in other parts of the IoT ecosystem—those with significant numbers of customers which require device or "thing" connectivity—can significantly remove substantial amounts of "friction" and inertia through removing fragmentation and uncertainty pertaining to the connectivity layer. The greater the scale of the connectivity requirement in terms of scale, geographic spread, and connectivity types deployed, the greater the management risk and cost, and the greater the relevance of IoT-X. This is equally applicable to enterprises for the same reason. For carriers, including (but not constrained to) cellular, WiFi, and satellite, the ecosystem we are creating provides a ready-to-go service for their existing and future end-customer need. As a result of ecosystem evolution, as well as in response to the requirements of customers using IoT-X, the supplementary services and technologies will continue to be further integrated, and this further extends the flexibility and options to all adopters and users in the ecosystem. Everyone benefits.

Jim Morrish: How do you think that the overall market would develop?

Nigel Chadwick: The Internet of Things is promising billions of connections. Due to the sheer scale of end point connections, their inevitable monetization will lead to emergent new organizations and clusters or partnerships comprising new service type organizations, as well as established players. The dynamics may change as to where value is created, including a potential shift of value and empowerment toward LPWA solutions, WiFi, and cable operators, as well as system integrator and solution provider–type organizations. We are still very much at the early stage of the IoT lifecycle.

There also remains the consumer sector—much anticipated and discussed, but yet to adopt en masse worldwide. Home security, personal asset management, and health and wellbeing are massive markets still to be affected by IoT. Connectivity management for this sector will equally be required across different wireless layers: security, reliability, and data routing; storage and accessibility; and sharing will move up the agenda, again introducing new challenges leading to the evolvement of companies and technologies that will usurp traditional legacy companies in the comms field and will likely shift control back to the consumer.

Finally, the all-important topic of total cost of ownership—imperative if billions of things are to be connected to the Internet. I expect new business models, possibly even some freemium type models, to start to emerge around platform connectivity management. If TOC is to reduce, then management of the connectivity layer is one obvious element whereby automation of systems and processes might result in some level of cost reduction. Conversely, currently "free" connectivity options such as WiFi (e.g., when used off the back of an already paid for broadband connection), or a public LPWA network, could also start to be simultaneously managed as a "private" network—thereby introducing the possibility of monetizing. This further introduces the somewhat radical notion of the creation of new national networks comprising multiple private networks within the unlicensed wireless spectrums.

Given these ideas, it soon becomes quite clear that the ability to effortlessly manage networks, monitor connections, and monetize/bill for connectivity to and from "things" is an incredible opportunity. And we really are at the very beginning of what is possible.

RECOMMENDATIONS. Ultimately, what the discussion in this section points to is the concept of "connectivity as a service," and the emergence of entities that support that proposition. This is an emerging, but particularly valuable concept as old M2M markets transition to IoT markets. It is highly consistent with the general technology agnosticism and abstraction that characterizes the IoT.

With that in mind, and with the emerging requirements of enterprises seeking to benefit from M2M and the IoT, connectivity support platform providers should:

- Continue their efforts in minimizing points of friction in M2M and IoT market growth and development by designing and building platforms that enable enterprises to create, build, and deploy agile, scalable, and flexible solutions for managing devices and connectivity, and developing and managing applications and data

- Create open and integrated systems that encourage and enable enterprises to deploy and manage end-to-end M2M and IoT solutions

- Remain aware of the evolving requirements of enterprises, and continue to explore how platforms can enable the strategic expansion of enterprises into new markets and opportunities

Finally, it is worth highlighting that the rise of connectivity support platforms does not relegate connectivity provision to commodity status. In reality, with the 12 capabilities and features outlined earlier in the "best practice" model, this new model of connectivity platform will be an important addition to the market. While connectivity may become a commodity, the provision of technology-agnostic, seamless connectivity as a service will become a highly valuable proposition.

We would like to thank Mike Prince, Principal Product Manager for M2M Platforms, Vodafone, for his support with this section.

[Big] Data and Process Management

The first part of this technology profile looks at the different kinds of data that have to be managed in the IoT, naturally with a strong focus on asset-related data. We will also discuss which kind of data management technology is suitable for each kind of project scenario.

The second part looks at how process management can be leveraged to streamline, optimize and partially automate operational aspects of IoT solutions. We will also discuss which kind of process management technology is suitable for which kind of process in the IoT, and how this relates to the different data types introduced in the first part. In particular, we want to understand how different kinds of IoT events and analytics results can trigger or signal processes.

[BIG] DATA MANAGEMENT. Big Data is seen as one of the most important enabling technologies for the IoT. In this chapter, we will talk about Big (and not-so-big) Data management for M2M and IoT applications. Because this is a complex topic and there is no one-size-fits-all solution, we will gradually construct the conversation by talking about scenarios of different complexity. But, before we get to that, we will set the stage by talking to one of the most respected figureheads of the Big Data movement: Mike Olson, Chief Strategy Officer and Founder of Cloudera.

Dirk Slama: Mike, Cloudera is the company behind Apache Hadoop, one of the most widely used Big Data frameworks. Can you talk about some of the most interesting IoT use cases that you've seen using your technology?

Mike Olson: Sure. You mentioned the Large Hadron Collider (LHC) at CERN as one of the case studies in your book, and how the LHC is not only capturing enormous amounts of sensor data, but is also building up an efficient, multitiered processing pipeline for the data from the experiments. As it turns out, at least one of the research facilities in tier 2 of this processing pipeline is using Hadoop: the University of Nebraska-Lincoln. They are using it to perform advanced physics analytics on the massive amounts of data generated by the particle collisions at CERN.

There are many other interesting cases. Take energy, for example; the smart grid is obviously an important IoT application using Big Data technology, and we know that Hadoop is being used by a number of those companies. A good example is Opower, which sells its services to utilities that want to capture, analyze, and use the smart grid observations streaming from their smart meters. Smart meters are now generating an observation every six seconds, which is vastly larger than the one reading per month that they used to collect. This means that they can establish a very fine-grained signal of demand over the course of a day. They can even determine when significant events happen, such as turning your washing machine or your refrigerator on. As such, they can observe demand in real time, and then use those observations to predict demand fluctuations, not just on the basis of smart grid activity, but also based on weather reports, forecasts, and significant upcoming events and celebrations. They can even use gamification to manage demand—for example, by letting customers know what their usage is as compared to their neighbor's usage and encouraging people to compete a little to preserve energy.

There's a pretty broad range of use cases, but generally, all of this data is being generated by sensors and machines at machine scale. Collecting and analyzing it using older technologies is a challenge. Big, scale-out infrastructure makes the processing and analysis of this data much cheaper.

Dirk Slama: So what challenges does the IoT present that haven't been faced by previous generations of computing and data management?

Mike Olson: My own view is that we are only seeing the very early days of IoT data flows, and already those data flows are almost overwhelming. Take the amount of information streaming from the smart grid, from taking readings once a month to 10 times a minute; that's 150,000 times more observations we're getting per meter per month. Those data volumes are guaranteed to accelerate. In the future, we will be collecting more data at finer grain, and from a lot more devices.

Look at the City of San Francisco: some estimate that we already have 2 billion sensors in the city. Not only in smartphones and cars, but in many other places, such as the city's many high-rise buildings, where they measure air pressure, temperature, vibration, etc. The most interesting thing about those sensors right now is that most of them are not connected to a network. I predict that most of them will be on a network within the next half decade; that those devices will be swapped out with network- and mesh-connected sensors. And that will bring about an absolute tsunami of data! So designing systems that can capture, process, summarize, manage, and then analyze this data is the big challenge for IT. We have never seen a flood of information like the one we are about to see.

Dirk Slama: So, are there any key advances in data management that are making the IoT a reality?

Mike Olson: We are building scale-out storage and compute platforms today that we didn't have a decade ago. We didn't need them then, because we weren't collecting information on this scale, and we weren't trying to analyze it in the way we are today. The emergence of machine-generated data has forced us to rethink how we capture, store, and process data; it's now completely commonplace to build very large-scale, highly parallel compute farms. So that transformation has already happened. If we look to the next 5 or 10 years of advances, the state of the software should continue to improve; we will have more and better analytic algorithms; we'll have cheaper scale-out storage architectures; we will be able to manage with less disk space, because we'll be smarter about how we encode and replicate data.

But the thing I think is going to be most interesting are advances in hardware. The proliferation of network-connected sensors in mobile devices and in the environment in general is going to continue or may even explode. That will produce a lot of new data. Think about the Intel Atom Chip-Line and its equivalent from all other vendors. On the data capture/storage/analysis side, we will see chips that are better suited to this scale-out infrastructure. Memory densities will increase of course, and we will see solid-state drives replace disks in many applications. Networking interfaces at the chip level will become more ubiquitous and much faster. We will see optical instead of just electrical networks available widely at chip level. The relative latencies of storage—that is, disk to memory—will shift; solid-state disk to RAM is going to be a much more common path in the future. The speed of optical networks will make remote storage much more accessible. So I think we will see a lot of innovation at the hardware level that will enable software to do way more with the data than was ever possible before.

Dirk Slama: What are the biggest risks for companies that want to build IoT solutions that leverage Big Data? How can they mitigate these risks?

Mike Olson: The technologies for generating this type of data—the scale-out proliferation of sensor networks—as well as the infrastructure to capture, process, and analyze this data, are new. Our experience has been that it is a very smart idea to start with a small-scale proof of concept. Instead of a million devices, maybe start with a thousand devices. And then build a data capture and processing infrastructure that can handle that. This should allow you to check that it works, and to educate your people and your organization about how these systems function, and what they are capable of. These are new technologies, and adoption of new technologies requires learning and new processes for successful deployment. It's important to learn those at small scale before you go for infinite-scale IoT.

We talk to a lot of people who are fascinated by IoT technology. They are excited about Big Data for its own sake. Those are bad people for us to work with because they are not fundamentally driven by a business problem. It's important when you start thinking about the IoT to think about why it matters. What questions do you want to answer with the sensor data streaming in? What are the business problems you want to solve? What are the optimizations you want to make? And then design your systems to address these problems. The "shiny object syndrome" of engineers who want to play with new technology—I totally get that, I am one of those guys, but those projects generally fail because they don't have clear success criteria.

Dirk Slama: Are there clear indicators that tell you when to recommend using Big Data technology, and when not?

Mike Olson: If you have a traditional transaction processing or OLAP workload, we will point you toward Oracle, SQL Server, Terra Data, etc., because those systems evolved to work on those kinds of problems. New data volumes and new analytical workloads are where Big Data technology works best. When the goal is, "we want to rip out our existing infrastructure and replace it with Hadoop," we generally walk away from those opportunities; they don't go well. If you have new problems or business drivers, and new data volumes, those are the cases where we are most successful. A wholesale, blind desire to rip and replace never works.

Dirk Slama: Can you quantify these indicators? How big does data really have to be to require Big Data technology?

Mike Olson: When the industry talks about Big Data, they always talk about *volume, variety, velocity;* meaning that you can have a very large amount of data, you can have wildly different types of data that you have never been able to bring together before, or you can have data that is arriving in at a furious pace. There is one other criterion that we see which doesn't fit under the Vs, but which is the analytic algorithm you should really be using, namely: What is the computational approach you want to take toward the data? Sometimes, if you need to do a lot of computation—such as for machine learning—based on modest amounts of data, a scale-out infrastructure like Hadoop makes sense. Satisfying any one of the volume, variety, velocity, or computational complexity requirements is enough to make a Big Data infrastructure attractive. In our experience, if you have two or more of those requirements, then the new platform is critical.

Dirk Slama: What advice would you give to readers who are developing their strategy and implementation for Big Data and the IoT?

Mike Olson: My consistent advice to organizations we work with is to take a use case or two—ones that really matter, where a successful result would be meaningful for the business—and then attack those on a modest scale. This will allow you to learn the necessary skills, and will demonstrate that the technology actually solves the problem. Once you have done that, scaling big—given the infrastructure—can be done for a simple linear cost, and works great.

Dirk Slama: Who stands to gain the most from the IoT and Big Data? And who stands to lose the most?

Mike Olson: My heartfelt conviction is that data will transform virtually every field of human endeavor. So, in your lifetime and mine, we will find cures for cancer, because we will be able to analyze genetic and environmental data in ways that we never could before. In the production and distribution of clean water; the production and distribution of energy; in agriculture—where we will be able to grow better, denser crops that feed 9 billion instead of 7 billion people; in every endeavor, I believe that data is going to drive efficiency. If organizations fail to embrace that opportunity, they risk losing out to the competition.

There has been a lot of discussion recently about privacy and Edward Snowden and the NSA, and one concern I have is that we will have an unfair backlash because of those examples. But think about the advantages if we could, for example, monitor student behavior at a very fine grain, and design courses that cater expressly to the learning modalities of individual students. We will have smarter people learning things faster and better than ever before. Think about the quality of the healthcare we could deliver.

Privacy does and will matter; we need sensible policy and meaningful laws and penalties to enforce reasonable guarantees of privacy. The "Data Genie" is kind of out of the bottle; I don't think we will be able to stuff it back in. Most of all, I think it would be a mistake for us to try to curtail the production and collection of data, because I believe that it is such an opportunity for good in society.

IOT DATA TYPES AND ANALYTICS CATEGORIES. As we discussed in "IoT Solution Lifecycle: Plan/Build/Run" on page 211, it is important to understand the distribution of and relationships between different data types within your distributed IoT application landscape. Figure 8-47 provides an overview of some of the most common data types found in an IoT environment. Data coming from remote assets typically includes meter data, sensor data, event data, and multimedia data (e.g., video data). Data uploaded to assets typically includes configuration data, work instructions, decision context (e.g., the weather forecast), and various multimedia files. In the backend, data coming from remote assets is usually managed in a dedicated IoT or M2M data repository, which includes basic asset and device data, status data, and status change history, as well as time series data (e.g., groupings of meter readings).

It's worth noting that, as in any good, heterogeneous enterprise application landscape, there will most likely be other applications that also contain asset-related data, some of which might be redundant. For example, the ERP system is likely to contain the Asset Master Data, including all data relating to the product configuration at sales time, as well as customer contract data. One or more ticket management systems will contain customer queries related to specific assets. Integrating this data into one, holistic view of the asset is usually a challenging task. In addition, there will be a lot of related data in other systems, including customer transaction history, customer social data, product data, and the like.

Building efficient applications based on this data is as challenging as in any heterogeneous enterprise application landscape, and can be tackled via well-established approaches like enterprise architecture management (EAM), enterprise application integration (EAI), service-oriented architecture (SOA), and business process management (BPM) [EBPM]. This is something we will look at in the next chapter.

Making sense of IoT data requires efficient analytics—this does not just apply to Big Data, as we will see in the following. There are different categories of analytics. Some of them simply review past events, while some more advanced analytics categories attempt to use historical data to forecast future events and developments.

Basic analytics include:

Descriptive analytics
"What is happening?" (Example: An engine stopped working)

Descriptive analytics
"Why did it happen?" (Example: Because of a faulty vault)

Advanced, forward-looking analytics include:

Predictive analytics
"What is likely to happen?" (Example: When is an engine likely to stop working?)

Prescriptive analytics
"What should be done to prevent this from happening?" (Example: Exchange the vault before it breaks)

Not all IoT solutions will leverage all of these data types and analytics categories. In fact, it is extremely important for a project manager to understand how they can ensure that the data management architecture and selected tools are limited to what is really needed. As we will see in the following, there are good ways to combine different technologies, so starting with a minimum viable product (MVP) philosophy often makes sense. Of course, choosing the right core data management technology—for example, relational versus NoSQL—must be based on careful analysis.

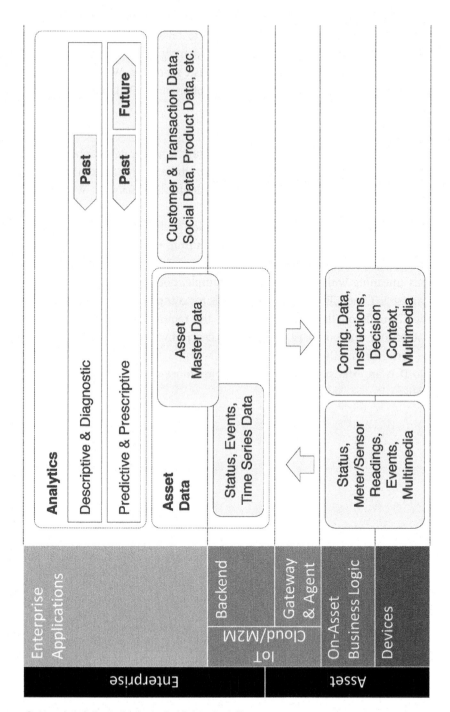

FIGURE 8-47. Data and analytics in the context of Enterprise IoT

FOUR IOT DATA MANAGEMENT SCENARIOS. In order to ensure that an IoT project manager using the Ignite | IoT Methodology can more easily identify the right architecture and technologies for data management, we have defined four basic scenarios. We will use these scenarios to gradually construct our discussion of different options for IoT data management architectures and technologies.

Figure 8-48 summarizes the four scenarios.

Scenario A is relatively straightforward, assuming a moderate number of assets in the field (a couple of thousand assets), with a very small number of events coming in per asset per hour. Analytics will be limited to basic reports and descriptive analytics. We call this scenario "Basic M2M."

Scenario B assumes a real Enterprise IoT solution with hundreds of thousands of assets in the field, and/or higher volumes of data coming in from the assets. The initial focus for this project is on analyzing the data stream from the assets and being able to react in "real time" to critical events (meaning within a second, for example, not hard real-time). We call this scenario "Enterprise IoT and CEP," where CEP stands for complex event processing.

Scenario C builds on this scenario, adding the requirement to store field data over a longer period of time and on a large scale. Basic descriptive and, potentially, diagnostics analytics will be performed on this data.

Scenario D is an extension of Scenario C, plus more advanced analytics, like predictive and prescriptive.

#	Scenario	# Assets	# Events/Hr	Analytics
A	Basic M2M	1000s	10,000s	Basic Reports/Descriptive Analytics
B	Enterprise IoT & CEP	> 100,000	> 100,000	"Real-Time" Stream Analysis
C	B + Big Data/Basic Analytics	> 100,000	> 100,000	Long-Term/Large-Scale, Basic Data Analysis (Descriptive, Diagnostics)
D	C + Advanced Analytics	>100,000	> 100,000	Advanced Data Analytics (Predictive, Prescriptive)

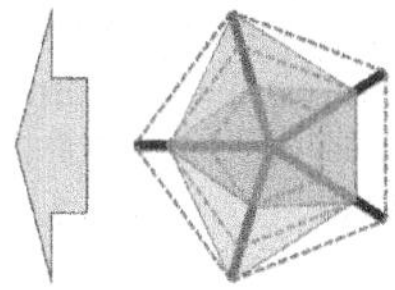

IoT project dimensions

FIGURE 8-48. Overview of four IoT data management scenarios

SCENARIO A: BASIC M2M. A typical application for Scenario A would be remote equipment monitoring, such as for a fleet of mobile industrial machines. A limited number of status updates and events would be expected per machine over time. Basic reporting will show machine status overview, machine utilization, and so on. The architecture will usually be relatively straightforward for the backend. The initial challenge will most likely center on integration of assets and having the required device interfaces for assets (see our discussion in "Asset and Device Interface Management" on page 380). Figure 8-49 shows the AIA for Scenario A.

In terms of technology selection, two key decisions have to be made: which data repository should be used to manage asset and field data, and which interface technology should be used to integrate the remote asset.

For the data repository, there are a number of different options, including RDBMS and NoSQL. Many traditional M2M application platforms are built on RDBMS technology, and this works perfectly well in most cases. One advantage is that one can build on the rich ecosystem of related tools, from reporting to backup management. Also, most organizations will have the required skills to build and operate RDBMS-based solutions.

However, if the scenario is likely to be extended over time; if slightly more complex applications have to be developed, for example, or the analytics requirements are likely to include some more advanced time series analysis in the future, then the solution architect might be well advised to consider a NoSQL database instead.

The second technology decision relates to the integration of the asset and the management of the events and other data streaming from it. If an M2M or IoT application platform is used, it will most likely have this functionality built in. If it is a custom development, there are multiple options. For very basic applications, an application server or a basic event processing technology like NodeJS could be used. There is no lack of established messaging and related technologies that could be used alternatively or in addition. Finally, some IoT-specific messaging solutions like MQTT have started to emerge, which should offer additional benefits due to their specific nature. Table 8-5 provides an overview.

TABLE 8-5. Basic event processing technologies

Category	Description	Pros/cons
AppServer	Lightweight, event-driven AppServer, e.g., NodeJS ("first frontier")	Easy to set up and use, asynchronous app-level event handling; none of the typical messaging advantages
Traditional messaging	JMS, MQ Series, AMQP, etc.	Queues/topics, scalability, persistent messages
IoT messaging	MQTT	Messaging for IoT

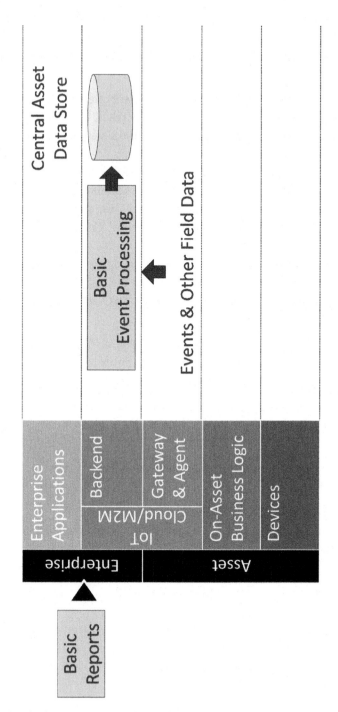

FIGURE 8-49. Architecture for data management in basic M2M

SCENARIO B: ENTERPRISE IOT AND CEP. Scenario B assumes that we are dealing with a much larger number of assets in the field, or that the assets are delivering a much higher data volume to the backend (or both).

In this scenario, close monitoring of data streams will often be required, as will the ability to react quickly to certain types of situations. In many cases, it will also be necessary to analyze data streams for certain patterns in real time—for a steep increase in temperature, for example.

In such cases, one technology that can be very useful is complex event processing (CEP). CEP allows data from multiple data streams to be tracked and analyzed in order to infer patterns that have a specific meaning on the business level—for example, a traffic light switching to red and a pedestrian crossing the road at the same time. Consequently, one interesting use case of CEP is in the area of sensor data fusion.

The overall goal of CEP is to identify the business logic of related events, and be able to respond to them in (near) real time. Figure 8-50 shows the basic principle of CEP.

Robin Smith, Director of Product Management at Oracle, has summarized the basic event patterns in CEP for us as follows:

Filtering

Data stream is filtered for specific criteria, such as temperature > 200 °F.

Correlation and aggregation

Scrolling, time-based window metrics, such as average heart pulse rate in the last three days.

Pattern matching

Notification of detected event patterns, such as machine events A, B, and C occurred within 15-minute window.

Geospatial, predictive modeling, and beyond

Immediate recognition of geographical movement patterns, application of historical business intelligence models using data mining algorithms.

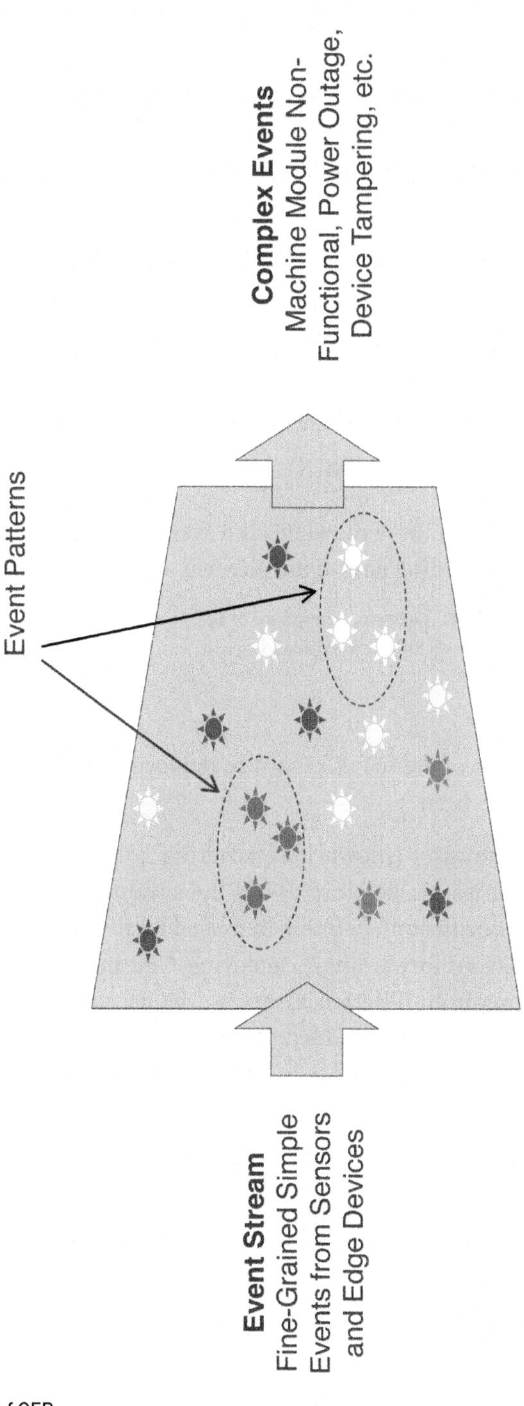

FIGURE 8-50. Basic principle of CEP

EXAMPLE: CONTINUOUS QUERY LANGUAGE (CQL). One good example of a well-established method for analyzing event streams in CEP is the Continuous Query Language (CQL), an extension to the standard SQL language. There are many other approaches, including a number of tools that use visual modelers to support CEP. We will use CQL as our example as it will allow us to illustrate the basic principles.

Robin Smith, Director of Product Management at Oracle, describes CQL as follows:

- CQL queries support filtering, partitioning, aggregation, correlation (across streams), and pattern matching on streaming and relational data.

- CQL extends standard SQL by adding the notion of stream, operators for mapping between relations and streams, and extensions for pattern matching.

- A window operator (e.g., RANGE 1 MINUTE) transforms the stream into a relation.

The simple example shown here calculates the average temperature in the last minute for all temperature sensors submitting data to the selected stream:

```
SELECT AVG(temperature) AS avgTemp, tempSensorId
FROM temperatureInputStream[RANGE 1 MINUTE]
GROUP BY tempSensorId
```

CEP AND IOT. In the context of the IoT, CEP can be deployed on the asset or in the backend, or both. Figure 8-51 shows the latter.

Deploying CEP on the asset (shown here covering both gateway and on-asset business logic, because the boundaries can be blurred) has the advantage that many events can be pre-filtered or combined (sensor fusion), before being used locally (assets autonomy) or being forwarded to the backend (event forwarding). Deploying CEP in the backend has the advantage that multiple data streams from different assets can be combined for analysis. Also, context data (such as weather forecasts) can be added more easily to the decision-making process.

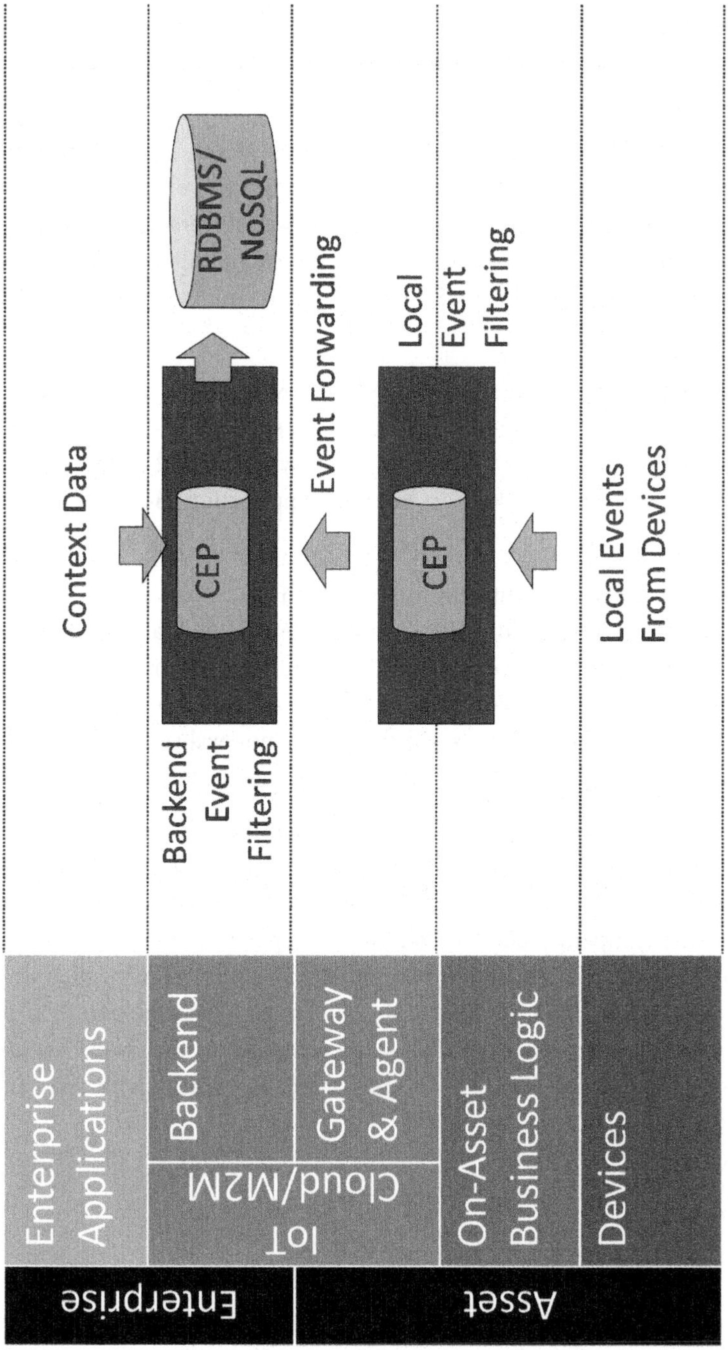

FIGURE 8-51. CEP and Enterprise IoT

CASE STUDY: EMERSON. Emerson is an American multinational corporation that manufactures products and provides engineering services for a wide range of industrial, commercial, and consumer markets.

The Emerson Trellis Platform is a data center infrastructure management solution, which combines inventory management, site management, and power management. The solution uses a local gateway appliance to connect to storage units, servers, power systems, and cooling equipment. CEP is used in this solution for data aggregation, filtering, and processing to support real-time decision making in a very large-scale environment. Figure 8-52 provides an overview of the solution architecture.

SCENARIO C: ADDING BIG DATA AND BASIC ANALYTICS. Scenario C assumes that the solution needs to be able to perform long-term analysis of asset data on a very large, Big Data scale. Here, the boundaries are often not clear. Many CEP systems will be able to scale to very large data volumes. However, as we will see in the following section, Big Data is about more than just volume.

BIG DATA. There are many different definitions of Big Data, which should generally be seen as a continuously evolving concept. Big Data usually refers to very large amounts of structured, semi-structured, and unstructured data which is stored with the intention to mine it for information. It is hard to get specific numbers on how *big* data has to be to count as "Big Data," but the general assumption is that it refers to petabytes, if not exabytes of data. Traditional, large enterprise applications such as ERP and CRM usually only reach terabyte level.

The driving forces behind Big Data have traditionally been large Internet companies, such as Google, Facebook, and the like. Google's engineers, for example, elaborated the initial concept of MapReduce, which allowed data and queries to be spread across thousands of servers. Together with other companies like Yahoo!, this concept was implemented as an open source product called Hadoop, which is now supported by startup companies such as Cloudera (see the interview with Mike Olson in "[Big] Data and Process Management" on page 320) and Hortonworks. Google, arguably the leading-edge company in this field, has also introduced next-generation technologies like its Cloud Dataflow, which is based on Flume and MillWheel.

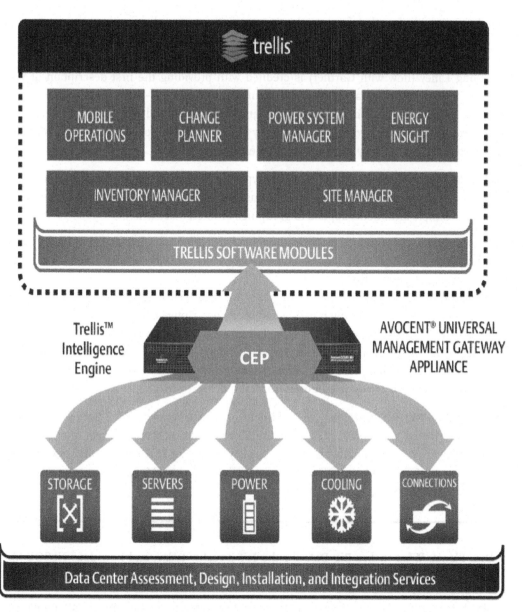

FIGURE 8-52. Emerson Trellis Platform (Source: Oracle)

Regardless of the technology used, Big Data has brought a lot of movement into the traditional RDBMS/OLAP market. One of the key changes is that Big Data is very well suited to manage very different types of data, from highly structured to completely unstructured.

Based on this infrastructure, for example, the emerging Data Lake concept is proposing to turn things upside down for enterprise; instead of defining a database structure first, and then populating it with data that fits into this structure, the Data Lake simply stores any and all kinds of data, and then makes this data available when it is needed, in whatever format is needed.

Doug Laney (now with Gartner) is credited with providing the first description of what many people see as the smallest common definition of Big Data—the three Vs: *volume* (dealing with large volumes of data), *velocity* (dealing with high-speed data streams in near real time), and *variety* (dealing with data in a variety of forms). Some people also add *variability* (or inconsistencies) and *veracity* (data quality) to the Big Data "Vs."

BASIC ANALYTICS. Basic analysis of Big Data typically involves descriptive and diagnostic analytics. Descriptive statistics involve counts, sums, averages, percentages, minimum and maximum, and simple arithmetic, applied to groupings or filtered datasets.

Some people claim that 80% of business analytics are descriptive analytics, especially in social media analytics [LI1]. Examples include page views, number of posts, mentions, followers, and average response time.

Because of the explorative nature of many IoT projects, it can be assumed that many projects will initially also heavily rely on such basic, descriptive analytics—for things such as analysis of statistics like mean time between failure (MTBF) of operational equipment.

Diagnostic analysis will also play an important role in the basic analysis of IoT data; in the event of a problem with a piece of operational equipment, it will be vital to be able to identify the root cause as soon as possible in order to fix it quickly.

ADDING NOSQL TO THE EQUATION. In addition to unstructured Big Data repositories, document-oriented and NoSQL databases are also starting to play an important role in the context of the IoT. In the following, we discuss key aspects of IoT, NoSQL, and big data with Max Schireson, CEO of MongoDB at the time of the interview. MongoDB is a leading opensource database for NoSQL data management.

Dirk Slama: What makes Big Data for the IoT a reality today, and how does NoSQL fit into this?

Max Schireson: In the past 5 years, there have been more developments in data management than we saw in the previous 30 years. With the rise of commodity computing, open source technologies, and the cloud, it is less expensive than ever to ingest, store, process, and analyze data.

These developments have seen the emergence of NoSQL databases to serve operational workloads, and Hadoop for analytical workloads, usually complementing existing technologies.

A lot of these concepts emerged from large web properties that hit scalability walls as their data requirements—both storage and processing—outgrew the limits of relational technology. They also discovered that the majority of their data did not fit a neat row and column format, and so couldn't easily be managed using tables in the relational data model. Application requirements changed radically and the static relational schema held back developer agility. These same problems confront architects and developers in the IoT. The ability to scale out NoSQL databases and Hadoop clusters on fleets of low-cost commodity servers and local storage, either in their own data centers or in the cloud, enables architects to address challenges relating to the data volumes generated by billions of sensors. New data models, such as the document model used by MongoDB, enable architects to store and process not just structured, but also semi-structured, unstructured, and polymorphic data—anything from events, to time-series data, geospatial coordinates, to text and binary data.

Advances in parallel programming have enabled complex algorithms to be distributed around clusters, moving compute to data, rather than the expense and time of moving data to compute. This means we can analyze much higher volumes of data faster than ever before. These fundamental changes in how we store, process, and analyze data provide the foundation for data management in the IoT.

Dirk Slama: What role do modern databases play in the IoT, and do more traditional databases still have a role?

Max Schireson: Many of the modern NoSQL databases serve the operational part of an IoT application. Sensor data is ingested and stored by the NoSQL database, where it can be queried and evaluated, often using business rules created in application middleware, to trigger actions and to feed online reporting dashboards.

Using an example from the world of retail, a network of in-store beacons can identify the location of a customer in a store and send them push notifications. For example, a user might create a shopping list on their smartphone and share it with the store app, where it is stored in the operational database. Upon entering the store, the store app will display a map to the customer, which highlights all the products on their shopping list. Every time the customer gets close to a position where a group of products from their shopping list is located, the app will notify them and make a recommendation for a particular brand. Again, these recommendations will be stored in the operational database. At the checkout point, the system could identify all the products in the shopping cart automatically via RFID, create and confirm an invoice, and use the smartphone to process the payment. The store's inventory system is automatically updated when the checkout process is complete.

In this scenario, the NoSQL database is storing the user's movements around the store, and serving up recommendations along with product information in real time. A more traditional relational database could be used in conjunction with the NoSQL database to handle the billing and invoicing. So, relational databases still have a role to play in IoT applications, often serving as the "system of record" for backend enterprise systems that are integrated into new IoT apps.

Dirk Slama: What role does Hadoop play in IoT, and do more traditional EDWs still have a role?

Max Schireson: This is best illustrated using an example: building on the retail use case from before, all actions taken by the customer are stored in the NoSQL database, and then loaded to Hadoop which combines the data with other sources, for example clickstreams from web logs, buying sentiment from social media, and historical customer data. All of these data points are analyzed to create deep behavioral models that can then be loaded back into the NoSQL database to serve real-time recommendations to customers when they return to the store.

Like the relational database, EDWs are limited in their capacity to scale to support new data sources, and are not efficient at handling exploratory questions which the data model hasn't been specifically designed to answer. These are problems addressed by Hadoop, which is deployed to complement the EDW, rather than replace it.

Dirk Slama: How do you integrate these modern databases and Hadoop enterprise data hubs to manage the lifecycle of IoT data?

Max Schireson: There are many ways IoT architects can integrate NoSQL databases and Hadoop, from custom scripts to productized and supported connectors. An example of the latter is the MongoDB Connector for Hadoop, which is certified for both Apache Hadoop and the leading commercial distributions. The MongoDB Connector for Hadoop allows users to integrate real-time data from MongoDB with the Hadoop platform and its tools. The connector presents MongoDB as a Hadoop data source, allowing a Hadoop job (MapReduce, Hive, Pig, Impala, etc.) to read data from MongoDB directly without first copying it to HDFS, thereby eliminating the need to move TB of data between systems. Hadoop jobs can pass queries as filters, thereby avoiding the need to scan entire collections and speeding up processing; they can also take advantage of MongoDB's indexing capabilities, including text and geospatial. The connector enables the results of Hadoop jobs to be written back out to MongoDB, including incremental updates of existing documents. In addition, MongoDB itself can be run on the same physical cluster as Hadoop, so there is very tight integration between the two platforms.

Dirk Slama: What role does stream processing play in these new IoT data architectures? How do you see established CEP concepts fitting in here?

Max Schireson: Stream processing such as Apache Spark and Apache Storm, as well as existing CEP, can be run against IoT data as it is streamed from sensors, devices, and assets, alerting against events and triggering automated actions. CEP is a well-proven and mature technology, typically correlating data from multiple sources to find patterns and apply business rules. The data and rules are stored in the operational database. Stream processing such as Spark and Storm are much more recent developments, typically operating against a single stream of data, and again working with an operational database for persistence of data, rules, and actions. Both have a role to play in the IoT, depending on use case and developer skills.

Dirk Slama: How do you analyze IoT data to gain new insight or automate new processes? Is this done in Hadoop, in the database, in the sensor data stream?

Max Schireson: It can be done in all three. Analytics can be run against data in flight (streams), in real-time processes controlled with a database using native data processing pipelines, and against Hadoop, which stores data ingested from multiple sources.

So, to go back to our retail example—stream analysis detects that a customer has returned from the store. The database retrieves the customer's details and matches them to a profile of preferences and product promotions. The customer's activity and purchases are tracked and stored in the database, and then loaded into Hadoop where the new data is used to tune the analytics models. This data is then loaded back into the database, so that when the customer returns, even more relevant offers can be served.

BUILDING UP THE BIG DATA INFRASTRUCTURE. Scenario C assumes that instead of (or in addition to) the real-time analysis of the asset data stream, we want to be able to keep this data for a longer time, in order to perform long-term pattern analysis on this "ephemeral" data. This scenario focuses on building up the required Big Data infrastructure in combination with stream processing, and introduces some basic algorithms that can be used to analyze this data.

Christopher Dziekan, Chief Product Officer at Pentaho, explains:

Everyone is anxious to turn data (or Big Data) into big value and big profit, often pointing to the three Vs of Big Data—volume, variety, and velocity. These Vs are driving an impetus for change architecturally; however, as companies build upon their Big Data infrastructures, more Vs come into play. A Big Data infrastructure is a necessary response to the first three Vs, but veracity and value also need to come into the equation.

To encompass all the Vs of Big Data, one must look to architectures and methodologies that enable large-scale production deployment.

To turn information into strategic advantage, a Big Data "orchestration" platform is needed that combines data integration with business analytics. Advanced analytic techniques are applied to the data generated by IoT devices, blending that data with both relational data and new data sources. The platform must fit into existing IT infrastructure and connect to business applications so that it is universally available at the point of impact, supporting line-of-business and operational decisions.

Examining the analytics needs of the different user communities that work with IoT systems, we can see that no single tool or repository perfectly fits all users' needs. Some need traditional data marts and data warehouses. Others may need a "Data Lake" repository that can be queried on an ad-hoc basis, along with a data refinery. Others need to analyze device states, perform streaming queries, and broadcast notifications. Still others need ad-hoc data transformation and an array of special tools for their data scientists.

Given these different requirements, how do we build a data architecture to meet all needs? First of all, we need a set of tools or a platform that will enable us to manage the entire architecture.

LAMBDA ARCHITECTURE. One approach for combining some of these elements into a single engine is known as the Lambda Architecture, which was introduced by Nathan Marz. The Lambda Architecture consists of a "batch layer" that stores all of the historic data, a "speed layer" that processes data in real time, and a "serving layer" that allows both of the other layers to be queried (Figure 8-53).

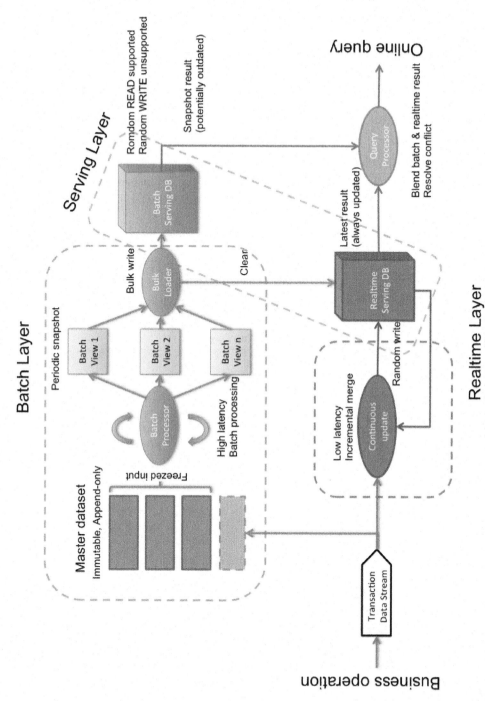

FIGURE 8-53. Lambda Architecture (Source: Ricky Ho [RH1])

We want all the layers to perform well, so the name "batch layer" is better thought of as a "Data Lake"—a term coined by James Dixon of Pentaho [FO1]. The speed layer should then be thought of as a "real-time layer."

The Lambda Architecture solves some of the data architecture issues for an IoT system, but it does not explicitly provide a way to store or query the state of one or all of the devices.

IOT DATA ARCHITECTURE. The Lambda Architecture can be used as the guiding principle to create an IoT system.

In Figure 8-54, you can see that the IoT data architecture contains the Real-Time Layer, the Data Lake/Historical Layer, and the Query Layer of the Lambda Architecture. It also has the State Layer, and the Blending/Transformation/Refinery/Data Mart layer.

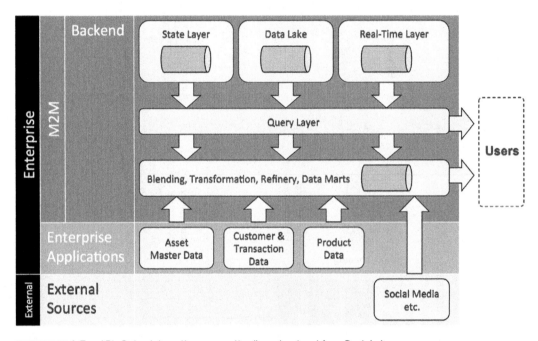

FIGURE 8-54. IoT and Big Data—integration perspective (based on input from Pentaho)

James Dixon of Pentaho elaborated on the importance between the State Layer and the Data Lake in his "Union of the State" concept. In a blog post on this topic, Dixon recommends capturing the initial state of an application's data and the changes to of all of the attributes, not just the main/traditional fields. He advocates applying this approach to multiple applications, each with its own Data Lake of state logs, storing every incremental change and event. This results in capturing the state of every field of (potentially) every business application in an enterprise across time, or, the "Union of the State."

This approach can be applied in many situations. For example, an e-commerce vendor can find out, for any specified millisecond in the past, how many shopping carts were open, what was in them, which transactions were pending, which items were being boxed or were in transit, what was being returned, who was working, how many customer support calls were queued, and how many were in progress. By its very nature, this approach supports processes like trend analysis and compliance.

To date, there are no off-the-shelf applications or tools that offer a Lambda Architecture product or the IoT extensions to it. This is something that the IoT implementation team needs to consider when designing, in order to maximize the abilities, efficiency, and effectiveness of their IoT system.

SCENARIO D: ADDING ADVANCED ANALYTICS. Once the infrastructure for Big Data management and the IoT has been built up, the next step is to increase the level of sophistication with which the data is analyzed. This includes predictive and prescriptive analytics. Predictive analytics uses historical data to make forecasts about future events and developments, while prescriptive analytics attempts to guide actions to achieve an optimized outcome.

Many people actually see these scenarios as extremely important in the IoT. In particular, industrial IoT scenarios will greatly benefit from use cases like predictive maintenance.

Because of the complexity of these use cases, many companies are now looking at creating new job roles, like a data scientist who combines the required business, technical, and data analytics skills required to support such user cases.

Predictive analytics includes a number of different techniques, such as modeling, machine learning, and data mining.

MACHINE LEARNING. Dr. Tapio Torikka is a Product Manager for Condition Monitoring at Bosch Rexroth. In this section, he provides an explanation of machine learning as an important element of predictive analytics, based on [ML1] and [ML2].

Machine learning is a field of artificial intelligence in which an algorithm constructs a model based on input data in order to make predictions. No explicitly programmed instructions are used to create the model, which enables problems to be solved where little or no domain knowledge is available. Figure 8-55 shows the process of training and applying a machine learning algorithm.

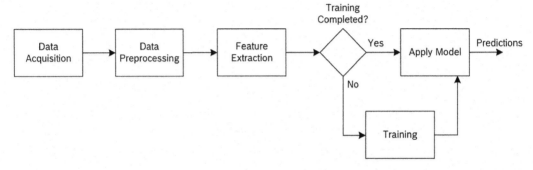

FIGURE 8-55. Machine learning (Source: Bosch Rexroth)

After data is acquired from a selected source, it has to be preprocessed—for example, by scaling the data and imputing missing values. After preprocessing, a feature extraction step extracts any significant information from the data in order to improve the subsequent training step. During the training phase, a learning algorithm is used to iteratively adjust the internal parameters of the machine learning model to improve itself. Once a desired accuracy or a preset training time has been reached, the model can be saved and later used to make predictions with unknown data.

The following types of learning can be identified:

- Supervised learning
  - Labeled training data is used to build a classifier model
  - Example Application: classification of emails ("normal" versus "spam")
- Unsupervised learning
  - Structure of the data is learned without labels
  - Example Application: credit card fraud detection
- Semi-supervised learning
  - Small amount of labeled data, larger volume of unlabeled data
  - Example Application: image recognition (a small number of manually labeled images available, a huge pool of unlabeled images available on the Internet)

Supervised learning is preferred when labeled example data (desired outputs for presented input data) is available. When labeled data is rare or unavailable, semi-supervised or unsupervised learning can be used. Figure 8-56 illustrates a simple unsupervised training process. The algorithm tries to adjust its parameters in such a way that the predictions given by the model match the input data. This kind of model can be used for anomaly detection—that is, the model will predict if a given piece of input data will exhibit the same structure as the training data.

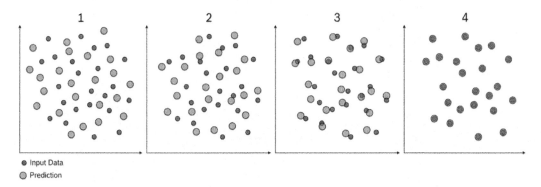

- Input Data
- Prediction

FIGURE 8-56. Example for unsupervised training process (Source: Bosch Rexroth)

Two distinct types of model can be built during the training phase of the machine learning process:

Classification
Output of the machine learning model (prediction) is discrete.

Regression
Output of the model is continuous.

A classifier separates the data into n categories as presented in the training data (e.g., a classifier built to categorize emails might classify them as normal or spam based on the content). A regression model can be used to predict continuous signals (e.g., the future values of a defined target signal).

CASE STUDY: MACHINE LEARNING FOR CONDITION MONITORING IN INDUSTRIAL APPLICATIONS.
The following case study is provided by Dr. Tapio Torikka, Product Manager for Condition Monitoring at Bosch Rexroth.

In condition monitoring, the health state of a machine is assessed based on collected sensor data. This allows the operator to optimize the maintenance activities of their assets and reduce the risk of unplanned downtime (see Figure 8-57). Typically, these systems are operated continuously (this is known as *online condition monitoring*).

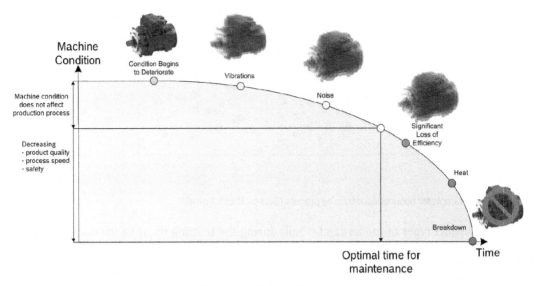

Machine
Condition

Condition Begins
to Deteriorate

Vibrations

Machine condition
does not affect
production process

Noise

Significant
Loss of
Efficiency

Decreasing
- product quality
- process speed
- safety

Heat

Breakdown

Optimal time for
maintenance

Time

FIGURE 8-57. Machine condition monitoring (Source: Bosch Rexroth)

Machines in industrial environments are very complex, so assessing their health state can be quite challenging. Many machines are purpose-built for a specific application and therefore exhibit a unique behavior. Additionally, environmental effects like temperature variations, noise, vibrations, and so on can influence sensor signals. To make matters worse, industrial machinery tends to produce very large volumes of data, partly due to the need for high-frequency measurements, as a result of the highly dynamic production cycles of the machinery. These characteristics mean that monitoring the maintenance status of machinery by manually inspecting individual sensor signals or simple rules is next to impossible.

Storing large amounts of data is no longer a problem and can be solved by implementing available Big Data solutions. The ability of machine-learning algorithms to generate models based on training data alone addresses the harder problem of making sense of this data. Data scientists are needed to create analytics pipelines for data preprocessing and learning algorithms. Furthermore, they are responsible for defining learning goals and determining action proposals based on the results, together with domain experts. Access to fast computers is important, as machine learning algorithms typically require a lot of computing power.

Anomaly detection is a typical approach to detect abnormal behavior in the data source. In an industrial context, this approach can be used to detect a deviation from normal machine behavior indicating a faulty condition. Anomaly detection requires training data from only one reference state (e.g., normal behavior).

In a real-world example, a mining operator was interested in monitoring the health of the Rexroth drive system of a conveyor belt, which is used to transport ore from the mine (Figure 8-58). This is a critical asset for the operator and is constantly in operation, as downtime translates directly into reduced revenue. Sensors were installed to collect data from the conveyor belt drive. A remote Big Data system was used to store the data from the system, and machine-learning algorithms were used to generate an index representing the general health state of the machine (this is an example of predictive analytics). No failure data was available from the system and therefore an anomaly detection algorithm was used to indicate the deviation from normal behavior.

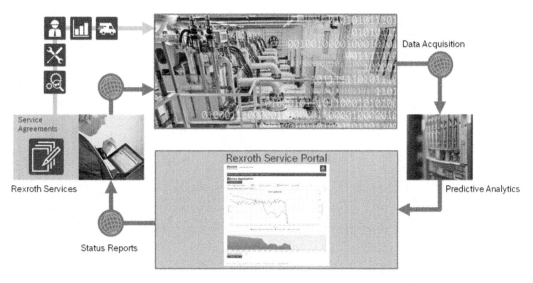

FIGURE 8-58. System architecture (Source: Bosch Rexroth)

A web portal was used to view the data and to monitor the system. Figure 8-59 shows the visualization screen of the portal.

An electric motor failure occurred in this drive unit. Figure 8-59 shows the result of the anomaly detection algorithm and the electric motor current over time. The electric motor current suddenly drops to zero after several months of operation without a significant change in the trend. Manual analysis of other sensor signals did not indicate any failure in the system. As can be seen in the image, the lower curve (the result of the anomaly detection algorithm) begins to deviate significantly from normal levels (90-100) well before the motor fails. This represents the capability of machine-learning algorithms to make sense of complicated data. Analyzing the data manually would have been an impossible task due to the large volume of data and the complexity of evaluating all the available sensor signals simultaneously.

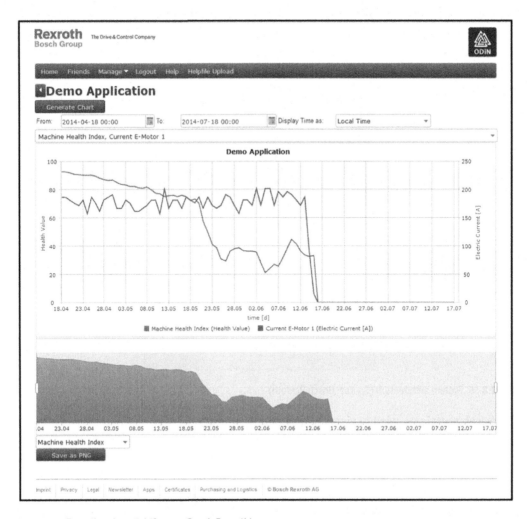

FIGURE 8-59. Rexroth web portal (Source: Bosch Rexroth)

CASE STUDY: AIRCRAFT ENGINE ANALYTICS. The following case study was provided by Ted Willke, Senior Principal Engineer and GM, Graph Analytics Operation at Intel Corporation.

Big Data systems are frequently used to calculate statistics from logs and other machine-generated data. This information may be used by engineers and data scientists to monitor operations, identify failures, optimize performance, and improve future designs. Aircraft engines are among the most complex machines in the world, bringing together many aspects of physics and having to operate over an extreme range of conditions [LYYJL]. They are often monitored for diagnostics to identify potential failures early, before they lead to safety concerns and interfere with flights.

Traditionally, snapshots of engine statuses and fault codes are taken during a flight and sent to a ground station for logging and monitoring. But with the availability of IoT systems that accommodate both streaming data and scale using Big Data technologies (Category C systems), engine data can be streamed off-board to fleet-wide ground stations, monitored continuously, and analyzed for deeper insights [DSAR]. The same stream of data can be collected on the same engine under the same flight conditions (altitude, velocity, temperature, operating time, etc.) time and time again. Simple statistics can be calculated based on this time series data to determine if the engine is operating as expected (when compared to design specifications), and to detect abnormal conditions, such as problems with the turbine pressure, exit air temperature, or fuel flow rate.

While Category C systems are able to detect anomalies and failures, they may not be able to isolate faults and uncover their root cause with high confidence and accuracy [LYYJL]. Furthermore, they may not be able to detect weak signals (subtle anomalies) that may develop into more apparent anomalies and serious faults over time. This is where machine learning comes in (Category D systems). Machine learning can create a model of the system under study (in this case, the aircraft engine), and then use the model to predict the behavior of the system. Machine learning is a data-centric approach. A prototype (generic form) of the model is selected and "trained" to improve predictive accuracy. A common training process involves supplying pairs of inputs (what the prediction will be based on) and known outputs (what is being predicted) so that patterns can be learned by the model. After the patterns are learned, accurate predictions can be made. In the case of engine diagnostics, the inputs are the operating characteristics of the engine and the prediction may be one of several engine fault codes ("normal" being one such code).

In one study [LYYJL], 49,900 flights' worth of data was analyzed to determine the ability of machine learning to predict 1 of 9 engine fault conditions from 8 engine measurements. The technique was shown to be able to detect the existence of a fault early on and to attribute the fault to a specific fault code.

CONCLUSIONS. As we saw in this chapter, there are many different levels of sophistication when it comes to data management in the IoT. The four scenarios that we have outlined should help a product manager to decide which solution architecture and technology is right for his particular need. In the following section, we shall provide some conclusions, first from the perspective of industrial applications, and then from the technological perspective.

INDUSTRY 4.0 PERSPECTIVE. Tobias Conz is a project manager in the industry team at Bosch Software Innovations. He is working at the intersection of advanced IT concepts and the harsh reality of today's manufacturing IT environments. He describes his experience as follows:

Data management in the area of manufacturing and Industry 4.0 is particularly challenging because many manufacturers are looking at investment cycles of 10–15 years, meaning that change doesn't come easily in existing environments. The good thing is that many machines are actually collecting a tremendous amount of data already, which is needed for machine control. However, before Industry 4.0, there were few requirements to actually make this data available to the outside world. This means that we are looking at a lot of very basic data integration scenarios that have to deal with the usual problems like heterogeneous interfaces, data types and protocols, software in different versions, etc.

Because most machine data was not integrated at a higher level, we are finding a much higher degree of heterogeneity in this space, compared, for example, to banks and insurance companies, who had to deal with integration much earlier.

New data management concepts like data mining, stream processing, etc., are of course extremely interesting in the context of manufacturing and Industry 4.0. Given the specificities of this space, we recommend a dual strategy: Individual machine data is a treasure trove for data mining which should be used wherever applicable. However, the integration of all machines for this purpose is nearly impossible. This is why we are also developing a near-real-time stream processing solution which will allow us to validate the process parameters of multiple machines at the same time. We are doing this one machine type at a time, to see which machine types this actually works best for. The biggest challenge we are facing is to find a time- and cost-efficient method for integration.

GENERAL RECOMMENDATIONS. As the CEO of MongoDB, Max Schireson was able to gain great insights into the deployment of NoSQL and Big Data technologies in general, as well as in the emerging IoT space. In this part of the interview, he provides some valuable recommendations for project managers:

Dirk Slama: What are the biggest risks associated with Big Data and the IoT? How can companies limit or avoid these risks?

Max Schireson: Because the IoT and Big Data are such hot topics right now, it is very easy to dive straight into the technology, rather than thinking first about the business objectives of the project. Much more important than the technology, you need to think about what it is the business is trying to achieve, and bring together the stakeholders (i.e., the business units, your customers, your partners, and the IT teams who will work on delivering the enabling technology). Maybe even competitors, as interconnectivity and integration are key in IoT ecosystems. You shouldn't be going to stakeholders, and especially not to customers, talking about the IoT itself. You need to frame the conversation around the benefits that IoT can deliver.

It is important that the project has strategic support at the most senior levels within the organization. Also, take time to learn from the success and failures of early movers. It

---

is important to be explorative. Remember there are very few people who can really predict what future business models will look like, in much the same way that few predicted what the most successful business models would look like in the early days of the Internet.

You need to upskill—either by taking existing staff and training them or by going to third parties outside of the company to leverage their expertise. We would recommend starting with pilot projects that have a defined use case and work on a subset of devices and data. Measure, optimize, and measure again. If the project is successful—with concepts being proven and staff being trained—then get more ambitious.

Dirk Slama: Who is likely to benefit most from the IoT? Who is liable to lose the most?

Max Schireson: There is sometimes a perception that it's just the makers of "things" that stand to benefit. This is completely wrong. Think about insurance companies who can optimize premiums by monitoring the behavior of their customers, or retailers who can optimize the entire farm-to-fork supply chain. *The Economist* estimates that 75% of companies are now planning for IoT at the most senior levels of the organization [Ref2]. Those companies that use the IoT and the data/insight it generates to create new business models and that can get closer to their customers will gain the most. Those that stick their heads in the sand will cease to exist.

Dirk Slama: What advice would you give to readers who are developing their strategy and implementation for Big Data and the IoT?

Max Schireson: First, I would go back to the discussion points mentioned earlier. When the team has selected the technologies that they plan to use, then there are some general best practices: give them ramp-up time to understand the technology (training, reading, and conferences). Engage resources from vendors and service providers to assist in development of new projects. As the development progresses, share progress and best practices internally with tech talks, hackathons, and project wikis. Then start to expand, build a CoE when multiple projects are underway so best practices are institutionalized. There is so much innovation happening in this space, and so many technology choices, you need to keep an open mind. Just selecting a data management platform because it has successfully run your ERP platform for the past 15 years is not a good idea!

IOT AND PROCESS MANAGEMENT. Process management might not be the first thing that comes to mind when talking about IoT solutions. This is because many IoT projects initially struggle with getting assets and devices connected, and then building the basic services in the backend. Also, as discussed in this chapter, many projects will focus on analyzing and managing inbound event streams, or building up basic analytics. However, once the initial IoT solution functionality is established and the system scales up in terms of connected devices and incoming data, process efficiency will eventually become a very important topic. In an IoT solution, many business processes will be triggered by individual events coming from devices and assets, or by the results of more advanced analytics that look at multiple, only indirectly related events (see Complex Event Processing in Chapter 7).

Take, for example, predictive maintenance. As discussed, for example, in "Case Study: Machine Learning for Condition Monitoring in Industrial Applications" on page 347, sophisticated machine-learning algorithms are applied to sensor data to identify situations which indicate that a machine breakdown is imminent. You can literally see the sensor network expert and the data scientist putting their heads together for weeks to figure out how to identify these trigger points. But what comes next? What do you do with the information that the conveyor belt at ACME mining has an 87.25% chance of breaking down between Monday and Wednesday of next week because of a problem with the liquids in a hydraulic component? And what do you do if this type of information actually comes in hundreds of times a week for the tens of thousands of customers who are using your machine components? This is exactly the point where business process management (BPM) comes in, to help ensure that these requests can be processed efficiently and that the field service team is utilized as well as possible.

Take, as another example, the eCall service that we have already used so many times: yes, the initial focus of the project is to correctly identify potential crash situations and send this information to a call center so that it can be processed. And this is exactly where BPM starts, at least from the call center manager's point of view. Managers must focus on two things: first, ensuring proper process execution (this means classifying the distress call and routing it to a call center agent with the right language skills), and secondly, call center utilization. These days, most call centers support multiple services. Implementing efficient call-routing processes is extremely important for ensuring SLAs, but also for ensuring profitability.

Or take, for example, the large telecom companies that build and operate large communication networks with hundreds of thousands of network elements and millions of customers. eTom, the TM Forum's blueprint for running a telecom company, identifies hundreds of critical business processes, from network management to customer-related processes such as sales, product activation, and customer service requests. After all, the IoT will not be so different.

So some interesting questions that we have to ask ourselves regarding BPM and IoT include:

- How do we identify the most critical processes in an IoT solution that should be addressed first, from a process automation point of view?
- How much automation will be possible (or desirable)?
- When should we use BPM tools for process automation, and when should we use other approaches like hard-coded business logic?
- What is the nature of these processes? For example, structured, unstructured, and so on.
- Is software provisioning and management on devices a BPM process or an application feature?
- What type of tools should be used? BPM engines, workflow management tools, or collaboration tools like Jira?
- Is it an advantage if my IoT application platform has a built-in BPM engine?
- What does the technical integration look like (Device2Process and Process2Device)?

In order to better understand these questions and the potential answers to them, let's take a closer look at how process management potentially fits into an IoT solution. Figure 8-60 is an AIA that builds on the AIA from Chapter 7, because at the end of the day, processes need to operate based on data, events, and the results of analytics.

In this example, we have positioned the BPM/workflow/case management component between the M2M/IoT application platform (see Chapter 9) on the one hand, and the existing enterprise application systems (ERP, CRM, PLM, etc.) on the other. A pattern that we call Device2Process and Process2Device is responsible for initiating new processes based on input that comes from assets and devices. The same pattern is also responsible for signaling to existing process instances if a relevant event from a device comes in that should potentially change the process flow. Similarly, processes can also be initiated by the results of the analytics engines. A use case for this would be predictive maintenance, where a predictive analytics algorithm comes to the conclusion that a machine breakdown is becoming likely, and then initiates a process to have customer service deal with this situation.

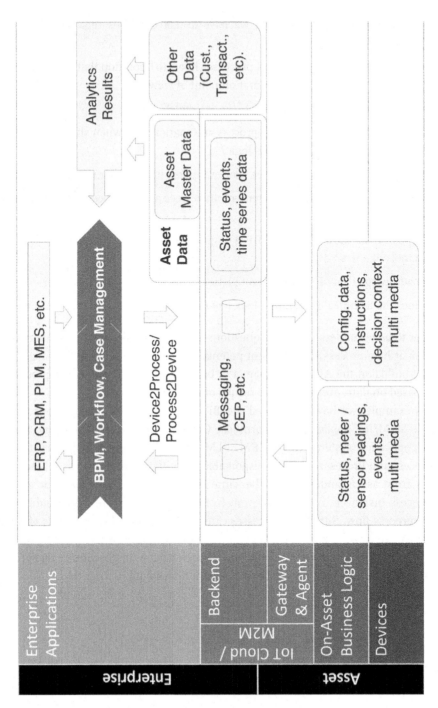

FIGURE 8-60. BPM, workflow, and case management in the context of the IoT

PROCESS DIVERSITY. Notice that we are differentiating between BPM, workflow, and case management. These are three different concepts that have been developed over time to address the fact that, in complex solutions, there are usually different subprocesses or process segments with very different characteristics. BPM is usually seen as being very strong in process automation, including orchestration of multiple backend systems (e.g., ERP, CRM, PLM, etc.). Workflow systems focus more on human workflows, and less on process automation. Finally, case management is adding a data-centric ("case folder") perspective with flexible workflow control.

If you think back to the discussion in the introduction about the impact of the IoT on the Distributed Assets Lifecycle, it becomes clear that it is important to understand the nature of the different subprocesses and to choose the right process management concept to support them. For example, the activation of IoT products is typically a highly automated process that could be implemented based on BPM. Service processes usually require a lot of human interaction, so they would usually rely on workflow management. In some situations, case management could also be interesting for support services, because case management is usually very good at gathering all related data and context information belonging to a case. For example, a service technician could get an information pack that tells her which support vehicle and support tools she should use and what time she should visit a customer, as well as providing details of the customer history and a description of the particular product.

Finally, the mapping between processes and events can also be quite complex and can require a lot of flexibility. Take the example in Figure 8-61, which is based on a scenario involving an industrial conveyor belt (similar to the use case provided by Bosch Rexroth in Chapter 7).

The conveyor is equipped with sensors that support a machine-learning approach in the backend. Let's assume that the analytics engine signals that there is a problem with one of the key components, and that the forecast indicates this part will break in 2-3 weeks (1). A process (or case, or workflow) should be initiated that creates a task for a call center agent to contact the customer and make an appointment within the next 2-3 weeks (2). Now let's assume that the situation at the customer site gets worse: our complex event processing (CEP) component has correlated a set of events that, in sum, indicate that the situation got worse much faster than forecasted (3). An internal rule decides that, based on these conditions, the conveyor belt will be shut down immediately to avoid further damage (4). The process must now advise the call center agent to urgently contact the customer again to agree on an emergency procedure (5).

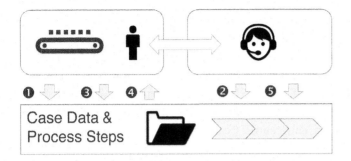

❶ Predictive analytics indicates problem will happen in 3 weeks
❷ Call center agrees date for visit of technician onsite
❸ CEP detects pattern that indicates conveyor belt breakdown is imminent
❹ Sytem automatically shuts down conveyor belt
❺ Call center contacts customer to agree on emergency procedure

FIGURE 8-61. Example of complex process

This scenario shows how important it will be in IoT environments to be able to deal with processes in a very flexible manner. One good way of doing this is by using adaptive case management (ACM), the most flexible version of case management.

EXPERT OPINION. In the following section, we will discuss this topic with Torsten Winterberg from Opitz Consulting. Torsten is also a very active member of the Enterprise BPM Alliance (www.enterprise-bpm.org), which develops and maintains a BPM methodology based on Enterprise BPM, the predecessor to this book.

Dirk Slama: Torsten, can you explain to us why applying process management to the IoT world is important?

Torsten Winterberg: Efficient process management might not be the first thing you think of in an IoT project. In fact, putting your Arduino experts in the same room with a bunch of Aris process analysts might not be a good idea. However, I believe we can learn from the evolution of the backend processes and systems of the large telcos. They have learned over the last couple of decades how to manage millions of remote devices used by end customers. Given the scale of their business, they were forced to look at process efficiency sooner rather than later. This includes many different types of processes, from sales and product configuration to product activation and customer service processes. At the moment, most IoT initiatives are focusing on solving basic problems like actually integrating devices and implementing the basic service functions. But as soon as these initiatives start upscaling, they will face the same problems. Managing millions of remote devices in the field, as well as their related end customers, means finding efficient ways of pre-filtering events and other information in order to deploy business rules to help with automated decision-making, and to ensure that only those problems which can't be automated reach the human support staff.

Dirk Slama: What is the easiest way to connect the device world to the BPM side of things?

Torsten Winterberg: The easiest way to derive benefit from an automated process in the IoT world is to identify an "interesting scenario," and then directly implement a process to handle that scenario. For example, think of some warehouses where temperature-sensitive goods are stored. If a temperature device detects that a threshold is exceeded, it can trigger a process in the backend that takes care of the problem. This process could try to find a solution by applying some predefined measures. If they fail, then a human can be notified to look into the problem. This leads to a much better and more efficient working environment; the employee responsible only has to react to deviations, maybe by means of an automated text message or a generated call.

Dirk Slama: OK, that's a very simple example. In reality, things are more complex. A process instance might have to react to several different incoming signals from devices. How would you solve this with BPMN?

Torsten Winterberg: Well, the BPMN engines have pretty good built-in mechanisms to handle signals, and therefore a process instance can react to a number of incoming events. But of course, this way of addressing the problem is not the BPMN's specialty. The process models tend to get polluted with a lot of event-handling symbols, which makes it hard to keep control of the complex business rules of the different events. Changing the environment will always necessitate changing the BPMN model. To sum up, the complexity of this scenario and the lack of flexibility to adapt to a change of environment will overstrain the BPMN paradigm. Therefore, we advise using a BPM discipline called ACM.

Dirk Slama: Can you explain what you mean by ACM?

Torsten Winterberg: ACM stands for adaptive case management, and is an interesting alternative to BPMN when process models get too complex, when you don't just have simple happy path models, or when you have to deal with lots of exception handling "code" which pollutes your nice BPMN models. ACM eliminates the need for transitions between activities in BPMN and typically replaces these transitions with a set of decision rules. ACM is goal-driven, for example, like in a navigation system in a car, where the goal is clear, but the path (the process itself) is unclear and full of escalation. BPMN, on the other hand, can be seen as a railway system with predefined tracks: if you need a shortcut or a new route, you can only use the existing tracks or prebuild new ones. When the IT world speaks about "unstructured processes"—this is the sense of ACM.

Dirk Slama: So ACM is a BPM discipline that can be used for unstructured processes. How does this help with IoT?

Torsten Winterberg: The term "unstructured" usually implies something chaotic, but this is not the case here. Many processes are goal-oriented or case-oriented, and the path the knowledge worker chooses to reach this goal is often not rigidly defined, and takes their evaluation of information into account. For example, think of a medical case: a patient enters a hospital and is routed by the expertise of different people through several stations. From a process perspective, the patient enters the hospital, then some unstructured things happen, and the goal is that the patient leaves the hospital again (hopefully healthy), and then a bill is sent.

With the emergence of the IoT, these types of cases will evolve. Remote health monitoring can provide additional inputs to the clinical case, like real-time events related to patient health. Usage-based insurance (UBI) will have an impact on how insurance companies deal with insurance-related cases in the future.

In ACM, you typically have a dashboard in your portal used by knowledge workers to view the "case." The UI highlights those activities, depending on the current state of the underlying knowledge base, that can be executed by the knowledge worker. An ACM engine in collaboration with an integration platform can easily collect all kind of incoming events from different devices. These events may or may not change the underlying knowledge base, thus implying a change to the adaptive process. So some signal signs can be "green" or "red," and some kinds of activities can be enabled or disabled, depending on the business effect an incoming event should have. The relation to the clinical case is simple. Each device with its messages can be viewed as a clinical appliance or clinical test measuring different values and implying and determining an appropriate response by the doctor.

Dirk Slama: Interesting approach. But doesn't this approach introduce an overly complex mechanism in the BPM world?

Torsten Winterberg: Yes and no! For the user of the system, ACM makes life much easier because the focus of the work is the business case, and the person working on the process has a new degree of freedom to perform the process in the most effective way. Again, compare this to the way you use a navigation system. The goal is to reach the target address, but you have the freedom to take the best possible route. In most cases, this might be the given, compiled route, but undefined circumstances might need a flexible reaction and a route change. This ease of use from the side of the "knowledge worker" necessitates higher complexity in designing the ACM engine case. But today's ACM engines are integrating business rule engines and are getting better through transparency of these underlying rules, so that this complexity isn't much of a hurdle anymore.

Dirk Slama: We learned that ACM is a very valuable approach for the Device2Process solution. But what about the other way around? Is there a correlation with Process2Device, too?

Torsten Winterberg: To complete a case successfully, you might perform a task that will manipulate the outside world, including the case data and the case status itself. You use small BPMN processes behind these tasks, as they are, in general, well defined and stable. A blood analysis as an example is a well-defined task, but the outcome and the necessary reaction in relation to the blood values are not so well defined. So the question is that if a process (which is executable in BPMN) is able to interact with a "thing" as in your earlier Process2Device example, what implications could this have? We think there is still some work to do to figure this out. Of course, a process could interact with a thing, such as adjusting the thresholds of alarm values. But we think it is more likely that a process will simply emit an event or a message, which is then consumed by some other system (like an IoT cloud), which will in turn interact with the single device. Normally you don't want too close a coupling between your process and your device world, because things will evolve extremely quickly over the next few years, so your architecture needs to be adaptive.

To sum up, having too much data and complexity to compile manually, analyze, and react to, and the wish to have a goal-oriented and flexible way to perform a business process makes a solid case for an ACM approach with BPMN subprocesses for well-defined subtasks and the integration of devices.

We are very excited, as this combined approach should be able to resolve many shortcomings of today's BPM implementations. Currently there is a gold rush atmosphere out there, looking forward to a large amount of still-unforeseen new business models, and perhaps also big, new players ready to leverage the possibilities presented by the availability of mass personal data.

User Interaction

Another area that plays an important role in the IoT is User Interaction, which in our definition includes both traditional User Interfaces (UI) as well as Human-Machine Interfaces (HMI). Traditionally, HMI was local to one machine or piece of equipment and describes the interface between the human and the machine, e.g., through membrane switches, rubber keypads, and touchscreens. With the proliferation of mobile devices and the ability to remotely control equipment, the boundaries between traditional HMI and UI start to become a little bit blurred. Take, for example, a user interface which combines remote access to an asset with central backend functionality. A good example for this is the interface provided by the real-time car sharing companies which we discussed in the introduction. They provide a mobile UI which allows users to find all available cars in their proximity. In addition, these mobile UIs often allow the user to make a reservation for an available car in real time. This function of the mobile UI could be seen as HMI, because it will directly interact with the car and lock it for other customers.

Mobile access to remote devices in general has the potential to revolutionize the way we interact with machines and equipment. Who wants to use a tiny and cryptic LCD display on the heating unit in his basement to change the program for his upcoming holiday when he can achieve the same thing with a nice looking and self-explanatory UI from his tablet in the living room? However, remote access might not become a reality for all industrial use cases in the near future. Consequently, traditional providers of HMI technologies for large industrial equipment have adapted their offerings in the last couple of years. CRTs have been replaced by flat-panel LCDs, some even adding 16:9 aspect ratios to the traditional 4:3. HMI touchscreens are now adding the multitouch capabilities found on smart phones and tablets.

Another key trend is the use of sensor technologies for HMI. Take, for example, a chain saw that uses sensors to stop the saw in a fraction of a second if the blade gets in touch with human skin. These kinds of sensor skins are also becoming increasingly important in an area called Men/Robot Cooperation (MRC). Today, almost all industrial robots are operated behind electric fences which automatically shut down the robot if a human crosses the fence. MRC aims to create work environments where men and robots can interact directly with each other. For example, a robot could support a human worker by doing the heavy lifting of workpieces. However, this requires a new approach for controlling robots. Modern robots like the Bosch APAS are thus deploying sensor skins that will automatically stop the movement of the robot in case a human is getting too close to it. For advanced MRC, the robot control algorithms will also have to be changed, e.g. to slow down a robot depending on sensor-based data about human proximity. This could be used to slow down the robot gradually if a human approaches.

Finally, another important technology for User Interaction in the IoT is Augmented Reality (AR). AR provides an augmented view of a real-world environment by adding computer-generated sensory data such as sound, video, graphics, or GPS data to the real, physical objects.

Security

There is no shortage of scary hacks and security breaches related to the IoT. Take Stuxnet, a computer worm designed to attack industrial PLCs and SCADA systems, reportedly used to destroy hundreds of centrifuges used by the Iranian nuclear research program [ST1]. Or consider the hack of a certain type of pacemaker that enabled high-voltage shocks to be sent to patients 50 feet away [DR2]. Or look at how Charlie Miller and Chris Valasek showed at the DEF CON Hacking Conference that they could take control of the electric steering, braking, acceleration, engine, and other features of two well-known car types. It seems pretty evident that the IoT will only be successful if we manage to secure the solutions that we build. Many people would also agree that it will never be 100% possible to secure a complex, distributed IT system—so thinking the unthinkable and being prepared for the consequences should also be part of the equation.

Many leading companies in the IoT field are taking a very proactive approach to IoT security. For example, the electric car manufacturer Tesla Motors has hired the renowned white hat hacker Kristin Paget to oversee vulnerability testing and security for its cars. As one of her first tasks, Paget brought a Tesla vehicle to the DEF CON Conference, where Tesla was looking to recruit more hackers to help identify security vulnerabilities in the software that controls the vehicles [DR1].

SECURING IOT SOLUTIONS. In the following section, we will start the discussion by looking at the different security concepts in the IoT. Figure 8-62 maps the main security concepts to our Asset Integration Architecture, each of which we will briefly discuss.

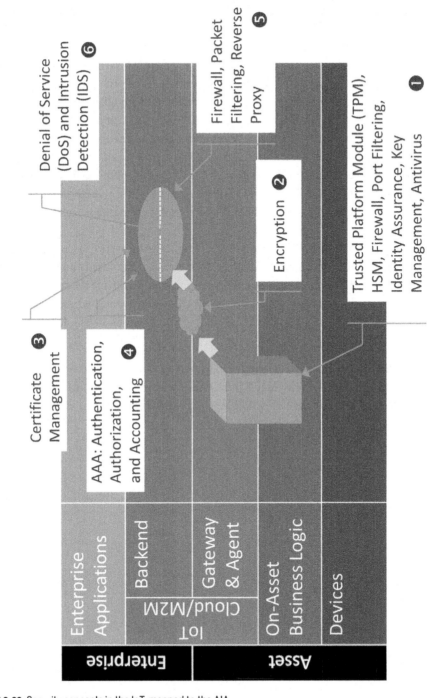

FIGURE 8-62. Security concepts in the IoT, mapped to the AIA

Securing the on-asset hardware (1)

Typically, it is relatively easy to prevent physical access to servers in a data center. However, this is very different in the IoT, as the assets in this case are deployed in the field, and it will often be impossible to prevent physical access to the on-asset hardware. One important approach here is the Trusted Platform Module (TPM)—an international standard for a secure crypto-processor that is designed to secure hardware by integrating cryptographic keys into devices. Hardware Security Modules (HSM) like the CycurHSM from Escrypt [ES1] are often used in the automotive industry. A HSM usually consists of a CPU core, different types of data storage, a memory protection unit, a memory encryption unit, sensors, and cryptographic accelerators. HSMs will usually support countermeasures against physical attacks, such as active sensors to detect fault and glitching attacks, and also employ cryptographic implementations that are hardened against side channel attacks [ES1].

Software-based security features that are deployed on the asset often include firewalls, port filtering, identity assurance, key management, and anti-virus functionality. The extending of traditional server-side security to operational technology in the IoT is an increasingly common strategy for companies such as Intel, whose strategic acquisition of McAfee allowed them to heavily extend their combined capabilities for the IoT.

Secure communication (2)

Ensuring secure communication between the asset and the backend is vital for many, if not most, IoT solutions. Most solutions utilize encryption technologies, either on the application layer (like Transport Layer Security, or TLS), or on the IP layer (like the Internet Protocol Security or IPsec). One key difference in these technologies is how they deal with firewall and NAT traversal, which has an impact on administration overheads for large-scale installations. In addition to encryption, technologies like Transparent Network Substrate (TNS) also deal with authentication.

Certificate management (3)

Certificates are an important part of Transport Layer Security (TLS). A certificate is an electronic document used to prove ownership of a public key. The certificate includes information about the key, about its owner's identity, and the digital signature verifies that the certificate's contents are correct. In large-scale IoT environments, efficient certificate management becomes essential so that assets and devices can authenticate themselves and communicate securely with the backend.

AAA (4)

Authentication, authorization, and accounting—often simply called AAA—is a framework designed for controlling access to applications, enforcing policies, and auditing usage. In the IoT, this will become very important. To use a simple example: Which piece of construction equipment is requesting to leave the construction site? Is this equipment permitted to do so according to the current schedule? If so, let's make a note that it has left.

Securing the backend (5 and 6)

And finally, we also have to secure the backend and its infrastructure. This will include prevention of denial-of-service (DoS) attacks, and employing intrusion detection systems (IDS), firewalls, packet filtering, and reverse proxies.

SECURITY BY DESIGN. As we can see from the previous section, there are many different technologies and concepts that can, or must, be used to make an IoT system secure. From the solution architect's perspective, it is important that security is built into the system from the ground up. This is also sometimes called Security by Design [SD1]. With Security by Design, malicious practices are taken for granted, and care is taken to minimize the impact when a security vulnerability is discovered. Another important feature is that everything works with the least amount of privileges possible.

In "IoT Project Initiation" on page 213, we actually recommend that security be a key element in the cross-cutting workstream. Only by explicitly manifesting this in the project organization will it be possible to achieve Security by Design across all the other workstreams in an IoT project.

IOT SECURITY TESTING. As much as we trust in the idea of Security by Design, every IoT project needs to have a solid security testing strategy. The best approach is to set up a dedicated team to perform what are known as penetration tests. These involve white-box testing, performed by staff from the project team with general knowledge about the systems, as well as black-box testing, involving an external, third-party team that performs security tests without internal knowledge, which is the more realistic scenario.

The Open Web Application Security Project (OWASP) Top Ten is the most popular list of potential risks in web applications. OWASP has now started to also publish an annual list of top 10 security issues in the Internet of Things [OW1]. Based on this list, the InfoSec Institute has proposed a concrete test strategy for IoT solutions [IS1]:

Testing an IoT device for insecure web interface

OWASP recommends looking specifically for default credentials on IoT devices that should be changed during initial setup, ensuring complex passwords are enforced, and checking for cross-site scripting, SQL injection, and cross-site request forgery vulnerabilities. A standard port scanner should be used to discover the web services that a particular device offers.

Testing an IoT device for poor authentication/authorization
Includes standard tests for weak passwords by checking the initial installation, testing if the device will accept weak passwords or no password, and use of proxies and sniffers to look for unencrypted or weakly encoded passwords.

Testing an IoT device for insecure network services
Includes the use of port scan tools like Nmap and penetration testing tools like Nessus or OpenVAS to look for critical services like Telnet, FTP, Finger, TFTP, or SMB.

Testing an IoT device for lack of transport encryption
Basic tests to ensure communication is properly encrypted.

Testing an IoT device for privacy concerns
Tests performed to prevent access to sensitive data like personal data (e.g., home address), financial data (e.g., credit card number), health information, and the like.

Testing an IoT device for insecure cloud interface
The backend services of an IoT solution can suffer from the same problems as any other web application and need to be tested accordingly, including basic tests such as checking for the use of HTTPS, but also for authentication problems like username harvesting or brute-force guessing attempts.

Testing an IoT device for insecure mobile interface
Some IoT devices may also act as wireless access points (WAPs) that need to be tested for security as well.

Testing an IoT device for insufficient security configurability
Basic checks for password policy enforcement, data encryption, and different levels of access.

Testing an IoT device for insecure software/firmware
This test has to ensure that all remote software updates are safely encrypted, to avoid installation of malware on the IoT device.

Testing an IoT device for poor physical security
This final test checks ease of storage media removal, encryption of stored data, physical protection of USB and similar ports, ease of disassembly, and removal or disabling of unnecessary ports.

IOT SAFETY PROGRAM. While the technologies and processes just listed are important in helping to secure the IoT, security will not come through the use of them alone. Developers of complex, highly security-relevant IoT solutions in particular will have to look at implementing an IoT safety program. This applies, for example, to the automotive industry: "I Am the Cavalry" is a grassroots organization focusing on the intersection between computer security and public safety. At the DEF CON Hacking Conference 2014, they proposed a five-point

Automotive Cyber Safety Program in an open letter to the automotive industry [FS1]. This program includes:

Safety by design (1)

The program should support published attestation of the Secure Software Development Lifecycle. Key elements include use of standards (ISO, NIST), traceable hardware and software supply chains, reduction of elective attack surface and complexity, and independent, adversarial resilience testing.

Third-party collaboration (2)

The program should have a published coordinated disclosure policy that invites contributions from third-party researchers acting in good faith, including a positive "recognition and reward" system for bug reporting.

Evidence capture (3)

Vehicles should support tamper-evident, forensically sound evidence capture and logging that help to facilitate safety investigations.

Security updates (4)

Remote software updates for vehicles in the field should be enabled to allow for prompt, reliable, and secure updates for critical bugs. This is of critical importance because increasing use of software is likely to produce the need for more updates and, with millions of vehicles deployed in the field, frequent factory recalls are not an option.

Segmentation and isolation (5)

Physical and logical isolation measures should be implemented and published to separate critical systems from noncritical systems.

IOT PRIVACY POLICIES. Finally, we need to take a look at IoT privacy policies (although strictly speaking they don't really belong in a Technology Profile). Assuming that security has been established to prevent malicious attacks, the IoT solution provider will also proactively have to look at how its privacy policies should be defined. The IoT Security Laboratory has created a nice summary of the Google Nest privacy policies, which are defined as follows [IL1]:

- The privacy policy is easy to find (this can be accomplished by, for example, putting a link to the privacy policy on every page).

- The privacy summary is written for humans, not for lawyers.

- A note that privacy depends on security.

- The buyer controls sharing and retention—that is, who can see the data (sharing) and how long it can be used (retention).

- Clear separation between web and device privacy policies.

- Data is made anonymous before publication, especially important in the age of Big Data.

- A real privacy contact is available (e.g., a direct email address to which customers can send all remaining questions).

For many consumers, privacy policies will determine their willingness to buy and use the product, so IoT solutions providers need to take great care in defining and implementing these policies.

SUMMARY AND OUTLOOK. In the following, we talk to Dr. Thomas Wollinger, Managing Director of ESCRYPT, a leading embedded security solutions provider, about his vision for security in the IoT.

Dirk Slama: What are the key elements for an end-to-end security solution for an IoT application?

Thomas Wollinger: Cryptographic primitives can be utilized to protect IoT applications. Different security objectives may be relevant, depending on the use cases. For instance, the confidentiality of transferred data can be protected by data encryption. Many applications also require protection against data manipulation, which can be achieved using mechanisms such as digital signatures.

All cryptographic primitives operate on keys that have to be managed throughout the whole lifecycle of the application. This means that secure key management is essential, including secure key generation (with a true random number generator), secure key distribution, and secure key storage.

Dirk Slama: Is all of this available today or are there missing pieces that still have to be built?

Thomas Wollinger: The technology is already there, but it needs to be adapted for the specific purpose of the IoT application. First, the cryptographic primitives and parameters (e.g., key length) have to be carefully selected to fit to the IoT platform. Most IoT platforms are quite restricted in terms of computing power and memory. Furthermore, in contrast to a desktop scenario, where you have user interaction, IoT applications usually operate without user input and thus are device-centric. Therefore, instead of user certificates, device certificates have to be used. But whatever the device or platform-specific requirements, security is not a feature that can be added to the device or application at a certain phase of its life. A truly secure device requires attention throughout the whole lifecycle, starting from design, through implementation, up to rollout. Each phase has its own relevance and challenges related to overall security.

Dirk Slama: How does a project manager address IoT security step by step? What does the checklist look like?

Thomas Wollinger: It is crucial to conduct a security analysis first, in order to identify all possible security threats and the appropriate countermeasures. From this analysis, the security requirements (primitives, protocols, parameters) can be derived, and these are then included in the design and architecture of the system. In addition, all supporting parts in the lifecycle need to be considered—the IT infrastructure, for example. Subsequently, the system is implemented and tested. Code reviews and security tests should be mandatory before shipping the IoT system to the customer.

Dirk Slama: What about security testing for the IoT? How should a project manager go about this?

Thomas Wollinger: Security tests should form an integral part of the application development. Besides unit tests and integration tests, penetration tests, including fuzz testing, should also be considered.

Dirk Slama: Assuming there will never be a 100% secure solution, what does the contingency plan look like? What does the project manager have to consider before rolling out the solution?

Thomas Wollinger: Just for clarification purposes and to avoid misunderstanding—there will never be a 100% secure solution. Software can contain bugs, some of which are very hard to detect. The firmware of IoT systems is no exception. Furthermore, new vulnerabilities might arise in the future (e.g., buffer overflows in common libraries). To make things worse, most IoT systems have quite a long lifecycle (several years, sometimes even decades) and are often not easily accessible (e.g., if they are embedded into a larger system). Therefore, the system should be prepared for secure firmware updates. The most convenient and cost-saving method is an over-the-air update. It is important that the firmware's authenticity is verified before it is written into the device, in order to ensure that the update originates from a legitimate manufacturer and to prevent malicious attacks. Again, cryptographic primitives and secure key management are the key factors here in the protection of the IoT device. We also recommend a frequent security analysis of the whole IoT system, for example every year. In this way, the latest attack vectors will be taken into account.

Platforms and Enablement

So far, we have looked at IoT gateways and edge devices, M2M/IoT communication services, data and process management in the IoT, IoT security, and user interaction. This section widens the perspective to give an overview of the platforms and other enabling technologies that combine some or most of these technologies to provide an integrated platform, or to support the enablement of IoT solutions in the broader sense. We will start by looking at the cloud and the IoT on the application level, before moving on to M2M/IoT application platforms, industrial data acquisition platforms, and indoor localization technology.

THE IOT AND THE CLOUD. For some people in the IT industry, the IoT and the cloud are inseparable, while for others, there are concerns in relation to privacy and security. Either way, the definition of the project's cloud strategy will be one of the most important tasks in an IoT project, because it will have a significant impact on the architecture, implementation, and operation of the solution.

For this section of the book we have turned to one of the pioneers in cloud services, Salesforce.com. Founded in 1999, the company has shaped the cloud CRM market, and has grown into a USD $4 billion business in 15 years. In the context of our earlier discussion about the machine camp versus the Internet camp, Salesforce.com, with its strong focus on purely Internet-based solutions centered on sales and services, could really be the blueprint for the Internet camp.

Our work with Peter Coffee, VP for Strategic Research at Salesforce.com, unearthed a number of very relevant perspectives. We have tried to map his views on the IoT and the cloud to the Ignite Asset Integration Architecture, the result of which is shown in Figure 8-63. Because this is a complex topic, we have assigned numbers to the most important elements of the cloud/IoT AIA, so we can refer back to them in the following interview.

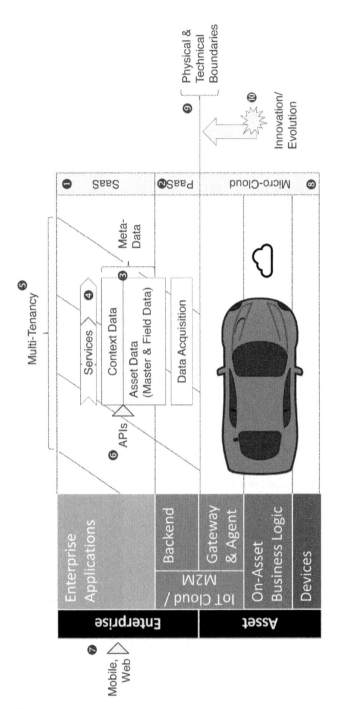

FIGURE 8-63. AIA for the IoT and cloud

Dirk Slama: Some argue that the cloud has been a massive effort in centralization, while the IoT is now exactly the opposite—a massive decentralization, with logic and data scattered across billions of distributed devices. So is the IoT killing the cloud?

Peter Coffee: I don't agree that the cloud is a massive effort in centralization. Yes, there has been a certain amount of centralization, people moving from local word processing to collaborative document management, for example. This is relevant, but it is not the most important aspect of the cloud. The most important aspect of the cloud is that it allows you to stop thinking about IT in terms of physical assets that have to be acquired and managed. The cloud is about building application services by orchestrating application programming interfaces (APIs), pulling data, and leveraging machine power in a highly location-independent manner. The way we work is completely decentralized, because everything is now abstracted and distributed in the cloud. Previously, taking things outside of data centers was difficult. Cloud is diffusion. So from that point of view, the IoT is only the next step in the ongoing decentralization effort!

Dirk Slama: What are the key drivers in this?

Peter Coffee: In the past, computers used to be scarce. Now they are ubiquitous. Then connectivity was scarce. Now connectivity is ubiquitous. What's scarce today is trustworthiness of data and of the partners with whom you are sharing data. What is relevant today is added value, or the potential you can leverage by securely operating on that data. This is the area of the enterprise cloud where we offer services to large businesses and government organizations, by leveraging a global pool of capabilities—placed where the availability of power, space, and network connectivity permit.

Dirk Slama: So how do you address the issue of trustworthiness?

Peter Coffee: It really starts at the core—data is born naked and defenseless. There is nothing that protects it from the world around it or proves its authenticity. We built a database where you cannot find a single data entity that does not have full traceability. Each entity is protected, privilege managed, and fully traceable. Having this kind of metadata (3) available for each entity is totally different from traditional databases. From an IoT point of view, this applies both to the core asset master data, as well as the context data, such as the customer related to the asset. And this is the foundation for our multitenancy capabilities (5). The ability to securely run many thousands of tenants on the same system, all securely sandboxed, is really the key differentiator of a cloud solution like ours. Yes, we are also a great CRM and Service Management Platform, but multitenancy is what enables this in the cloud, and provides the technical foundation for trustworthy data management.

Dirk Slama: Putting the data from assets and devices in the right context is also important?

Peter Coffee: Yes. Andrew Rosenthal from Jawbone [a wearable devices company] once said that getting the data from the devices is actually not that interesting. What matters is putting it in context. Data only starts to become meaningful if you start putting a story around it. Counting your steps is not important. Being able to tell you how many calories you have burned today compared to your wife—now that is interesting!

Dirk Slama: So what is Salesforce.com's IoT strategy?

Peter Coffee: Salesforce has never been a mixed strategy company. We have always been a cloud service provider, not a software company. So there is no need to discuss our transition. We were born "cloudy." We have recently been listed in the top 5 of MIT Technology Review's "50 Smartest Companies," together with Illumina, Tesla Motors, Google, and Samsung. The reason MIT gave for our ranking was that our "tools will be crucial in helping companies incorporate new data from the Internet of things" [MI1]. The IoT will generate an enormous amount of multidimensional, textured data. For us, this is an incredibly rich opportunity to help our customers find out what their customers would find delightful before the customer can even articulate this themselves.

And we are obviously not a device company. Take Apple with its upcoming Apple Watch product. Apple Watch will trigger an ecosystem of apps that will each generate data. This is of interest to us. Or take Scania. They recently launched the Scania Watch, which provides truck drivers with information like transport metrics, fuel data, and driver support scoring [SC1]. This is not only brilliant in terms of brand building and customer loyalty, it is also a great example of the potential of wearable technology. Providing the right tools to allow integration with any kind of wearable is a key part of our IoT strategy. We recently announced Salesforce Wear Developer Pack, a collection of tools that let you design and build wearable apps that connect to the Salesforce1 Platform.

Dirk Slama: And what about the Industrial IoT?

Peter Coffee: Yes, also extremely important. But again, for us this comes down to putting data from assets and devices in context and then adding services. I mean, collecting data, analyzing it, summarizing, and taking action is not a new concept. I worked in the oil and gas industry and saw the first digital control rooms in refineries emerge in the 1980s. You would be amazed how much added value you can create by adding the right context to what is actually very little data to begin with. Take an oil field with hundreds of pumps, spread tens of miles wide. The most useful thing to know is whether the pump is actually pumping or not, so that you can give the field workers directions on where they need to go to do something useful. Or take repairing a wind turbine: this requires climbing up a 100-foot tower. So it would be nice to climb up with the right tools and instructions in the first place, instead of having to climb up twice.

This is exactly the role that cloud-based services like ours can play in the IoT: bringing data from the IoT into processes and putting it into context (4). So if the telemetry data is telling us that the wind turbine needs fixing, we can find an available service technician, tell him what equipment to take with him, and what vehicle to use from the repair truck fleet. Ideally, this would actually be done even before anything breaks down, because a breakdown is a customer experience that can never again be repaired after it's happened. So developing the capability to predict maintenance situations will also become important.

Dirk Slama: So what kinds of features does a cloud application platform have to support to enable these kinds of IoT scenarios?

Peter Coffee: I think this is all about the cloud engine APIs (6). Many cloud applications have traditionally been built around web-based UIs. Later, mobile capabilities were added. However, in the IoT, in many cases the first line of contact will not be a human user, but a machine or some other kind of asset. For this, it is important that the data coming from the asset can be processed automatically—and this requires direct access to the cloud engine APIs. Salesforce.com has completed the migration of all cloud applications to open APIs in 2013. This gives us a great deal of flexibility for developing mobile and web UIs that aggregate different types of applications (7). And I also think this was a milestone for us in terms of IoT preparedness.

Dirk Slama: What about the technology required for data acquisition and device control?

Peter Coffee: I think it is unlikely that we will be in that marketplace. We have many partners in our ecosystem that provide these kinds of capabilities, such as Etherios [recently acquired by Digi]. I also think it is important to realize that the IoT will not be implemented on a green-field environment. Similar to our situation when we started in an existing ERP market, this is about adding value, not replacement. But of course, new cloud solutions can also add value in the integration space. Take, for example, cloud-based SCADA. I think in the next decade we will see a lot of growth in boutique manufacturing, factories that are able to produce small amounts of highly customized goods. They would not be able to afford a full-blown, self-administered on-site SCADA. But with cloud-based SCADA, connected to services such as ours, this becomes a different ball game. And we are quite happy with this. At the end of the day, we are not an industrial automation company: our job is to add value to data, not to originate it.

Dirk Slama: So the IoT integration layer will be more like a Platform-as-a-Service (2) (PaaS) model that integrates with a Software-as-a-Service (1) (SaaS) model such as yours?

Peter Coffee: Yes. Think of it as the "last mile" problem. Somebody needs to address this, but it will always be more low-level, integration stuff, including protocol bridging, data stream analysis, and so on. Except that it will become much easier to address the last mile in the future because of the advances in technology. In the past, the local carrier owned the cable into the basement of your house. Nowadays it has become very easy to attach a box to a street lamp pole to provide the required bandwidth to the houses in the vicinity. Of course for trucks and container ships this is still a different story. So yes, PaaS in this context is relevant from an integration perspective.

Dirk Slama: What kind of logic do you see residing on the asset in the future, and how much in the cloud?

Peter Coffee: I like to compare this to how the human body works. The sensory neurons do not exclusively pass information to the brain. Local spinal motor neurons can trigger reflex actions almost without delay. So if you touch something hot, your hand moves away automatically, while your brain starts putting the information into context and thinking about finding an emergency exit route. In the IoT, we see poppy-seed-sized microchips that can do amazing things when deployed on an asset. But putting things in context and making strategic decisions is something I will always see in the cloud.

Dirk Slama: So physical and technical boundaries (9) remain important?

Peter Coffee: It is extremely important to understand the latency and bandwidth restrictions in your specific environment to make decisions about data and logic distribution.

Dirk Slama: Time sensitivity is also often cited as a big issue. It seems unlikely that an application like controlling a high-speed manufacturing robot with hard real-time requirements can be done out of a cloud environment. Or take the CERN case study from this book, which describes a massive, multitiered analog/digital data conversion, data collection, distribution, and analytics application. Another unlikely cloud candidate?

Peter Coffee: This might be true at the moment. But I don't think the accomplishments of the cloud should be viewed in terms of physical distances or economies of scale. Don't forget that we are living in a world of constant technical evolution. The existing boundaries are moved, every day (10)! In this world, the cloud should always be the goal. So instead of the silo being the default, the cloud should be the default.

At the point of data origination, you can first decide if you need to process it locally, or make it available over a bus, or a local network in a building, or globally to all devices of that type—at which point you are on the Internet and in the cloud. If you originate the data in a form that it is accurate and trustworthy, the best way to put it into context is in the cloud.

Also, think of emerging concepts like micro-clouds (8), which can be deployed locally. In your discussion about the connected vehicle, you talk about the future, sandboxed application platform for the car. The foundation for this will be nothing other than a local micro-cloud, connected to the Internet cloud.

Dirk Slama: So what is your advice for the IoT project manager and the solution architect who have to decide on a cloud strategy today?

Peter Coffee: Understand today's technical boundaries. But design your system in such a way that it anticipates and allows the continued movement of these boundaries instead of engraving the current boundaries into the design. The question of "what is cloud and what is not" is not an answerable question: micro-clouds, personal clouds, clouds of communities of devices are emerging. Think of them all with the same cloud perspective. Don't build silos, but clouds instead. Allow for departures from the original strategy, but anticipate that, over time, the need for change will disappear.

M2M/IOT APPLICATION PLATFORMS. The next platform category that we are going to look at are platforms that enable the development and operation of basic M2M solutions and more advanced IoT mashups. M2M solutions typically focus on basic remote asset monitoring and management, while IoT mashups add more semantically rich application logic. We have explicitly excluded very high throughput, hard real-time-type data acquisition solutions. These types of solutions are described in "Industrial Data Acquisition Platforms" on page 390.

The main goal of M2M/IoT application platforms is to streamline the development process and provide as much out-of-the-box functionality as possible in order to make application development and maintenance as efficient as possible. Figure 8-64 describes the key elements of such a platform:

1. The core M2M/IoT application platform in our definitions consists of a backend plus different technologies that enable asset integration such as agents, libraries, and interfaces. In our standard AIA, these are the two middle tiers that together, are always called IoT cloud/M2M.

2. Asset interface definitions. Ideally, the platform will provide a consistent way of describing all functional interfaces of the assets and devices in an abstract format that can be used in all tiers of the AIA, from device integration to application development in the backend.

3. The backend, which usually contains a central database or repository for managing all asset-related data, as well as a set of services that help to manage the distributed assets.

4. A set of asset integration technologies, including sophisticated agent technologies, basic libraries for less powerful hardware, as well as remote interfaces for direct integration of assets.

5. Support for a set of protocols, such as MQTT, CoAP, XMPP, and many other protocols that enable remote communication between the asset and the backend.

6. IoT application development and mashup capabilities that leverage the data and services of the backend.

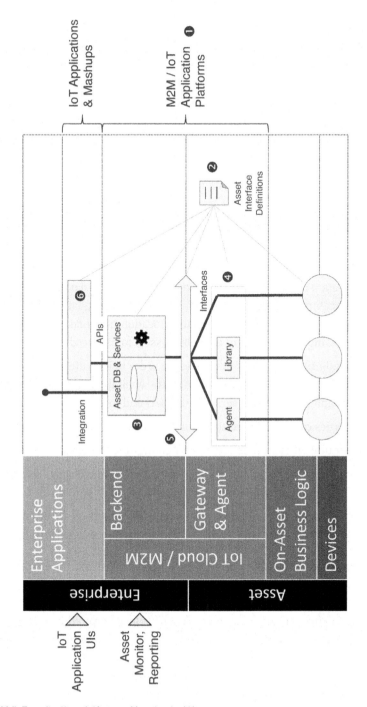

FIGURE 8-64. M2M/IoT application platforms—Mapping to AIA

ASSET AND DEVICE INTERFACE MANAGEMENT. As described by Roman Wambacher in the "Recommendations" on page 294, managing heterogeneity is probably one of the biggest challenges for any company that has large numbers of assets of different types and versions deployed in the field. In order to address this problem, most platforms support some form of standard for defining and managing asset and device interfaces. This is also important for the platforms themselves, because a standardized mechanism for the definition of asset and device interfaces can be used to ensure that all elements in the platform are functioning properly together, from asset integration and asset data persistence, to asset-related UIs.

Figure 8-65 shows the main elements that should be supported by a generic device and asset model:

- Assets and devices should be modeled explicitly: it should be possible to define aggregation hierarchies (multiple devices per asset, asset groups, etc.). In the previous example, a "managed entity" is used to describe the common characteristics of assets and devices.

- The mobile location of a managed entity can be used to store data about the current location. The time stamp is used to indicate when this was last updated. This is important for mobile equipment. In the backend, the mobile location information can be stored as a time series, allowing the movement of mobile assets to be traced.

- Events can be submitted by assets or devices, in order to indicate an error situation, for example. Again, they are timestamped to indicate when the event was submitted. Again, this should be captured as a time series in the backend to ensure full traceability.

- Multiple properties can be defined individually, such as temperature, pressure, etc.

- Many assets require efficient management of configuration data and other files.

- Many assets will also support different operations that can be triggered remotely from the backend (e.g., "increase temperature," "increase pressure," "shut down," "restart," etc.).

- Finally, the model also needs to reflect user access rights, which are often role-based. For example, only the super-user role might have the permission to perform a restart.

There are a number of initiatives underway to define standards for the definition of interfaces to assets and devices in the IoT. For example, the IPSO Alliance has defined the specification of Smart Objects for interoperability between devices in the IoT. Or take OSGi RFC 196, which aims to define a device abstraction layer for Java-powered gateways running OSGi. Another interesting example is the Vorto project, recently initiated by Bosch Software Innovations at the Eclipse Foundation. Vorto aims to define the meta-information model for devices and assets, support for code generators, an open source toolset to create and manage interfaces, and an information model repository to store and manage these.

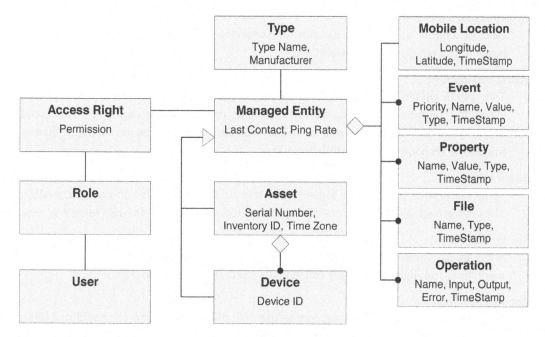

FIGURE 8-65. Sample model of asset and device interface definitions

The whole area of higher level interface definitions will most likely be a key factor in the success of interoperability in the IoT, and as such, will also play an important role in the success of the IoT overall. As usual, we don't expect the world to agree on one unified standard; however, agreement on a small number of widely established standards in different vertical application domains would be helpful.

M2M BACKEND/IOT CLOUD. The M2M backend (often rebranded as the IoT cloud today) usually provides central management of asset-related data, as well as a set of generic support functions that allow assets to be managed and monitored in the field. Key functions include:

Asset database or repository

Stores asset definition and configuration data, as well as status information and time series data (e.g., event history, metering data, etc.). The database schema should be generic and allow support for many different versions of the generic asset interface definitions, as discussed in Chapter 7.

Asset monitoring and management UI

A generic UI for administrators that provides an overview of all registered assets, including asset health and history. The asset admin UI will read data from the local asset database or repository, but will also allow users to update values by getting new readings directly from the asset. Also, if the asset supports operations, the UI will list all available operations and allow the user to dynamically invoke them.

Reporting and dashboards

Basic descriptive analytics functions will be provided in an—ideally—customizable dashboard (e.g., average machine health, etc.).

Alarm management

The system should ideally provide a scripting or business rules–based mechanism that allows the definition of actions for certain events or alarms. For example, a rule could define that a text message is sent to an administrator if a machine takes longer than 15 minutes to respond to a regular ping message.

Remote access

Many assets will provide some form of remote login mechanism for on-asset diagnostics. The platform should support remote diagnostics tools and firewall-friendly remote access.

Content distribution

Many assets require regular updates of content such as configuration files, test data, documentation, and digital marketing collateral that is to be displayed locally.

Software distribution

The platform must be able to support secure and efficient management and distribution of firmware, operating system updates, and application logic.

Security management

Includes certificate management, as well as user and role management (or integration with external systems), and management of permission assignments between users (or roles) and assets (or specific data or functions on the assets).

Logging and tracing

All actions must be fully logged in an efficient and transparent manner.

Automation

The platform should provide support for automation of tasks, such as through the support of APIs and scripting engines. For example, instead of manually checking the right version of a certain configuration file on ten thousand remote assets, a simple script should be able to automate this task.

ASSET INTEGRATION. There are many different strategies for integrating the backend with assets, but the main categories include:

Agent-based integration

Allows for deployment of sophisticated integration and business logic on the asset (usually in combination with a relatively powerful gateway).

Local libraries

In case only less powerful hardware is available on the asset, many platforms will provide libraries (e.g., in C/C++ or JavaScript) that allow for highly optimized, custom integration of the backend. These libraries will understand the remote interfaces supported by the backend, and will also support the local interfaces expected by the backend. However, they will often be much simpler and will only support a subset of the interfaces.

Interface-based integration

In some cases, it will not be possible or will not make sense to use one of the two approaches described previously. If the backend supports a set of well-documented online interfaces based on open standards, then it will also be possible to integrate assets via other means.

With the ever-decreasing cost of hardware and an ever-increasing need for more services on the assets, the agent-based approach would seem to have great potential in the IoT. Smart homes was one area in which there was early adoption of on-asset agent technology for integration purposes, but also for the provision of local business logic. Another area where an agent-based approach could be of interest in the future is the automotive industry. See our discussion about open car app platforms in Chapter 5.

Key features that this type of agent software would need to support include:

- A secure environment (application sandbox) to execute local applications in such a way that they don't interfere with each other or with the environment.

- A device abstraction layer must provide support for integration with local devices, mapping to the abstract interface definitions, and support for the interfaces required by the backend to read asset status data, to execute operations on the asset, and so on.

- Management agent as a counterpart for the software distribution mechanism on the backend.

- Support for key protocols, both for different device types and local wireless communication, as well as for backend communication.

- User and role management, compatible with the same functions on the backend

- Local data collection and filtering (see "Process Diversity" on page 357).

- Local automation, similar to automation on the backend.

Probably the most advanced open standard out there for agent technology is OSGi. OSGi offers very sophisticated support for application isolation, resource allocation, application lifecycle management, application dependency management, and so on.

IOT APPLICATIONS AND MASHUPS. So far, we have mainly been focusing on features that are required to integrate with assets, remotely monitor assets, and react to events received from assets. However, we have not spoken about how to leverage these capabilities in order to actually build those semantically rich, new applications that will differentiate Enterprise IoT from basic M2M. Fortunately, most platforms will, by default, provide a set of open interfaces and APIs that can be used to build such applications. There are also products becoming available that promise rapid development of IoT applications and mashups by integrating with the basic M2M platforms (or the "IoT cloud," depending on the terminology used).

Rick Bullotta, CTO of ThingWorx, feels very passionately about this, as can be seen from the following interview.

Dirk Slama: Rick, how do you see the future of application enablement in the IoT?

Rick Bullotta: We see this as two distinct tiers: the device/machine cloud and the application enablement layer. We find that many of our large global customers already have connected devices—you'd be amazed how many devices out there are connected via dial-in modems and other techniques. We have designed our platform in such a way that the application enablement layer can work with other device clouds. It's really a matter of supporting customer choice and the reality that they might be using different technologies in different business units. While we also offer a world-class device cloud of our own, we also chose to "play well with others." An application platform must also embrace the systems and people involved, as well as the machines.

Dirk Slama: So, the IoT is not just about machines...

Rick Bullotta: Any IoT application that is doing anything interesting is integrating with lots of other lines of business applications, as well as integrating with human elements. This is an important capability to have for the application enablement platform: bring in assets such as your ERP system, CRM system, field service management, weather data, and energy pricing and make that composable functionality available at an application platform level. Composition can be applied to user interface, analytics, and business processes.

Dirk Slama: Let's talk a little bit about strengths and potential limitations of this approach.

Rick Bullotta: Let me give you an example: I want a consumer device that controls a smart vacuum in my home. That's a very focused, linear application. Not a lot of complexity. Many companies are developing their own end-to-end technologies where they use standard development tools to create the applications. Where the traditional development approaches do not work, in my opinion, is the moment there is any complexity, or integration with other systems or data. In particular, if the application is to be dynamic in

---

nature, if you want to add new services and capabilities, want to be able to tailor it to different customers and use cases, or if you want to have a very iterative development approach. You need a different model for developing applications. The number one thing to note is: if it's a static app that's not going to change very often, you have lots of choice in what you can use. If it's a very dynamic application, or a business model that's constantly adding new capabilities, an environment like ThingWorx provides substantial initial and ongoing advantages in terms of productivity. We've found that the vast majority of IoT applications fit those criteria.

Dirk: So to conclude, what are the key enablers for IoT platforms?

Rick Bullotta: You need to start with powerful out-of-the-box functionality from device to cloud. You need to enable others to enhance and extend your platform. Let others innovate. Let others create innovative solutions. But let them leverage our development environment, transport, security, and the high-level services we provide. Let people plug in their own algorithms, business logic, connectors, and user interface components. It's not an either/or situation. If people prefer to use our software development kits to integrate their unique intellectual property, we let them do it in a sustainable way and in a way that enables rapid composition, as we discussed earlier.

INTEGRATING SUBNETS OF THINGS. As we discussed in the introduction, many Enterprise IoT solutions will initially focus on a relatively well-defined, often closed ecosystem, or Subnet of Things (SoTs). Integration within and between SoTs will become one of the key challenges for the evolution of the IoT.

There are many companies addressing this on different levels. One of them is woit.io, a New York–based startup that aims to assist with interconnection between devices, data services, and owners of data in order to unlock business opportunity. While the company does not actually provide data services, it aims to streamline the technical, legal, and business processes involved in end users availing themselves of third-party data services. From a customer perspective, wot.io aims to "look like" a Salesforce.com for the IoT. From a technical backend perspective, it is more analogous to the Object Management Group's DDS standards (more on this momentarily). The main value that the company adds is in the development and maintenance of the legal and business frameworks and agreements that are needed to bridge the gap between that Salesforce.com shop window and a supporting technical integration with data services partners. Put another way, the company competes on the basis of its business facilitation capabilities, while underpinning technical capabilities are a qualifier for competing in the marketplace.

The following interview with Allen Proithis, President & Founder of wot.io, explores this interesting market positioning in more detail.

Jim Morrish: wot.io is somewhat of a new player in the IoT space. Can you summarize why you founded the company, and characterize the opportunity that you see?

Allen Proithis: Almost everyone who wants to participate in the incredible opportunities around IoT is struggling at some level. This struggle to fully realize IoT-driven products, services, and cost efficiencies is caused by the number of participants it takes to create value, and by the technical, business, and legal friction that needs to be addressed to define a successful, working relationship between these players. We remove much of that friction.

Jim Morrish: Can you give me some examples?

Allen Proithis: We often find that end customers struggle with who to call for an IoT solution, which vendors to choose, and how to justify the massive custom integration effort, including consideration of risks, costs, and time. Companies that add value to IoT data struggle to access the market thanks to massive market fragmentation, complex integration requirements, and the challenge of maintaining relationships with other companies required to add different value to the same data. And systems integrators attempting to sell professional services are losing deals where the majority of the work is custom. Successful SIs will need to focus on where they can add the most value, and will partner for pieces of the solution that can be productized.

Jim Morrish: And you don't think that standardization, or the simple fact that many IoT players are already building those interfaces is going to solve these problems anytime soon?

Allen Proithis: It is generally recognized that the IoT is going to be huge in terms of both the impact that it will have on our daily lives and also new commercial opportunities. What is not nearly so well recognized is that the future IoT is going to be somewhat "lumpy." To put a little more flesh on those bones, we think that the next stage of development of the IoT will be driven by common data standards, association with common providers of data services, common ownership of data sources, or common cause among the owners of data, and will be characterized by relatively tightly integrated islands of connected devices, which we term "Subnets of Things." The connections and interfaces *between* these islands of connected devices can be expected to develop significantly more slowly than connections and interfaces *within* these islands. That's where wot.io comes in. We can quickly connect, for example, users of ARM's mbed platform, or the ARM mbed Subnet of Things, with Rackspace, or scale DB, or Stream Technologies.

Jim Morrish: But Object Management Group is doing something pretty similar with their Data Distribution Service (DDS) standards, right?

Allen Proithis: Real Time Publish-Subscribe (RTPS) DDS would be analogous to the wot.io message bus and adapter framework. Just as we create adapters for other Pub/Sub streaming protocols; AMQP, MQTT, XMPP, Kafka, and even cloud services like Pubnub, we will create a transport adapter for RTPS DDS and bridge the message routing worlds. But message routing is not what wot.io is about, message routing is a sub-service to make things work. wot.io is a data service exchange for connected device platforms. Data services are integrated applications that operate on data from connected device platforms, and yes, we use a pubsub SOA to make it happen.

Jim Morrish: OK, that sounds like Rackspace marketplace?

Allen Proithis: Yes, Rackspace offers hosted applications, but they are not integrated into data services that can operate on and add value to data from connected device platforms without significant engineering. wot.io and Rackspace are partners. Not only can we deploy our data service to the Rackspace infrastructure, we can also integrate services from the Rackspace marketplace.

Jim Morrish: So what's the wot.io proposition, in a nutshell?

Allen Proithis: wot.io is a data service exchange for connected device platforms. We help clients meet the challenge of rapidly and flexibly extracting business value from connected data. Our solution is independent of individual technologies, and compliments existing vendor platforms for organizations already operating in the Internet of Things and Machine-to-Machine industry. The fact is that many of those Subnets of Things that I described earlier could benefit from being connected together somehow, and it makes sense for a small number of market participants, like wot.io, to focus on making those connections, rather than have each of the individual Subnets of Things build their own bilateral relationships. There's a lot of scale benefits to be had from this approach. But, in truth, establishing those connections is the first step toward a wider concept of liquidity in the provision of data services. This is why we characterise wot.io as a Data Services Exchange, or DSE.

Jim Morrish: You mean decreasing the friction associated with connecting together providers of data services with potential consumers of those services?

Allen Proithis: Correct, having built all those connections to those Subnets of Things, a Data Services Exchange is ideally positioned to offer clients access to a range of services provided by partners that are already integrated into the DSE's ecosystem. For instance, a DSE might offer access to Volt, Hadoop, Cassandra, SAP, or MongoDB database services, or even some hybrid combination of these, all in an essentially pre-integrated and off-the-shelf commercial package. And from the data service supplier's perspective, applications are at the core of the IoT opportunity. Every connected device must have an associated application, possibly several, and the development of those applications and the provision of supporting capabilities—such as, for example, data analytics, data mining and other data services—represent real commercial opportunities for a range of players. A DSE helps those specialized and differentiated providers connect to potential customers.

Jim Morrish: And you think that this freer exchange and interconnection of more differentiated services is what will characterize the IoT in the coming years?

Allen Proithis: We expect that this more horizontal perspective on M2M markets will become a dominant theme. Up until now, the M2M market has been dominated by industry behemoths. As Tier 2 and other smaller players enter the market, they will naturally look for ways to differentiate by developing specific capabilities. The mass market phase of M2M and IoT adoption will be characterized by a more differentiated "horizontal first" approach.

Jim Morrish: And that's the dynamic that you are looking to support?

Allen Proithis: Exactly, the wot.io data service exchange is a marketplace of integrated, third-party data services. By already integrated, we mean that the developer does not need to focus on the technical, business, or legal aspects of integrating with new data services, and can hit the ground running. In general, we believe that data service exchanges are the entities that will provide the underpinnings required so that the future M2M and IoT markets can function. Entities like wot.io will allow differentiated and specialised providers to easily "plug-in" to larger and less differentiated service providers, and vice versa. This will usher in a phase of development of the IoT that is characterized by the establishment of an ecosystem of differentiated data service and platform players. Ultimately, products are better than services in the IoT market, and the market as a whole will be strengthened when participants play to their strengths.

OPEN SOURCE. In addition to the many different commercial platforms available in this space, there is also a lot happening in the open source community. To take just one example, see Figure 8-66, which provides an overview of the different IoT projects that are currently active at the Eclipse Foundation (recall that the Ignite | IoT Methodology described in this book is now also an official open source project, hosted by the Eclipse Foundation).

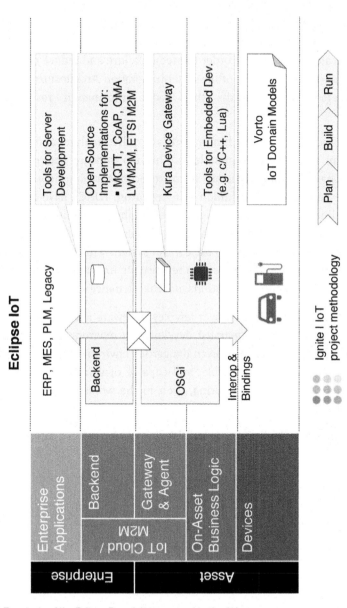

FIGURE 8-66. Key IoT projects of the Eclipse Foundation mapped to the AIA

The Eclipse Vorto project was established to manage interface definitions for the IoT. For embedded development, Eclipse aims to provide open source development tools for C, C++, and Lua. The Kura device gateway is an exciting open source hardware initiative. On the protocol level, Eclipse already supports, or plans to support, MQTT, CoAP, OMA LWM2M, and ETSI M2M. Finally, Eclipse plans to support open source tools for server development.

INDUSTRIAL DATA ACQUISITION PLATFORMS. Industrial data acquisition and control (IDAC) systems are powerful, headless, distributed systems designed to increase efficiency through monitoring and control. Through high-speed monitoring and analytics, IDACs can provide insight into the health of an asset in order to predict failure and reduce downtime. These systems can interface with every aspect of the Asset Integration Architecture (AIA) to form a vast network of interconnected systems that distill information for fast and reliable decision-making.

From smart grids to smart machines, IDACs acquire, analyze, and communicate information on both an asset and enterprise level. Through onboard heterogeneous processing, IDACs can make hard real-time decisions in microseconds, saving time, network bandwidth, and central processing power. In addition to monitoring, IDACs have the input/output and processing capabilities needed to perform advanced, high-speed control, based on information obtained through monitoring. These capabilities also enable IDACs to acquire, analyze, and communicate processed information to the control system without slowing down the control loop. In turn, this information can be used in real time to improve asset health, efficiency, and throughput by optimizing control algorithms and maintenance schedules.

BASIC ELEMENTS. IDACs are defined by a few key hardware and software elements that are tied together through a unified integrated development environment. Because many assets are often located in remote, rugged, or even dangerous environments, this hardware and software solution has to be durable, reliable, and capable of standalone operation in order to ensure continuous control and monitoring, even in the worst conditions, including loss of network communication.

Figure 8-67 maps the key features of an IDAC to our Asset Integration Architecture.

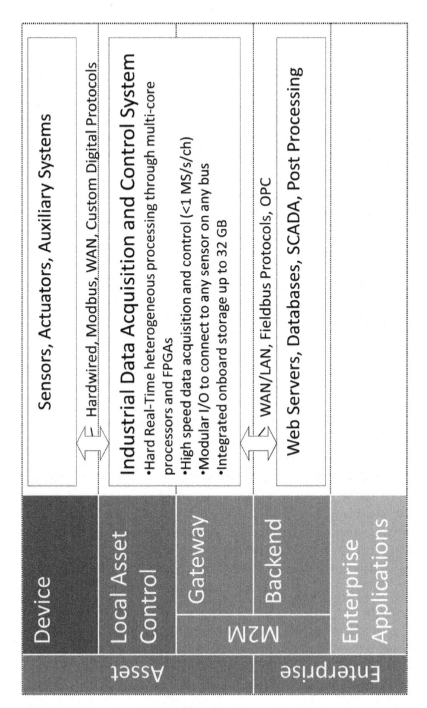

FIGURE 8-67. Key elements of an IDAC mapped to the Ignite AIA

The primary elements of an IDAC are:

Heterogeneous processing

In order to get the best response time and throughput, IDAC systems combine a host of processing options to optimize performance for various tasks. These processing elements include multicore processors, digital signal processors, field-programmable gate arrays (FPGAs), and lookup tables. Each of these elements stores and processes information using different methods, which makes them suitable for different tasks. Low-level tasks such as high-speed parallel processing can be moved to the FPGA, which is optimized for such tasks. High-level tasks like communication and software architecture can be run on the processors. Each element is user-programmable so the hardware can be combined in many different ways to achieve the flexibility of a custom design with an off-the-shelf solution. To further simplify a custom design, many of these elements have been integrated into a single chip known as a system on a chip (SoC). Because they integrate many types of processing elements, IDACs also can be configured to act as vision, motion, or human–machine interface (HMI) systems without changing any core components. For this reason, these IDAC systems are often described as "software defined," in that it is the software that defines the hardware functionality.

Software and operating system

The Internet of Things adds a lot of complexity to system design, so to remain efficient, simplifying in every way possible becomes paramount. Having an integrated software package that is hardware-aware is key to reducing such complexity. This software abstracts low-level, low-value tasks so the user can create a framework of reusable code that can be leveraged across many applications. When the software and hardware are tied together, the hardware can then be upgraded to the latest processing elements with maximum code reuse. Security is another challenge presented by the Internet of Things. When assets can be manipulated from almost anywhere in the world, the need for security grows. To address this, IDACs are based on an IT-friendly operating system that can be securely provisioned and configured to properly authenticate and authorize users, to maintain system integrity, and maximize system availability. They are also based on an open OS, so developers around the world can unite and develop the latest in embedded security.

Input/Output (I/O)

In order to be effective, IDACs need to get information to and from the asset in the most accurate and efficient way possible, which is usually through a network of sensors and actuators. The I/O of an IDAC system offers the means to translate these real-world signals into the digital world for processing, through analog-to-digital and digital-to-analog converters. As important as processing is, the calculations are only as good as the I/O generating the data. For this reason, the I/O in an IDAC is capable of very precise and high-speed sample and update rates (>1 kS/s) for a high-fidelity insight into an asset's performance. A common application in which such rates are required is condition monitoring of spinning machinery, where sample rates can reach hundreds of kilo-samples per second. The I/O has been modularized so that a single IDAC system can adapt to many different assets and changing sensor requirements. The I/O modules feature a wide range of signal conditioning in order to accommodate any sensor required by the asset. In many ways, the I/O acts as both an analog and digital means of communication between the asset and the processing.

Communication

In addition to the communication between the asset and the processing layer, Ethernet-based communication protocols allow asset systems to communicate with other assets and with the enterprise. In the past, these protocols were proprietary to the individual manufacturers, which made it difficult to maintain a vast network of assets. IDACs solve this problem by supporting many communication protocols. There remains, however, a need for a standard universal communications protocol to allow further simplification and increased performance.

APPLICATIONS. Many applications require I/O and processing. In the following section, we discuss three types of application in which IDACs have been successful:

Condition monitoring

Condition monitoring is the monitoring of assets in order to prevent and predict failure so as to prevent unscheduled outages, optimize asset performance, and reduce repair time. It is the quintessential application for an IDAC system. From power generation to industrial manufacturing, IDACs can be configured to acquire and process data to prevent and predict asset failure.

Smart machines

Smart machines are high-performance machines with built-in intelligence that enable them to adapt to changing conditions and tasks. They come in many shapes and sizes, and usually integrate many disparate features such as motion, vision, custom protocols, HMI, control, and monitoring. Because IDACs are so versatile in their processing and I/O, they can provide a single platform from which to build such a machine.

Smart grid

The idea of creating an electrical grid that can react to changing grid conditions in order to reroute power, improve power quality, or self-heal is becoming a reality. The smart grid and its related standards are evolving to meet these changing conditions. IDAC systems are one of the key technologies behind the smart grid because they have the I/O, processing capability, and open architecture needed to adjust to the changing power standards and to perform power calculations.

EXAMPLES. One example of an IDAC system is the CompactRIO system from NI. Powered by LabVIEW reconfigurable I/O (RIO) architecture, CompactRIO combines a processor, user-programmable FPGA, and modular I/O with the LabVIEW integrated development environment. Because the system is so versatile, CompactRIO can communicate with open and proprietary protocols to integrate with existing systems or operate as a standalone solution. The CompactRIO hardware's software-designed functionality runs on an open, real-time Linux OS that allows the system to be customized as a monitoring and/or control solution.

Other examples of IDAC systems can be found in both custom hardware and high-performance programmable automation controllers, or in a combination of the two types of systems.

DIFFERENTIATION. Table 8-6 shows the key differences between an IDAC, wireless sensor networks, and PLCs.

TABLE 8-6. Comparison of IDAC, WSN nodes, and PLC

Category	IDAC	WSN nodes	PLC
Real-time	Yes	No	Yes
Speed	ns–μs	ms–s	ms–s
Data returned	Waveform or single point	Single point	Single point
Processor	Best	Good	Better
Primary applications	Advanced control and big analog data systems	Distributed monitoring	Machine automation
Common programming language	LabVIEW, C, C++	C, C++	61131

Here are further differences in the technologies used:

Wireless sensor network technologies
  Both IDACs and wireless sensor network (WSN) technologies can be used for monitoring, but they differ in terms of performance and channel count. WSN nodes acquire data from a few channels at regular intervals at a relatively slow rate (<1 kS/s), perform some minor processing, and then send that data back to a central processor for more in-depth processing. These systems are great for monitoring fairly static conditions that do not require quick decisions. On the other hand, IDACs can handle hundreds of channels at rates up to 1 MS/s, perform more in-depth processing, and report changes as they occur. IDACs, consequently, are designed to monitor more dynamic systems that require on-asset processing to make decisions quickly. The two types of technologies can operate

together, with the IDAC acting as a central hub to collect and process data, and the WSN nodes supplementing the main application.

Programmable logic controllers

Both IDACs and programmable logic controllers (PLCs) can be used for control, but they differ in performance. PLCs run at relatively slow loop rates (<1 kHz) and are designed for simple control tasks. Users must tack on other systems to add more advanced functionality for things like vision, motion, or custom protocols. IDACs, on the other hand, can achieve higher loops (>100 kHz) and can handle more advanced control algorithms, vision, motion, and customer protocols. PLCs offer an industry standard and can be easier to program and use for simple tasks. However, for more complex functions involving high-performance control or integrating other tasks, IDACs are more useful. The two are often paired together to communicate with one another, with PLCs providing the main control loop and the IDAC tackling specialized tasks.

RECOMMENDATION. When considering an IDAC system, take both current and future needs into account. No one can predict the future, but it is important to be prepared for it. Black box solutions may solve today's challenges but they do not have the flexibility to adapt to changing standards, sensors, or applications in the future. Choose an IDAC that is flexible with an open platform to adapt to these ever-changing variables. Otherwise, you will need to replace whole systems instead of performing simple firmware and component updates.

OUTLOOK. One of the biggest challenges facing the Internet of Things in the industrial sector is the lack of an open, universal, Ethernet-based communication protocol that has the bandwidth and determinism to meet the needs of today's high-performance machines and networks, and can grow with advancements in Ethernet technology to meet the needs of tomorrow. One promising technology that could eventually meet these needs is the Time-Sensitive Network (TSN). The Institute of Electrical and Electronics Engineers (IEEE) has formed a TSN task group to evolve IEEE Standard 802.1 to meet these requirements. There is still much work to do to ensure that these standards meet the needs of your application—get involved with organizations like the IEEE and the Industrial Internet Consortium to make your voice heard.

We would like to thank James Smith and Brian Phillippi from National Instruments for the contribution of this section on Industrial Data Acquisition Platforms.

WIRELESS INDOOR LOCALIZATION. Established GPS systems are opening up vast opportunities in the area of localization, particularly in relation to the ever-increasing prevalence of mobile end devices. Use of these devices in car navigation or in vehicle tracking for goods transport is now an everyday occurrence. However, there are still environments known as "GPS-denied areas" in which GPS-based localization does not work—for example, inside buildings or street canyons. This is why many sectors today are experiencing an increasing need for seamless localization in both indoor and outdoor areas (e.g., for large infrastructures such as airports and company premises). The use and continued development of wireless communication technologies have allowed the emergence of various WiFi-based indoor localization solutions that close these gaps in localization coverage, thus generating new opportunities and added value across all levels of the value chain.

CROSS-SECTOR APPLICATIONS OF INDOOR LOCALIZATION SYSTEMS. Indoor localization solutions are employed whenever traditional GPS-based systems cannot be used due to signal blockage and reflection within buildings and large infrastructures. For indoor applications, different technologies come into play, such as WiFi, optical sensors, and motion sensors. The diverse fields of application of WiFi-based indoor localization systems cover the entire value chain in the following sectors: sports, security, production, logistics, automotive, healthcare, and entertainment.

In the context of Industry 4.0, for example, new opportunities are emerging thanks to the integrated capturing and networking of infrastructures, processes, and products via indoor localization systems across all levels of the value chain. The Internet of Things is an essential prerequisite for Industry 4.0. It will allow new potential benefits to be reaped in optimizing processes, speeding up work processes, and increasing industrial and corporate safety.

Indoor localization in the manufacturing sector will enable the application of concepts such as geofencing, which makes it possible to check whether people or vehicles are located in specific areas, such as near machines. You can also verify whether people in a specific area are authorized to be there. This is particularly useful in terms of ensuring transparency and safety for work processes.

Another application of indoor localization systems is the optimization of logistics processes, as it allows the automatic location of pallets, products, forklifts, and even people in real time. This makes it possible to speed up, connect, and improve logistics processes as well as make them more secure, both at a single location and across several locations. Finally, a complete localization solution paves the way for new services.

Indoor localization systems also support coordination and operational safety in large infrastructures like airports. Critical situations such as near collisions can be recorded centrally using collected location data in combination with camera monitoring to prevent accidents and hazardous situations. An additional application scenario is the localization of passengers and employees in airports, or employees and visitors on company premises.

In the sporting field—for example, in football—indoor localization systems are used to analyze games and process the data collected. By linking sporting performance with athletes' vital data, training strategies and games can be objectively assessed and optimized. For instance, technical aids based on indoor localization technology can provide visually impaired people with support in their training programs and their day-to-day mobility and accessibility. The Fraunhofer Institute for Integrated Circuits IIS is developing a positioning system that uses a sensor belt worn by the visually impaired person to transmit tactile and acoustic warning signals and instructions whenever the person leaves a predefined path.

In the context of ambient assisted living (AAL), indoor localization solutions are being developed to support elderly people, people with disabilities, and people in need of care, while also ensuring full localization coverage by means of WiFi and Bluetooth, for instance. In this field of application, experts are creating intelligent environments and seamlessly integrating different components and solutions. This will enable medical condition monitoring and geofencing. Specific incidents such as a fall can thus be detected and carers notified. Different radiolocation technologies can be used for a wide variety of assistance systems, allowing people to lead independent lives to the greatest possible extent and to improve their health and overall quality of life. Researchers at Fraunhofer IIS have demonstrated that systems for monitoring vital body functions can help to locate people quickly in the event of emergencies.

In the area of public transport, an intelligent combination of satellite positioning (GPS), WiFi positioning, and motion sensors via sensor fusion can facilitate door-to-door navigation. In particular, this makes it easier for passengers to find their bearings when changing buses, trams, trains, and subway systems.

DIVERSE REQUIREMENTS OF INDOOR LOCALIZATION SOLUTIONS. Because they have such a wide range of applications, the various indoor localization solutions have to fulfill different requirements in each field of application to ensure reliability and user-friendliness. Accuracy and availability are particularly important for these systems, which are employed whenever traditional GPS-based solutions do not work. The different levels of availability range from the basic feasibility of identifying a given position, to the degree of accuracy to which this can be determined across all areas. Availability is paramount for both individuals and companies in areas such as logistics, production, or AAL.

In addition, a technical distinction is made in terms of infrastructure function. One option is for the infrastructure to enable a device to locate itself (self-positioning), as seen in museum navigation systems based on WiFi networks, for example. Alternatively, the infrastructure can locate the device (remote positioning), whereby data is captured and processed centrally. Size and the physical attributes of an area play an important role in large infrastructures, logistics, and manufacturing, as both line of sight and radio-wave transmission are frequently interrupted by obstacles (e.g., machines or thick walls).

Likewise, specific indoor localization solutions can be defined based on the number and speed of the objects to be located, or depending on whether it is objects and/or people that are to be located. The incorporation of sensor technology in localization systems is particularly beneficial for sports and AAL systems that assist individuals in need of support (e.g., to monitor vital data or detect a fall). In this context, transmission speed and frequency for additional sensor data, such as temperature data for medical supplies, can be defined according to specific users' needs. It may also be necessary to use a real-time analysis system that responds appropriately to specific events—by triggering an alarm in the event of an emergency, for instance.

Other critical issues include battery life as well as transmitter form and weight, as these properties are subject to different considerations depending on the application. Indeed, in a variety of situations, transmitter operation is crucial for the effective deployment of an indoor localization system. In addition, the update rate must be optimized for the relevant application, as both positioning speed and frequency can be varied depending on the application. While the goal is to achieve the best possible design for indoor localization solutions that are tailored to customer requirements, both cost issues and the availability of the required system must be factored in for implementation. To meet the considerable demands placed on indoor localization systems, Fraunhofer IIS is working to combine these diverse technologies and develop them further.

TECHNICAL FOUNDATION. The indoor localization technologies discussed in the previous section use different techniques to determine the position of objects or people. The following provides an overview of the most important indoor localization techniques and the possibilities these techniques offer.

Overview

Field intensity measurement—which works inside buildings such as museums using existing infrastructure like WiFi or Bluetooth networks—measures field intensity distribution and compares it with a field intensity map stored in a database in order to calculate a position. These systems, which have an accuracy of several meters, can be used for guidance and information systems in museums or shopping malls, for instance, or to ensure the safety of rescue workers in crisis situations. The beacon solution also enables positioning by using short-range radio systems such as Bluetooth low energy (BLE) or radio-frequency identification (RFID) to determine the area in which a person or a device is located. This is useful for theft prevention or navigation in shopping malls.

For angle measurement techniques, the position of the transmitter is calculated to an accuracy of one meter based on the angle of incidence of a radio signal on an antenna array. This system can be used to locate rescue forces, or for security applications in airports, for example.

Travel-time-based radiolocation enables a position to be determined by measuring the time it takes a radio signal to travel between the transmitter and the receiver. This positioning solution, which offers centimeter-scale accuracy, is used in sports and in satellite navigation (GNSS) for vehicles.

Sensor networks use proximity relationships to measure the relationships or distances between sensor nodes, and then calculate their own position on the basis of nodes whose positions are known.

The different localization technologies can be combined, which means they can be supported by other technologies and techniques such as inertial sensor technology and event detection. Combining the systems ensures higher accuracy, reliability, and availability. Environment models also incorporate a position's environs, which is useful for applications such as route planning. Depending on the technique, positioning data comprises both the position at which something is located, as well as its destination and the speed at which it is moving there. Depending on the sensor technology used, people's vital functions or device functionality can also be conveyed.

THE FUTURE OF WIFI-BASED INDOOR LOCALIZATION. Overall, the entire field of indoor localization is a major up-and-coming trend that is now set to conquer internal spaces. In addition to basic indoor availability, one of the primary concerns is improving performance, in particular, accuracy. One major goal here is to achieve localization using as little infrastructure as possible, or even without any infrastructure at all. This would allow the seamless, reliable location of objects both indoors and outdoors.

Due to the widespread availability of smartphones and the resulting development of new markets, such as direct marketing, we can expect seamless indoor/outdoor localization and navigation to become available in the next few years. In terms of integration, a central role is played by the availability of increasingly high-quality sensors on the one hand, and the large quantities of these sensors on the other.

Another promising approach concerns the use of "pseudolites." These "pseudo-satellites" are transmitters that amplify satellite signals inside buildings, thus enabling indoor localization via normal GPS receivers. In addition, we anticipate that an increasing number of miniaturized, localization-enabled components will be integrated within devices, infrastructures, and vehicles as standard, enabling them to communicate with each other. This will give rise to new standards, protocols, and interfaces. Increasing standardization, integration, and networking will improve technology performance and enable new applications and services—in the area of Industry 4.0, for example, or by connecting cars together (Car2Car) or with infrastructures such as parking garages or machinery (Car2X).

We would like to thank Dr. Stephan Otto from Fraunhofer IIS for his contribution of this section on Wireless Indoor Localization.

CASE STUDY: KLM. KLM Royal Dutch Airlines, in cooperation with indoo.rs, enhanced their KLM app with an indoor positioning and navigation prototype functionality to be used by its transit passengers at Amsterdam Airport Schiphol. The application, running on iOS and Android, shows the position of the user as a dot on the map and the route from their current position to the next gate. The application also calculates the time needed to walk there.

The primary aim of the project was to improve gate closing times and decrease transfer times by providing additional services to their customers. Also, by providing the airline's customers with map directions, the journey from their arrival gate to their connecting flight should be much easier.

In order to enable accurate positioning within the transit area, iBeacons were installed at KLM kiosks. When a customer who has the KLM app installed on her phone passes an iBeacon, a push notification is sent to her smartphone if route information is available. If the user decides that she would like this information, the app then opens and displays the route to next gate starting from her current position.

The navigation service is available in the newest release of the KLM app, which can be downloaded from the Apple and Android app stores.

PROJECT MANAGEMENT PERSPECTIVE. The project-specific challenges can be summarized as follows:

- The solution put in place at Schiphol Airport requires BLE beacons to be installed in the transit area and reception of these signals by users' smartphones. Historically, Bluetooth has been known for being battery draining. Thus, KLM feared that app users wouldn't turn on Bluetooth 4.0 (Bluetooth Low Energy/BLE) to use the navigation feature. Also, not all users own smartphones that support BLE as standard.

- The latter constraint will become irrelevant over time as newer generations of smartphones support BLE as standard. It is common that new and upcoming technologies would encounter some compatibility issues with older devices. Compared to earlier Bluetooth versions, Bluetooth 4.0 is characterized by very low power consumption (e.g., iBeacons can run for up to four years off a single coin cell). Having Bluetooth connections enabled on newer smartphones accounts for only a small fraction of total battery consumption compared with earlier Bluetooth versions. Explanation of the core benefits of BLE helped to overcome the opposition to a Bluetooth-based solution.

- Small iBeacons have been installed at the KLM kiosks in the transit area. Interestingly, the beacons attracted the curiosity of people passing by these kiosks and were sometimes removed or taken away. The installation of iBeacons at the airport is subject to several restrictions for a variety of reasons due to the fact that the project is partnered with the airline and not the airport. Thus, beacons could not be installed anywhere but at KLM kiosks (e.g., in higher places). The small iBeacon devices have been firmly mounted with adhesive to prevent loss.

LEARNING AND BEST PRACTICES. Several stakeholders are involved in an airport's business operating environment, including airport operators, airlines, and retail operators. Successful indoor navigation systems in airports require the cooperation of various players: a technology company, building facility management, passenger services.

Every building has unique characteristics and these need to be taken into consideration for the installation of BLE beacons. Airports can be considered a building site 365 days a year: appearance and arrangement of airport areas are subject to ongoing changes (temporary promotions, additional stands, etc.). Bluetooth signals are affected by objects with insulation and absorption properties. Hence, beacons should be installed in places that guarantee high visibility so that the impact caused by an ever-changing environment can be minimized.

The high degree of innovation involved means that IoT projects and initiatives require users in the market to be educated about the potential of such technologies. Only then can the value to both operators and users be fully realized.

We would like to thank Bernd Gruber, COO of indoo.rs, for his support with this case study.

PART III

Detailed Case Study

The Ignite | IoT Methodology presented in Part II was developed by analyzing best practice and M2M/IoT case studies, such as the ones discussed in Part I. Naturally, these projects did not use the Ignite | IoT Methodology, because it was not available at the time. So, the next important step for Ignite | IoT is to enter a validation phase where we can identify the strengths and weaknesses of the proposed methodology and fine-tune it based on what we learn. One of the first projects to be fully developed based on the Ignite | IoT Methodology is the IIC Track & Trace testbed.

Track & Trace is a solution that Bosch Software Innovations is currently developing with its partners Tech Mahindra, Bosch Rexroth, and Cisco. The goal is to enable management of handheld power tools in manufacturing and maintenance environments. This "management" involves efficiently tracking and tracing these tools to ensure their proper use, prevent their misuse, and collect data on their usage and status. A phased approach will be used.

The next chapter (Chapter 9) provides general background information about the Track & Trace testbed. The subsequent chapter (Chapter 10) describes the full Plan/Build/Run cycle for the testbed.

Background Information

THE TRACK & TRACE CASE STUDY IS AN OFFICIAL TESTBED OF THE INDUSTRIAL INTERNET CONsortium (IIC). To better understand how this fits together, we will first provide an overview of IIC testbeds in general, followed by a high-level overview of Track & Trace. Next, we will look at the key drivers for this testbed, first from the perspective of an end user (Airbus), then from the perspective of a power tools vendor (Bosch Rexroth).

Industrial Internet Consortium Testbeds

As this is an IIC testbed case study, we first want to explain what an IIC testbed actually is. A more detailed description of the IIC itself can be found in "Industrial Internet Consortium" on page 80. To learn more about testbeds, we spoke to Michael Lee, Director of Testbeds for the IIC. In this role, Michael assists members with the identification, specification, creation, and adoption of testbeds. He also facilitates the creation of policies and procedures for these activities.

Dirk Slama: Testbeds are a key element of the Industrial Internet Consortium strategy. What exactly is a testbed?

Michael Lee: At its simplest, a testbed is a controlled experimentation platform where applications can be deployed and tested in an environment that resembles real-world conditions. The approximation of, but insulation from, the real world allows the issues of safety, security, reproducibility, etc. to be managed during an experiment. The experimentation itself can explore untested technologies or existing technologies working together in an untested manner. And, most importantly for the Industrial Internet Consortium, testbeds should result in the creation of new products, services, and technological innovations. The Track & Trace testbed, for example, should result in open tool interfaces and proven localization technologies that drive innovation on the factory floor and create opportunities for new products and services.

Dirk Slama: How does a project qualify to become a testbed?

Michael Lee: For an Industrial Internet Consortium testbed, it has to be approved by the Industrial Internet Consortium Steering Committee. Their overriding approval criteria are the perceived degree to which the testbed can successfully lead to innovative and new products, and how it can verify or extend our technical capabilities. To assess these criteria, numerous characteristics of the testbed are considered, including business case, technology requirements, social and cultural impacts, research requirements, timeline, etc.

Dirk Slama: What type of testbeds are you looking for, and how many?

Michael Lee: Tough question. I'm not sure we know enough to set a limit on either the type or the number of testbeds at this point. The Internet of Industrial Things is here. And member companies of the Industrial Internet Consortium are already driving many usages in industry. It's a massive enterprise, and it will be decades before we know exactly where it may lead. Sir Tim Berners-Lee didn't predict all of today's uses of the Internet when he invented the World Wide Web in 1989, and I don't think we can predict all the uses of the Industrial Internet, or how many testbeds will be required going forward. Our current focus is therefore more on qualifying and approving Industrial Internet Consortium testbeds rather than on limiting their number.

Dirk Slama: The Industrial Internet Consortium says it does not do any standardization work. What does this mean for a testbed?

Michael Lee: That's correct, the Industrial Internet Consortium does not create standards. However, standards are important to us, and it is an area we are very involved in. To make this a little clearer, let me briefly explain the Industrial Internet Consortium's major activities and how standards fit into them. Broadly speaking, there are three main activities, as shown in Figure 9-1.

The first element (on the left of Figure 9-1) relates to the ecosystem in general and membership in particular. The business needs from the ecosystem drive ongoing work in the security and technology groups, and all of that leads to the creation of innovative products and services by means of the Industrial Internet Consortium testbed. The security and technology references in the middle element are either based on existing, hopefully open, standards or help to identify a gap or lack of standards. In the latter case, the Industrial Internet Consortium will work to clarify the requirements for missing standards and assist members in standardization efforts along with appropriate (external) organizations. Likewise, the testbed activities may help refine these requirements and possibly vet a potential technology for standardization. This is reflected in the lessons learned-improvements feedback loop.

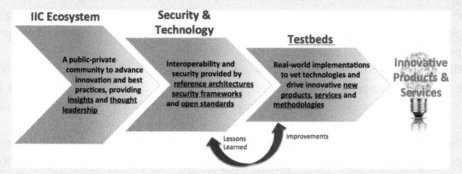

FIGURE 9-1. Overview of the Industrial Internet Consortium testbed (Source: Industrial Internet Consortium)

Dirk Slama: What does the current testbed pipeline look like, and what's next?

Michael Lee: The testbeds are member-driven and thus reflect the needs and expectations of the consortium's members. In practice, they are typically driven by multiple, collaborating members. There are currently a variety of testbeds in various stages of consideration. While it is too early to comment on specifics, I can comment on some patterns we're seeing. One is "Horizontal" testbed initiatives. These tend to be technology driven and focus on things like software-defined networks, cross-domain connectivity, and ultra-high-speed networking. There are also "Vertical" testbed initiatives. These tend to be market driven and focus on things like remote patient healthcare and smart tools on the factory floor (as the Track & Trace testbed is doing). And finally, there are "Grand Challenge" initiatives, which have a much broader and longer-term focus and may drive the need for multiple testbeds. These are a popular topic in the IoT world and include subjects like healthcare, transportation, energy, smart cities, etc. Additional effort is required to maintain a sustained and coordinated approach when working on this kind of initiative. I expect we will soon see new Industrial Internet Consortium testbed initiatives reflecting all three of these patterns.

Track & Trace Testbed

The Track & Trace testbed from the Industrial Internet Consortium (Figure 9-2) will provide solutions for the manufacturing and maintenance of safety-critical products such as machines, vehicles, aircraft, and the like. Another application area is the construction and maintenance of buildings or industrial structures like oil rigs.

In many of these sectors, more and more advanced industrial power tools are being used. In the past, such tools were generally connected to a base station via cables and tubes. The base station provided electricity and compressed air, as well as central control of the tool and the work process. Because of the advancements in battery and computer technology, a whole new generation of completely cordless industrial power tools is now emerging, with powerful battery packs and onboard computers. Examples include measurement, riveting, and tightening tools. Their ability to communicate wirelessly via the IP protocol has made these intelligent power tools the poster children of the IoT movement.

These types of cordless, handheld power tools are often used in environments where cables would be a hindrance, such as inside an aircraft body. However, because of their flexibility, they can also be found in many other environments, including automotive manufacturing.

Despite the many benefits of this newly won flexibility, there are also some disadvantages to cordless power tools. Managing larger fleets of these tools becomes more difficult because they are difficult to locate. It is also trickier to ensure that the tools are used in the right place at the right time, and with the right configuration. And finally, while it is great that intelligence is now located directly on the tools—allowing for finer-grained work control and tracing—it is vital that the tools don't operate in isolation; integration with manufacturing execution systems (MES), product lifecycle management (PLC), and other enterprise systems therefore becomes essential.

PHASED APPROACH

The Track & Trace testbed will provide solutions in a phased approach, as well as other value-added features, too. Phase 1 can be summarized as follows:

- Takes a pragmatic approach, focusing on go-to-market strategy, and leveraging existing technologies for innovative use
- Key deliverables will include a proven benchmark solution and a physical testbed with associated documentation
- The first tool to be integrated will be the Bosch Rexroth Nexo
- A set of open interfaces will be published that allow flexible access to all components of the testbed, allowing partners to integrate different power tools and software/hardware components
- Go-to-market is planned for 2015
- First important milestone is the keynote demo at Bosch ConnectedWorld (February 2015)

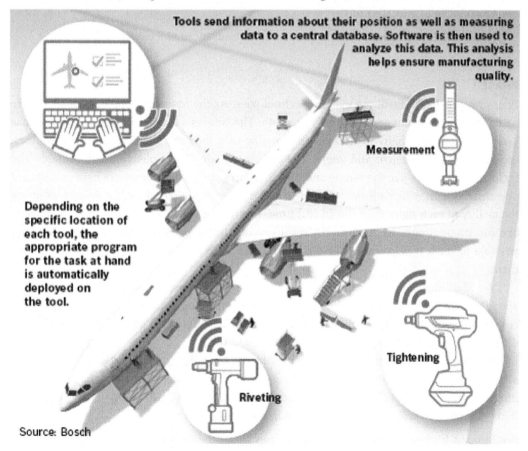

Connected tools in manufacturing

In the international Track and Trace project, Bosch and its partners in the Industrial Internet Consortium are exploring the interconnection and management of industrial tools.

Tools send information about their position as well as measuring data to a central database. Software is then used to analyze this data. This analysis helps ensure manufacturing quality.

Measurement

Depending on the specific location of each tool, the appropriate program for the task at hand is automatically deployed on the tool.

Tightening

Riveting

Source: Bosch

FIGURE 9-2. Overview of the Track & Trace testbed from the Industrial Internet Consortium (Source: Bosch)

Phase 2 takes a much longer-term perspective, with a focus on the advanced aspects of Track & Trace, such as high-precision indoor localization (sub-centimeter accuracy), deployment of customizable logic on the power tools, and advanced vertical integration.

TESTBED SPONSORS

Each Industrial Internet Consortium testbed has a set of designated testbed sponsors who are responsible for the development and go-to-market of the testbed. The sponsors of Track & Trace Phase 1 are:

- **Bosch Software Innovations** as the industry solution leader and provider of the underlying IoT application platform
- **Bosch Rexroth** as provider of industry expertise and test tools like the Nexo nutrunner
- **Tech Mahindra** for solution development
- **Cisco** for indoor localization
- **National Instruments** will join in Phase 2 for the advanced tool control

PHASE 1

Phase 1 of the testbed will use existing technologies. As the first tool to be integrated, we are using the Nexo nutrunners from Bosch Rexroth. The Nexo is a high-end tool for industrial use cases. It offers the ability to measure the quality of a tightening run via multiple sensors, including torque, wrench, and angle. The tightening run is completely programmable and includes parameters like the torque and timing information. The nutrunners have an onboard operating system, which allows workers to choose from multiple programs as well as to see the quality of each tightening run in real time. Furthermore, the tools are connected via WiFi and can be configured to transmit the results in real time to a backend component. It is also possible to push new programs to the nutrunners as well as to remotely enable or disable them.

We place the nutrunners in a setting where a fleet of assets is used within one or more shop floors or even out in the field. In Phase 1, the implementation will be able to *track* devices inside buildings via WiFi triangulation. Additionally, we are able to *trace* the actions of the different handheld tools remotely in real time (Figure 9-3).

The ability to track the locations of handheld tools and trace their actions in real time offers three major benefits in Phase 1 that go beyond the current industry offering (see the interview in "Industrial Power Tools: Vendor Perspective (Bosch Rexroth)" on page 415). In particular, Phase 1 will deliver the following benefits for customers:

- **Support for new, flexible assembly processes** where the tools are brought to the work item by the operator at any point in the product's lifecycle. This allows for flexibility regarding the space and time where the actual work is carried out.

- **Zero defect and early fault detection** guarantees factory-level quality and traceability in the field. This benefit will be enabled through direct integration with existing product lifecycle management (PLM) systems used in the industry.

- **Creation of new business models** that lower CAPEX and provide improved SLA management, such as "Bill per Drill" or "Power by the Hour," where the equipment manufacturer is in charge of providing the necessary tools at the right place and time.

1 Connected Asset: Handheld power tools

Intelligent tools capture the quality of their work done and transmit the results in real time. They are also remotely reconfigurable and can be enabled/disabled as required.

2 Track Fleets of Assets

All the tools in the factory halls and in the field can be tracked for their location. They will be programmed and enabled regarding to the specific macro and micro-location.

3 Trace Actions

Trace the action of all your tools and map them with the connected product's lifecycle inside your factory and out in the field.

Source: www.enterprise-iot.org

FIGURE 9-3. Track & Trace overview

PHASE 2

The vision for Phase 2 takes the concept of Track & Trace much further. The idea is to be able to track all work tools, products, and semifinished products in a factory or similar environment with a very high level of precision, and to map this localization data in real time to a 3D model. For example, the 3D model can provide information about the different joints that need to be worked on—in a large aircraft, this can number more than 400,000 (see the interview in "Industrial Power Tools: End-User Perspective (Airbus)" on page 412). The data associated with the 3D model can help to identify which program needs to be used for a tightening process at a selected joint. This program can then be automatically activated (or even uploaded) to the power tool in use. Likewise, after the tightening process has finished, the details of this process—a curve that records torque and angle—can be read from the tool and written back to the quality management database, creating a quality lot for the particular joint based on the localization and 3D PLM data.

One limiting factor currently is the lack of cost-efficient, high-precision indoor localization technologies for industrial environments. This is one of the key problems that must be addressed in Phase 2 of this testbed. Some trials in this area have already started, as we will discuss later.

In order to get a better feel for the current status of available technologies and how they can be used in Phase 2 of the testbed, the testbed sponsors agreed to take the basic Track & Trace functionality of Phase 1 and use it as the foundation for an advanced prototype showcasing some of the features that should be developed for Phase 2. These are, in particular, high-precision indoor localization and mapping to 3D PLM data. The task was to complete this in time to be used as a keynote demo at Bosch ConnectedWorld 2015 (February). The Track & Trace sponsors invited the following companies to contribute to the demonstration system:

- **Dassault Systèmes** to provide support for the 3D element of the demo

- **Haption** to help connect a real tool operator to a virtual 3D avatar

- **Xsens** for their expertise in 3D motion tracking

The Ignite | IoT Methodology was used to structure the development of this system. We will discuss the results and experience of this approach later. But, before this, we will provide some more background on the testbed scenario from the perspective of two industry experts.

Industrial Power Tools: End-User Perspective (Airbus)

To better understand the future usage scenarios of intelligent power tools in an industrial environment, we spoke to Sébastien Boria from Airbus. Sébastien is R&D Mechatronics Technology Leader for the Airbus Factory of the Future. The interviewer is Dirk Slama from Bosch Software Innovations.

Dirk Slama: Sébastien, you are working on the Airbus Factory of the Future project. This sounds like a very ambitious venture. What areas does the project cover?

Sébastien Boria: There are currently more than 8,000 Airbus aircraft in operation, with 15,276 orders for aircraft logged as of January 31, 2015 [AB1]. Each aircraft is a complex product consisting of millions of parts that have to be assembled to perfection. Integrating innovative production techniques is vital for our productivity. Today, digital mock-ups, laser projections onto aircraft bodies, and complex 3D environments have already been fully integrated into our processes. Because each generation of our manufacturing lines has a lifetime of more than a decade, the Future Factory has to adopt an outlook that goes well beyond just one year. There are a variety of important considerations here, including robotic exoskeletons for assembly, advanced robots (from standard to cobotics), ALM technology, the virtual plateau and digitization of the shop floor, integrated production, and so on [AB2]. The aim is to leverage emerging lab technologies that can be adapted or matured in order to improve our manufacturing processes.

Dirk Slama: But the focus of your own work is a bit more specific, isn't it?

Sébastien Boria: Yes, I mainly focus on smart production and advanced robotics. We are in the process of implementing a "smart workshop" that uses intelligent, connected production tools to streamline processes and provide error-proof processes for shop floors.

Dirk Slama: Can you give a concrete example?

Sébastien Boria: Sure. Think of the hundreds of thousands of point-based process steps that need to be completed in order to assemble an aircraft. Because of the sheer volume of process steps involved, it's not possible to have an individual task for each step at work-cell level. Instead, these process steps need to be managed collectively as process sequences. Most assembly tasks involve a drilling process, a point-checking (i.e., measurement) process, and a tightening process. These processes can involve multiple stages within one takt, be spread over several workcells or assembly lines, or even shared by various production operators. For example, different torque and angle parameters are used in different phases of the same tightening process, at a single 3D location, for example. Therefore, if something goes wrong with one of these processes, it could lead to costly, dedicated fixes, just because the part is not in the correct workcell on the shop floor. So there is enormous potential for improving these processes by making the relevant handheld tools more intelligent and connected, by dynamically configuring the tools for the specific task at hand, for example.

Dirk Slama: What types of tool are you looking at specifically?

Sébastien Boria: Currently, we are focusing on smarter handheld drilling, tightening, and measurement processes, either through standard tools with embedded intelligence or through wearable computer intelligence embedded in operator suits, such as belt systems, for example. Later, we will also look at integration with robots and CNC machines using the same architectural design.

Dirk Slama: And what does your solution look like?

Sébastien Boria: Everything is linked to a platform which combines specialized hardware and software. In other words, we are using an architecture that is linked to distributed intelligence that is embedded in every system involved in our processes. First of all, there is the tool intelligence itself. Handheld power tools used in our Future Factory environment will have to either have an onboard control unit or at least be able to support wearable controllers. This is important for ensuring local processing of process input data, in combination with onboard sensors and actuators linked to the physical tool process. And leveraging wireless connectivity for the most part too, of course.

Dirk Slama: And what about tool integration?

Sébastien Boria: In the past, we took a more traditional, centralized approach, but this is not efficient enough to manage heterogeneous systems in real time, given the imperative for lower infrastructure costs. This is why we are now looking more closely at solutions that work as a mashup of interconnected tools. We need to transfer data from one system to another or perform the relevant synchronization, but only when requested by the local intelligence, or when it serves a purpose for the overall process. In other words, not every tool is connected to a central backend all the time. But tools can connect with each other to exchange information and instructions. This solves many problems—for example, if you are working inside an aircraft where there is no wireless network available.

Dirk Slama: How do you track tools and map tool information to production data?

Sébastien Boria: Indoor localization is important, and so is integration with data from MES and PLM systems. Automatically reconciling localization data for tools and work items with PLM data is also important. Reconciliation is requested based on various trueness values (see ISO 15725) and depending on the application. Tracking a tool on the shop floor or within a workcell is not the same task as tracking a handheld tool tip from one position to another when carrying out processes on an individual part. In the first case, inaccuracy in tracking data can correspond to tens of centimeters or even meters, while in the second case, inaccuracy can be a matter of tenths of millimeters. Again, system integration has to take into account context-based adaptive behaviors in order to avoid errors and nonquality outcomes.

Dirk Slama: So you're integrating localization data with 3D PLM data?

Sébastien Boria: Well, not exactly. We have learned from experience that CAD/CAM data models coming directly from engineering can sometimes be too detailed and fine-grained for our purposes. So we are currently developing an intermediate layer that works with a simplified XML dataset for geo data. This layer helps to integrate the power tools with the 3D PLM layer. Also, you can't expect shop-floor workers to use a full 3D modeling environment to configure their working environment. This means that we need to build a simpler configuration application.

Dirk Slama: It sounds like a lot of different types of production equipment and IT systems have to interact and work together. How do you roll this out in a very heterogeneous environment with a large number of different suppliers?

Sébastien Boria: Dissemination is important, as is a clear focus on open interfaces and interface-based integration. Software openness through an API is the main enabler of efficient integration. We are therefore defining neutral interfaces based on robust standards, which will enable our own engineers as well as suppliers and partners to develop tools and applications that fit into our overall shop-floor support system. Because of the high level of heterogeneity we have here, this type of integrative approach is central to our future production system.

Dirk Slama: Sébastien, that was very insightful—thanks a lot!

Industrial Power Tools: Vendor Perspective (Bosch Rexroth)

To better understand the current status and future evolution of industrial power tools, we spoke to Martin Doelfs, an expert in this area. Martin is responsible for Product Management for Bosch Rexroth Tightening and Welding Systems. He has degrees in Mechanical Engineering from the University of Stuttgart and Michigan Technological University, and joined Robert Bosch in 1992 to focus on the interface between customer, engineering, and sales. Prior to his current position he was Director of the Production Tools business unit in Bosch's Power Tools division.

Frank Puhlmann: Martin Doelfs, Industry 4.0 is an interesting application of the Internet of Things and Services. Besides intelligent parts that actively drive automation within the factory, what other improvements do you believe the Internet of Things can offer in this regard?

Martin Doelfs: In terms of Industry 4.0, I find handheld tightening tools especially interesting. Modern battery and drive technology means that the worker is no longer bound to a specific place by cables and hoses. While this may have been the case for consumer and professional tools for years (as can easily be seen in the sophisticated products offered by Bosch power tools) the industry perspective is quite a different story.

Frank Puhlmann: Can you elaborate a bit on this difference? As a consumer, I have been using cordless, battery-driven tools for years.

Martin Doelfs: Sure! First of all, we should identify the different industrial use cases. According to the German engineering association (VDI guideline 2862), there are three different cases: Class A covers screw connections which might pose a risk to life and safety. If the connection fails to hold, there is a risk of injury or death. Class B covers a connection that is crucial to functionality. If the connection fails, the machine could stop working. Class C covers the kind of "annoyances" that can result from the failure of a connection, such as a rattling sound from a loose part. If you look at use cases A and B, industrial applications require a controlled tightening process with a well-defined torque/angle curve and speed. Sensors also need to be able to capture the results of the tightening operation. Each tightening operation produces a lot of log data that needs to be captured and transferred to a server for later analysis and storage. If you consider the required level of accuracy and the amount of data generated by just one of these screws and then think of the number of Class A and B screws required to produce a passenger car, it becomes clear that the relevant tool will need to be of a different caliber to your average consumer tool.

Frank Puhlmann: Can you think of any other requirements for industrial tightening tools? As far as I remember, these tools used to be based on air-compression mechanisms in the past.

Martin Doelfs: That's right. Historically, tightening tools used to be powered by compressed air. Nowadays, these tools have been replaced by electrically or even battery-driven tools. Battery and drive technology have made huge steps toward more power and efficiency, as well as allowing for significant reduction in weight in recent years, and this trend will continue. Battery-powered tools also allow more flexibility for a worker. This enables new manufacturing processes which, in turn, directly lead to higher productivity.

Frank Puhlmann: Do you have an idea of what a new manufacturing process could look like?

Martin Doelfs: I foresee a scenario where workers can move more flexibly on the shop floor, and can do more, and more varied, jobs with a single tool, without having to return to a "base." If this is taken into consideration when designing the manufacturing process, it should lead to increased productivity.

Frank Puhlmann: Where do you see handheld tightening tools heading with regards to IoT?

Martin Doelfs: That's an interesting question. As I said previously, the foremost change I see happening is a new, more flexible process for A- and B-class tightening operations. We can already see more worker autonomy as a result of the controlled tightening process offered by handheld tools. But, to secure this process and ensure that high quality is maintained, we need to know how and where tools are used (i.e., something is tightened). This information is obvious when dealing with wired tools but more of a challenge for mobile tools. For instance, some tools are not allowed in certain environments (e.g., electric tools must be kept away from hazardous environments to prevent fire). We also need to ensure that we correctly match the tightening log data produced by the tools with a specific part or—at an even more detailed level—with a certain screw in the part. In general, we can distinguish three levels of granularity: (1) Where is the tool in the factory or construction site? In general, assessing if the tool is within or outside a given geolocation is sufficient. (2) If you are working with a larger part, such as an airplane body or passenger car: Which section of the part am I working on? This might require accuracy within a meter. (3) If I have exact knowledge of the screw I'm working on, I can automatically program the tightening tool with the right parameters and process the tightening order, which might be important. So geotracking is a vital functionality to help unlock the full potential of wireless tightening tools with respect to increased productivity at even higher levels of process quality. Combining these elements is what will create truly "intelligent tools."

Frank Puhlmann: Intelligent tightening tools—that sounds very promising. I'm interested to know what kind of services you envision for these tools.

Martin Doelfs: As you can already see from the kind of Big Data that I mentioned earlier, any tightening run produces a lot of analysis data. This needs to be stored on a server and used to assess production quality. If I extend this data with additional process data and have the data available in the backend, I can run automated analysis in real time and provide action items and tasks to improve process and productivity (e.g., to allow engineers to analyze tightening runs and detect problems like an oily screw or a missing shim). However, as is generally the case with Big Data–based services, these ideas are just the beginning. As soon as we start rolling them out, new ideas will emerge and, hopefully, using IoT technology, we will have the means to implement them quickly and easily. In the end, making cordless tools intelligent, having sensor data available in backend systems, and implementing intelligent data-mining algorithms will have a big impact on the way handheld tightening tools are used in the future industry. Users and suppliers of these tools will need to have the foresight and the courage to try new things and create new solutions. I'm greatly looking forward to the new opportunities they make available to us all.

Developing Track & Trace with the Ignite | IoT Methodology

THE FOLLOWING SECTIONS DOCUMENT HOW WE DEVELOPED THE FIRST MILESTONE OF THE Track & Trace testbed—the keynote demo for Bosch ConnectedWorld—with the help of the Ignite | IoT Methodology. We chose this scenario for Part III for the following reasons:

- First, the scenario should represent the complexity of a typical IoT project as described by the Ignite | IoT Solution Delivery methodology. Hence, we decided to select a case study that involves multiple stakeholders from different application domains. In our case study, we included Bosch Rexroth as a connected tool manufacturer, Cisco as a wireless/localization expert, Bosch Software Innovations as a provider of IoT middleware and industrial solution design, Dassault/Haption/XSENS as 3D visualization and interaction experts, and Tech Mahindra as the system integrator to build the complete solution.

- Second, the scenario should be simple enough to be described in a couple of pages (we hope that we managed to do this!). Those without much knowledge of the domain should be easily able to follow its core idea. So we used a well-known thing (i.e., nutrunners) and investigated their professional usage in industry.

- Finally, the case study should not be a one-off demo, but should have the potential to be developed into a professional solution over multiple steps (as outlined by the phased approach earlier). The collaborative approach taken with the IIC to build the partner ecosystem for Track & Trace has been working very well so far.

Alignment of the Ignite | IoT Methodology with the IIC Reference Architecture: The main goal of Part III is to provide a concrete example for the use of the Ignite | IoT Methodology, as described in Part II. Because Part III is also a description of an IIC testbed, another key requirement involved compliance with the IIC Reference Architecture (RA). The IIC RA is based on a four-layer structure, as opposed to the three-layer structure proposed by Ignite in Part II. So what we did was to rearrange the Ignite artifacts to match the IIC RA Viewpoints. Figure 10-1 describes this mapping. This example also highlights the flexibility of the Ignite | IoT Methodology in matching different architectures.

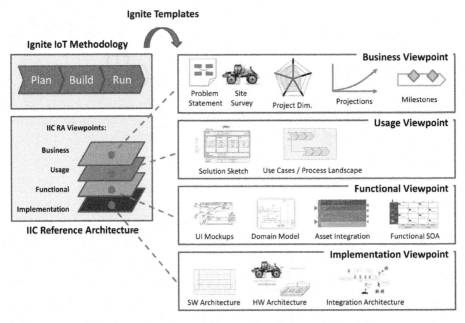

FIGURE 10-1. Alignment of Ignite | IoT Methodology with IIC Reference Architecture

Note that projects don't always have to use all of the Ignite artifacts. In this example, neither the quantity structure (projections) nor the hardware design from Ignite is used. The former is due to the fact that Track & Trace is currently a testbed without a commercial rollout (as of yet), while the latter is due to the fact that the applied hardware from Rexroth is already fully functional and doesn't need any enhancements to be integrated in the solution.

IIC RA: Business Viewpoint

The initial project idea was conceived by the business development teams at Bosch Software Innovations, Tech Mahindra, and Bosch Rexroth; experts from the service domain and the "machine camp" worked together to create an exemplary use case in the area of connected industry and manufacturing. In the next step, Cisco added cloud-based localization services based on their managed routers, while Dassault Systèmes provided an environment for virtual product support.

PROBLEM STATEMENT

The joint team depicted the problem domain and key solution elements as per Figure 10-2. The righthand side of the figure shows the target customers—in this case, industries that produce complex products that need to be serviced in the field, such as airplanes, cars, or trains. The solution therefore targets the maintenance industry and should provide three major features, including the introduced tracking solution as well as asset management and dashboard capabilities (shown in the top-left part of the figure). An overview of the design and the partners involved is provided in the bottom-left pane of the figure. The IoT middleware is provided by Bosch Software Innovations and includes components for M2M/device connectivity, BPM/Business Process Management, and BRM/Business Rules Management. The integrated ESB connects to the systems from Dassault Systèmes and Cisco's Prime Infrastructure. Technologies from MongoDB and Amazon Web Services are also used to provide data persistence as well as cloud-based hosting of the solution.

1 Connected Asset: Hand-Held Power Tools

Intelligent tools capture the quality of the work they do and transmit the results in real time. They are also remotely reconfigurable and can be enabled/disabled as required.

2 Track Fleets of Assets

All tools in the factory and in the field can be tracked for location. They are programmed and enabled based on the specific macro- and micro-location.

3 Trace Actions

Trace the actions of all your tools and map them to the connected product's lifecycle in your factory and in the field.

FIGURE 10-2. Track & Trace overview

STAKEHOLDER ANALYSIS

The key stakeholders are represented in Figure 10-3. The assets/devices are handheld nutrunners provided by Bosch Rexroth. These nutrunners are IP-enabled devices that include a local operating system that can be configured for different programs by the solution users. The enterprise services for these companies are provided as a cloud-based solution from Tech Mahindra. Companies use the provided services, such as smart indoor asset tracking or dashboard functionality, while devices are managed by and connected to the enterprise services.

Depending on specific customer needs, the provider of the enterprise services can partner with different service providers to offer tracking, visualization, or tool hardware. In this case study, the testbed partners were Cisco for macro-level tracking, Haption for micro-level tracking, Dassault Systèmes for 3D visualization, with Rexroth providing the handheld nutrunners.

Tool Operator
- One portal for accurate tracking of all hand-held tools
- Integration of existing processes and systems

Solution Users

Shop Floor
- Improved productivity
- Efficient use of tools based on over-the-air configuration
- Increased quality

Enterprise Services

Tools
- Analysis and logging of process data to ensure quality
- Automatic tool configuration

Assets/Devices

Tool Supplier
- Optimized service offering
- Revenue through new services
- Increased margins by offering services remotely

Partner Ecosystem

FIGURE 10-3. Stakeholder analysis

SITE SURVEY

We decided to document a public "instance" of the Track & Trace testbed that was showcased at the keynote demonstration of Bosch ConnectedWorld 2015. Hence, the "factory shop floor" was represented by the audience hall of the BCC Berlin, Germany (Figure 10-4). Early visits to the site revealed that the location had more than 50 wireless Cisco routers installed that might be usable for macro-level localization within the building. Unfortunately, the running servers were incompatible with the required software from Cisco's side, so we needed to install 12 additional routers to enable tracking of the nutrunners.

The project partners visited the Bosch Rexroth production site early on to clarify possible issues regarding the assets (nutrunners) and also held several meetings focusing on the solution parts from Bosch Software Innovations, Cisco, and Dassault Systèmes. Several integration workshops took place at Tech Mahindra in Bengaluru, India.

Source: bcc-berlin.de/de/downloads

FIGURE 10-4. Site survey

PROJECT DIMENSIONS

After sketching out the core project ideas, the team worked on assessing the key project dimensions and comparing them with other existing projects. For the context of this book, we compared the Track & Trace testbed with three case studies introduced earlier: sFDA ("Systematic Field Data" on page 132), CERN ("Case Study: LHCb Experiment at CERN" on page 107), and Daimler eCall ("eCall" on page 122).

Assets and devices

 It might be assumed that the Track & Trace testbed (which is designed for around 1,000 devices only) would have a lower complexity score for this dimension than the eCall project (which has to support millions of assets). However, this was not the case, as the Track & Trace testbed needs to address a very heterogeneous environment with many different tools from different manufacturers. Also, these tools can have complex onboard logic that needs to be integrated, increasing the complexity of the interfaces. However, Track & Trace scores lower compared to the requirements for structured field-data capturing from vehicle components (sFDA) and to the complexity of the assets found at CERN.

Communications and connectivity

 The team worked on the assumption that full WiFi/Bluetooth integration would be available for the tools tracked with the solution. This integration will either be supported by onboard WiFi controllers for IP-enabled devices that can push data or by iBeacon-style stickers attached to nonconnected tools for tracking capabilities. Both technologies are used with advanced access points that can triangulate the position of the assets within a range of 30 cm to 1 m. It is thus more sophisticated than connecting via the existing CAN bus in the car or using integrated 3G components from mobile networks.

Backend services

The planned backend services for Track & Trace introduce a complete shift in application strategy within factories. They have a high business complexity due to the introduction of new end-to-end processes that will disrupt numerous existing solutions. From the team's perspective, the backend services are the most challenging part of the testbed.

Standards and regulatory compliance

Because the testbed needs to navigate regional-, industry-, and technology-specific regulatory requirements for wider adoption, the score for this dimension is comparable to the eCall solution. On the other hand, the current proposal relies on approved standards like WiFi and Bluetooth, which should enable straightforward implementation.

Project environment

The environment for the project has been classified as having medium complexity. While it is worked on as time-to-budget, the geographic distribution of the contributors and the highly technical skills required make it challenging.

Note that the summary provided here (and shown in Figure 10-5) is on a very high level. Refer to *www.enterprise-iot.org* to download the full Excel template of Ignite | IoT Project Dimensions, which contains more than 40 detailed dimensions and their explanations.

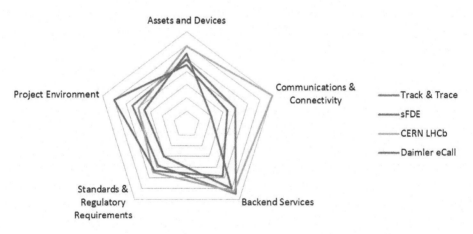

FIGURE 10-5. Comparing Track & Trace with other projects by leveraging Ignite project dimensions

IIC RA: Usage Viewpoint

The IIC RA Usage Viewpoint is represented by the Use Case Analysis and the Ignite Solution Sketch, which depicts the key stakeholders and assets as well as the core business processes, rules, and data.

USE CASES

The initial use cases for the Track & Trace testbed have been captured in the form of UML use case diagrams, as shown Figure 10-6. The team decided to include two actors as key users: a factory worker and a production engineer. While the factory worker should be able to execute tightening runs via their handheld nutrunner, the engineer should be able to analyze and manage the nutrunners. Note that we omitted actions like geofence-based enabling of nutrunners from the use case diagram, as this is internal system functionality.

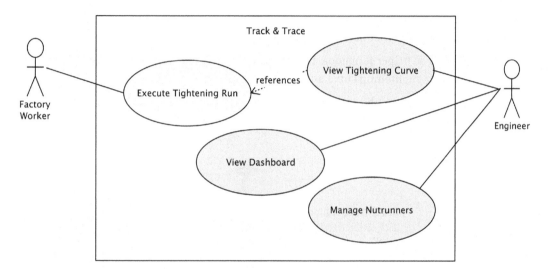

FIGURE 10-6. Track & Trace use cases

SOLUTION SKETCH

The Track & Trace testbed is depicted in a standard Ignite | IoT solution sketch (Figure 10-7). The event section captures the most important events:

- The Bosch Rexroth Nexo nutrunner sends the tightening result via WiFi immediately after each tightening run. The data transmitted includes the program used, success status, and detailed data from the tightening run, including torque and angle.

- The Cisco Prime Server (not depicted) generates geofencing alerts each time the tool is moved within the coverage of the WiFi network.

The UI sections provide an overview of the primary interfaces for the customer and system operator:

- The Tool Fleet Management UI provides an overview of the states of all assets managed by the system. In the case of the nutrunners, this includes the last-known positions, online status, battery levels, programs used, utilization ratios, etc.

- The Tool Tracking UI provides a visualization of the shop floors via 2D/3D map views with the tools displayed accordingly.

- The Tightening Curve UI provides tool-specific details regarding a single asset, including a visualization of the last tightening runs for a specific nutrunner.

The Processes, Rules, and Data sections provide corresponding business middleware functionality:

- The Processes section describes the business processes that should be run if, for example, a nutrunner requires maintenance or needs to be assigned.

- Rules are used as helper functions, focusing on complex calculations like evaluating device data (e.g., tightening curve analysis) or complex geofencing algorithms.

- Data persistence covers the configuration of the assets as well as tracking and tightening histories as configured by the customer.

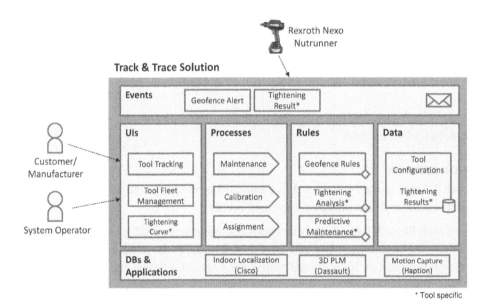

FIGURE 10-7. Solution sketch for the Track & Trace testbed

The complete solution is packaged as a single application that can be deployed in cloud environments. The services provided by Cisco, Dassault, and Haption are integrated via external cloud services.

IIC RA: Functional Viewpoint

As indicated in the corresponding section of Part II, the functional design focused on a lightweight analysis suitable for an Agile development approach, as opposed to a fully fledged, detailed specification. In particular, there was a strong focus on UI mock-up creation for the users of the system.

GETTING STARTED: UI MOCK-UPS

The initial UI mock-ups created during this phase are shown in the following figures. The team decided to focus on three main screens and put the more complex configurations into a specific menu (shown in the top-right corner of the UI mock-ups).

The first screen, shown in Figure 10-8, depicts the assets within the different shop floors (e.g., asset tracking). Usually, a factory is split into different halls or areas, which can be easily selected. The map shown at the righthand side allows for scroll and zoom operations. Currently active nutrunners are shown in green in the interface, while disabled nutrunners are shown in red. The user should be able to click on a specific nutrunner location to obtain more information. If they click the link within this information, they are directed to the tool-specific screen within asset management.

The tool-specific screen (Figure 10-9) shows the data transmitted by the assets. The user can select an asset and see the available data transmissions sorted by time, as in the following image. A detailed view is shown on the righthand side. In the case of the Nexo nutrunner, this includes a visualization of the tightening run data (tightening curve), the program used, the status, as well as the time and location information.

The last UI mock-up screen (Figure 10-10) discussed focused on the KPI dashboard. Interestingly, the team was initially unsure about the core KPIs. While the experts from Tech Mahindra discussed more than 60 different manufacturing-specific high-level KPIs, other partners wanted to cut these to fewer than 10 of the most important ones, as the testbed implementation should focus on the core ideas of the Track & Trace scenario and not become too industry specific. It was decided to move this discussion to a later date, which was made easy due to the Agile implementation approach selected.

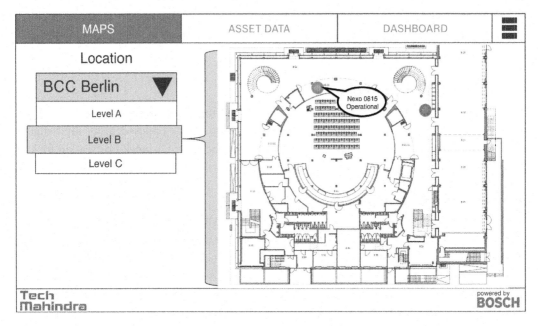

FIGURE 10-8. Mock-up for map overview

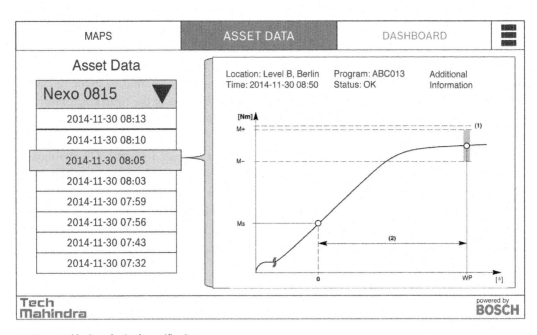

FIGURE 10-9. Mock-up for tool-specific view

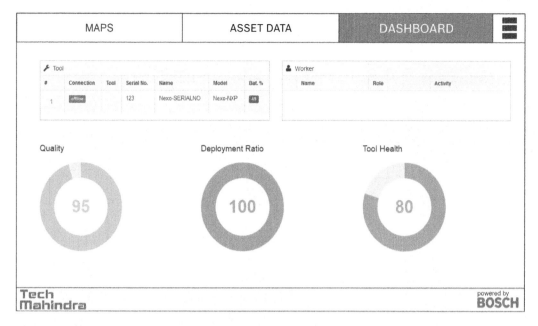

MAPS	ASSET DATA	DASHBOARD	≣

Tool

#	Connection	Tool	Serial No.	Name	Model	Bat. %
1	offline		123	Nexo-SERIALNO	Nexo-NXP	45

Worker

Name	Role	Activity

Quality
95

Deployment Ratio
100

Tool Health
80

Tech Mahindra

powered by
BOSCH

FIGURE 10-10. Mock-up for dashboard

DOMAIN MODEL

The team created a high-level Domain Model, as shown in Figure 10-11. For the sake of clarity, we omitted most of the detailed attributes. The model follows a formal style that requires one root node (stereotype "root_instance") under which all nodes are subsumed. Because the Track & Trace solution should be operated by different parties as instances of the testbed, an operator was defined. Each instance is made up of three core elements: assets, maps, and geofences.

The assets represent the tools managed; in the current phase, the focus is on power tools (shown by an inheritance). Each power tool has to provide a battery status and an operational status as well as a MAC and IP address, as discussed earlier. The Domain Model highlights the possibility to support different power tools, again depicted by inheritance. The nutrunner power tool has a submodel attached, according to the definition from Rexroth (simplified view). Basically, each nutrunner has a set of tightening programs as well as tightenings (runs), each of which is associated with a specific program. A tightening program is made up of several tightening steps, which define different target angles, torques, and so on. An individual tightening is composed of multiple tightening curves, each representing a concrete run of a tightening step.

Each asset has one or more assigned geofences. A geofence is a geographic polygon that describes the inclusive or exclusive area in which the tool is allowed to operate. To enable visualization, maps are used to provide visual representations of where geofences are located. One example would be a map of the different shop floors in a factory.

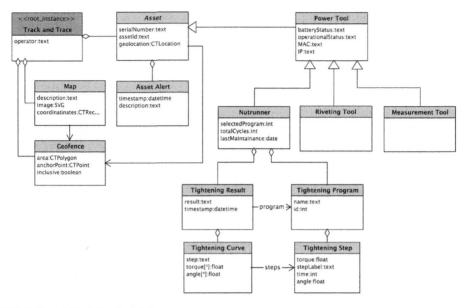

FIGURE 10-11. Domain Model for Track & Trace

ASSET INTEGRATION ARCHITECTURE

The initial Asset Integration Architecture (AIA) for the Track & Trace testbed is depicted in Figure 10-12.

Basically, the Bosch Rexroth nutrunner already provides all the functionality required for the devices and the on-asset business logic level. Furthermore, its integrated FTP client and web server place it in the gateway domain in the AIA. The nutrunner communicates via wireless 802.11a/b/g with Cisco 3700 access points and with a router that centralizes the management of these access points.

The WiFi router forwards wireless visibility metadata from all devices connected to the managed access points to a Cisco Prime Server with Mobility Service Engine (MSE). The physical location of the access points is configured in such a way that every WiFi device is always visible within the scope of multiple range-overlapping access points. Based on the different signal strengths for a single device received by multiple access points, the MSE can triangulate the position of each particular device within the WiFi coverage area using the metadata received.

The nonmetadata communication of the nutrunners (e.g., TCP/IP traffic) is routed to the Bosch M2M middleware, which manages the nutrunners from a logical point of view. The M2M backend hub provides an abstract information model that represents the capabilities of the nutrunners. The information model is connected to specific drivers representing different types of nutrunner. The Bosch M2M central repository manages the information models as well as all devices connected to agent hubs, and provides a REST-full interface to the Track & Trace operations.

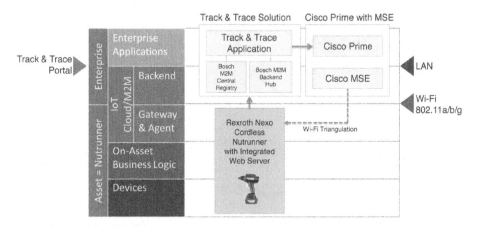

FIGURE 10-12. AIA for Track & Trace

MAPPING THE DOMAIN MODEL TO THE AIA

The mapping of the Domain Model to the AIA is important, because it shows how the data will be distributed in the system. Figure 10-13 shows how this mapping has been carried out for Track & Trace. The following can be observed:

- All asset-related data is centrally managed by the central asset registry component in the backend.

- Asset details (e.g., tightening curve, etc.) are distributed between the backend and the assets themselves. The backend stores this data for all assets for a long time, while the assets only store their own data, and for a limited time only.

- Geolocation data is managed by the Cisco component in the backend.

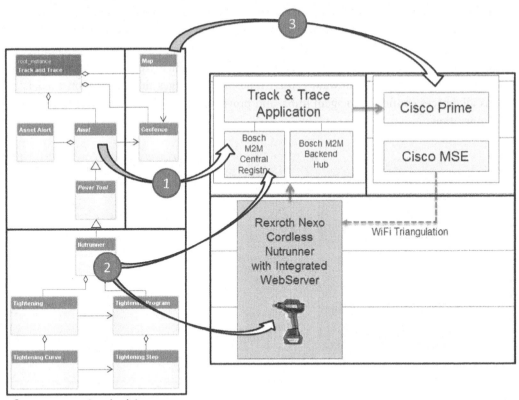

Source: www.enterprise-iot.org

FIGURE 10-13. Data distribution in the AIA

SOA

The definition of a set of open interfaces is one of the key deliverables of the Track & Trace testbed. The goal is to have a modular architecture, which allows integration with different industrial power tools, but also with different indoor localization technologies.

To achieve this goal, the interfaces will be grouped into three main areas:

- Asset-specific data and functions, such as asset location, geofence definitions, geofence violation events, and so on, as introduced in the asset, map, and geofence entities in the Domain Model.

- Data and functions specific to handheld power tools, such as tool status, battery load, battery life, emergency shutdown, and so on, represented by the power tools entity of the Domain Model.

- And finally, tool domain-specific data and interfaces, such as for nutrunners, riveting tools, measurement tools, and the like.

Figure 10-14 provides an overview of the layering of these three sets of interfaces.

FIGURE 10-14. Layering of Track & Trace

As discussed in the interview with Roman Wambacher in "Recommendations" on page 294, managing large numbers of complex interfaces to highly heterogeneous assets and devices is one of the biggest challenges in an IoT project. In Track & Trace, we are looking at integrating different tools from different vendors, such as drilling, tightening, and riveting tools. Each tool interface can be quite complex, with hundreds of different properties and functions. In addition, the interfaces are likely to evolve over time, meaning that we will have to deal with multiple versions of interfaces. To address this challenge in the Track & Trace testbed, we decided to standardize on a common language for defining tool interfaces. This language is based on the Vorto Open Source standard, which is managed by the Eclipse Foundation as part of their IoT stack (more details here: *https://projects.eclipse.org/proposals/vorto*). Vorto is a standard that supports the definition of interfaces for complex hierarchies of assets and devices in the IoT. Technically, Vorto defines a DSL that can be used as an Interface Definition Language (IDL) for the IoT. Vorto comes with a set of valuable tools such as code generators to support different communication protocols like MQTT, as well as a repository to manage asset and device interfaces.

One key deliverable of the Track & Trace testbed is a repository of interfaces for different tools that can be integrated in the solution (Figure 10-15). This enables tool vendors to provide implementations of these interfaces for their individual tools. Or, alternatively, manufacturers can use this mechanism to integrate tools from different vendors themselves. Because of the importance of providing a set of open standards for Track & Trace, the project plans to work with the Object Management Group (OMG) on the standardization of tool interfaces, as well as with the Eclipse Foundation on managing the associated open source aspects.

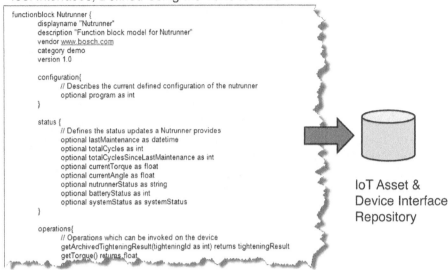

Tool Interfaces, Defined Using the Vorto IoT/IDL

```
functionblock Nutrunner {
        displayname "Nutrunner"
        description "Function block model for Nutrunner"
        vendor www.bosch.com
        category demo
        version 1.0

        configuration{
                // Describes the current defined configuration of the nutrunner
                optional program as int
        }

        status {
                // Defines the status updates a Nutrunner provides
                optional lastMaintenance as datetime
                optional totalCycles as int
                optional totalCyclesSinceLastMaintenance as int
                optional currentTorque as float
                optional currentAngle as float
                optional nutrunnerStatus as string
                optional batteryStatus as int
                optional systemStatus as systemStatus
        }

        operations{
                // Operations which can be invoked on the device
                getArchivedTighteningResult(tighteningId as int) returns tighteningResult
                getTorque() returns float
```

IoT Asset &
Device Interface
Repository

FIGURE 10-15. Interface definitions for Track & Trace tools

IIC RA: Implementation Viewpoint

The Track & Trace testbed will be deployed in a number of different environments. Usually, each factory has a production or shop-floor network that connects the machines being used. The business systems are usually located in a different network called the service network. For the BCW keynote demo, this distinction was not made.

SOFTWARE ARCHITECTURE

The high-level software architecture and connectivity model is shown in Figure 10-16. It depicts how the data is sent from the Nexo power tool via "open protocol" to the agent hub software after each tightening run. Furthermore, the tool transmits the tightening curve directly to an FTP server. The Nexo driver implementation of the agent hub fetches the curve data each time a tightening is registered and stores the event data within a MongoDB. The central registry is then notified of a new event. The Track & Trace solution itself is made up of two core applications and an additional application for the BCW keynote demo. The first application ("Connect App") retrieves the current location of all registered assets from the Cisco servers and forwards it to registered clients. The "T&T App" represents the core business application. For the purposes of showcasing the testbed at the BCW keynote, a simplified UI was developed that leverages the existing functions of the "T&T App."

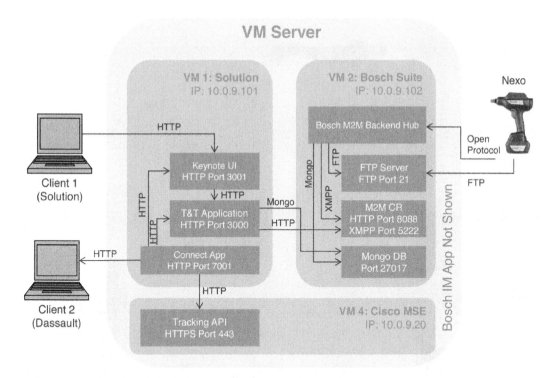

FIGURE 10-16. Track & Trace software architecture for Bosch ConnectedWorld

TECHNICAL INFRASTRUCTURE VIEW

The final deployment of the BCW Track & Trace instance is shown in Figure 10-17. The shop-floor network is represented as a private C-class network within the IP range 192.168.0.x. It only includes the production machines (e.g., nutrunners) and the sensors required for micro-level tracking. All other systems are deployed on a services network, represented by the IP addresses 10.0.9.x. The gap between both networks is bridged by the Cisco router depicted at the bottom of the figure, which can be configured based on different firewall settings.

Another important aspect of the technical deployment view is shown in Figure 10-18. It highlights the positioning of access points within the conference venue. The nutrunner tools can be tracked inside every triangle that can be created by three different access points. As we can see, the entire conference hall is covered, as well as two specific areas outside.

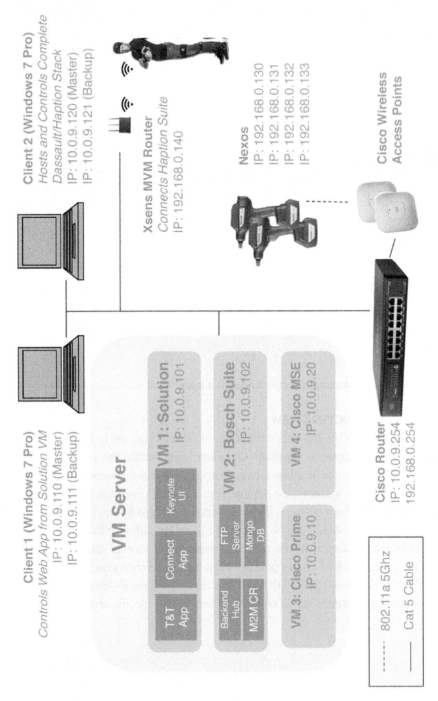

Client 2 (Windows 7 Pro)
Hosts and Controls Complete
Dassault/Haption Stack
IP: 10.0.9.120 (Master)
IP: 10.0.9.121 (Backup)

Xsens MVM Router
Connects Haption Suite
IP: 192.168.0.140

Nexos
IP: 192.168.0.130
IP: 192.168.0.131
IP: 192.168.0.132
IP: 192.168.0.133

Cisco Wireless Access Points

Client 1 (Windows 7 Pro)
Controls Web App from Solution VM
IP: 10.0.9.110 (Master)
IP: 10.0.9.111 (Backup)

VM Server

VM 1: Solution
IP: 10.0.9.101

T&T App | Connect App | Keynote UI

VM 2: Bosch Suite
IP: 10.0.9.102

Backend Hub | FTP Server
M2M CR | Mongo DB

VM 3: Cisco Prime
IP: 10.0.9.10

VM 4: Cisco MSE
IP: 10.0.9.20

Cisco Router
IP: 10.0.9.254
192.168.0.254

- - - - - 802.11a 5Ghz
――― Cat 5 Cable

FIGURE 10-17. Track & Trace technical infrastructure for Bosch ConnectedWorld

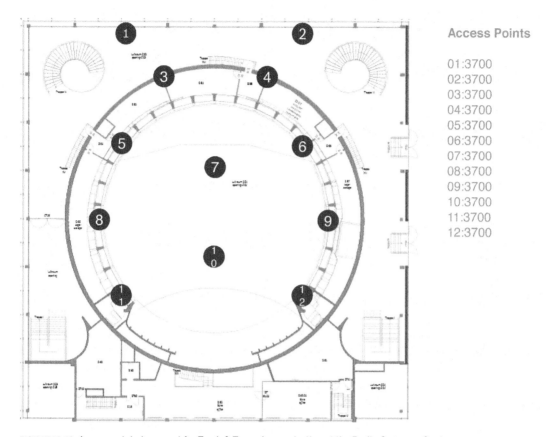

Access Points

01:3700
02:3700
03:3700
04:3700
05:3700
06:3700
07:3700
08:3700
09:3700
10:3700
11:3700
12:3700

FIGURE 10-18. Access point placement for Track & Trace demonstration at the Berlin Congress Center

Results

Figure 10-19 provides an overview of the digital models that were created using Dassault Systèmes' 3DExperience products (CATIA and DELMIA mainly), including the conference site BCC, the engine that we used as a work item, and, of course, the Nexo nutrunner. On the lower righthand corner of the conference site model, you can see three smaller circles. These represent the position of the Nexo. Using Cisco indoor localization technology, we are able to track the movement of the Nexo in the 3D model.

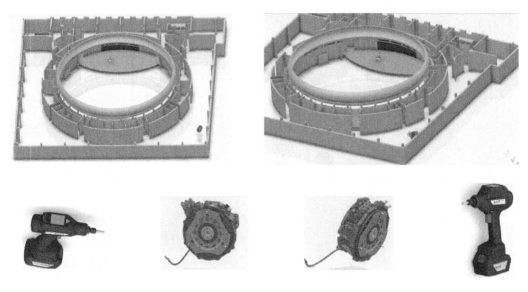

FIGURE 10-19. Test environment—3D models

The next thing we wanted to demonstrate was the ability to use high-precision localization technology for tracking tool positions relative to the work item. For the demo, we also wanted to show the movement of the person operating the tool. We achieved this by combining technology from Haption and Xsens. In Figure 10-20, you can see an operator wearing a number of Xsens sensors. This operator is also depicted in the 3D model, which was enabled by the Dassault Systèmes 3DExperience platform and updated using Haption technology. Each movement carried out by the physical operator is mirrored by an identical movement by the avatar in the 3D model. The system also provides a virtual training facility that allows the pre-recording of certain movements. The system follows the movement of the operator and then sends an error message if the predefined sequence of movements is not followed correctly.

Once they have successfully completed basic tightening training, the operator performs the actual tightening move itself. In Figure 10-21, we can see the corresponding tightening performance data from the portal. This data is transferred via WiFi from the Nexo to the back-end in real time.

Figure 10-22 (an extract from the dashboard) shows four selected KPIs for operational equipment efficiency (OEE) and tool fleet performance.

And finally, Figure 10-23 provides an overview of the tool fleet as well as the status of the individual tools.

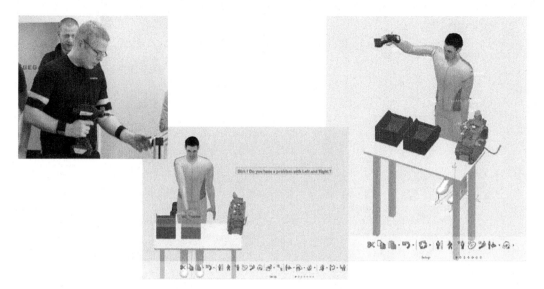

FIGURE 10-20. Physical operator and virtual avatar

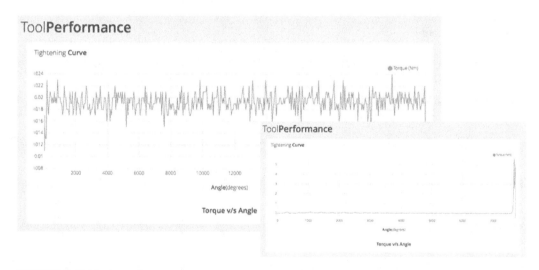

FIGURE 10-21. Tightening performance

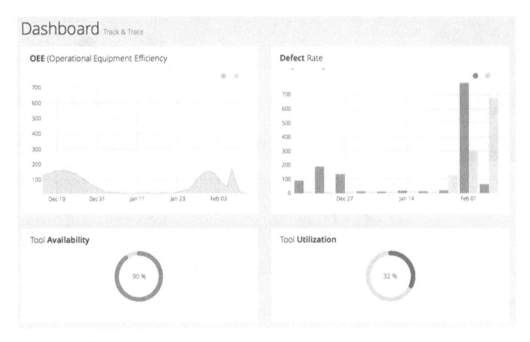

FIGURE 10-22. Dashboard

FIGURE 10-23. Tool fleet overview and details

Of course, none of this would have been possible without a great team. As discussed many times (e.g., see "Clash of Two Worlds: Machine Camp Versus Internet Camp" on page 9), one of the main challenges of an IoT project is the need for a multidisciplinary approach—this project was no exception. In Figure 10-24, you can see experts from many disciplines who worked together to make this project happen: N. Ramanathan ("NR") and C. Rajeswaran from Tech Mahindra; C. Thiemich, F. Puhlmann, and D. Slama from Bosch SI; J. Veaux-Logeat and G. Shenoy from Dassault; D. Vasilev ("Mitko") from Cisco; and A. Geneslay, and Q. Parent from Haption.

FIGURE 10-24. The team

The final demo was successfully showcased at Bosch ConnectedWorld 2015 in Berlin, with Bosch Group Chairman Dr. Volkmar Denner (Figure 10-25).

FIGURE 10-25. Track & Trace demo at Bosch ConnectedWorld 2015

| **CHAPTER 10: DEVELOPING TRACK & TRACE WITH THE IGNITE | IOT METHODOLOGY**

CHAPTER 11

Conclusions and Outlook

IN THE FOLLOWING DISCUSSION WITH CHRISTIAN THIEMICH (SENIOR SOLUTION ARCHITECT at Bosch SI) and Narayanan "NR" Ramanathan (VP & Global Head – Connected Engineering & Analytics at Tech Mahindra), we review their experience of implementing the first milestone of the Track & Trace testbed based on the Ignite | IoT Methodology.

Dirk Slama: Christian, what was the key learning from this project for you so far?

Christian Thiemich: Working in an internationally distributed team, spanning Singapore, Bangalore, Germany, and Canada, is not always easy. Because we all speak different languages, it was important that we at least agreed on one methodology, to help us focus on what was most important.

Dirk Slama: NR, what else?

Narayanan Ramanathan: The Ignite framework provides a checklist of the main points that need to be covered in order to bring your business ideas to life. This helped us with Phase 1 of the development of the Track & Trace testbed.

Dirk Slama: Did the fact that this was also an Industrial Internet Consortium testbed have a role to play in this project?

Christian Thiemich: Because the focus of the Industrial Internet Consortium is a fast, go-to-market strategy, there is always room for improvement. This approach lent itself well to the Ignite framework, which allows for an Agile or more classical development strategy. It provided the structural support we needed to start splitting up the different work packages and get things done.

Dirk Slama: What's next?

Narayanan Ramanathan: In addition to the existing framework, what we'd like to get out of Ignite in the future is an approach that will help us to keep track of the Ignite artifacts and requirements that have been defined at a high level during the implementation phase.

Dirk Slama: NR, Christian—thank you so much!

APPENDIX A

References

- [BoschCH14] *http://www.bosch-softtec.com/connected_horizon.html.*

- [Van88] Vandermerwe, S., Rada, J. 1988. Servitization of Business: Adding value by adding services, *European Management Journal* 6 (4): 314-324.

- [Aston14] Aston Business School. "Servitization Impact Study. *https://connect.innova-teuk.org/documents/416351/3926914/Servitization+impact+study.pdf/.*

- [HSG14] *http://www.iot-lab.ch/.*

- [TH1] *http://www.automotivetimes.com/chinese-students-successfully-hack-tesla-model-s/.*

- [MR13] Machina Research. 2013. "Research Note: What's the Difference Between M2M and IoT?"

- [MR14] Machina Research. 2014. "Research Note: More of a Network of Subnets of Things than an Internet of Things."

- [OR14] *http://radar.oreilly.com/2014/02/the-industrial-iot-isnt-the-same-as-the-consumer-iot.html.*

- [NI1] U.S. Energy Information Administration. Form EIA-860 Annual Electric Generator Report, and Form EIA-860M. (See Table ES3 in the March 2011 *Electric Power Monthly*).

- [NI2] NI Week 2013 Conference. Cook, Bernie. "Duke Energy Asset Monitoring."

- [NI3] NI Week 2013 Conference. Cook, Bernie. "Duke Energy: Deploying Smart Maintenance and Diagnostics Update for Electrical Power Generation."

- [NI4] NI 9068 CompactRIO System. *http://www.ni.com/compactrio/whatis/.*

- [LBL1] *https://building-microgrid.lbl.gov/microgrid-definitions.*

- [SCR14] *http://www.bosch.com/en/com/boschglobal/virtual_power_plants/smart_city_rheintal/smart-city-rheintal.html.*

- [AB1] *http://www.airbusgroup.com/int/en/story-overview/factory-of-the-future.html.*

- [OP1] *https://opcfoundation.org/.*

- [TS1] *http://www.ieee802.org/1/pages/tsn.html.*

- [TY1] *http://www.wsj.com/articles/SB10001424052702303704304579378592734446798.*

- [I41] *http://www.acatech.de/fileadmin/user_upload/Baumstruktur_nach_Website/Acatech/ root/de/Material_fuer_Sonderseiten/Industrie_4.0/Final_report__Industrie_4.0_accessible.pdf.*

- [DF1] *http://www.smartfactory-kl.de/.*

- [LT1] *http://www.intellion.com/fileadmin/user_upload/ 2006-03_LotTrack_IEEE_Pervasive_Computing_02.pdf.*

- [FS09] *http://de.slideshare.net/FrostandSullivan/cleaning-industry-a-strategic-analysis-of-asia-pacific-markets.*

- [CERN09] CERN faq – LHC the Guide. *http://cds.cern.ch/record/1165534/files/CERN-Brochure-2009-003-Eng.pdf.*

- [MI1] *http://www2.technologyreview.com/tr50/2014/.*

- [SC1] *http://www.scania.com/watch/.*

- [AB2] *http://www.airbus.com/company/market/orders-deliveries/.*

- [IL1] *http://iotsecuritylab.com/nest-privacy-policy-7-best-practices/.*

- [IS1] *http://resources.infosecinstitute.com/test-security-iot-smart-devices/.*

- [OW1] *https://www.owasp.org/index.php/OWASP_Internet_of_Things_Top_Ten_Project#tab=OWASP_Internet_of_Things_Top_10_for_2014.*

- [SD1] *http://en.wikipedia.org/wiki/Secure_by_design.*

- [FS1] *https://www.iamthecavalry.org/domains/automotive/5star/.*

- [ES1] *https://www.escrypt.com/fileadmin/escrypt/pdf/CycurHSM-Whitepaper.pdf.*

- [Ref2] *https://www.arm.com/files/pdf/EIU_Internet_Business_Index_WEB.PDF.*

- [ST1] *http://en.wikipedia.org/wiki/Stuxnet.*

- [DR1] *http://www.darkreading.com/vulnerabilities—threats/hiring-hackers-to-secure-the-internet-of-things/d/d-id/1318107.*

- [DR2] *http://www.darkreading.com/attacks-breaches/lost-in-translation-hackers-hacking-consumer-devices/d/d-id/1140272.*

- [AN1] *http://www.autonews.com/article/20150114/OEM09/150119807/bosch-outlines-10-year-path-to-door-to-door-driverless-car.*

- [CAN1] *http://en.wikipedia.org/wiki/CAN_bus.*

- [BSI1] *https://www.bosch-si.com/solutions/mobility/mobility.html.*

- [LL1] Yeomans, Gillian. 2014. "Autonomous vehicles." Lloyd's Exposure Management.

- [FC1] *http://www.driverless-future.com/?page_id=384.*

- [TI1] Mujica, Fernando. "Scalable electronics driving autonomous vehicle technologies." Texas Instruments. *http://www.ti.com/lit/wp/sszy010a/sszy010a.pdf.*

- [IE1] *http://spectrum.ieee.org/automaton/robotics/artificial-intelligence/how-google-self-driving-car-works.*

- [LA11] L. Alonso, et al. "Ultrasonic Sensors in Urban Traffic Driving-Aid Systems." Open Access Sensors, ISSN 1424-8220. *http://www.mdpi.com/1424-8220/11/1/661.*

- [MI2] "One Way Google's Cars Localize Themselves." *http://mappingignorance.org/2014/04/07/one-way-googles-cars-localize/.*

- [ST2] *http://www.bosch-presse.de/presseforum/details.htm?txtID=6424&locale=en.*

- [UBI1] *http://money.usnews.com/money/personal-finance/articles/2014/01/13/should-you-try-pay-as-you-drive-insurance.*

- [UBI2] *http://www.insurancenetworking.com/news/mobility/auto-insurance-usage-based-premiums-apps-telematics-34833-1.html.*

- [OBD1] *http://en.wikipedia.org/wiki/On-board_diagnostics.*

- [LN1] Kendall, T., Crandown, C., and Hassib, A. "Data Management: The Key to Unlocking the Potential of Usage-Based Insurance." CSMG and LexisNexis.

- [ST4] *http://www.statista.com/statistics/200002/international-car-sales-since-1990/.*

- [JC1] Hybrid Cars. Cobb, Jeff. 2014. "Global Plug-in Car Sales Now Over 600,000." *http://www.hybridcars.com/global-plug-in-car-sales-now-over-600000/.*

- [AN2] *http://www.autonews.com/article/20140904/OEM01/140909919/tesla-picks-nevada-for-giant-battery-plant.*

- [WSJ1] *http://blogs.wsj.com/moneybeat/2014/03/27/analyst-on-tesla-we-see-rising-gigafactory-risks/.*

- [WC1] *http://wallstcheatsheet.com/automobiles/top-10-electric-vehicles-with-the-longest-driving-range.html/?a=viewall.*

- [WI2] *http://en.wikipedia.org/wiki/Tesla_station.*

- [DB1] *http://blog.bosch-si.com/categories/smart-city/2014/10/connected-city-get-out-of-the-silos/.*

- [BM1] *http://www.bmi-lab.ch/.*

- [AE1] *https://agileelements.wordpress.com/2008/10/29/what-is-a-center-of-excellence/.*

- [PM1] *http://en.wikipedia.org/wiki/A_Guide_to_the_Project_Management_Body_of_Knowledge.*

- [EC1] "Commission takes first step towards rollout of eCall system," TRL (Transport Research Library, UK). 2011. *http://www.trl.co.uk/trl-news-hub/transport-news/latest-transport-news/commission-takes-first-step-towards-rollout-of-ecall-system_800724486.htm.*

- [EC2] *http://pr.euractiv.com/pr/ecall-mandatory-1st-march-2018-122453.*

- [OB1] *https://en.wikipedia.org/wiki/On-board_diagnostics.*

- [SI1] *http://www.siemens.com/press/de/pressemitteilungen/?press=/de/pressemitteilungen/2010/corporate_communication/axx20101003.htm&content[]=CC&content[]=Corp.*

- [IP1] *http://www.innovationprojectcanvas.com.*

- [SPS] *https://www.scrum.org/Resources/What-is-Scaled-Scrum.*

- [LeSS] *http://less.works/.*

- [SAFe] *http://www.scaledagileframework.com/.*

- [AS] *http://www.agilesoc.com/2012/09/30/guest-blog-a-heretic-speaks-why-hardware-doesnt-fit-the-agile-model/.*

- [EBPM] *http://bpm-alliance.org.*

- [LYYJL] Jaw, Link, and Lee, Yuh-Jye. "Engine Diagnostics in the eyes of machine learning." Proceedings of the 2014 ASME Turbo Expo. June 16-20, 2014: Dusseldorf, Germany.

- [DSAR] Donald Simon and Aidan Rinehart, "A model-based anomaly detection approach for analyzing streaming aircraft engine measurement data," Proceedings of the 2014 ASME Turbo Expo, June 16-20, 2014, Dusseldorf, Germany.

- [FO1] *http://www.forbes.com/sites/danwoods/2015/01/26/james-dixon-imagines-a-data-lake-that-matters/.*

- [LI1] *http://community.lithium.com/t5/Science-of-Social-blog/Big-Data-Reduction-1-Descriptive-Analytics/ba-p/77766.*

- [RH1] *http://horicky.blogspot.de/2014/08/lambda-architecture-principles.html.*

- [ML1] Duda, Richard O., Peter E. Hart, and David G. Stork. *Pattern Recognition.* New York: Wiley & Sons, 2001.

- [ML2] *https://en.wikipedia.org/wiki/Machine_learning.*

Index

Symbols

E

e-education projects (Boston), 159

EAI (enterprise application integration), 73, 243, 325

eCall services, 8, 75, 122, 172

    as example of Enterprise IoT solution, 31

    Asset Integration Architecture, 122, 229

    business case, 195

    executive summary, 216

    mandatory, in the EU, 124

    project management, 207

Eclipse Foundation, 389

economic development (Chicago), 156

EDI (Electronic Data Interchange), 267

electric power grids, 39

    smart grid, 393

    smart grid IoT connections, 47

    smart grids and microgrids, overview of, 56

    traditional grids versus future smart grids, 40

Electric Power Research Institute (EPRI), 51

electric vehicles

    and cross-energy management, 140

    as power consumers, 60

    as power storage units, 60

    charging services, 134

    eMobility movement, 134

    outlook, 152

    remote management, 138

electromobility infrastructure, 59

    in Smart City Rheintal project, 60

electronic control units (ECUs), 118

Elfrink, Wim, interview with, 162-165

embedded generation, 56

embedded systems, 274

emergency services (see eCall services)

Emerson case study, 336

eMobility

    electric vehicle (EV) charging services, 134

    eRoaming, 137

    EV remote management, 138

    EVs and cross-energy management, 140

employee incentives encouraging innovation, 186

encryption technologies, 365

end-to-end solutions, 193

energy trading, 44

energy, smart, 39-66, 77

    digitization and its influence, 41

        adoption of smart energy technologies, 46

        customers, 46

        distribution and metering, 44

        generation of power, 43

        marketing, sales, and service, 45

        storage of electricity, 45

        transmission of energy, 44

    traditional grids versus future smart grids, 40

engine control units (ECUs), 263

engineering, digital, 71

enterprise application integration (EAI), 73, 243, 325

enterprise applications (in Enterprise IoT solution), 31

Enterprise BPM (business process management), 231

Enterprise BPM Alliance, 358

Enterprise IoT, 23-32

    CEP and, 334

    definitions of key terms, 29

    differences between M2M and IoT, 23

    focus and scope of solutions, 27

    Subnets of Things (SoTs) in evoluion from M2M, 26

Enterprise IoT architecture pattern, 286

Enterprise IoT solutions

    components of, 30

    eCall example, 31

enterprise resource planning (ERP), 263

Enterprise SOA (service-oriented architecture), 231

enterprise tier (in AIA), 228

enterprise, definition in Enterprise IoT, 30

EPRI Asset Fault Signature Database, 52

EPRI Remaining Useful Life Database, 52

European Research Cluster on the Internet of Things (IERC), 77

EVs (see electric vehicles)

executive summary (initial design phase), 216

extended field tests milestone, 222

F

fail fast, fail often, fail cheap VC business model, 10

field data analytics, 132

field intensity measurement, 398

field tests, 222

    extended field tests milestone, 222

field-programmable gate arrays (FPGAs), 52

    in LHCb experiment at CERN, 114

filtering, intelligent, 108

firewalls, 366

first integrated release milestone, 221

combining with manufacturing, 74
operating, 74
IoT Solution Lifecycle (Plan/Build/Run), 209,
211-213
assumptions, 211
descriptions of Plan/Build/Run phases, 211
project structure, 212
IoT Solution Sketch, 216
creating in initial design phase, 218
IoT solutions (see Ignite | IoT Solution Delivery)
key elements of, 217
IoT strategy, 182
IoT Technology Profiles, 268-401
IoTS (Internet of Things and Services), 166
IoTS formula, 12
IP (Internet Protocol), industrial bus systems and,
73
IrDA, 277
IT infrastructure for IoT-based services, 7

J

Jarp, Sverre, 108

K

Kallenbach, Rainer, 152
Kärcher Fleet Management solution, 92-99
role-based web portal, 94
key performance indicators (see KPIs)
Kiviat diagrams, 220, 257
Klemd, Olaf (Bosch), 78
KLM case study, 399
learning and best practices, 400
project management perspective, 400
Kodak, inability to deal with disruptive technologies, 179
KPIs (key performance indicators), 94
for smart cities, 161, 165
Kryszak, Bernard, 43, 47

L

Lamanna, Massimo, 110
Lambda Architecture, 342
Large Hadron Collider (LHC), 107
Lee, Michael, 405
LHC (Large Hadron Collider), 107
LHCb experiment at CERN (case study), 107-115,
321
Asset Integration Architecture, 112
data management, 108

lessons learned and outlook, 114
physical data analysis, 111
Li-Fi, 315
LIDAR, 145
lightbulbs, remote-controlled, 12
load management
consumer devices in Rheintal Smart City
project, 60
electromobility infrastructure, 60
local compute and storage, 272
logistics systems, adaptive, 76
lot-tracking solutions (intelligent), 87-90
LotTrack, 89
low-power, wide-area (LPWA) network providers,
315
low-power, wide-area (LWPA) networks, 277, 300
LWM2M protocol, 284
LWPA (see low-power, wide-area networks)

M

M2M (Machine-to-Machine)
conclusions and outlook, 171
data management scenario, basic M2M, 330
deciding whether to use M2M middleware,
228, 236
Enterprise IoT versus, 27
evolution to IoT, Subnets of Things (SoTs), 26
global cellular M2M connections, 174
IoT versus, 23
M2M application in Tech Mahindra UBI solution, 127
M2M architectural pattern, 265, 285
M2M backend/IoT cloud, 381
M2M tier in IoT solutions, 261
M2M/IoT communication services, 298
M2M/IoT gateways, 271
mobile M2M communication, 302
momentum of IoT versus, 14
scalable opportunities for MNOs in automotive, 171
M2M Alliance, 77
M2M Communication Module, 303
M2M Device, 303
M2M/IoT application platforms, 378
M2M/IoT communication services
defining best practices for IoT connectivity
platforms, 312
recommendations and outlook, 311
outlook, 315
recommendations, 319

ultrasonic technology (for automated driving), 145
UML elements for domain models, 227
Unified Access Connectivity Environment (U-ACE), 316
unsupervised learning, 346
usage-based insurance (UBI), 125, 141
 AIA for Tech Mahindra UBI solution, 125
use cases
 for Track & Trace testbed, 425
 gathering for functional design in initial
  design phase, 223
user interaction, 361
user interfaces (see UIs)

V

validation milestone, 222
value added (IoT business model), 191
value proposition (IoT business model), 191
value-added networks, adaptive logistics and, 76
Vasilev, Mitko, 290
vehicle area networks (VANs), 316
vehicle control unit (VCU), 263
vehicle state data, 130
vehicle-to-grid concept (electricity storage), 45
Vehicle2X, 145
vehicles, connected, 117-153
 car dashboard and infotainment, 119
 car sharing, 140-141
 connected enterprise solutions, 129-134
  fleet management, 129-132
 eMobility, 134-140
 intermodal services, 142
 outlook, 152-153
 overview, connected vehicle and related services, 117
 value-added services, 121-129
  bCall, 124
  eCall, 122
  reasons for no open car app platform, 128
  stolen vehicle recovery, 124
  usage-based insurance, 125
 vehicle functions, parking, 150
 vehicle functions, toward automated driving,
  142-150
venture capital (VC) business model for Internet
 camp, 10
vertical integraton, production modules and business appliications, 84
verticals, M2M versus IoT, 25
virtual power plants (VPPs), 56-63

VPP/MMS, 57
visual light communications (VLC), 315
Vodafone portal Dashboard for M2M connectivity,
 309
Vogel, Silke, 189, 189
VPP/MMS (virtual power plant/microgrid management system), 57
 consumer devices, load management, 60
 electromobility infrastructure, 60
 forecasting photovoltaic energy, 59
VPPs (see virtual power plants)

W

Wambacher, Roman, 274, 295, 380
waterfall development, 211
 combining with agile, 255
wearable electronics (see smart wearables)
wearables, 271
Web 3.0 Platform (Bosch), 185
Weiss, Christian, 251
Westcott, Brian, 101
WiFi, 276
Willke, Ted, 350
wind turbines, 56
Winterberg, Torsten, 358
wireless communication, 237
 device integration through, 267
wireless connectivity
 M2M and IoT solutions' reliance on, 171
 satellite, 300
wireless personal area network (WPAN), 271
wireless technologies, 15
 for sensor networks, 289
 for sensors in transport and logistics, 286
 in smart home sector, 283
 indoor localization, 395-401
 key local wireless technologies, 275
 M2M/IoT communication services, 299
 metropolitan area networks (MANs), 300
 sensor networks in industrial sector, 290
 wireless sensor networks, 277
  comparison to IDACs, 394
  connectivity technologies, 279
Wollinger, Thomas, 369
work environment, Industrial IoT and, 76
workflows, 357
workstreams, 213
 asset preparation, 250
 backend integration, 249
 backend services, 243

About the Authors

Dirk Slama, Director of Business Development at Bosch Software Innovations, has 20 years experience in large-scale distributed system design (EAM, SOA, BPM, M2M). He is also coauthor of *Enterprise CORBA*, *Enterprise SOA*, and *Enterprise BPM*.

Frank Puhlmann, Head of Project Methodology and Solution Architecture at Bosch Software Innovations, has a strong background in distributed systems design, including research, project execution, and methodology.

Jim Morrish, Founder and Chief Research Officer at Machina Research, is a respected M2M and IoT industry expert with over 20 years experience in strategy consulting, operations management, and telecoms research.

Dr. Rishi Bhatnagar, VP Digital Enterprise Services at Tech Mahindra, has around 20 years experience in managing global customers in the United States, the UK, Germany, Africa, and India. He is an IoT thought leader and recognized business planning and strategy expert.

Community Members

Veronika Brandt joined Bosch Software Innovations in 2010. As Senior Expert for Solution Architecture & Methodology, she focuses on implementing the IoT methodology in projects with respect to requirements analysis and solution design. Before joining Bosch, she worked as an IT consultant for Siemens and BearingPoint. She holds an MBA from the LMU Munich.

Peter Busch is Senior Expert for Corporate Research of Robert Bosch with 20+ years experience in international project management, coaching, and training in SW/HW development. He holds a diploma in computer science and business administration and has worked for, among others, JP Morgan, Sun Microsystems, and the Bosch Group. His current research topics are new business models and ecosystems for all engineering disciplines.

Tobias Conz has been working for Bosch Software Innovations since 2011. As Senior Solution Architect, he is responsible for one of the company's Industry 4.0 solutions for machine monitoring. Before joining Bosch, he worked as consultant for Software AG and IDS Scheer AG.

Peter Fürst's expertise in innovation and innovation management is built on 15+ years of experience. As a managing partner of five i's innovation consulting, he supports companies in their aim to grow through new products, services, and businesses. Peter also trains individuals and teams in innovation management through open seminars, and is a lecturer at the University of Applied Sciences – Vorarlberg.

Jason Garbis, Director of Product Marketing for Identity Management, RSA, has over 25 years of experience in roles that span engineering, professional services, product management, and marketing at various technology companies. Currently, he's responsible for RSA's go-to-market initiatives for Identity and Access Management, and the Internet of Things. He has a BS in computer science from Cornell, an MBA from Northeastern, and is also a published author.

Anuj Jain is a Managing Director at Bosch Software Innovations. He is an entrepreneurial executive with experience in general management, sales, business development, marketing, and alliances. His previous work experience includes Oracle, Nucleus Software, and Honda Cars India.

Michael Jungmann, Managing Director, Dr. Wehner, Jungmann & Wambacher, has a strong background in the development of distributed systems and seven years' experience in the delivery of international large-scale IoT projects. As a co-founder and managing director of WJW, Michael works closely with customers in Industrial and Consumer IoT projects to derive requirements from business goals, leads system architecture, project, and supplier management.

Sven Kappel joined Robert Bosch in 2014. As Senior Expert for Embedded Software & Connected Services, he focuses on IoT Ecosystems within the Bosch business sector Mobility Solutions with respect to requirements engineering and coordination. He is also responsible within the corporate department for the open ideation community. Before joining Robert Bosch, he worked as project leader and senior manager at Bosch Engineering.

Dr. Stephan Otto, Group Manager, Fraunhofer-Gesellschaft, studied computer science and economics. From 2006 to 2009 Mr. Otto gained professional experience in software engineering in different industrial projects (logistics, automotive, healthcare). In 2009, he entered Fraunhofer as a senior researcher. In parallel, he finished his PhD thesis. Since 2010, he is a group manager and is active in the areas of sensor fusion, real-time analysis, and positioning.

Brian Phillippi, Product Marketing Manager for the Embedded Control and Monitoring team at National Instruments, helps manage the I/O modules for the company's industrial, embedded, and data acquisition platforms. Phillippi joined NI in 2011 as an applications engineer and moved to product marketing in 2012. He holds a bachelor's degree in mechanical engineering from Brigham Young University.

Christiane Prager, Business Development Intern, Bosch Software Innovations, has several years' professional experience in strategic management and business development in IT and the Internet industry. Currently, she is responsible for organizing the book project *Enterprise IoT* and its marketing program at Bosch Software Innovations. Christiane holds a BA in business communication management from the University of Applied Sciences Berlin and is working toward an MA in business management.

Mike Prince, Principal M2M Platform Product Manager, Vodafone Group, has 20 years' international experience in telecoms technology and product management with equipment vendors and mobile network operators. He has been working in Vodafone M2M since 2009, initially as the technical architect for the connectivity management platform. Today he leads the product management team responsible for Vodafone's expanding range of global M2M platform products.

Narayanan Ramanathan is VP & Global Head of the Connected Engineering & Analytics Practice at Tech Mahindra and has been instrumental in building this practice as one of the fastest growing global engineering service providers. NR has more than 17 years of professional experience in product design and engineering management. Widely recognized as a thought leader among customers, industry analysts, and media, he has published 31 technical papers in national and international conferences.

Adi Reschenhofer is the founder and CEO of Wyconn. After working for many years on M2M, branch connectivity, and management of enterprise networks for some of Europe's largest firms, Adi launched Wyconn in 2013 with the vision of a radically simpler approach to meeting the needs of OEMs and enterprises, telecom companies, and solution providers in the area of IoT.

Jamie Smith, Director of Embedded Systems, National Instruments, is the global leader of product management and go-to-market strategies for the company's industrial and embedded products, including NI CompactRIO, Vision, Motion, and Wireless. Since joining NI in 1996, Jamie has held key leadership positions in sales, engineering, product strategy, corporate development, and marketing. He has been recently recognized as a Top Embedded Innovator by Embedded Computing Design and received an R&D 100 Award.

Robin J. Smith, Product Management/Strategy Director at Oracle Corporation, is responsible for the Oracle Stream Explorer Event Processing Platform encompassing real-time, event-driven architecture and complex event processing technologies. Evolving and delivering award-winning, innovative products, including the latest Oracle Stream Explorer (a business user friendly visual tool), foundational technologies of Oracle OSGi Fast Data (real-time streaming analytics), and IoT strategies.

Christian Thiemich is located in Singapore and is responsible for shaping the future of manufacturing in Asia by delivering Industry 4.0 solutions. As Senior Solution Architect at Bosch Software Innovations, he is closely working together with customers and Bosch industry experts. Being an Agile development enthusiast, he is clearly driven by business value. Over the last few years, he supported quite a number of complex projects across industries as coach and consultant.

Mitko Vasilev has worked in high technologies since 1996. He has worked for service providers, industrial companies, and lately (since 2003), for Cisco Systems. As of 2013, Mitko is Technology Leader in the EMEA IoT team and CTO/co-founder at openBerlin, Cisco IoT Innovation Platform.

Arthur Viegers joined MongoDB in 2013. As Manager Central Europe & Solutions Architecture, he leads the pre-sales team for MongoDB in central Europe. With over 20 years of experience in logistics, fleet, and engine management systems, he specializes in IoT/M2M solutions. Prior to joining MongoDB, Arthur ran his own fleet management software company with operations in Europe, USA, Brazil, and China.

Silke Vogel joined Bosch Corporate Marketing & Sales in 2012. As Strategic Marketing Manager, she integrates market and customer expertise, enabling new business models and quick decisions. The Web3.0@BBM is one key initiative in this scope. Before joining Bosch, she has worked for 10 years as product marketing manager in an innovation incubator called "Domain Driving Assistance" with the Tier 1 supplier Valeo.

Wolfgang Volz is Senior Project Manager Smart City at Bosch Software Innovations. Wolfgang joined Bosch in 2000. He started within the cooperate research group as project manager and moved on to setting up activities in Asia Pacific in the energy field and managing startup investments. Since 2013, he has been responsible for Smart City projects at Bosch Software Innovations and the strategic alignment of Smart City activities within the Bosch Group worldwide.

Roman Wambacher is Co-Founder and Managing Director, Dr. Wehner, Jungmann & Wambacher. Roman has a technical background in designing embedded systems. Supplemented by deep domain knowledge of the machinery industry, he has 8 years' experience in the delivery of international large-scale industry IoT projects. As a cofounder and managing director of WJW, Roman has specialized in development of value-based business cases, embedded system architecture, as well as project and supplier management.

Dr. Ted Wilke is Senior Principal Engineer at Intel Labs. Ted leads a team that researches large-scale machine learning and data mining techniques for Intel Labs. He developed his expertise in data center technologies over his 17 years with Intel. Ted holds a doctorate in electrical engineering from Columbia University. He won Intel's highest award in 2014 for starting a venture focused on the processing of graph-shaped data.

Colophon

The cover was designed by Edie Freedman. The cover fonts are URW Typewriter and Guardian Sans. The text font is Scala Pro; the heading font is Benton Sans Condensed and URW Typewriter; and the code font is Dalton Maag's Ubuntu Mono.

Get even more for your money.

Join the O'Reilly Community, and register the O'Reilly books you own. It's free, and you'll get:

- $4.99 ebook upgrade offer
- 40% upgrade offer on O'Reilly print books
- Membership discounts on books and events
- Free lifetime updates to ebooks and videos
- Multiple ebook formats, DRM FREE
- Participation in the O'Reilly community
- Newsletters
- Account management
- 100% Satisfaction Guarantee

Signing up is easy:

1. Go to: oreilly.com/go/register
2. Create an O'Reilly login.
3. Provide your address.
4. Register your books.

Note: English-language books only

To order books online:
oreilly.com/store

For questions about products or an order:
orders@oreilly.com

To sign up to get topic-specific email announcements and/or news about upcoming books, conferences, special offers, and new technologies:
elists@oreilly.com

For technical questions about book content:
booktech@oreilly.com

To submit new book proposals to our editors:
proposals@oreilly.com

O'Reilly books are available in multiple DRM-free ebook formats. For more information:
oreilly.com/ebooks

Lightning Source UK Ltd.
Milton Keynes UK
UKOW07f0719170217
294569UK00002B/6/P